Beginning XML with DOM and Ajax

From Novice to Professional

Sas Jacobs

Apress®

Beginning XML with DOM and Ajax: From Novice to Professional

ISBN-13 (pbk): 978-1-59059-676-0

ISBN-10 (pbk): 1-59059-676-5

Printed and bound in the United States of America 9 8 7 6 5 4 3 2 1

Lead Editors: Charles Brown, Chris Mills
Technical Reviewer: Allan Kent
Editorial Board: Steve Anglin, Ewan Buckingham, Gary Cornell, Jason Gilmore, Jonathan Gennick, Jonathan Hassell, James Huddleston, Chris Mills, Matthew Moodie, Dominic Shakeshaft, Jim Sumser, Keir Thomas, Matt Wade
Project Manager: Beth Christmas
Copy Edit Manager: Nicole LeClerc
Copy Editor: Nicole Abramowitz
Assistant Production Director: Kari Brooks-Copony
Production Editor: Kelly Winquist
Compositor: Dina Quan
Proofreader: Dan Shaw
Indexer: Brenda Miller
Artist: Kinetic Publishing Services, LLC
Cover Designer: Kurt Krames
Manufacturing Director: Tom Debolski

Distributed to the book trade worldwide by Springer-Verlag New York, Inc., 233 Spring Street, 6th Floor, New York, NY 10013. Phone 1-800-SPRINGER, fax 201-348-4505, e-mail `orders-ny@springer-sbm.com`, or visit `http://www.springeronline.com`.

For information on translations, please contact Apress directly at 2560 Ninth Street, Suite 219, Berkeley, CA 94710. Phone 510-549-5930, fax 510-549-5939, e-mail `info@apress.com`, or visit `http://www.apress.com`.

The source code for this book is available to readers at `http://www.apress.com` in the Source Code section.

Contents at a Glance

Contents

About the Author

SAS JACOBS is a web developer who set up her own business, Anything Is Possible, in 1994, working in the areas of web development, IT training, and technical writing. The business works with large and small clients building web applications with .NET, Flash, XML, and databases.

Sas has spoken at such conferences as Flashforward, webDU (previously known as MXDU), and FlashKit on topics related to XML and dynamic content in Flash.

In her spare time, Sas is passionate about traveling, photography, running, and enjoying life.

About the Technical Reviewer

ALLAN KENT is a born-and-bred South African and still lives and works in Cape Town. He has been programming in various and on diverse platforms for more than 20 years. He is currently the head of technology at Saatchi & Saatchi Cape Town.

Acknowledgments

I want to thank everyone at Apress for their help, support, and advice during the writing of this book. Thanks also to my family who has provided much support and love throughout the process.

Introduction

This books aims to provide a "one-stop shop" for developers who want to learn how to build Extensible Markup Language (XML) web applications. It explains XML and its role in the web development world. The book also introduces specific XML vocabularies and related XML recommendations.

I wrote the book for web developers at all levels. For those developers unfamiliar with XML applications, the book provides a great starting point and introduces some important client- and server-side techniques. More experienced developers can benefit from exposure to important coding techniques and understanding the workflow involved in creating XML applications.

The book starts with an explanation of XML and introduces the different components of an XML document. It then shows some related recommendations, including Document Type Definitions (DTDs), XML schema, Cascading Style Sheets (CSS), Extensible Stylesheet Language Transformations (XSLT), XPath, XLink, and XPointer. I cover some common XML vocabularies, such as Extensible HyperText Markup Language (XHTML), Mathematical Markup Language (MathML), and Scalable Vector Graphics (SVG).

The middle section of the book deals with client-side XML applications and shows how to display and transform XML documents with CSS and XSLT. This section also explores how the current web browsers support XML, and it covers how to use JavaScript to work with XML documents. In this section, I also provide an introduction to the Asynchronous JavaScript and XML (Ajax) approach.

The book finishes by examining how to work with XML on the server. It covers two server-side languages: PHP 5 and .NET 2.0. The last chapters of the book deconstruct two XML applications: a News application and a Community Weather Portal application.

The book includes lots of practical examples that developers can incorporate in their daily work. You can download the code samples from the Source Code area of the Apress web site at `http://www.apress.com`. I hope you find this book an invaluable reference to XML and that, through it, you see the incredible power and flexibility that XML offers to web developers.

CHAPTER 1

Introduction to XML

This chapter introduces you to Extensible Markup Language (XML) and explains some of its basic concepts. It's an ideal place to start if you're completely new to XML. The concepts that I introduce here are covered in more detail later in the book.

Web developers familiar with Extensible HyperText Markup Language (XHTML) are often unsure about its relationship with XML; it's not always clear why they might need to learn about XML as well. Be assured that both technologies are important for developers.

XML is a metalanguage used for writing other languages, called XML vocabularies. XHTML is one of those vocabularies, so when you understand XML, you'll also understand the rules underpinning XHTML. XHTML is HTML that conforms to XML rules, and you'll find out more about this shortly.

XHTML has a number of limitations. It's good at structuring and displaying information in web browsers, but its primary purpose is not to mark up data. XHTML can't carry out advanced functions such as sorting and filtering content. You can't create your own tags to describe the contents of an XHTML document. The fixed XHTML tags usually don't bear any relationship to the type of content that they contain. For example, a paragraph tag is a generic container for any type of content.

XML addresses all of the limitations evident in HTML. It provides more flexibility than XHTML, as it works in concert with other standards that assist with presentation, organization, transformation, and navigation. XML documents are self-describing; their document structures can use descriptive tags to identify the content that they mark up.

I'll cover these points in more detail within this chapter. I'll explain more about XML and show why you might want to use it in your work. The chapter will cover:

- A definition and a short history of XML
- A discussion of how to write XML documents
- Information about the processing of XML content

When you finish this chapter, you should have a good understanding of XML and see where you might be able to use it in your work. I'll start by explaining exactly what XML is and where it fits into the world of web development.

What Is XML?

The first and most important point about XML is that it's not a language itself. Rather, it's a metalanguage used for constructing other languages or vocabularies. XML describes the rules for how to create these vocabularies. Each language is likely to be different, but all use tags to mark up content. The choice of tag names and their structures are flexible, and it's common for groups to agree on standard XML vocabularies so that they can share information.

An example of an XML language is XHTML. XHTML describes a standard set of tags that you must use in a specific way. Each XHTML page contains two sections described by the `<head>` and `<body>` tags. Each of those sections can include only certain tags. For example, it's not possible to include `<meta>` tags in the `<body>` section. Web developers around the world share the same standardized approach, and web browsers understand how to render XHTML tags.

XML is a recommendation of the World Wide Web Consortium (W3C), making it a standard that is free to use. The W3C provides a more formal definition of XML in its glossary at `http://www.w3.org/TR/DOM-Level-2-Core/glossary.html`:

> *Extensible Markup Language (XML) is an extremely simple dialect of SGML. The goal is to enable generic SGML to be served, received, and processed on the Web in the way that is now possible with HTML. XML has been designed for ease of implementation and for interoperability with both SGML and HTML.*

A Brief History of XML

XML came into being in 1998 and is based on Standard Generalized Markup Language (SGML). SGML is an international standard that you can think of as a language for defining other languages that mark up documents. HTML was based on SGML. One of the key points about SGML is that it's difficult to use. XML aims to be much easier.

XML also owes much of its existence to HTML. HTML focused on the display of content; you couldn't use it for more advanced features such as sorting and filtering. HTML wasn't a very precise language, and it wasn't case-sensitive. It was possible to write incorrect HTML content but for a browser to display the page correctly.

XML addresses many of the shortcomings found in HTML. In 1999, HTML was rewritten using the XML language construction rules as XHTML. The rules for construction of an XHTML document are more precise than those for HTML. The strictness with which these rules are enforced depends on which Document Type Declaration (DOCTYPE) you assign to the XHTML page. I'll explain more about DOCTYPEs in Chapter 3.

Since 1998, it's been clear that XML is a very powerful approach to managing information. XML documents allow for the sharing of data. A range of related W3C recommendations address the transformation, display, and navigation within XML documents. You'll find out more about these recommendations in Chapter 2.

Let's summarize the key points:

- XML isn't a language; its rules are used to construct other languages.
- XML creates tag-based languages that mark up content.
- XHTML is one of the languages created by XML as a reformulation of HTML.
- XML is based on SGML.

The Goals of XML

After the complexity of SGML, the W3C was very clear about its goals for XML. You can view these goals at `http://www.w3.org/TR/REC-xml/#sec-origin-goals`:

1. XML shall be straightforwardly usable over the Internet.
2. XML shall support a wide variety of applications.
3. XML shall be compatible with SGML.
4. It shall be easy to write programs which process XML documents.
5. The number of optional features in XML is to be kept to the absolute minimum, ideally zero.
6. XML documents should be human-legible and reasonably clear.
7. The XML design should be prepared quickly.
8. The design of XML shall be formal and concise.
9. XML documents shall be easy to create.
10. Terseness in XML markup is of minimal importance.

A few things about these goals are worth noting. First, the W3C wants XML to be straightforward; in fact, several of the goals include the terms "easy" and "clear."

Second, the W3C has given XML two targets: humans and XML processors. An XML processor or parser is a software package that processes an XML document. Processors can identify the contents of an XML document; read, write, and change an existing document; or create a new one from scratch.

The aim is to open up the market for XML processors by keeping them simple to develop. Stricter construction rules mean that less processing is required. This in turn means that the targets for XML documents can be portable devices, such as mobile phones and PDAs.

By keeping documents human-readable, you can access data more readily, and you can build and debug applications more easily. The use of Unicode allows developers to create XML documents in a variety of languages. Unfortunately, a necessary side effect is that XML documents can be verbose, and describing data using XML can be a longer process than using other methods.

UNICODE

XML supports the Unicode character set to enable multilanguage support. Unicode provides support for 2^{31} characters. It includes every character you're likely to need, as well as many that you'll never see.

You can use 8-bit Unicode Transformation Format (UTF-8) to encode Unicode characters so that the characters use the same codes as they do in ASCII. Obviously, this provides good compatibility with older systems. Languages such as Japanese and Chinese need UTF-16 encoding. You can find out more about Unicode at `http://www.unicode.org`.

Third, note the term *XML document*. This term is broader than the traditional view of a physical document. Some XML documents exist in physical form, but others are created as a stream of information following XML construction rules. Examples include web services and calls to databases where the content is returned in XML format.

Now that you understand what XML is, let's delve into the rules for constructing XML languages.

Understanding XML Syntax

XML languages use tags to mark up text. As a web developer, you're probably familiar with the concept of marking up text:

```
<p>Here is an introduction to XML.</p>
```

The previous line is XHTML, but it's also XML. In XHTML, you know that the `<p>` tag indicates a paragraph of text. All of the tags within XHTML have predefined meanings.

XML allows you to construct your own tags, so you could rewrite the previous markup as:

```
<intro>Here is an introduction to XML.</intro>
```

In this example, the `<intro>` tag tells you the purpose of the text that it marks up. One big advantage of XML is that tags can describe their content—that's why XML languages are often called *self-describing*.

XML is flexible enough to allow for the creation of many different types of languages to describe data. The only constraint on XML vocabularies is that they be well-formed.

Well-Formed Documents

XML documents are well-formed if they meet the following criteria:

- The document contains one or more elements.
- The document contains a single document element, which may contain other elements.
- Each element closes correctly.
- Elements are case-sensitive.
- Attribute values are enclosed in quotation marks and cannot be empty.

I'll describe all of these criteria throughout this chapter, but it's worthwhile highlighting some points now. XML languages are case-sensitive; this means that the tag `<intro>` is not the same as `<Intro>` or `<INTRO>`. In XML, these are three different tags. Prior to the days of XHTML, HTML was case-insensitive, so `<body>` and `<BODY>` were equivalent tags.

All XML tags need to have an equivalent closing tag written in the same case as the opening tag. So the `<intro>` tag must have a matching `</intro>` tag. If no content exists between the opening and closing tags, you can abbreviate it into a single tag, `<intro/>`. Again, contrast this with HTML, where it was possible to write a single `<p>` tag to add a paragraph break.

The order of tags is important in XML. Tags that are opened first must close last:

```
<chapter><intro>Here is an introduction to XML.</intro></chapter>
```

HTML pages had no such requirement. The following would have been correct in HTML, although unacceptable in XML:

```
<p><strong>Paragraph text</p></strong>
```

In XML, attributes always use quotation marks around their values:

```
<intro type="chapter">
```

It doesn't matter whether these are single or double quotation marks, but they must be present. This wasn't a requirement in HTML. Similarly, some HTML attributes, such as the `nowrap` attribute in a `<td>` tag, didn't need to contain an attribute name and value pair:

```
<td nowrap>A table cell</td>
```

This type of tag construction isn't possible in XML. You must replace it with something like this:

```
<td nowrap="true">A table cell</td>
```

Understanding the Difference Between Tags and Elements

You may have noticed that I've used the terms *tag* and *element* when talking about XML documents. At first glance, they seem interchangeable, but there's a difference between the terms.

The term *element* describes opening and closing tags as well as any content. A *tag* is one part of an element. Tags start with an opening angle bracket and end with a closing angle bracket. Elements usually contain both an opening and closing tag as well as the content between.

The following line shows a complete element that contains the `<intro>` tag.

```
<intro>Here is an introduction to XML.</intro>
```

Now that you understand the construction rules, it's time to look at a complete XML document.

Viewing a Complete XML Document

A complete piece of XML is referred to as a document. It doesn't matter whether you're dealing with XML that marks up text, information requested from a server, or records received from a database—all of these are documents.

Each XML document is made up of markup and character data. In general, the character data comprises the text between a start tag and an end tag, and everything else is markup. You can further divide markup into elements, attributes, text, entities, comments, character data (CDATA), and processing instructions.

The following document illustrates the different parts of an XML document. You can download it, along with the other resource files, from the Source Code area of the Apress web site (`http://www.apress.com`). The document, called `dvd.xml`, describes the contents of a small DVD library:

```
<?xml version="1.0" encoding="UTF-8"?>
<!-- This XML document describes a DVD library -->
<library>
  <DVD id="1">
    <title>Breakfast at Tiffany's</title>
    <format>Movie</format>
    <genre>Classic</genre>
  </DVD>
  <DVD id="2">
    <title>Contact</title>
    <format>Movie</format>
    <genre>Science fiction</genre>
  </DVD>
  <DVD id="3">
    <title>Little Britain</title>
    <format>TV Series</format>
    <genre>Comedy</genre>
  </DVD>
</library>
```

I'll walk you through each part of the document. The document starts with an XML declaration:

```
<?xml version="1.0" encoding="UTF-8"?>
```

This declaration is optional and can contain a number of attributes, as you'll see shortly.

This XML document also includes a comment describing its purpose:

```
<!-- This XML document describes a DVD library -->
```

I've added this comment as a guide for anyone reading the XML document. As with XHTML, developers normally use comments to add notations.

The document or root element is called `<library>`. You'll notice that all elements within the document appear between the opening and closing `<library>` tags.

The document element contains a number of `<DVD>` elements, and each `<DVD>` element contains `<title>`, `<format>`, and `<genre>` elements. The `<DVD>` element also contains an `id` attribute:

```
<DVD id="1">
  <title>Breakfast at Tiffany's</title>
  <format>Movie</format>
  <genre>Classic</genre>
</DVD>
```

The `<title>`, `<format>`, and `<genre>` elements each contain text.

You can understand the structure and the contents of this document easily by looking at the tag names. It's obvious, even without the comment, that this document describes a list of DVDs. You can also easily infer the relationship between all of the elements from the document.

Understanding the Structure of an XML Document

Each XML document is divided into two parts: the prolog and the document or root element. The prolog appears at the top of the XML document and contains information about the document. It's a little like the `<head>` section of an XHTML document. In the XML document example, the prolog includes an XML declaration and a comment. It can also include other elements, such as processing instructions or a Document Type Definition (DTD). You'll find out more about these later in the "Processing Instructions" and "DTDs and XML Schemas" sections.

Well-formed XML documents must have a single document element that may optionally include other content. Any content within an XML document must appear within the document or root element. In the example XML document, the document element is `<library>`, and it contains all of the other elements.

You might wonder about the names that I've chosen for the elements within the XML document. You're free to use any name for elements and attributes, providing that they conform to the rules for XML names.

Figure 1-1 shows the structure of an XML document.

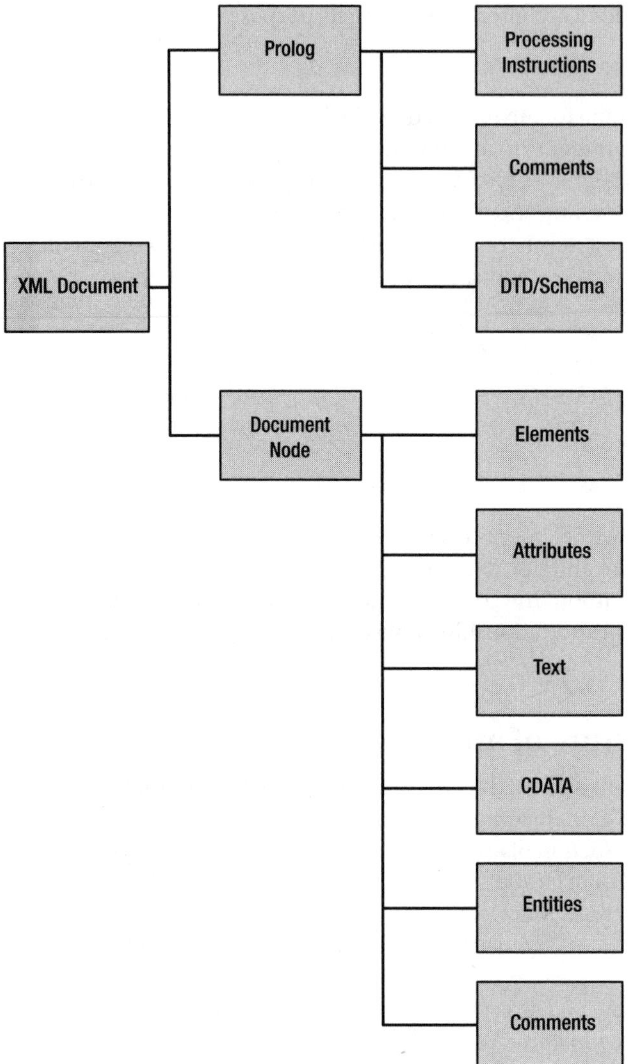

Figure 1-1. *The structure of an XML document*

Naming Rules in XML

Elements, attributes, and some other constructs have names within XML documents. A name is made up of a starting character followed by name characters. Don't forget that XML names are case-sensitive.

The starting character must be a letter or underscore; it can't be a number. The name characters can include just about any other character except a space or a colon. Colons indicate namespaces in XML, so you shouldn't include them within your names. You'll learn more about namespaces in Chapter 2. To be sure that you're using legal characters, it's best to restrict yourself to the uppercase and lowercase letters of the Roman alphabet, numbers, and punctuation, excluding the colon.

If you're authoring your own XML content as opposed to generating it automatically, it's probably a good idea to adopt a standardized naming convention. You should also use descriptive names.

I prefer to write in CamelCase and start with a lowercase letter, unless the element name is capitalized normally:

```
<camelCaseElementName>Here is an element name</camelCaseElementName>
```

I tend to avoid using underscore characters in my names because I think it makes them harder to read.

The use of descriptive names makes it easier for humans to interpret the content. Imagine the difficulty you'd have with this:

```
<zyxtr>Some content</zyxtr>
```

Let's summarize the rules for XML names:

- XML names cannot start with a number or punctuation.
- XML names cannot include spaces.
- Don't include a colon in a name unless it indicates a namespace.
- XML names are case-sensitive.

I'll describe the contents of an XML document in more detail. I'll start by showing you the elements that can appear in the prolog.

Understanding the XML Document Prolog

The prolog of an XML document contains metainformation about the document rather than document content. It may contain the XML declaration, processing instructions, comments, and an embedded DTD or schema.

The XML Declaration

XML documents usually start with an XML declaration, although this is optional:

```
<?xml version="1.0" encoding="UTF-8"?>
```

It's a good idea to include the declaration because it tells an application or a human to expect XML content within the document. It also provides processors with additional information about the document, such as the character-encoding type.

If you include the XML declaration, it must appear on the first line of the XML document. Nothing can precede an XML declaration—not even white space. If you accidentally include white space before the declaration, XML processors won't be able to parse the content of the XML document correctly and will generate an error message.

The XML declaration may also include attributes that provide information about the version, encoding, and whether the document is standalone:

```
<?xml version="1.0" encoding="UTF-8" standalone="yes"?>
```

At the time of writing, the current XML version is 1.1. However, many processors don't recognize this version, so it's best to stick with a version 1.0 declaration for backward compatibility.

The `encoding` attribute describes the character set for the XML document. If you don't include an `encoding` attribute, it's assumed that the document uses UTF-8 encoding.

The `standalone` attribute can have either the values `yes` or `no`. The value indicates whether external files are required to process the XML document correctly.

Each of the attributes in the XML declaration is optional, but the order is important. If you choose to include an `encoding` attribute, it must appear after the `version` attribute. The `standalone` attribute must appear as the last attribute in the declaration.

Processing Instructions

The prolog can also include processing instructions (PIs) that pass information about the XML document to other applications. The XML processor doesn't process PIs, but rather passes them on to the application unchanged.

PIs start with the characters `<?` and finish with `?>`. They usually appear in the prolog, although they can appear in other places within an XML document.

■ **Note** An XML declaration also starts with the characters `<?xml`. Even though the XML declaration looks similar, it's worth remembering that it's quite different from a PI.

The following PI indicates a reference to an XSL stylesheet:

```
<?xml-stylesheet type="text/xsl" href="stylesheet.xsl"?>
```

The first item in a PI is a name, called the PI target. The preceding PI has the name `xml-stylesheet`. Names that start with `xml` are reserved for XML-specific PIs. The PI also has the text string `type="text/xsl" href="stylesheet.xsl"`. Although this looks like two attributes, the content isn't treated that way. You'll see more examples of stylesheet PIs in Chapters 6 and 7.

Comments

Comments can appear almost anywhere in an XML document. The example XML document included a comment in the prolog, so let's look at comments with the other prolog contents.

XML comments look the same as XHTML comments. They begin with the characters `<!--` and end with `-->`:

```
<!-- Here is a comment -->
```

Comments don't affect the processing of an XML document. They're normally intended for human readers. If you add a comment, you must be aware of the following rules:

- A comment may not contain the text -->.
- A comment may not be included within tag names.
- A comment should not hide either the opening or closing tags in an element.
- An XML processor isn't obliged to pass a comment to an application, although most do.

DTDs and XML Schemas

DTDs and XML schemas provide rules about which elements and attributes can appear within the XML document. In other words, they specify which elements and attributes are valid and which are required or optional.

The prolog can include declarations about the XML document, a reference to an external DTD or schema, or both. I'll explain more about DTDs and schemas in Chapter 2.

Understanding Sections Within the XML Document Element

The data within an XML document is stored within the document or root element. This element contains all other elements, attributes, text, and CDATA within the document and may also include entities and comments.

Elements

Elements serve many purposes in an XML document. They

- Mark up content
- Provide a description of the content they mark up
- Provide information about the order of data and its relative importance
- Show the relationships between data

Elements include a starting and ending tag as well as content. The content can be text, child elements, or both text and elements. The starting tag for an element can also contain attributes. You can position comments inside elements.

In the earlier example, you saw the following structure within the `<DVD>` element:

```
<DVD id="1">
  <title>Breakfast at Tiffany's</title>
  <format>Movie</format>
  <genre>Classic</genre>
</DVD>
```

The opening `<DVD>` tag contains an `id` attribute and includes three other elements: `<title>`, `<format>`, and `<genre>`. Each of these elements contains text.

You saw earlier that it's necessary to open and close tags in the correct order. It would be wrong to write the following:

```
<DVD id="1">
  <title>Breakfast at Tiffany's</title>
  <format>Movie</format>
  <genre>Classic</DVD>
</genre>
```

There are four types of elements:

- Empty elements
- Elements containing only text
- Elements containing only child elements
- Elements containing a mixture of child elements and text, or mixed elements

You'll see how important it is to distinguish between these different types when I cover XML schemas in Chapter 2.

Empty Elements

If an element doesn't contain any text, it's an empty element, and you can write it in two different ways. The following code shows two equivalent examples:

```
<elementName></elementName>
<elementName/>
```

The tag in the second line uses the shortened form that adds a forward slash at the end before the closing angle bracket. The XHTML <br/> tag is another example of an empty element. Using the empty element syntax can save file size and improve legibility.

Elements Containing Only Text

Some elements only contain text content. You'll recall from the previous example that the <title>, <format>, and <genre> elements contain only text:

```
<title>Breakfast at Tiffany's</title>
<format>Movie</format>
<genre>Classic</genre>
```

Elements Containing Other Elements

It's possible for an element to contain only other elements. The container element is called the *parent*, while the elements contained inside are the *child* elements. The <DVD> element is an example of an element that contains child elements:

```
<DVD id="1">
  <title>Breakfast at Tiffany's</title>
  <format>Movie</format>
  <genre>Classic</genre>
</DVD>
```

The family analogy is often used when describing element structures in XML.

Mixed Elements

Mixed elements contain both text and child elements. The DVD example doesn't include any of these types of elements, but the following code block shows a mixed element:

```
<mixedElement>This element contains both text and child elements
  <childElement>This element contains text</childElement>
  <emptyElement/>
</mixedElement>
```

To summarize, elements have the following requirements:

- Elements must contain starting and ending tags, unless there is no content, in which case you can use the shorthand form.
- The tag names must obey the XML naming rules.
- Elements must be nested correctly.

Attributes

Another way to provide information in XML documents is by using attributes within the opening tag of an element. Attributes normally provide additional information about the element that they modify. There is no limit to the number of attributes that can appear inside an element.

Attributes consist of name and value pairs, with the value enclosed in either double or single quotation marks:

```
<elementName attributeName="attributeValue"/>
```

Attributes provide additional information about an element:

```
<p style="text-align:center;">Introduction to XML</p>
```

In this case, the data `Introduction to XML` is enclosed in a `<p>` element. This element tells a web browser to display the information in a separate paragraph. The `style` attribute provides additional information about how to display the data. Here, you're telling the browser to center the text.

Two common uses of attributes are to convey formatting information and to indicate the use of a specific format or encoding. For example, you could convey a date as

```
<Date Format="mmddyyyy">06081955</Date>
```

or indicate use of an International Organization for Standardization (ISO) date format using

```
<Date Code="ISO8601">1955-06-08</Date>
```

When an element contains an attribute, it's said to be a *complex type* element. As you'll see later, this is important when writing XML schema documents.

You can use either a pair of double or single quotes for different attributes within the same element:

```
<elementName att1="value1" att2='value2'>Here is an element</elementName>
```

Make sure you don't include one of each in a single attribute, or the document won't be well formed.

Caution Be careful when cutting and pasting attributes from a word-processing document into an XML document. Word processors often use smart quotes, which cause an error in an XML document.

You can also write an attribute as a nested child element. For example, you could rewrite the <DVD> element

```
<DVD id="1">
  <title>Breakfast at Tiffany's</title>
  <format>Movie</format>
  <genre>Classic</genre>
</DVD>
```

as

```
<DVD>
  <id>1</id>
  <title>Breakfast at Tiffany's</title>
  <format>Movie</format>
  <genre>Classic</genre>
</DVD>
```

There's no clear rule about which is the better option. Both alternatives are acceptable. Let's summarize the rules relating to attributes:

- An attribute is made up of a name/value pair.
- You must enclose the attribute value in single or double quotes.
- Attributes cannot contain an XML tag.
- Attribute names must follow the XML naming rules.

Text

All text within an XML document is contained inside opening and closing tags. Unless you mark the text as CDATA, it will be treated as if it were XML and processed accordingly. This means an opening angle bracket will be treated as if it were part of an XML tag.

If you want to use reserved characters within text, you must rewrite them as character entities. For example, you can write the left angle bracket < as `<`. You can also embed the reserved characters within CDATA.

CDATA Sections

CDATA allows you to mark blocks of text so that they're not processed as XML. As I mentioned before, this is useful for text that contains reserved XML characters:

```
<title><!CDATA[ Why 9 is < 10 ]]</title>
```

This CDATA section starts with <!CDATA[and ends with]]. The character data is contained within the opening and closing square brackets. Obviously, the string]] can't appear within a CDATA section.

You can use CDATA sections in XML documents for embedding code, such as JavaScript, and for adding content that doesn't need processing. For example, an application that reads data from a database and marks it up in XML might embed all content in CDATA sections to avoid the need to process the reserved characters explicitly. I'll show you an example of using CDATA with JavaScript in Chapter 3.

Entities

Character entities are symbols that represent a single character. In XHTML, character entities are used for special symbols such as an ampersand (&) and a nonbreaking space ( ).

You can use character entities to replace the reserved characters in XML documents. All tags start with a left angle bracket, so it isn't possible to include this character in the text within an element:

```
<expression>10 < 25</expression>
```

If you try to process this element, the presence of the left angle bracket before the text 25 causes a processing error. Instead, you could replace this symbol with the entity <:

```
<expression>10 &lt; 25</expression>
```

You need to consider the following reserved characters:

- <, which indicates the start of a tag name
- &, which indicates the first character of an entity
- xml, which is reserved for referring to parts of the XML language, such as xml-stylesheet

Table 1-1 summarizes the character entities that you need to use.

Table 1-1. *Character Entities Used in XML Documents*

Character	Entity
&	&
'	'
>	>
<	<
"	"

Sometimes you can't include a literal character in an XML document, perhaps because the character doesn't exist on a keyboard or because it's a graphic character. Instead, you can add these as character entities using Unicode or hexadecimal numbers. For example, you can encode the copyright symbol © as `©` or `©`.

If the reference starts with &# and ends with a semicolon, it's a character reference. The number between is the Unicode code for the character required. If the code is written as a hexadecimal, then it's prefixed with the character `x`.

You can also define your own entities. For example, you could define the reference `©right;` to mean `Copyright 2006 Apress`. Each time you want to include this text in the XML document, you could use the entity reference `©right;`. This makes the text easier to manage and update.

Let's move on to look at the processing of XML documents.

The XML Processing Model

The XML recommendation assumes that an XML document will be processed in a particular way. The model indicates that an XML processor passes the content and structure of the XML document to an application. XML processors are usually called XML parsers, as they parse the XML document; see Figure 1-2.

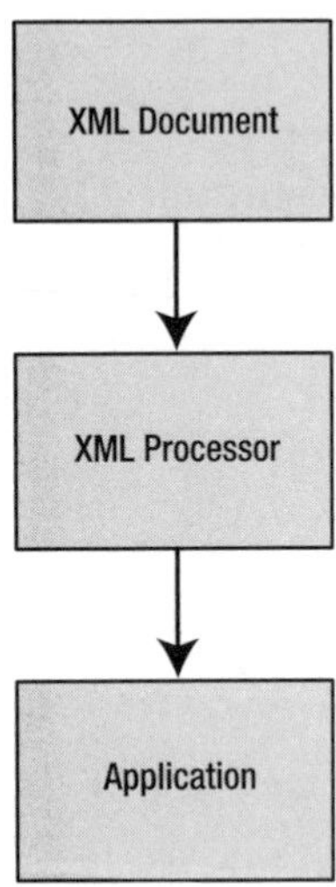

Figure 1-2. *The XML document-processing model*

Common XML processors include Microsoft XML Parser (MSXML), Apache Xerces2, and the Oracle XML parser. You can write an application that uses any of these parsers. Some XML parsers are also available as prepackaged software that install automatically. Extensible Stylesheet Language Transformations (XSLT) processors used to display XML in a web browser fall into this category. MSXML contains both an XML parser and an XSLT processor, and is both an XML processor and an application. It installs automatically with Internet Explorer and other Microsoft software.

XML Processing Types

There are two categories of XML processing: tree-based and event-based. Many XML parsers, including later versions of MSXML, support both models. You'll often hear tree-based parsers referred to as Document Object Model (DOM) parsers, while event-based parsers are referred to as Simple API for XML (SAX) parsers. Both are named after the specifications they support.

The DOM is a W3C recommendation that provides an application programming interface (API) to an XML document. Any application can use this API to manipulate an XML document, read information, add new nodes, and edit the existing content. You can find out more about this recommendation at `http://www.w3.org/TR/REC-DOM-Level-1/`.

SAX is not a W3C recommendation, but it does enjoy support from both large and small software companies. A SAX-based parser reads an XML document sequentially, firing off events as it reaches important parts of the document, such as the start or end of an element. You can find out more at `http://www.saxproject.org/`.

DOM Parsing

Figure 1-3 shows the `dvd.xml` document that you've been working with represented as a tree structure.

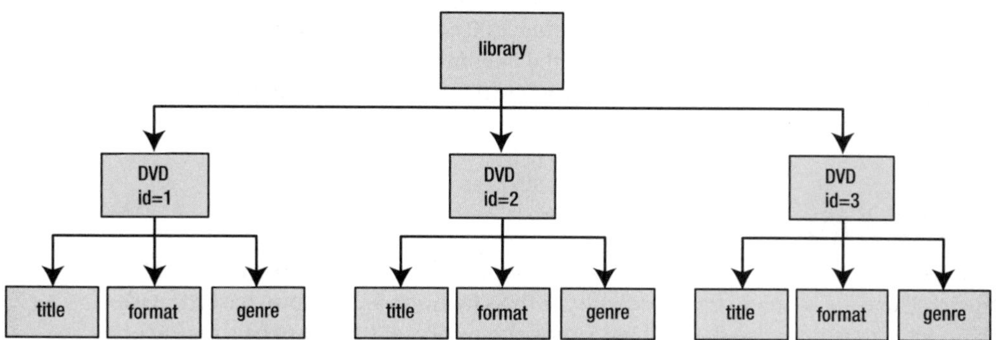

Figure 1-3. *The dvd.xml document shown as a tree structure*

Displaying the document in this way reinforces the relationship between the elements, as in a family tree. The `<library>` element is the parent of the `<DVD>` element and the grandparent of the `<title>`, `<format>`, and `<genre>` elements. The `<DVD>` elements are siblings and have the `<library>` element as a parent or ancestor. The `<title>`, `<format>`, and `<genre>` elements are descendants of the `<library>` element.

DOM parsing allows access to these elements, their values, and all other parts of an XML document through either a programming language or a scripting language such as JavaScript.

SAX Parsing

A SAX-based parser presents an XML document as a string of events. You must write handlers for each event so that something suitable occurs when the event triggers the handler.

This type of parsing works well with languages that have good event-handling properties. For instance, SAX parsing is used extensively with Java. It's less suitable for the scripting languages often employed on the web, so I don't cover it in detail here.

Why Have Two Processing Models?

Both processing models offer advantages. DOM-based parsing provides full read-write access to an XML document, and you can traverse the document tree to access nodes within the document. It can also validate a document against a DTD or XML schema to determine that the document is valid.

However, DOM-based parsing must read the full XML document into memory, so DOM parsing can be slow and memory-intensive when working with large XML documents. It's difficult to determine exactly what constitutes a large XML document, because processing time depends on computing power, memory, time available, and whether it's working in a single-user environment or a multiuser environment such as a web server. As a rule, most systems cope with documents up to tens of megabytes in size, but you need to take care with files above this size.

The SAX-based model, on the other hand, is sequential in operation. Once a node has been processed, it is discarded and cannot be processed again. The whole document isn't loaded into memory at once, so you can avoid problems associated with processing large XML documents. This method of processing puts the onus on you to store any information from the XML document that might be required later.

SAX is ideal, for example, as an intermediate routing product in a communications system. An incoming XML document is likely to consist of a small routing header and a larger document for delivery to the end point. Using SAX, a routing device can read the routing information and ignore the document, as the document is irrelevant to its delivery. A DOM-based parser, however, must parse the complete document to be able to deliver it to its ultimate destination.

Some XML Tools

Developers commonly want to know what tools are available for working with XML documents. There are so many tools available, both as freeware and for purchase, that it's impossible to summarize them all here. Your choice of tool is likely to be a matter of personal preference.

In general, XML development tools fall into several categories:

- Extensions to existing programmers' IDEs
- XML-specific IDEs
- Individual tools

Tools such as Microsoft Visual Studio (`http://msdn.microsoft.com/vstudio/`) fall into the first category. They have good XML support aimed specifically at developers. At the time of writing, the latest version is Visual Studio 2005 and includes the following features:

- It helps you create and edit XML documents, including checking whether a document is well formed.
- It offers XML schema support, including the ability to infer a schema from an instance document, validation of documents, and conversion from a DTD.
- It offers XSLT support, including the ability to view the results of a transformation.

The dedicated XML IDEs tend to cover similar ground and differ in the depth of their support and their user interfaces. Most of these tools have an XML editor, tools for creating DTDs and XML schemas, and support for XSLT development. Several such tools are available, including this small sample of common ones:

- Altova's XML Suite: `http://www.altova.com/suite.html`
- TIBCO Software's suite of XML tools: `http://www.tibco.com/software/business_integration/xml_tools.jsp`
- DataDirect Technologies' Stylus Studio: `http://www.stylusstudio.com/`

Many of the suites mentioned include individual tools that you can use for editing XML documents. These include

- Altova's XMLSpy: `http://www.altova.com/products_ide.html`
- Blast Radius' XMetal: `http://www.xmetal.com/index.x?products/xmetal/`
- SyncRO Soft's <oXygen/>: `http://www.oxygenxml.com//`

There are many other excellent tools available that I haven't mentioned here. You can find out more by searching the Internet or subscribing to mailing lists such as XML-DEV (`http://xml.org/xml/xmldev.shtml`).

Summary

In this chapter, you've been introduced to some of the basic concepts relating to XML. I've covered XML syntax in some detail, and I've shown you the benefits that XML provides for web developers. I've also shown you some of the tools that you can use to work with XML documents.

In Chapter 2, I'll show you some of the related XML recommendations. You'll learn how to work with DTDs and XML schemas. You'll also find a brief introduction to XSLT, XPath, XLinks, and XPointer.

CHAPTER 2

Related XML Recommendations

In the previous chapter, you learned about XML documents and their rules for construction. XML is one in a set of related recommendations from the World Wide Web Consortium (W3C). In this chapter, I'll show you some of the recommendations that you're likely to encounter when working with XML applications.

Specifically, I'll discuss

- The role of namespaces in XML
- Defining XML vocabularies with Document Type Definitions (DTDs) and XML schemas
- Displaying XML with XSLT
- Navigating XML documents using XPath
- Linking to XML documents with XLink and XPointer

You can download the files referred to in this chapter from the Source Code area of the Apress web site (`http://www.apress.com`). Let's start by looking at the importance of namespaces when working with XML documents.

Understanding the Role of XML Namespaces

XML documents allow you to create your own vocabularies of elements and attributes to describe data. As XML documents become more complex or draw content from other sources, it's possible that you'll want to use more than one vocabulary in the same document, and that the same element name will appear in both vocabularies with different meanings.

For example, say you want to produce a furniture catalog that contains some embedded XHTML information:

```
<?xml version="1.0" encoding="UTF-8"?>
<catalog>
  <table>
    <size>
      <length>2.0</length>
      <width>0.9</width>
```

```
      <height>1.2</height>
    </size>
    <description>
      <table>
        <tr>
          <td>This is a lovely table</td>
          <td>And this is a picture of it</td>
        </tr>
      </table>
    </description>
  </table>
</catalog>
```

In this XML document, the two elements called <table> have completely different meanings.

Namespaces allow you to show which elements belong to which vocabulary. You can identify each vocabulary with a unique prefix that you then apply to elements in the XML document:

```
<?xml version="1.0" encoding="UTF-8"?>
<cat:catalog>
  <cat:table>
    <cat:size>
      <cat:length>2.0</cat:length>
      <cat:width>0.9</cat:width>
      <cat:height>1.2</cat:height>
    </cat:size>
    <cat:description>
      <xhtml:table>
        <xhtml:tr>
          <xhtml:td>This is a lovely table</xhtml:td>
          <xhtml:td>And this is a picture of it</xhtml:td>
        </xhtml:tr>
      </xhtml:table>
    </cat:description>
  </cat:table>
</cat:catalog>
```

The prefix you choose isn't significant, although you can follow some conventions. In the previous example, the first prefix, `cat`, refers to catalog items. You could equally call this `dog` or `catalog`. The second prefix, `xhtml`, refers to XHTML elements within the document. This is an example of a namespace convention.

Namespaces use Uniform Resource Identifiers (URIs) to identify each vocabulary. In the case of the previous XHTML content, the W3C controls the URI because it controls the XHTML standard. However, you can associate the `cat` prefix with any URI under your control.

It's important to note that the URI doesn't have to point to an actual document or directory. The only requirement is that it's unique in the XML document. However, many processors, including XML schema, XHTML, and XSLT processors, use the URI to indicate that they must process certain parts of the document. Therefore, you must use the correct URI for these applications.

You can find the W3C's "Namespaces in XML" recommendation at `http://www.w3.org/TR/REC-xml-names/`.

Adding Namespaces to XML Documents

You reference a namespace by adding it as an attribute of any node that contains elements belonging to the namespace. Frequently, you add the namespace to the document element, because it contains all other elements. In the previous XML document, you could rewrite the opening element as follows:

```
<cat:catalog xmlns:cat="http://www.apress.com/ns/furniture"
xmlns:xhtml="http://www.w3.org/1999/xhtml">
```

This determines that the `cat` namespace refers to the URI `http://www.apress.com/ns/furniture`. The `cat` namespace can precede any element name, providing it is separated by a colon:

```
<cat:catalog>
```

Adding Default Namespaces

Quite often, a large portion of an XML document belongs to a single XML vocabulary. In this case, you can define a default namespace instead of repeating the namespace prefix for each element. You can use the `xmlns` keyword to define a default namespace. If you do this, you don't need to assign a prefix to elements within this namespace.

For example, you can set the `catalog` namespace as the default namespace:

```
<catalog xmlns="http://www.apress.com/ns/furniture"
xmlns:xhtml="http://www.w3.org/1999/xhtml">
```

Because this is now the default namespace, you don't need to use a prefix in front of element names from this namespace.

You can define a default namespace at any point in the document. When you do this, the default applies to the element containing the namespace declaration and any descendants. The declaration overrides any earlier default declarations.

The following XML document shows how to use multiple default namespaces:

```
<?xml version="1.0" encoding="UTF-8"?>
<catalog xmlns="http://www.apress.com/ns/furniture" >
  <table>
    <size>
      <length>2.0</length>
      <width>0.9</width>
      <height>1.2</height>
    </size>
    <description>
      <table xmlns="http://www.w3.org/1999/xhtml">
        <tr>
```

```
          <td>This is a lovely table</td>
          <td>And this is a picture of it</td>
        </tr>
      </table>
    </description>
  </table>
</catalog>
```

The default catalog namespace applies to all elements except those contained within the second <table> element. Because you added the namespace declaration, the following elements use the XHTML namespace as the default:

```
<table xmlns="http://www.w3.org/1999/xhtml">
  <tr>
  <td>This is a lovely table</td>
  <td>And this is a picture of it</td>
  </tr>
</table>
```

A final point on namespaces is their use with attributes. By default, an attribute belongs in the same namespace as its containing element. Unless you use an attribute defined in a different namespace from its containing element, it doesn't need to be qualified.

You'll see the importance of namespaces as I show you how to define XML vocabularies using DTDs and XML schemas.

Defining XML Vocabularies

Languages based on XML are called vocabularies, and you can define them using a DTD, XML schema, or some other schema language. Many industry groups have come together to define their own XML vocabularies.

If you want to use an XML vocabulary, you need to know the rules for its construction. The rules ensure that you can generate valid XML documents that match the language construction criteria.

Knowing the rules also allows XML processors to check that the XML document conforms. This process is called *validation*, and processors that do this are called *validating parsers*. Chapter 1 provides information about how XML documents are processed.

You can share the rules for XML vocabularies by writing a schema. This is a formal description that people or validating parsers can use. If you're using an XML document for a one-off application, it's probably overkill to document the vocabulary. The real benefit comes when you want to share the language with other people or applications so that either can check that the document is constructed correctly.

There are two common types of schemas: the DTD and the XML schema. The W3C defines and controls both of these. In fact, the DTD is part of the XML recommendation itself.

I'll use the DVD library example from Chapter 1:

```
<?xml version="1.0" encoding="UTF-8"?>
<!-- This XML document describes a DVD library -->
<library>
  <DVD id="1">
    <title>Breakfast at Tiffany's</title>
    <format>Movie</format>
    <genre>Classic</genre>
  </DVD>
  <DVD id="2">
    <title>Contact</title>
    <format>Movie</format>
    <genre>Science fiction</genre>
  </DVD>
  <DVD id="3">
    <title>Little Britain</title>
    <format>TV Series</format>
    <genre>Comedy</genre>
  </DVD>
</library>
```

Let's start by looking at how you could construct a DTD to describe this vocabulary.

The Document Type Definition

A DTD describes the structure of a document. Among other things, it indicates how many times an element can appear, whether it's optional, and whether it contains attributes.

Validating parsers can check an XML document against its DTD to see if it's valid. If it isn't, the parser will report an error. An XML document that complies with a DTD is called a document instance of that DTD.

This book isn't intended as a complete reference to DTDs, but it includes enough information so you can understand how to construct a DTD. The following DTD defines the DVD library document:

```
<?xml version="1.0" encoding="UTF-8"?>
<!ELEMENT library (DVD+)>
<!ELEMENT DVD (title, format, genre)>
<!ELEMENT title (#PCDATA)>
<!ELEMENT format (#PCDATA)>
<!ELEMENT genre (#PCDATA)>
<!ATTLIST DVD id CDATA #REQUIRED>
```

You'll find the document saved as `dvd.dtd` with your resources. I've called the XML document that refers to this DTD `dvd_dtd.xml`, but the name isn't significant.

This DTD shows two types of declarations: one for declaring elements and the other for attributes. You can also add entity and notation declarations. Notation declarations are uncommon, so I'll cover only entity declarations later in the "Entity Declarations" section.

Element Type Declarations

An element type declaration gives information about an element. The declaration starts with the `!ELEMENT` text and lists the element name and contents. The content can be a data type or other elements listed in the DTD:

```
<!ELEMENT elementName (elementContents)>
```

Empty elements show the word `EMPTY`:

```
<!ELEMENT elementName (EMPTY)>
```

In the sample DTD, the `<DVD>` element contains three other elements: `<title>`, `<format>`, and `<genre>`:

```
<!ELEMENT DVD (title, format, genre)>
```

The order of these elements dictates the order in which they should appear within an XML document instance.

Parsed Character Data (PCDATA) indicates that the element's content is text, and that an XML parser should parse this text to resolve character and entity references. The `<title>`, `<format>`, and `<genre>` declarations define their content type as `PCDATA`:

```
<!ELEMENT title (#PCDATA)>
<!ELEMENT format (#PCDATA)>
<!ELEMENT genre (#PCDATA)>
```

You can use several modifiers to provide more information about child elements. Table 2-1 summarizes these modifiers.

Table 2-1. *Symbols Used in Element Declarations Within DTDs*

Symbol	Explanation
,	Specifies the order of child elements.
+	Signifies that an element must appear at least once (i.e., one or more times).
|	Allows a choice between a group of elements.
( )	Marks content as a group.
*	Specifies that the element is optional and can appear any number of times (i.e., zero or more times).
?	Specifies that the element is optional, but if it's present, it can appear only once (i.e., zero or one times).
	No symbol indicates that an element must appear exactly once.

The declaration for the `<DVD>` element includes a + sign, which indicates that the element must appear at least once, but can appear more often:

```
<!ELEMENT library (DVD+)>
```

Attribute List Declarations

Attribute declarations, which appear after element declarations, are a little more complicated. You can indicate that an element has attributes by including an attribute list declaration:

```
<!ATTLIST DVD id CDATA #REQUIRED>
```

In this line, the element `<DVD>` has a required attribute called `id` that contains CDATA.

■ **Note** Setting a required attribute doesn't affect any of the other element declarations within the DTD. It would be entirely possible to include another child element, also called `id`, within this element.

The most common type of attribute is CDATA, but you can declare other types as well:

- `ID`: a unique identifier
- `IDREF`: the ID of another element
- `IDREFS`: a list of IDs from other elements
- `NMTOKEN`: a valid XML name
- `NMTOKENS`: a list of valid XML names
- `ENTITY`: an entity name
- `ENTITIES`: a list of entity names
- `LIST`: a list of specified values

The keyword `#REQUIRED` indicates that you must include this attribute. You could also use the word `#IMPLIED` to indicate an optional attribute. Using the word `#FIXED` implies that you can only use a single value for the attribute. If the XML document doesn't include the attribute, the validating parser will insert the fixed value. Using a value other than the fixed value generates a parser error.

If you need to specify a choice of values for an attribute, you can use the pipe character (`|`):

```
<!ATTLIST product color (red|green|blue) "red">
```

This line indicates that the `<product>` element has a `color` attribute with possible values of `red`, `green`, or `blue` and a default value of `red`.

Entity Declarations

In Chapter 1, you saw how to use the built-in entity types, and I mentioned that you can define your own entities to represent fixed data. For example, you could assign the entity reference `©right;` to the text `Copyright 2006 Apress`. You'd use the following line to define this as an entity in the DTD:

```
<!ENTITY copyright "Copyright 2006 Apress">
```

This is a simple internal entity declaration. You can also reference an external entity and use it to include larger amounts of content in your XML document. This is similar to using a server-side include file in an XHTML document.

The following XML document refers to several entities:

```
<book>
  <content>
    &tableOfContents;
    &chapter1;
    &chapter2;
    &chapter3;
    &appendixA;
    &index;
  <content>
</book>
```

This XML document takes its content from several entities, each representing an external XML document. The DTD needs to include a declaration for each of the entities. For example, you might define the `tableOfContents` entity as follows:

```
<!ENTITY tableOfContents SYSTEM "entities/TOC.xml">
```

Associating a DTD with an XML Document

So far, you've seen how to construct a DTD, but you haven't yet seen how to associate it with an XML document. You can either embed the DTD in the XML document or add a reference to an external DTD.

You can reference an external DTD from the XML document in the prolog:

```
<?xml version="1.0" encoding="UTF-8"?>
<!DOCTYPE library SYSTEM "dvd.dtd">
```

You can also embed a DTD within the prolog of the XML document:

```
<?xml version="1.0" encoding="UTF-8"?>
<!-- This XML document describes a DVD library -->
<!DOCTYPE library [
<!ELEMENT library (DVD+)>
<!ELEMENT DVD (title, format, genre)>
<!ELEMENT title (#PCDATA)>
<!ELEMENT format (#PCDATA)>
<!ELEMENT genre (#PCDATA)>
<!ATTLIST DVD id CDATA #REQUIRED>
]>
<library>
  ...
</library>
```

You can find this example saved as `dvd_embedded_dtd.xml` within your resources files.

It's possible to have both an internal and external DTD. The internal DTD takes precedence if a conflict exists between element or attribute definitions.

It's probably more common to use an external DTD. This method allows a single DTD to validate multiple XML documents and makes maintenance of the DTD and document instances easier.

You can then use an embedded DTD if you need to override the external DTD. This approach works much the same way as using embedded Cascading Style Sheets (CSS) declarations to override external stylesheets.

If you're creating a one-off document that needs a DTD, it may be easier to use embedded element and attribute declarations. Even if you don't want to define the elements and attributes, you might want to define entities.

Note If you include a reference to an external DTD that includes entities, you must change the `standalone` attribute in the XML declaration to `no`:

```
<?xml version="1.0" encoding="UTF-8" standalone="no"?>
```

Let's turn to the other commonly used XML validation language, XML schema.

XML Schema

XML schemas share many similarities with DTDs; for instance, you use both to specify the structure of XML documents. You can find out more about XML schemas by reading the W3C primer at `http://www.w3.org/TR/xmlschema-0/`.

DTDs and XML schemas also have many differences. First, the XML schema language is a vocabulary of XML. XML schemas are more powerful than DTDs and include concepts such as data typing and inheritance. Unfortunately, they're also much more complicated to construct compared with DTDs. A further disadvantage is that XML schemas offer no equivalent of a DTD entity declaration.

One important aspect of XML schemas is that a schema processor validates one element at a time in the XML document. This allows different elements to be validated against different schemas and makes it possible to examine the validity of each element. A document is valid if each element within the document is valid against its appropriate schema.

A side effect of this element-level validation is that XML schemas don't provide a way to specify which is the document element. So, providing the elements are valid, the document will be valid, regardless of the fact that a document element may not be included.

Let's start by looking at the schema that describes the `dvd.xml` document:

```
<?xml version="1.0" encoding="UTF-8"?>
<xs:schema xmlns:xs="http://www.w3.org/2001/XMLSchema">
  <xs:element name="library">
    <xs:complexType>
      <xs:sequence>
        <xs:element name="DVD" minOccurs="0" maxOccurs="unbounded">
          <xs:complexType>
```

```
          <xs:sequence>
            <xs:element name="title" type="xs:string"/>
            <xs:element name="format" type="xs:string"/>
            <xs:element name="genre" type="xs:string"/>
          </xs:sequence>
          <xs:attribute name="id" type="xs:integer" use="required"/>
        </xs:complexType>
      </xs:element>
    </xs:sequence>
  </xs:complexType>
 </xs:element>
</xs:schema>
```

Straight away, you can see some big differences between this schema and the previous DTD. The most obvious difference is that the schema is tag-based and uses a namespace. By using XML to create the schema vocabulary, you can take advantage of standard XML creation tools. The XML schema also includes data types for both the elements and attribute. For example, the `id` attribute uses the type `xs:integer`.

Let's work through this schema document. The schema starts with a standard XML declaration. The document element is called `schema`, and it includes a reference to the XML schema namespace `http://www.w3.org/2001/XMLSchema`:

```
<?xml version="1.0" encoding="UTF-8"?>
<xs:schema xmlns:xs="http://www.w3.org/2001/XMLSchema">
```

By convention, this namespace is usually associated with the prefixes `xsd` or `xs`. This example uses the `xs` prefix.

This schema uses *Russian doll* notation, where element declarations are positioned at the appropriate position in the document. In other words, the element declarations nest to indicate the relative position of elements. It's possible to organize schema documents differently.

The first element defined is the document element `<library>`. It has global scope because it's the child of the `<xs:schema>` element. This means that the element definition is available for use anywhere within the XML schema. You might reuse the element declaration at different places within the schema document. Global elements can also be the document element of a valid document instance.

The definition includes the following:

```
<xs:element name="library">
  <xs:complexType>
    <xs:sequence>
```

These statements define the element as a *complex type* element and indicate that it contains child elements in some order (<xs:sequence>). Complex type elements contain other elements or at least one attribute. Because the <library> element contains the remaining elements in the document, you must declare it as a complex type element. I'll show you an example of declaring simple type elements shortly.

You've declared that the <library> element contains a sequence of child elements by using <xs:sequence>. This seems a little strange, given that it only contains a single element that may be repeated. You could also select one element from a choice of elements using <xs:choice>, or you could select all elements in any order using <xs:all>.

The <library> element contains a single <DVD> element that appears at least once and can appear multiple times. You specify this using

```
<xs:element name="DVD" minOccurs="0" maxOccurs="unbounded">
```

If the element can occur exactly once, omit the minOccurs and maxOccurs attributes.

The <DVD> element contains child elements, so it's a complex type element containing other elements, also in a sequence:

```
<xs:element name="DVD" minOccurs="0" maxOccurs="unbounded">
  <xs:complexType>
    <xs:sequence>
```

The child elements are simple type elements because they contain only text. If they included an attribute, they would automatically be complex type elements, but the only attribute in the document is included in the <DVD> element.

Define simple type elements by specifying their name and data type:

```
<xs:element name="title" type="xs:string"/>
<xs:element name="format" type="xs:string"/>
<xs:element name="genre" type="xs:string"/>
```

The XML schema recommendation lists 44 built-in simple data types, including string, integer, float, decimal, date, time, ID, and Boolean. You can find out more about these types at http://www.w3.org/TR/xmlschema-2/. You can also define your own complex data types.

The <DVD> element also includes an attribute id that is defined after the child element sequence. All attributes are simple type elements and are optional unless otherwise specified:

```
<xs:attribute name="id" type="xs:integer" use="required"/>
```

It's also possible to add constraints to the attribute value to restrict the range of possible values.

Figure 2-1 shows the XML document and schema side by side in Altova XMLSpy.

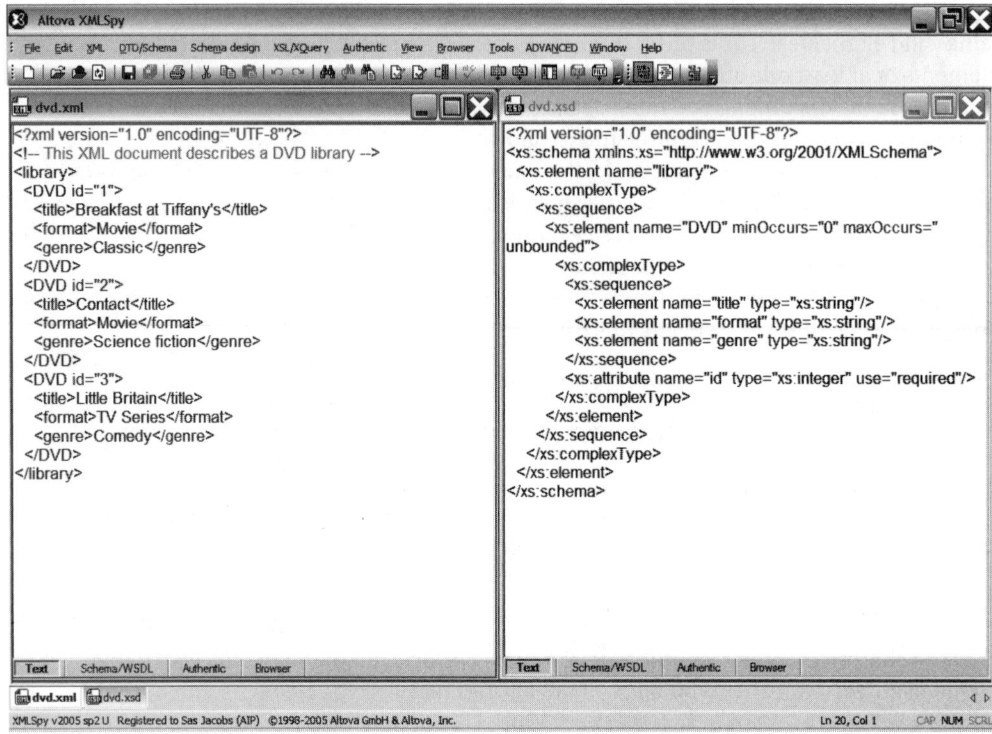

Figure 2-1. *The XML document and related schema*

An Alternative Layout

In the previous example, only the `<library>` element was declared as a child of the `<xs:schema>` element, so this is the only element available globally. If you want to be able to use other elements globally, you can change the way they're declared by using the `ref` attribute.

The following code shows the schema document reworked to make the `<DVD>` element global:

```
<?xml version="1.0" encoding="UTF-8"?>
<xs:schema xmlns:xs="http://www.w3.org/2001/XMLSchema">
  <xs:element name="library">
    <xs:complexType>
      <xs:sequence>
        <xs:element ref="DVD"  minOccurs="0" maxOccurs="unbounded"/>
      </xs:sequence>
    </xs:complexType>
  </xs:element>
  <xs:element name="DVD">
    <xs:complexType>
      <xs:sequence>
```

```
      <xs:element name="title" type="xs:string"/>
      <xs:element name="format" type="xs:string"/>
      <xs:element name="genre" type="xs:string"/>
    </xs:sequence>
    <xs:attribute name="id" type="xs:integer" use="required"/>
  </xs:complexType>
 </xs:element>
</xs:schema>
```

You can find this document saved as dvd_global.xsd with your resources.

The changes are relatively small. Instead of the complete <DVD> declaration being included within the <library> declaration, it is now a child of the <xs:schema> element. This means that any other definition can access the declaration using the ref keyword. The changed lines appear in bold in the code listing. You can see both the XML document and alternative schema within Figure 2-2.

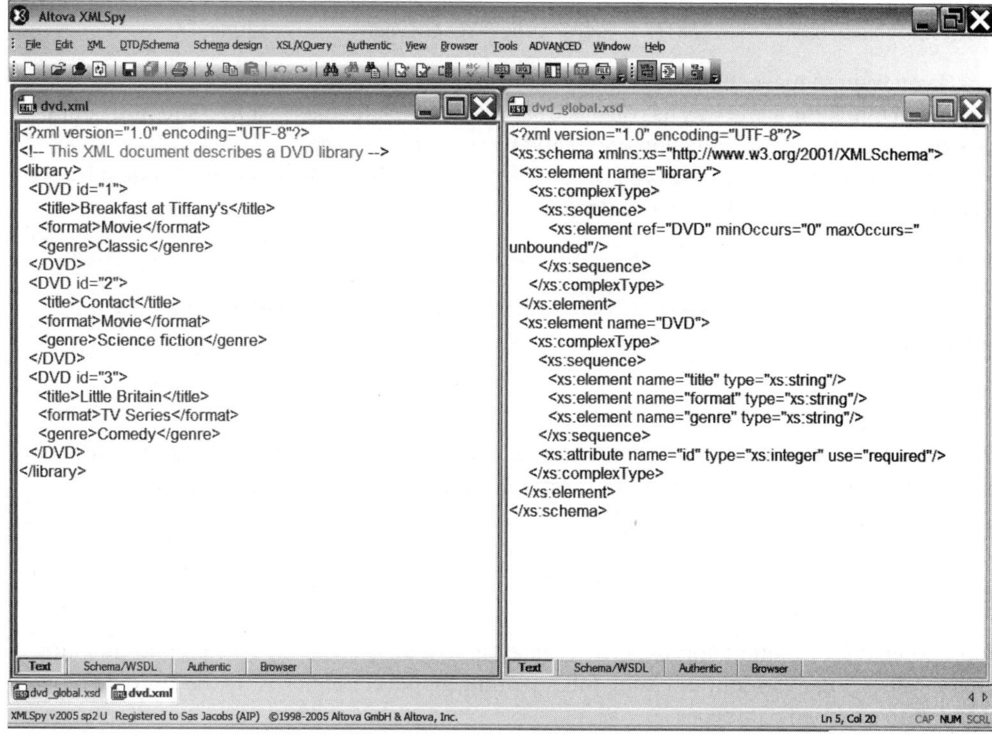

Figure 2-2. *The XML document and alternative related schema*

Creating schema documents with this structure is useful if the same element appears in more than one place. The XML schema has no concept of the document element of an instance document, so you can include more than one global element. The downside is that a validating parser could accept either element as the document element.

Defining Data Types

The sample XML schema uses only the built-in simple data types included in the XML schema recommendation. You can also define your own data types. For example, if an attribute can only have a value of yes or no, it might be useful to define a custom data type to reflect this:

```
<xs:simpleType name="YesNoType">
  <xs:restriction base="xs:string">
    <xs:enumeration value="no"/>
    <xs:enumeration value="yes"/>
  </xs:restriction>
</xs:simpleType>
```

These declarations create a simple type element with the name YesNoType. The element is based on the xs:string data type and has two possible values: yes and no.

Once defined, declarations can then access the data type in the same way as the built-in data types:

```
<xsd:attribute name="availableForLoan" type="YesNoType" use="optional"/>
```

If you want to make this data type available to other schemas, you can include the schema in much the same way as you'd use server-side include files in a web site. You could save the data type in a schema document and use the <xs:include> statement.

The data type definition is saved in the file customDataType.xsd. You can include it by using the following statement in your schema document:

```
<xs:include schemaLocation="customDataType.xsd"/>
```

You can find the files customDataType.xsd and dvd_include.xsd with the resource file downloads.

■ **Note** An included schema is sometimes referred to as an architectural schema, as its aim is to provide building blocks for the document schemas against which documents will be validated.

Schema Structures

You've seen three different approaches for creating schemas: declaring all elements and attributes within a single element (Russian doll), defining global elements using the ref data type, and defining named data types.

In general, if you're creating a schema specific to a document, the Russian doll approach works well. If you're creating a schema that you might use for several different document instances, it may be more flexible to use global definitions for at least some of your elements.

If you always want an element to be referenced by the same name, then define it as an element. Where there's a chance that elements with different names might be of the same structure, define a data type.

For example, say you have a document that contains an address that you use for multiple purposes, such as a postal address, a street address, and a delivery address. One approach would be to reuse an <address> element throughout the document. However, if you want to use the sample element structure with different element names, it would be more appropriate to define a global address data type and use it for <postalAddress>, <streetAddress>, and <deliveryAddress> elements.

Schemas and Namespaces

The subject of XML schemas is so complex that it could take up an entire book. For now, let's discuss the relationship between schemas and namespaces.

When defining a schema, it's possible to define the namespace within which an instance document must reside. You do this by using the targetNamespace attribute of the <xs:schema> element. If you do this, any reference to these elements within the schema must also use this namespace. It avoids complications if you define this as the default namespace of the XML schema. An example follows:

```
<xs:schema targetNamespace="http://www.apress.com/schemas"
xmlns="http://www.apress.com/schemas"
xmlns:xs="http://www.w3.org/2001/XMLSchema"
elementFormDefault="qualified"
attributeFormDefault="unqualified">
```

The example also sets the elementFormDefault attribute to qualified and the attributeFormDefault to unqualified. These attributes determine whether locally declared elements and attributes are namespace-qualified. A locally declared element is one declared inside a complex type element.

Setting the elementFormDefault attribute to qualified means that the local elements in the instance document must not be qualified. The attributeFormDefault setting ensures that attributes are treated as belonging to the namespace of their containing element, which is the default for XML.

Assigning a Schema to a Document

Once you create a schema document, you need to reference it from the instance document so that a validating XML parser can validate the document. You can do this with either the schemaLocation or noNamespaceSchemaLocation attribute. Use the latter if the schema has no target namespace.

These attributes are part of a W3C-controlled namespace known as the XML Schema Instance namespace. This is normally referred to with the prefix xsi. You need to declare this namespace within the document instance.

The schema document is not within a namespace, so use the noNamespaceSchemaLocation attribute as the example document element:

```
<library xmlns:xsi=http://www.w3.org/2001/XMLSchema-instance
xsi:noNamespaceSchemaLocation="dvd.xsd">
```

You can find the completed document saved as dvd_schema.xml with your code download files.

Note the syntax of the xsi:noNamespaceSchemaLocation attribute. In this case, the document uses a local reference to the schema document, but it could have used a fully qualified URI to find the schema document on the Internet.

If you use the schemaLocation attribute, the value is made up of a namespace URI followed by a URI that is the physical location of the XML schema document for that namespace. You can rewrite the document element to reference a namespace:

```
<library
xmlns="http://www.apress.com/schemas"
xmlns:xsi="http://www.w3.org/2001/XMLSchema-instance"
    xsi:schemaLocation="http://www.apress.com/schemas
    http://www.apress.com/schemas/dvd.xsd">
```

You can use either a local reference or a fully qualified URI, as shown in the preceding example. It's worth noting that the value of the xsi:schemaLocation attribute can be any number of pairs of URIs, with the first part being the URI of a namespace and the second being the location of the associated XML schema. This allows you to associate several XML schema documents with one document instance.

Schemas and Entity Declarations

One of the advantages of using DTDs is that they provide a way to define custom entity references. As mentioned, these are not available when you use an XML schema to declare XML vocabularies. If you need to include entity references when using an XML schema, you can also include a DTD in your document instance. The XML schema is used for validation while the DTD declares entity references:

```
<?xml version="1.0" encoding="UTF-8"?>
<!DOCTYPE library [
<!ENTITY copyright "Copyright 2006 Apress">
]>
<library xmlns:xsi=http://www.w3.org/2001/XMLSchema-instance
xsi:noNamespaceSchemaLocation="dvd.xsd">
```

Comparing DTDs and Schemas

You've seen how DTDs and XML schemas specify the rules for an XML vocabulary. While both types of documents serve the same purpose, there are some differences between them. A comparison of the two follows:

- DTDs and XML schemas both allow you to define the structure of an XML document so you can check it with a validating parser.
- DTDs allow you to define entities; you can't do this within XML schemas.
- XML schemas allow you to assign data types to character data; DTDs don't.
- XML schemas allow you to define custom data types; you can't do this within DTDs.
- XML schemas support the derivation of one data type from another; you can't derive data types in DTDs.
- XML schemas support namespaces; DTDs don't support namespaces.

- XML schemas allow for modular development by providing `<xsd:include>` and `<xsd:import>`; DTDs don't offer similar functionality.
- XML schemas use XML markup syntax so you can create and modify them with standard XML processing tools; DTDs don't follow XML vocabulary construction rules.
- DTDs use a concise syntax that results in smaller documents; XML schemas use less concise syntax and usually create larger documents.
- The XML schema language is newer than the DTD specification and has addressed some of DTDs' weaknesses.

DTDs and XML schemas are two of the many available schema languages. In some circumstances, it can be useful to consider alternative types of schemas.

Other Schema Types

Both DTDs and XML schemas are examples of closed schema languages. In other words, they forbid anything that the schema doesn't allow explicitly. The XML schema language offers some extensibility, but it's still fundamentally a closed language.

Other schema languages are open, allowing additional content that the schema doesn't forbid explicitly. You can use these languages either as an alternative to DTDs or XML schemas, or as an addition. Their processing occurs after the processing of the closed schema.

You may wish to use an alternative schema type if you wish to impose a constraint that isn't possible using a DTD or XML schema. For example, a tax system may have the following rule: "If the value of gender is male, then there must not be a MaternityPay element." An application often includes such business rules, but a different schema type might allow you to represent the constraint more easily.

Examples of these alternative schema languages include

- Schematron `http://www.ascc.net/xml/resource/schematron/schematron.html`
- REgular LAnguage for XML Next Generation (RELAX NG): `http://www.oasis-open.org/committees/tc_home.php?wg_abbrev=relax-ng`
- XML-Data Reduced (XDR): `http://www.ltg.ed.ac.uk/~ht/XMLData-Reduced.htm`

Schematron uses XSLT and XPath, so you can embed Schematron declarations in an XML schema document to expand its scope. I'll explain more about XSLT and XPath in this chapter's "Understanding XSLT" and "XPath" sections.

There are currently many different XML vocabularies in use. The next section introduces you to some popular vocabularies.

XML Vocabularies

In this chapter, you've seen how to define an XML vocabulary using a DTD or XML schema. Many XML vocabularies have become industry standards, so before defining your own language, it might be worthwhile to see what vocabularies already exist.

You've already seen some XML vocabularies such as XHTML and XML schema, and I'll show you more in Chapter 3. Table 2-2 lists some common XML vocabularies.

Table 2-2. *Common XML Vocabularies*

XML Language	Use	Reference
Architecture Description Markup Language (ADML)	Provides interoperability of architecture information	`http://www.opengroup.org/architecture/adml/adml_home.htm`
Chemical Markup Language (CML)	Covers macromolecular sequences to inorganic molecules and quantum chemistry	`http://www.xml-cml.org/`
Common Picture eXchange environment (CPXe)	Enables the transmission of digital pictures, orders, and commerce information	`http://www.i3a.org/i_cpxe.html`
Electronic Business XML (ebXML)	Allows enterprises to conduct business using the Internet	`http://www.ebxml.org/`
Flexible Image Transport System Markup Language (FITSML)	XML specification for astronomical data, such as images, spectra, tables, and sky atlases	`http://www.service-architecture.com/xml/articles/nasa.html`
Open Building Information Exchange (oBIX)	Enables enterprise applications to communicate with mechanical and electrical systems in buildings	`http://www.oasis-open.org/committees/tc_home.php?wg_abbrev=obix`
Mathematical Markup Language (MathML)	Describes mathematics	`http://www.w3.org/Math/`
Meat and Poultry XML (mpXML)	Used for exchanging business information within the meat and poultry supply-and-marketing chain	`http://www.mpxml.org/about/`
Market Data Definition Language (MDDL)	Enables sharing of stock market information	`http://www.mddl.org/default.asp`
Synchronized Multimedia Integration Language (SMIL)	Coordinates the display of multimedia on web sites	`http://smw.internet.com/smil/smilhome.html`
Scalable Vector Graphics (SVG)	Describes vector shapes	`http://www.w3.org/TR/SVG/`
eXtensible Business Reporting Language (XBRL)	Enables electronic communication of business and financial data	`http://www.xbrl.org/Home/`

Now that you've seen some examples of XML vocabularies, it's time to discover how to display the content within XML documents.

Displaying XML

At some stage, you're likely to need to display the contents of an XML document visually. You might need to see the contents in a web browser or print them out. In the DVD example, you also might want to refine the display so that you see just a list of the titles. You might even want to sort the document by alphabetical order of titles or by genre.

In this section, I'll introduce the XML document display technologies: CSS and XSLT.

XML and CSS

You can use CSS with XML in exactly the same way that you do with XHTML. This means that if you know how to work with CSS already, you can use the same techniques with XML. I'll discuss CSS and XML in more detail in Chapter 5; this section just covers some of the main points.

To display an XML document with CSS, you need to assign a style to each XML element name just as you would with XHTML. In XML, one difference is that the stylesheet is associated with an XML document using a processing instruction placed immediately after the XML declaration:

```
<?xml-stylesheet type="text/css" href="style.css"?>
```

In XHTML pages, the text that you wish to style is character data. With XML, that might not be the case. For example, the content might consist of numeric data that a human can't easily interpret visually. When working in CSS, it's not easy to add explanatory text when rendering the XML document. This limitation might not be important when you're working with documents that contain only text, but it might be a big consideration when you're working with other types of content.

Another limitation of CSS is that it mostly renders elements in the order in which they appear in the XML document. It's beyond the scope of CSS to reorder, sort, or filter the content in any way. When displaying XML, you may need more flexibility in determining how the data should be displayed. You can achieve this by using XSL.

XSL

Extensible Stylesheet Language (XSL) is divided into two parts: XSL Transformations (XSLT) and XSL Formatting Objects (XSL-FO). The former transforms the source XML document tree into a results tree, perhaps as an XHTML document. The latter applies formatting, usually for printed output. Figure 2-3 shows how these two processes relate.

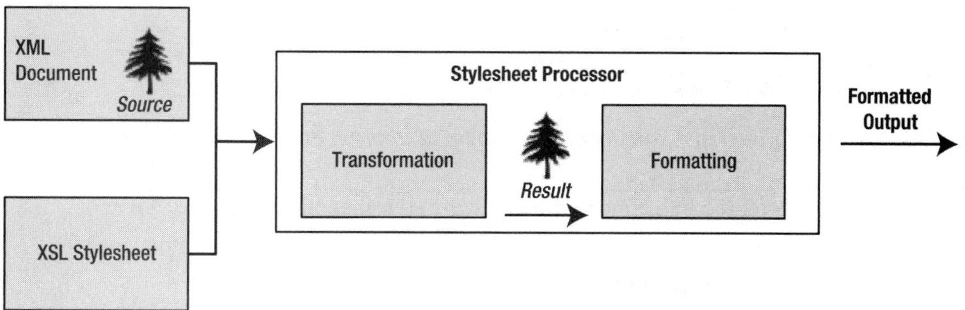

Figure 2-3. *Applying a transformation and formatting to an XML document*

Once the XSLT processor reads the XML document into memory, it's known as the *source tree*. The processor transforms nodes in the source tree using templates in a stylesheet. This process produces result nodes, which together form a result tree.

The result tree is also an XML document, although you can convert it to produce other types of output. The conversion process is known as serialization. As I mentioned earlier, the result tree will usually be serialized as XHTML. You can also produce printed output from the result tree with XSL-FO.

Nowadays, when someone refers to XSL, they're usually referring to XSLT. You can use XSL-FO to produce a printed output, a PDF file, or perhaps an aural layout.

Understanding XSLT

I'll delve into XSLT in much more detail in Chapters 6 and 7, but here I'll work through a simple example so you can see the power of XSLT. You'll see how to use XSLT to convert your DVD document into an XHTML page that includes CSS styling. This process is different from styling the XML content directly with CSS, which I'll cover in Chapter 5.

Earlier, you saw that CSS styles the source document using a push model, where the structure of the input defines the structure of the output. XSLT allows both a push model and a pull model, where the structure of the stylesheet defines the structure of the output.

In this example, you'll see how to use both. You'll use the source document to define the display order, but the stylesheet will provide the structuring information. You'll create a list of all DVDs to display in a table on an XHTML page, and you'll add a little CSS styling to improve the appearance. You can find the files used in the example saved as `dvd_XSLT.xml` and `dvdtoHTML.xsl`. They are saved within this chapter's ZIP file in the Source Code area of the Apress web site (`http://www.apress.com`).

Figure 2-4 shows the web page produced by the XSLT stylesheet.

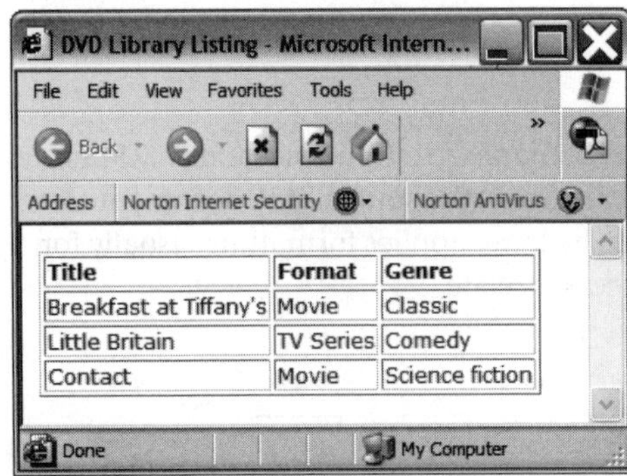

Figure 2-4. *The transformed dvd.xml document shown in Internet Explorer*

The web page is created by applying the following stylesheet to the source XML document:

```
<?xml version="1.0" encoding="UTF-8"?>
<xsl:stylesheet version="1.0" xmlns:xsl="http://www.w3.org/1999/XSL/Transform">
  <xsl:output method="html" version="4.0"/>
  <xsl:template match="/">
    <html>
      <head>
      <title>DVD Library Listing</title>
      <link rel="stylesheet" type="text/css" href="style.css"/>
      </head>
      <body>
```

```
    <tal
      <
      <
      <                                  )">
                                         le"/></td>
                                         nat"/></td>
                                         re"/></td>
      </
    </ta
  </body
 </html>
</xsl:temp
</xsl:styles
```

The style ... ation. It uses the xsl prefix to denote the XSLT namespace, which is declared in the document element, <stylesheet>. You're also required to declare the version of XSLT that you're using—in this case, 1.0:

```
<?xml version="1.0" encoding="UTF-8"?>
<xsl:stylesheet version="1.0" xmlns:xsl="http://www.w3.org/1999/XSL/Transform">
```

Next, the stylesheet declares the output type—in this case, HTML 4.0:

```
<xsl:output method="html" version="4.0"/>
```

You could also choose the output method xml or text. If you choose the output type xml, you can generate well-formed XML or XHTML. The output type text is useful if you want to create a comma-delimited file for import into a spreadsheet or database.

The next section of the stylesheet uses a template to generate the <html>, <head>, and opening <body> tags. I left out the DOCTYPE declaration to simplify the example:

```
 <xsl:template match="/">
  <html>
  <head>
    <title>DVD Library Listing</title>
    <link rel="stylesheet" type="text/css" href="style.css"/>
  </head>
  <body>
  <table width="40%">
    <tr>
      <th>Title</th>
      <th>Format</th>
      <th>Genre</th>
    </tr>
```

The first line specifies what nodes in the source tree the template matches. It uses an XPath expression to determine the node. You'll find out more about XPath a little later in the chapter. In this case, you're matching the root node, which is indicated by a slash (/).

■ **Note** Technically, the root node isn't the same as the root element. The root note is at a higher level in the document and has the root element as a child. This allows the stylesheet to access information in the prolog and epilog, as well as information in elements.

The template specifies what should happen when the XSLT processor encounters the root. In this case, the result tree includes the HTML tags indicated within the template. It should generate the following output:

```
<html>
  <head>
   <title>DVD Libarary Listing</title>
    <link rel="stylesheet" type="text/css" href="style.css"/>
  </head>
  <body>
    <table width="40%">
      <tr>
        <th>Title</th>
        <th>Format</th>
        <th>Genre</th>
      </tr>
```

The result tree sets up the HTML document and adds a link to an external CSS stylesheet called `style.css`. The closing `<table>` and `<body>` tags appear after the other content that you include.

The next section within the stylesheet includes each `<DVD>` element as a row in the table using another template. This time the template matches each `<DVD>` element. Because there are multiple `DVD` elements, it's appropriate to use an `xsl:for-each` statement:

```
<xsl:for-each select="/library/DVD">
  <xsl:sort select="genre"/>
  <tr>
    <td><xsl:value-of select="title"/></td>
    <td><xsl:value-of select="format"/></td>
    <td><xsl:value-of select="genre"/></td>
  </tr>
</xsl:for-each>
```

The `xsl:for-each` statement finds the `<DVD>` node using the XPath expression `/library/DVD`. In other words, start with the root node, locate the `<library>` element, and move to the `<DVD>` node. This statement retrieves all of the `<DVD>` nodes in the XML document.

The next statement dictates the sorting for the group of nodes using the `xsl:sort` statement. In this case, the stylesheet sorts in order of the genre. Because the template refers to the `/library/DVD` path, it's appropriate to use a relative path to specify the `<genre>` node.

Within the `xsl:for-each` statement, the `xsl:value-of` element selects a specific element for inclusion in the table cell. The stylesheet repeats the statement three times—one for each of the `<title>`, `<format>`, and `<genre>` elements.

This transformation results in the following results tree:

```
<html>
  <head>
    <title>DVD Library Listing</title>
    <link rel="stylesheet" type="text/css" href="style.css" />
  </head>
  <body>
    <table width="40%">
      <tr>
        <th>Title</th>
        <th>Format</th>
        <th>Genre</th>
      </tr>
      <tr>
        <td>Breakfast at Tiffany's</td>
        <td>Movie</td>
        <td>Classic</td>
      </tr>
      <tr>
        <td>Little Britain</td>
        <td>TV Series</td>
        <td>Comedy</td>
      </tr>
      <tr>
        <td>Contact</td>
        <td>Movie</td>
        <td>Science fiction</td>
      </tr>
```

The remaining section of the stylesheet adds the closing `</table>`,`</body>`, and `</html>` tags:

```
        </table>
      </body>
    </html>
  </xsl:template>
</xsl:stylesheet>
```

If you want to see some of the power of XSLT, you can modify the stylesheet to change the sort order. You can also filter the content to display specific records; you'll see this in Chapters 6 and 7.

XSLT Summary

This section shows some of the functionality of XSLT, and you should remember these key points:

- CSS applies styles to an XML document based on the current structure of the document tree. This is called a push model.
- XSLT can transform a source XML document into any well-formed XML document that can be serialized as XML, HTML, or text.
- XSLT stylesheets can produce a result tree in a different order from the source tree.
- XSLT can add text and markup during the transformation.
- XSLT is template-based, making it mainly a declarative language.
- XSLT makes extensive use of XPath to locate nodes in the source tree.

I've mentioned XPath during this discussion of XSLT, so it's worthwhile exploring it in a little more detail.

XPath

You saw that the XSLT stylesheet relied heavily on the use of XPath to locate specific parts of the source XML document tree. Other recommendations, such as XPointer, also rely on the XPath specification, so it's useful to have an understanding of the basics. One important thing to realize is that XPath doesn't use XML rules to construct expressions.

You use XPath by writing expressions that work with the XML document tree. Applying an XPath expression to a document returns one of the following:

- A single node
- A group of nodes
- A Boolean value
- A floating point number
- A string

XPath expressions can't address the XML declaration in a document because it isn't part of the document tree. They also don't address embedded DTD declarations or blocks of CDATA.

XPath treats an XML document as a hierarchical tree made up of nodes. Each tree contains

- Element nodes
- Attribute nodes
- Text nodes

- Processing instructions
- Comments
- Namespaces

The root node is the starting point for the XML document tree, and there's only one root node in an XML document. The XML document itself is a node in the tree, and it's a child of the root node. Other children of the root node include processing instructions and comments outside of the document node. You write XPath expressions to locate specific nodes in the tree.

XPath Expressions

XPath expressions use an axis name and two colon characters (::) to identify nodes in the XML document:

```
/axis::nodetest[predicate]
```

XPath expressions include location paths that you read from left to right to identify the different parts of an XML document. The expression separates each step in the path with a slash (/):

```
/axis::nodetest[predicate]/axis::nodetest[predicate]
```

These paths indicate how nodes relate to each other and their context. The starting point of the path provides the context for the node. Using a slash means that the root element provides the context. The processor evaluates XPath expressions without this character against the current node.

The axis or axes used in the path describe these relationships. The `nodetest` identifies the node to select. It may optionally include one or more predicates that filter the selection.

The following expression refers to any `<DVD>` descendants of the root element. The root element provides the context. The descendant axis specifies that the expression should select the descendants of the `<DVD>` node:

```
/descendant::DVD
```

XPath recognizes the following axes:

- `ancestor`
- `ancestor-or-self`
- `child`
- `descendant`
- `descendant-or-self`
- `following`
- `following-sibling`
- `preceding`

- `preceding-sibling`
- `parent`
- `self`

The axis names are self-explanatory; it's beyond the scope of this book to go into them in too much detail. It's worth mentioning, however, that you can write a shortened form of XPath expressions for the `child`, `parent`, and `self` axes. Table 2-3 provides some examples of the long and short forms of expressions.

Table 2-3. *Examples of Long and Short Forms of XPath Expressions*

Long Form	Abbreviation
`child::DVD`	`DVD`
`DVD/attribute::id`	`DVD/@id`
`self::node()`	`.`
`parent::node()`	`..`

You saw the use of abbreviated XPath expressions in the previous section on XSLT. For example, you could refer to the `<DVD>` nodes using `/library/DVD`. When you want to refer to a child node, use `title` rather than `child::title`.

Identifying Specific Nodes

XPath allows you to navigate to a specific node within a collection by referring to its position:

```
/library/DVD[2]
```

This expression refers to the second `<DVD>` node within the `<library>` node.

You also can apply a filter within the expression:

```
/library/DVD/[genre='Comedy']
```

The preceding expression finds the `<DVD>` nodes with a child `<genre>` node containing `Comedy`.

Including Calculations and Functions

XPath expressions can include mathematical operations, and you can use the + (addition), – (subtraction), * (multiplication), `div` (division), and `mod` (modulus) operators. Obviously, you can't use the / symbol for division because it's included in the location path. These expressions might be useful if you want to carry out calculations during a stylesheet transformation.

You can also include functions within XPath expressions. These include node set, string, Boolean, and number functions. Again, it's beyond the scope of this book to explore these in detail, but it's useful to know that they exist. If you want to find out more about the XPath recommendation, visit `http://www.w3.org/TR/1999/REC-xpath-19991116`.

XPath Summary

The following list summarizes the main points to consider when working with XPath expressions:

- You can use XPath in XSLT stylesheets and XPointers to specify a location in an XML tree.
- XPath expressions identify the location using an axis name, a node test, and, optionally, a predicate. The expressions read from left to right with each point in the path separated by a forward slash (/).
- You can abbreviate some XPath expressions to use a shortened form.
- You can include mathematical operators and functions within an XPath expression if you want to perform calculations during a transformation.

You saw earlier that XPath expressions specify locations in XSLT stylesheets. These expressions can also be used in XPointers, which point to a specific location within an XLink. Before we see this, let's look at XLinks.

Linking with XML

XLinks provide a powerful alternative to traditional XHTML links. XHTML links allow you to link from a source to a destination point, in one direction. XLinks allow you to

- Create two-way links
- Create links between external documents
- Change the behavior of links so that they trigger when a page loads
- Specify how the linked content displays

You can find out more about the W3C XLink recommendation at `http://www.w3.org/TR/2001/REC-xlink-20010627/`. The XPointer recommendation is split into the element (`http://www.w3.org/TR/2003/REC-xptr-element-20030325/`), the framework (`http://www.w3.org/TR/2003/REC-xptr-framework-20030325/`), and the xmlns scheme (`http://www.w3.org/TR/2003/REC-xptr-xmlns-20030325/`). At the time of writing, a fourth recommendation is in development—the xpointer() scheme (`http://www.w3.org/TR/2002/WD-xptr-xpointer-20021219/`). This recommendation adds advanced functionality to XPointer, including the ability to address strings, points, and ranges within an XML document.

Currently, XML tools offer very limited support for XLink and XPointer. However, the recommendations are important and their usage is likely to be extended in the future, so it's worthwhile having an understanding of how they fit into the XML framework.

Let's start by looking at the two different types of XLink that you can create: simple and extended.

Simple Links

A simple link connects a single source to a single target, much like an XHTML link. Before you can include an XLink, the XML document that includes the XLink must also include a reference to the XLink namespace. You can do this in the document element as follows:

```
<?xml version="1.0"?>
<library xmlns:xlink="http://www.w3.org/1999/xlink">
```

By convention, developers use xlink to preface this namespace.

In XHTML, the <a> element indicates a link. Web browsers understand the meaning of this element and display the link accordingly. In XML, you can add a link to any element within the XML document.

Let's look at an example of a simple link:

```
<elementName
  xlink:type="simple"
  xlink:href="http://wwww.apress.com"
  xlink:title="Apress"
  xlink:show="replace"
  xlink:actuate="onRequest">
  Here is a linked element
</elementName>
```

This XLink provides a link to http://www.apress.com. It includes an xlink:type attribute indicating that it's a simple link. It uses the attribute xlink:href to provide the address of the link. The link has a title that is intended to be read by humans.

The XLink includes an xlink:show behavior of replace, which indicates that the link should replace the current URL. You could also specify xlink:show = "new", which is akin to the XHTML target="_blank".

Other values include embed, other, and none. Choosing embed is similar to embedding an image in an XHTML page—the target resource replaces the link definition in the source. A value of other leaves the link action up to the implementation and indicates that it should look for other information in the link to determine its behavior. The value none also leaves the behavior up to the implementation, but with no hints in the link.

The xlink:activate attribute determines when the link opens. In this example, using onRequest indicates that the document will await user action before activating the link. The attribute could also use values of onLoad, other, or none. Setting the attribute value to onLoad causes the link to be followed immediately after the resource loads. You could use this value with xlink:show="embed" to create a display from a set of linked source documents. The values other and none have the same meanings as in the xlink:show attribute.

The preceding example creates a link that's very similar to a traditional XHTML link, with some additional capabilities. An extended XLink offers much more powerful capabilities.

Extended Links

Extended links provide much more complex linking abilities. You can

- Link more than two resources
- Create a link between resources outside of the source (out-of-line linking)
- Separate the direction of the link from the definition of the resources being linked

Currently, no web browser supports extended XLinks, so I'll give you a brief introduction only. To use extended links, you must use more than one element and several attributes. Let's start by looking at how you could link more than two resources.

Linking More Than Two Resources

Web developers often create links that effectively move from a single point to multiple destinations. You can see this in the following analogy.

Consider a web site for DVD movies. Any page providing information about a single DVD might contain references to other pages about the actors or the director. For example, if you're looking at *The Lord of the Rings: The Fellowship of the Ring*, you might want to see other films starring Sir Ian McKellen. The link from this page goes to multiple destinations, each referring to a film including the actor.

In XHTML, you could write several links to the other films starring Sir Ian McKellen. In XML, you can use a single extended link. XLink doesn't define the presentation of these links. You could use an XSLT stylesheet to display them as a list of XHTML links or a drop-down list.

Out-of-Line Linking

When you use XHTML links and simple XLinks, you define the link at its source point. With an extended XLink, you can define both the source and destination from an unrelated point. You don't need to include the link in either the source or the destination document. This could be useful if you need to add links from documents where you don't have write permission.

You can effectively build your own links to other people's documents. Out-of-line links are likely to be useful to build up a set of information resources. You can also update links more easily because they're stored in a single location.

Separating the Direction of the Link from the Resource Definitions

In an extended link, the `xlink:type="locator"` attribute identifies elements participating in the link. Elements with the `xlink:type` of `arc` define the connections. This construction allows you to traverse links in both directions, rather than having the fixed source and target present in the simple link.

Returning to the DVD example, you can define extended XLinks that can be followed either way. You can use the link to find out which actors appeared in a film. You can also follow a link from the actors to the films they've appeared in or see which other actors appeared in the same film. All you need to do is build a "link database" containing a list of all the linked resources and the definitions of a set of arcs to be followed. A simple example follows:

```
<allFilms xlink:type="extended">
  <film xlink:type="locator"
  xlink:href="fellowshipofthering.xml" xlink:label="fellowship"/>
  <actor1 xlink:type="locator"
  xlink:href="ianmckellen.xml" xlink:label="actor1"/>
  <actor2 xlink:type="locator"
  xlink:href="elijahwood.xml" xlink:label="actor2"/>
  <arcName xlink:type="arc"
  xlink:from="fellowship" xlink:to="actor1"/>
  <arcName xlink:type="arc"
  xlink:from="fellowship" xlink:to="actor2"/>
  <arcName xlink:type="arc"
  xlink:from="actor1" xlink:to="actor2"/>
  <arcName xlink:type="arc"
  xlink:from="actor2" xlink:to="actor1"/>
</allFilms>
```

So far, you've seen XLinks that link to a complete resource. Now it's time to discuss the role of XPointers, which allow you to link to a specific section within an XML document.

XPointer

In the preceding section, all links examples referred to complete documents. However, you may want the source or destination to be a point within a document or a part of a document. You can achieve this using XPointers. In a way, this is similar to using an anchor within an XHTML link:

```
<a href="movies.htm#fellowshipofthering">
```

When someone clicks this link, the document loads and positions the screen at the named anchor `fellowshipofthering`.

If you use an XPointer, you don't need to mark part of the document with a named anchor. Instead, you can use the following construction:

```
<xlink:simple xmlns:xlink="http://www.w3.org/1999/xlink"
  xlink:href="movies.xml#xpointer(/library/DVD/title[5])"
  xlink:title="Fellowship of the Ring"
  xlink:show="replace"
  xlink:actuate="onRequest"/>
```

The XPointer appears at the end of the `xlink:href` attribute and uses the keyword `#xpointer`. It includes an XPath expression to identify the destination for the link. In this case, you're linking to the fifth `<title>` node within the `<DVD>` node in the `<library>` node.

Because you don't need to add a named anchor to the destination link, you can be more flexible when creating out-of-line extended links. XPointer also allows you to specify a range of locations to view a small part of a large document. You can use the `xlink:show="embed"` attribute with an XPointer to embed a specific fragment of one XML document within another. You can do this without altering any of the source documents. I'm sure you can see how much more flexibility this approach to linking offers.

XML Links Summary

XLink and XPointer combine to provide powerful linking opportunities, which, unfortunately, aren't yet supported in web browsers. In this section, I've only scratched the surface of what's possible. The following list summarizes the main points about XML links:

- In XHTML, a link has a fixed behavior. You click on the link to arrive at a destination. In XML, you can specify additional behaviors.
- XHTML links have a single source and a single destination. XML links can have multiple destinations.
- XHTML links always link from the anchor (<a>) element to a destination. XML links can be bidirectional from any element.
- XHTML links use source and destination points that are embedded in documents. XML links can be completely separate from either end point.
- To link to a specific location in the destination point, XHTML links require the inclusion of a named anchor in the destination document. XLinks can use an XPointer containing an XPath expression instead and don't need to modify the destination document in any way.
- In XTML, a named anchor refers to a single point in the destination document. In XML, you can use XPointers to refer to a portion of the document.

Summary

In this chapter, I've covered some of the related XML recommendations from the W3C, including the role of namespaces, the use of DTDs and XML schemas in specifying XML vocabularies, and the application of XSLT in transforming XML documents for different purposes. I've also provided a brief introduction to XPath and shown you some of the main points about XLinks and XPointers.

In Chapter 3, I'll show you some web-specific XML vocabularies and examine XHTML, Mathematical Markup Language (MathML), Scalable Vector Graphics (SVG), and web services in detail.

CHAPTER 3

Web Vocabularies

As XML grows in popularity, the number of XML vocabularies used within various industry and community sectors increases. These groups use XML to store database information, exchange structured information, and even describe concepts.

XML is a mechanism for storing data. When first applied to the web, XML addressed many of the shortcomings associated with HTML. Although you can view any XML document on the web, some vocabularies were created specifically for this medium.

In this chapter, I'll focus on web vocabularies such as

- XHTML
- Mathematical Markup Language (MathML)
- Scalable Vector Graphics (SVG)
- Web services (WSDL and SOAP)

You can use these vocabularies in web browsers and other web-enabled devices.

You can download the files referred to in this chapter from the Source Code area of the Apress web site (`http://www.apress.com`).

Let's start with a closer look at XHTML.

XHTML

XHTML is probably the most widespread web vocabulary of all; web developers have been using it for several years. XHTML enjoys support in modern web browsers such as Internet Explorer 6 for Windows, Mozilla Firefox 1.x for Windows, and Safari 1.x for Macintosh.

The W3C states that XHTML is HTML *reformulated* in XML. XHTML 1.0 is nothing other than HTML 4.01 in XML syntax. It's an XML-compliant version of HTML. XHTML is a great starting point for a discussion of XML vocabularies.

XHTML provides a number of benefits compared with HTML. First, XHTML separates presentation from content. In XHTML, content is made up of data as well as the structural elements that organize that data. HTML was concerned with both information and its display, whereas its replacement, XHTML, is concerned with both information and the way it's structured. XHTML also uses much stricter construction rules compared with HTML, as XHTML web pages must be well formed. You learned about well-formed documents in Chapter 1.

Because XHTML is based on XML, you can use XML-specific tools and technologies to create modular documents. Throughout the chapter, I'll show you how to merge other vocabularies into XHTML.

Let's begin by looking more closely at the benefits of XHTML.

Separation of Presentation and Content

The separation of content from presentation is perhaps the single most important concept in web development today. This fundamental principle underpins most modern web specifications.

Content refers to the basic data and structures that make up a document. Within XHTML, this includes elements such as headings, paragraphs, tables, and lists. Presentation determines how these structures appear within the viewing device and might include font faces, colors, borders, and other visual information. Cascading Style Sheets (CSS) control the presentation of a document.

■ **Note** When working with XML applications, you can separate the content into both data and data structures. In XML applications, an XML document supplies the data, while XSLT stylesheets provide the structure. You still apply styling through CSS stylesheets.

It's important to separate content from presentation because it allows you to repackage the content for different audiences. If you want to provide the same information to a web browser, a mobile phone, and a screen reader, the presentation layer must be different for each device. You can achieve this by excluding the presentation of information from web documents.

Separating presentation from content has four major benefits:

- Accessibility
- Targeted presentation using stylesheets
- Streamlined maintenance
- Improved processing

Let's look at each of these benefits in more detail.

Accessibility

In recent times, the W3C has focused on making XHTML more accessible to people with disabilities. For example, people with visual impairments can use screen readers and voice browsers when working with XHTML documents. Documents that follow the XHTML construction rules often require little or no change, so users can access them with a screen reader.

Many countries have legislation requiring web sites to be accessible to people with disabilities. In the United States, Section 508 of the Rehabilitation Act of 1973 requires people with disabilities to have access to federal agency electronic information. You can find out more about this regulation at `http://www.usability.gov/accessibility/`.

The W3C Web Accessibility Initiative web site (`http://www.w3.org/WAI/`) provides information about how to make web sites accessible. The site includes quick tips for accessibility (`http://www.w3.org/WAI/References/QuickTips/`), as well as a list of tools to help you evaluate whether your site is currently accessible (`http://www.w3.org/WAI/ER/existingtools.html`).

By separating the visual elements from the actual content of your page, you make the content instantly more accessible. Screen readers and other text-based browsers, such as Lynx for Unix and Linux, can interpret the flow of the document easily. Ultimately, users of your site will have a better experience.

Targeted Presentation

If you separate the presentation layer from your content, you'll be able to target its appearance for specific devices. You can do this by storing all style information within a stylesheet and linking a specific stylesheet for each device that you want to support. Storing the style information in one place makes it easier to reuse stylesheets and maintain a consistent look.

Several types of stylesheets exist, but the most popular are CSS and XSLT. I'll explain these stylesheets in detail in Chapters 5 to 7.

Streamlined Site Maintenance

Storing the content and structure separately from the presentation layer makes it easier to maintain your web site. Pages no longer contain presentational elements mixed in with the XHTML structures and data. When working through long blocks of code, you only need to concern yourself with the structural elements because the presentation layer exists elsewhere. This streamlines the site maintenance process and speeds up workflow.

Improved Processing

Accessibility and targeted presentation were important concerns in HTML even before XHTML was introduced. XHTML, however, directly addresses the need for an improved processing model. Because the rules for XML are so strict, processing XHTML documents becomes easier than processing its predecessor HTML. Software programs can perform XML-related tasks, such as designing XSLT stylesheets. See the WYSIWYG XSLT Designer by Stylus Studio (`http://www.stylusstudio.com/xhtml.html`) for one such example.

Because the rules for constructing HTML were less strict than XHTML rules, it was possible for HTML pages to contain mistakes that didn't affect their display. For example, you could leave out a closing `</body>` tag but still be able to view the page within a browser.

In addition, some web browsers rendered elements slightly differently, so browser manufacturers started adding proprietary extensions to their browsers. Ultimately, this led to incompatible browsers and lack of compliance with the HTML specification.

You can instruct more recent browser versions and software tools to discard XHTML documents that aren't authored correctly and don't use valid, well-formed XHTML. Modern browsers feature improved page processing because they don't need to deal with malformed documents.

Cell phones and personal digital assistants (PDAs) are capable of viewing web documents using either Wireless Markup Language (WML) or XHTML Basic. WML is an XML vocabulary for Wireless Application Protocol (WAP)-enabled phones, and XHTML Basic is a cut-down version of XHTML that includes only basic markup and text. XHTML Basic was created using XHTML's modularization framework, which I'll discuss in more detail in the "XHTML Modularization" section.

XHTML Construction Rules

The rules for constructing XHTML pages are a little different compared with HTML pages. You must follow these rules in XHTML:

- Include a DOCTYPE declaration specifying that the document is an XHTML document.
- Optionally include an XML declaration.
- Write all tags in lowercase.
- Close all elements.
- Enclose all attributes in quotation marks.
- Write attributes in full (i.e., don't minimize attributes).
- Use the `id` attribute instead of `name`.
- Nest all tags correctly.
- Specify character encoding.
- Specify language.

You'll see how these rules are applied in the following section, which covers DOCTYPE declarations. I'll also work through some sample XHTML documents.

DOCTYPE Declarations

In any web vocabulary, you need to determine which elements and attributes are valid. In Chapter 2, you saw how you can do this using Document Type Definitions (DTD) and XML schemas. XHTML 1.0 allows for three different DOCTYPE declarations that determine which DTD to use. You can write the following XHTML documents:

- Transitional
- Strict
- Frameset

A DOCTYPE declaration tells a validator how to check your web page. It also instructs a web browser to render your page in standards-compliant mode. Using an outdated or incorrect DOCTYPE makes browsers operate in "Quirks" mode, where they assume that you're writing old-style HTML.

XHTML 2.0

At the time of writing, the W3C had prepared a working draft of the XHTML 2.0 specification (`http://www.w3.org/TR/xhtml2/`). This vocabulary removes backward compatibility and all presentation elements in favor of stylesheets. It allows for more flexible organization using sections and headers, and it introduces separator and line elements, as well as navigation lists. It introduces links to every element and overhauls tables and forms.

The most recent XHTML specification, XHTML 1.1, became a recommendation in May 2001. It has only one document type to choose from: XHTML 1.1, which is very similar to XHTML 1.0 strict.

Each of these four document types has a slightly different set of allowable elements. Choosing the right type of document should be the first step in building your XHTML page. I'll explain each of these document types in more detail.

The examples in this chapter show you how to create pages for an imaginary web site called "Mars Travel." I'll keep the examples simple so you can focus on the XHTML content.

Transitional XHTML Documents

You use the transitional document type for web sites that need to work in many different web browsers, because it supports the deprecated elements not allowed in the strict DTD. If you're not ready or able to remove all presentation from your documents, you should use the transitional DTD.

Let's look at an example of some transitional markup:

```
<?xml version="1.0" encoding="UTF-8"?>
<!DOCTYPE html PUBLIC "-//W3C//DTD XHTML 1.0 Transitional//EN"
"http://www.w3.org/TR/xhtml1/DTD/xhtml1-transitional.dtd">
<html xmlns="http://www.w3.org/1999/xhtml">
  <head>
    <title>Mars Travel</title>
  </head>
  <body bgcolor="#FFFFFF">
    <h1 align="center">Mars Travel<br />
      <i>Visits to a faraway place </i>
    </h1>
    <hr width="100%" />
    <h2 align="center">Your spacecraft</h2>
    <p align="center">
      Your spacecraft is the Mars Explorer, which provides the latest in
      passenger luxury and travel speed.
    </p>
    <hr width="100%" />
    <p align="center">XHTML 1.0 Transitional Document</p>
  </body>
</html>
```

You can find this document saved as `marstransitional.htm` with your code download.

The document begins with an XML declaration:

```
<?xml version="1.0" encoding="UTF-8"?>
```

XHTML documents don't require an XML declaration, but it's recommended that you include one. If you include the declaration, web browsers can check that the document is well formed.

Immediately following the XML declaration, a DOCTYPE declaration tells the web browser exactly what kind of document you're writing:

```
<!DOCTYPE html PUBLIC "-//W3C//DTD XHTML 1.0 Transitional//EN"
"http://www.w3.org/TR/xhtml1/DTD/xhtml1-transitional.dtd">
```

The document root `<html>` contains a reference to the XHTML namespace:

```
<html xmlns="http://www.w3.org/1999/xhtml">
```

The markup is well-formed XML, but it still contains some presentational information—in particular, `align` and `bgcolor` attributes.

You can download this example, called `marstransitional.htm`, in the Source Code area of the Apress web site (`http://www.apress.com`). If you open the file in a web browser, you should see something like the screen shot shown in Figure 3-1.

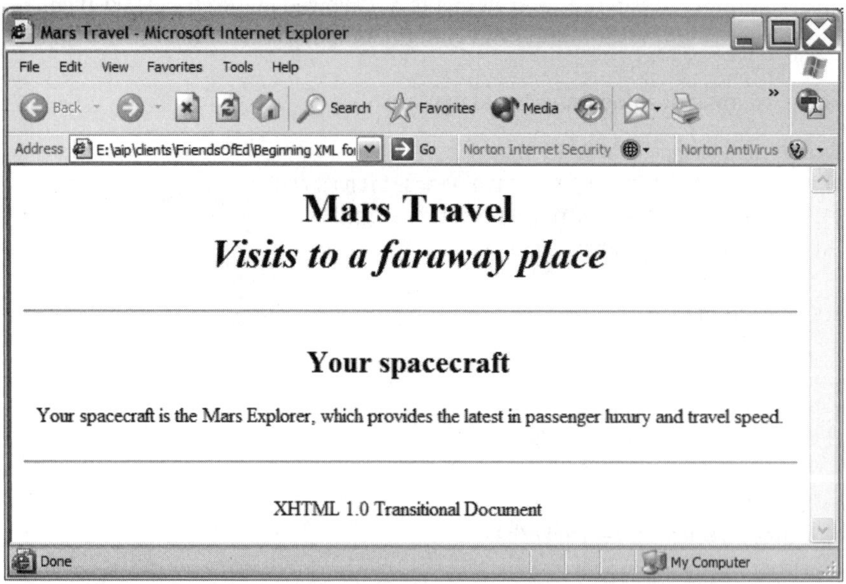

Figure 3-1. *The marstransitional.htm page displayed in Internet Explorer*

The XHTML transitional DTD can be useful if you need to support older browsers. Otherwise, you should try to use the strict or XHTML 1.1 document types.

Strict XHTML Documents

Strict XHTML documents allow you to work with only structural tags, such as headings (<h1>, <h2>, <h3>, <h4>, <h5>, <h6>), paragraphs (<p>), and lists (<ul>, <ol>, <dl>). All of the presentational elements and attributes, such as align and bgcolor, are removed. The XHTML 1.1 specification has also completely removed presentational markup. In both strict and XHTML 1.1 document types, you should always use stylesheets to control how your document appears in various browsers.

Let's look at a sample of a strict XHTML document:

```
<?xml version="1.0" encoding="UTF-8"?>
<!DOCTYPE html PUBLIC "-//W3C//DTD XHTML 1.0 Strict//EN"
"http://www.w3.org/TR/xhtml1/DTD/xhtml1-strict.dtd">
<html xmlns="http://www.w3.org/1999/xhtml">
  <head>
    <title>Mars Travel</title>
    <link href="styles.css" type="text/css" rel="stylesheet" />
  </head>
  <body>
    <h1>Mars Travel<br />
      <em>Visits to a faraway place </em>
    </h1>
    <hr />
    <h2>Your spacecraft</h2>
    <p class="centered">
      Your spacecraft is the Mars Explorer, which provides the latest in
      passenger luxury and travel speed.
    </p>
    <hr />
    <p class="footer">XHTML 1.0 Strict Document</p>
  </body>
</html>
```

You can find this file saved as marsstrict.htm with your resources.

The strict XHTML document is much shorter and doesn't contain any presentational markup. Instead, it contains a link to a stylesheet called styles.css, which includes the presentational elements. It also replaces the presentational <i> element with the structural <em> element. If you view the file in a web browser, it will look much the same as the first XHTML document.

The styles.css stylesheet contains the following presentational elements:

```
h1 {
  font-weight: bold;
  font-size: 24px;
  text-align: center;
}
h2 {
  font-weight: bold;
  font-size: 20px;
```

```
  text-align: center;
}
hr {
  width: 100%;
}
.centered {
  text-align: center;
}
.footer{
  text-align: center;
}
```

The declarations redefine the <h1>, <h2>, and <hr> elements and create classes called centered and footer. I'll explain CSS in more detail in Chapter 5.

You can change the look of the web page easily by modifying the CSS. If you apply the same stylesheet to multiple pages, you can update all pages at once by making changes. Figure 3-2 shows the same web page with a modified style sheet.

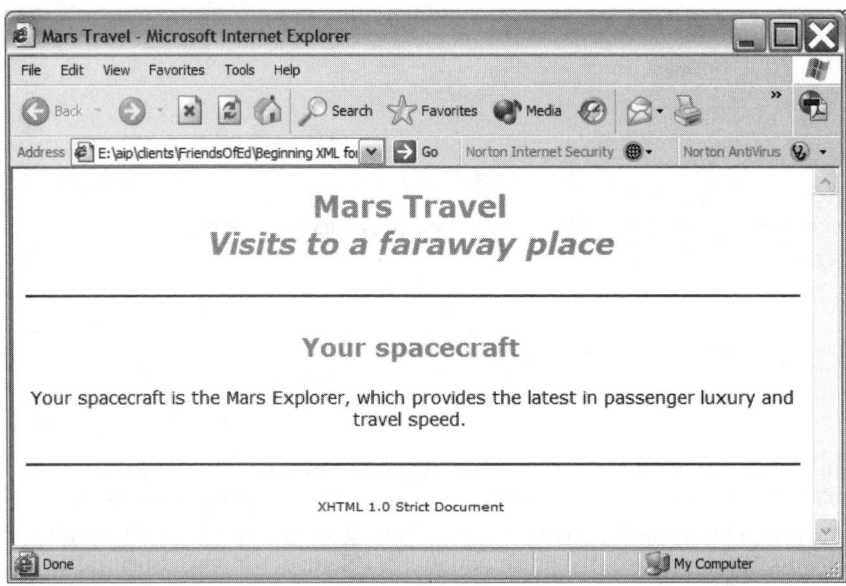

Figure 3-2. *A revised presentation of the marsstrict.htm file*

You can find these files saved as marsstrict2.htm and styles2.css.

The stylesheet tells the browser to set the sizes and colors for the <h1> and <h2> elements. It also changes the font for the entire page and defines a color for the <hr> element. The two classes centered and footer inherit the default font and center the text. The footer class uses a smaller font size.

Frameset XHTML Documents

XHTML allows you to write a third kind of document called a frameset document. You use frameset documents with web pages that use frames. Frames are no longer recommended for a variety of reasons, so I'll discuss this topic only briefly.

Use the following DOCTYPE declaration to reference a frameset DTD:

```
<!DOCTYPE html PUBLIC "-//W3C//DTD XHTML 1.0 Frameset//EN"
"http://www.w3.org/TR/xhtml1/DTD/xhtml1-frameset.dtd">
```

■ **Note** A frameset can include both transitional and strict documents. You can also include one frameset document within another, allowing you to have nested frames.

XHTML 1.1 Documents

XHTML version 1.1 is a modular version of the XHTML 1.0 strict document type. As it's based on the strict document type, you can't include any presentation elements or attributes; you need to declare these in a stylesheet. Frames, which are often presentational, have been moved to a separate "module" that is not enabled by default.

XHTML is modular, which means that parts of the XHTML document have been divided into separate modules that you can add or remove. When I discuss XHTML Modularization later in the chapter, I'll show you how to mix web vocabularies using different XHTML 1.1 modules.

Take a look at this simple XHTML 1.1 document:

```
<?xml version="1.0" encoding="UTF-8"?>
<!DOCTYPE html PUBLIC "-//W3C//DTD XHTML 1.1//EN"
"http://www.w3.org/TR/xhtml11/DTD/xhtml11.dtd">
<html xmlns="http://www.w3.org/1999/xhtml">
  <head>
    <title>Mars Travel</title>
    <link href="styles.css" type="text/css" rel="stylesheet" />
  </head>
  <body>
    <h1>Mars Travel<br />
      <em>Visits to a faraway place </em>
    </h1>
    <hr />
    <h2>Your spacecraft</h2>
    <p class="centered">
      Your spacecraft is the Mars Explorer, which provides the latest in
      passenger luxury and travel speed.
    </p>
    <hr />
    <p class="footer">XHTML 1.1 Document</p>
  </body>
</html>
```

This document is saved as `marsxhtml-1.htm` with your resources.

As you can see, the XHTML 1.0 strict and XHTML 1.1 documents are almost identical. The major difference is the DOCTYPE declaration that specifies which DTD to use. Although most of the internal reorganization is invisible to you, web browsers can understand the modular structure much more easily. Viewing the document gives almost the same results as shown in Figure 3-1.

You could modify the display by changing the stylesheet declarations, exactly as you did with the strict document.

The next requirement for XHTML documents is that tags are written in lowercase.

Case Sensitivity

Unlike HTML, XHTML is a case-sensitive vocabulary. This means that you must write all elements and attributes in lowercase in order to make them valid. Of course, the text within the element and attribute values is not case-sensitive.

In HTML, you had to write element names in uppercase. However, this wasn't enforced, so any of the following was allowable:

```
<HTML>
<Html>
<html>
```

In XHTML, however, the only allowable element construction is

```
<html>
```

Likewise, you must specify attributes using lowercase names. In HTML, any of the following were allowable:

```
<IMG SRC="images/flower.gif">
<img src="images/flower.gif">
<Img Src="images/flower.gif">
```

In XHTML, all element and attribute names must be lowercase:

```
<img src="images/flower.gif">
```

XHTML is case-sensitive because it's a requirement in XML. Case sensitivity is a major step in internationalization efforts. Although you can easily convert uppercase English characters to lowercase ones, or lowercase characters to uppercase, it's not so easy in other languages. Often there are no equivalent uppercase or lowercase characters, and some case mapping depends on region. Case sensitivity is important in order to allow the specification to use other languages and character sets.

Closing Elements

In HTML, you didn't need to close some elements, including `<img>`, `<br>`, `<hr>`, and `<input>`. These elements didn't mark up text, so they didn't have a corresponding closing element.

In XML, this type of element, referred to as an empty element, may contain attributes but doesn't mark up text. You must close all elements for an XHTML document to be well formed.

In HTML, empty elements appeared like this:

```
<IMG SRC="flower.gif">
```

In XHTML, empty elements can either appear with an immediate opening and closing tag, such as

```
<img src="flower-.gif"></img>
```

or in the short form, such as

```
<img src="flower.gif"/>
```

In the short form, you add a forward slash (/) before the closing angle bracket (>). This tells the XML or XHTML parser that the element is empty. Although both forms are legal XHTML, very old browsers have problems reading opening and closing tags for elements that are empty. It's much better to use the short form for empty elements. These browsers also may have difficulty with the forward slash character, so, if you're targeting them, it's also good practice to add a space before the character (<br />).

Attributes

In addition to using the proper case for attribute names, you also need to make sure that you write them correctly. In HTML, you could write attribute values without quotation marks. For example, the following was legal in HTML:

```
<TD colspan=4>
```

HTML also allowed you to minimize attributes:

```
<OPTION selected>An option</OPTION>
```

Neither of these options is acceptable in XHTML. All attributes must have a value, even if it's blank, and you must enclose all values in matching quotation marks:

```
<td colspan="4">
<option selected='selected'>An option</option>
```

In the preceding <td> element, you add quotation marks around the attribute value 4. In the <option> element, you remove the minimization of the selected attribute and use single quotes around the attribute value. The value for the selected attribute is selected.

Names and IDs

In HTML, the name attribute identified an element within the document. Later versions also allowed the use of id to replace the name attribute. In HTML 4.0 and XHTML 1.0, you can use the name attribute, the id attribute, or both. For example, you can identify the anchor element, <a>, with either attribute:

```
<a name="Section1" />
<a id="Section1" />
<a name="Section1" id="Section1" />
```

In XHTML 1.1, however, the W3C permits only the id attribute:

```
<a id="Section1" />
```

Again, older browsers expect you to use the name attribute. Because of this, some XHTML 1.1 pages don't work in early browser versions.

Nesting Tags

The HTML language didn't specify how you should nest tags, so writing something like the following didn't cause an error:

```
<H1><EM>A heading</H1></EM>
```

This doesn't work in XHTML; you need to rewrite the code so the tags close in the correct order:

```
<h1><em>A heading</em></h1>
```

Character Encoding

Specifying the document encoding is very important, and in some cases required, so that the document displays correctly within different web browsers. Document encoding defines a numeric value for each character. Different encoding schemes sometimes use these values in different ways.

Most browsers and computers support ASCII encoding, which assigns values to the 128 most commonly used characters. These characters are compatible across different platforms. If you're using characters with values higher than 128, you must specify the character set so that the browser knows which character to display for a given value.

Within XHTML, you can specify the character set that your document is using in several ways, including

- Using the XML declaration
- Using the <meta> element
- Using external means

You can use any of these methods alone or in combination. Using all methods together ensures that the browser understands the document's encoding, even if it doesn't support that encoding. Again, including encoding declarations may confuse some older browsers.

Let's look at each of the methods more closely. Specifying encoding using the XML declaration is very easy, and you've seen it in the examples in Chapter 1:

```
<?xml version="1.0" encoding="UTF-8"?>
```

You can specify encoding in a <meta> tag by adding the following element to the <head> section of your XHTML document:

```
<meta http-equiv="Content-Type" content="text/html; charset=UTF-8" />
```

CHOOSING AN ENCODING

UTF-8 is a Unicode character set that supports the first 128 ASCII characters, as well as additional characters. Documents using only simple ASCII characters can use UTF-8 encoding. The basic ASCII character set doesn't include European characters that include accents, and the numeric values for each character may vary depending on the specified encoding.

If you're running an English version of Windows, your default encoding is compatible with ISO-8859-1. This encoding is supported widely, so changing the encoding declaration to ISO-8859-1 allows European characters to display correctly.

Encoding rules are often complex. XML supports UTF-8 and UTF-16 encoding by default. UTF-16 is a large character set that includes many Chinese and Japanese characters, among others. In order to have numeric values for all of the characters, it uses two or more bytes for each character, instead of one byte as in UTF-8 and ASCII. Simple text editors may not support encoding other than UTF-8 or ASCII. For more information about different encoding specifications, visit `http://www.unicode.org/`.

Again, this line tells the browser what type of content the document contains. In the preceding `<meta>` tag, you specify `text/html` as the document type and `ISO-8859-1` as the encoding. If a document contains both the XML declaration and the `<meta>` element, the browser uses the encoding value in the XML declaration. Browsers that don't support the XML declaration use the `<meta>` value.

You can also use the HTTP header `Content-Type` to specify encoding on the web server. This approach provides the most reliable way to specify the encoding in an XHTML document. You can set the header using any server-side technology.

Specifying Language

HTML 4.0 and XHTML 1.0 allow you to specify the language for a document or element using the `lang` attribute. Web browsers can use this information to display elements in language-specific ways. For example, hyphenation may change depending on the language in use. Additionally, screen readers may read the text using different voices, depending on the language specified. The following `lang` attribute specifies the U.S. version of English as the language for the document:

```
<body lang="en-US">
```

You can find out more about which attribute values to use at `http://www.w3.org/TR/REC-html40/struct/dirlang.html`.

XHTML 1.1 replaces the `lang` attribute with `xml:lang`. In addition to XHTML, many other web vocabularies use this attribute from the `xml` namespace. This makes XHTML much more compatible with other XML applications. If you want a quick refresher on namespaces, see the section, "Understanding the Role of XML Namespaces," in Chapter 2.

XHTML Tools

You can use three kinds of tools to edit your XHTML documents:

- Simple text editors
- XML editors
- XHTML editors

Each of these tool types offers different benefits. Let's explore these types in more detail.

Text Editors

Because XHTML is a text-based format, you can create document markup in text editors, including Notepad on Windows, SimpleText on Macintosh, and Vim on Linux. These editors aren't specifically designed to create XHTML or XML documents, so they have very few features that can assist with authoring. They can't provide information about whether a document is well formed or valid, and they don't provide any type of color-coding for the text.

Although they have significant limitations, text editors are often useful because they exist on almost all computers and start up very quickly. The most useful text editors can display line numbers, which are invaluable for tracking down parser errors.

XML Editors

Many XML editors are designed to work specifically with XML documents. These editors offer many advantages over text editors, not the least of which is automatic color coding for elements within the document.

Although not written specifically for XHTML, XML editors can still provide tag completion so your elements close automatically. In addition, XML editors allow you to check that your document is well formed and valid, based on its DTD or XML schema.

Some popular XML editors include

- Altova's XMLSpy: `http://www.altova.com/products_ide.html`
- Stylus Studio's XML Editor: `http://www.stylusstudio.com/xml/editor/`
- Topologi's Markup Editor: `http://www.topologi.com/products/tme/index.html`
- TIBCO's Turbo XML: `http://www.tibco.com/software/business_integration/turboxml.jsp`
- SyncRO Soft's <oXygen/>: `http://www.oxygenxml.com/index.html/`
- Blast Radius' XMetal: `http://www.xmetal.com/en_us/products/xmetal_author/index.x`
- Wattle Software's XMLwriter: `http://www.xmlwriter.net/`

Most of these products offer a trial version so that you can test whether they'll suit your needs.

XHTML Editors

Editors written specifically for XHTML documents can provide the most features. These tools often come with XHTML document templates and can warn you about potential display problems. Most importantly, many XHTML editors allow you to design XHTML visually without needing to see the markup. This can be very useful when designing complex layouts.

Some common XHTML editors include

- Adobe's (formerly Macromedia) Dreamweaver: `http://www.macromedia.com/software/dreamweaver/`
- Microsoft's FrontPage: `http://www.microsoft.com/frontpage/`
- W3C's Amaya: `http://www.w3.org/Amaya/`
- Chami.com's HTML-Kit: `http://www.chami.com/html-kit/`
- Adobe's (formerly Macromedia) HomeSite: `http://www.macromedia.com/software/homesite/`
- Belus Technology's XStandard: `http://xstandard.com/?program=google1`
- Bare Bones Software's BBEdit: `http://www.barebones.com/products/bbedit/index.shtml`
- NewsGator Technologies' TopStyle: `http://www.bradsoft.com/topstyle/`

Again, you can often download a trial version so you can test the software against your needs.

Well-Formed and Valid XHTML Documents

Even if you follow the XHTML construction rules, you need to make sure that the document is both well formed and valid. These concepts are critical regardless of which XML vocabulary you use.

In Chapter 1, you learned that an XML document must be well formed before it can be processed by an XML parser. Well-formed means that

- The document contains one or more elements.
- The document contains a single document element, which may contain other elements.
- Each element closes correctly.
- Elements are case-sensitive.
- Attribute values are enclosed in quotation marks and cannot be empty.

A document is valid if, in addition to being well formed, it uses the correct elements and attributes for the specified vocabulary. In XHTML, the DOCTYPE declaration determines which DTD is used and hence, the validity of elements and attributes.

Validity is an important concept for web developers because creating valid documents guarantees that your web site is interoperable with virtually any XML application. A number of online tools can check XHTML documents for validity.

Online Validators

In addition to the tools I mentioned previously, several web sites offer free online validation services. You can use them to check that your document is valid against specific versions of the XHTML specification. Two popular online validators include

- W3C Markup Validation Service: `http://validator.w3.org/`
- WDG HTML Validator: `http://www.htmlhelp.com/tools/validator/`

I'll validate one of the XHTML documents that you saw previously to show you how the W3C Markup Validation Service works. You need to use the `Validate by File Upload` option to validate an offline file.

Open the web site (`http://validator.w3.org/`) and click the `Browse` button to select your file. In Figure 3-3, I'm validating the file `marsstrict.htm`.

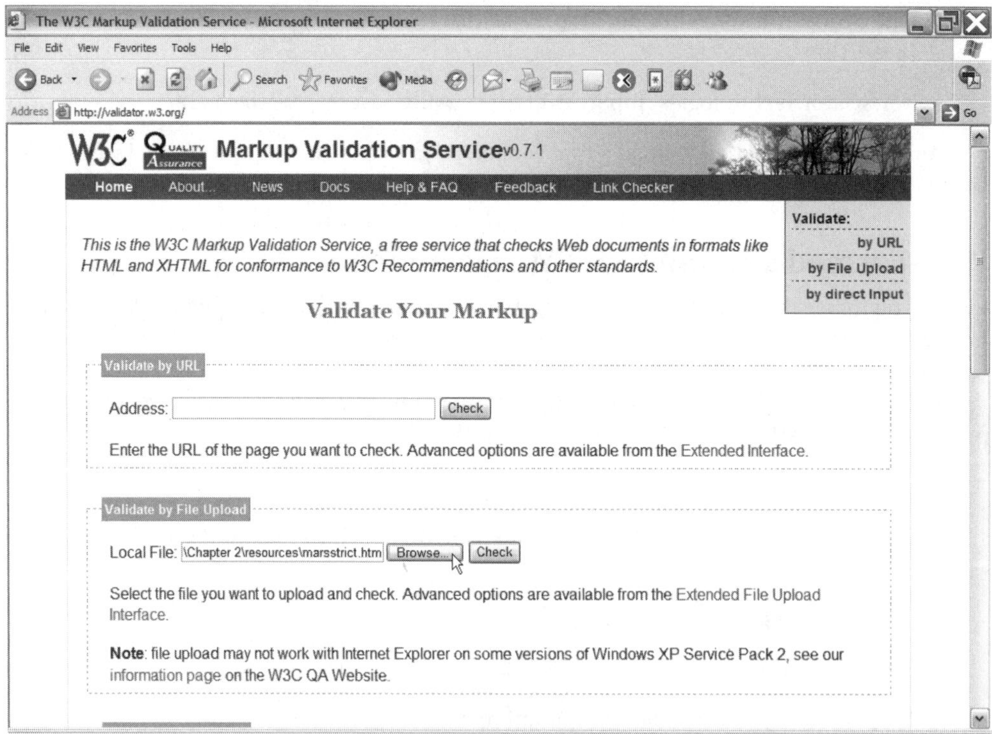

Figure 3-3. *Uploading a file for validation at the W3C Markup Validation Service*

Click the `Check` button to validate the document. After validating, you can see whether the document is valid. You also might see some other messages about the page, as shown in Figure 3-4.

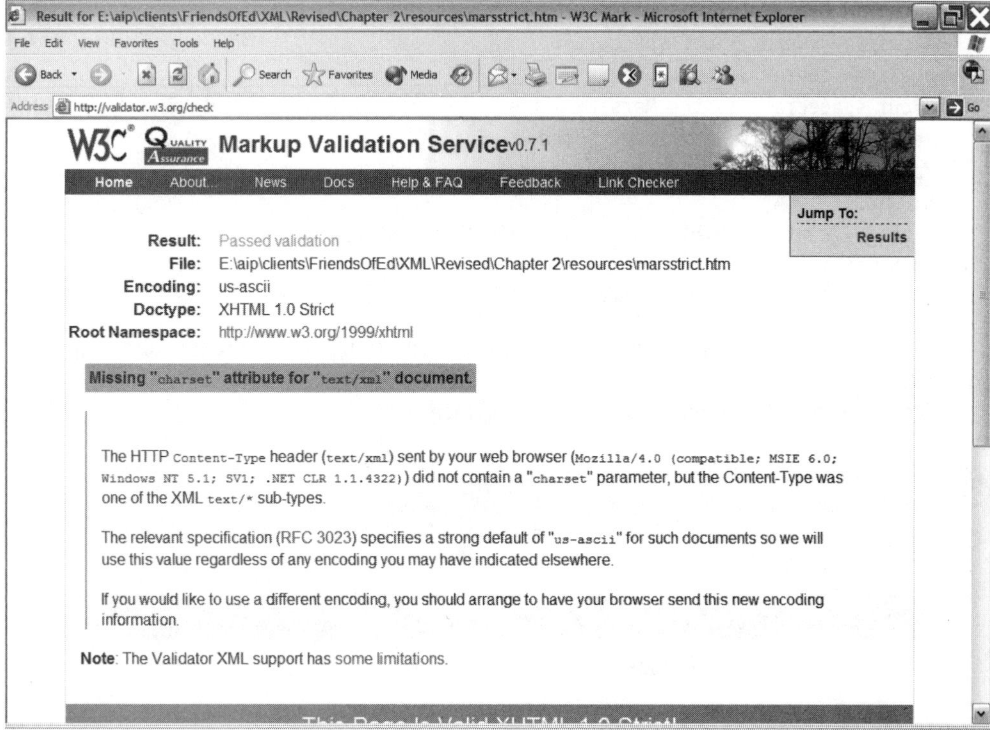

Figure 3-4. *The validation results*

In addition to errors, the W3C validator may return warnings. Often, these warnings refer to possible character encoding or DOCTYPE problems. The warnings normally offer suggestions that allow you to address the issues. If you're able to validate your entire site, you can display the W3C XHTML logo on your web page.

If your validation produces an error message, fix the error and validate the document again. Where you're notified of multiple errors, it's usually easier to revalidate after fixing each error, because a single error can often cause multiple errors later in the document.

I'll deliberately introduce errors into the `marstransitional.htm` page so you can see the effect on validation. I've left out the closing `</h1>` tag and introduced an `<unknown>` element. The document now reads like this:

```
<?xml version="1.0" encoding="UTF-8"?>
<!DOCTYPE html PUBLIC "-//W3C//DTD XHTML 1.0 Transitional//EN"
"http://www.w3.org/TR/xhtml1/DTD/xhtml1-transitional.dtd">
<html xmlns="http://www.w3.org/1999/xhtml">
  <head>
    <title>Mars Travel</title>
  </head>
  <body bgcolor="#FFFFFF">
    <unknown>Some text</unknown>
    <h1 align="center">Mars Travel<br />
      <i>Visits to a faraway place </i>
```

```
    <hr width="100%" />
    <h2 align="center">Your spacecraft</h2>
    <p align="center">
      Your spacecraft is the Mars Explorer, which provides the latest in
      passenger luxury and travel speed.
    </p>
    <hr width="100%" />
    <p align="center">XHTML 1.0 Transitional Document</p>
  </body>
</html>
```

I've saved this document as `marstransitionalerror.htm` if you want to try validating it yourself.

Figure 3-5 shows the effect of validating this document.

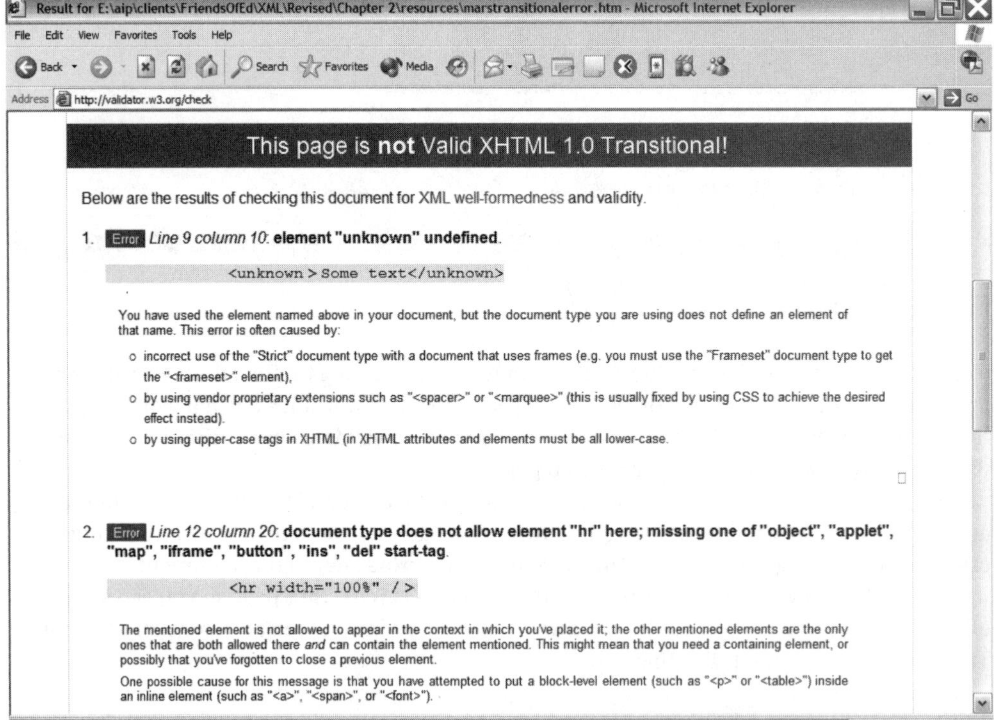

Figure 3-5. *Validation errors*

Validating a web site is an important step. The next section looks at some common practices that can cause validation errors.

Validation Errors

Unfortunately, the everyday practices of web professionals can cause validation errors. Some common issues involve

- Including JavaScript in your page
- Embedding advertising information
- Including unsupported elements and attributes

In this section, I'll show you some practical tips to address these issues. Many of these tips may be helpful when working with other web vocabularies.

Including JavaScript in Your Page

For validity, it's best to store your JavaScript in a separate file and refer to it with the `<script>` element:

```
<script type="text/javascript" src="mars.js" />
```

If you can't avoid embedding JavaScript in an XHTML document, place the JavaScript code within a `<![CDATA[...]]>` element so that it is not interpreted as XHTML by the browser. JavaScript can include characters that otherwise cause the document to fail the well-formed test. Instead of using the following code

```
<script type="text/javascript">
<!--
  function maxnumber(a, b) {
    if (a > b) then
      return a;
    if (a < b) then
      return b;
    if (a = b) then
      return a;
  }
-->
</script>
```

rewrite it like this:

```
<script type="text/javascript">
<![CDATA[
  function maxnumber(a, b) {
    if (a > b) then
      return a;
    if (a < b) then
      return b;
    if (a = b) then
      return a;
  }
]]>
</script>
```

Embedding Advertising Information

Many web sites display advertising information on their pages. If the advertisement isn't valid XHTML, you must make sure that you're using the XHTML 1.0 transitional DTD. You can also add the advertiser information to the page using JavaScript. This ensures that the content displays in the browser, but at the same time, you can ensure that the XHTML page is valid. Make sure that you follow the preceding JavaScript guidelines. I'll cover some advanced JavaScript techniques in Chapter 8.

Including Unsupported Elements and Attributes

In some cases, you may need to add invalid content to the XHTML page. Using unsupported elements isn't good practice, because it ultimately limits your audience. However, there might be times when you want to add

- Elements or attributes that existed in earlier versions of HTML
- Elements or attributes that are specific to one browser
- New elements or attributes

The first two situations commonly occur when you're trying to build a web site for a specific browser, or when you're trying to convert an older web site to XHTML. You can add this kind of information in several ways. As I discussed in the previous section, you can add the content using JavaScript after the page loads.

Another more complex option is to test for the browser type and version and return appropriate pages to the user. By maintaining templates on the web server, you can quickly transform your web page to support various browsers using XSLT.

XHTML Modularization

A primary goal of XML is to create a simple markup language that you can extend easily. XHTML 1.1 simplifies the process of extending the XHTML definition. You can add any vocabulary to XHTML through a process called modularization.

Although XHTML modularization is complex, you can still enjoy the benefits. The W3C has released a working draft of a modularization that supports the MathML and SVG vocabularies. These two vocabularies are commonly embedded within XHTML and vice versa. You can find out more at `http://www.w3.org/TR/XHTMLplusMathMLplusSVG/`.

You might need to limit rather than extend the XHTML specification. XHTML Basic provides a subset of the basic modules of XHTML for use on mobile devices; find out more at `http://www.w3.org/TR/xhtml-basic/`.

Using these new vocabularies is very similar to using the other document types you've seen in this chapter. You need to follow the rules of the new document type and declare the appropriate DOCTYPE. The DOCTYPE declaration for XHTML plus MathML plus SVG is

```
<!DOCTYPE html PUBLIC
"-//W3C//DTD XHTML 1.1 plus MathML 2.0 plus SVG 1.1//EN"
"http://www.w3.org/2002/04/xhtml-math-svg/xhtml-math-svg.dtd">
```

The DOCTYPE declaration for XHTML Basic is

```
<!DOCTYPE html PUBLIC "-//W3C//DTD XHTML Basic 1.0//EN"
"http://www.w3.org/TR/xhtml-basic/xhtml-basic10.dtd">
```

I've introduced you to the basics of XHTML, examining it as a vocabulary of XML. Now let's move on to examine some of the other popular web vocabularies, starting with MathML and SVG.

MathML

Mathematical Markup Language (MathML) is a popular XML vocabulary that describes mathematical notation. It was developed to include mathematical expressions on web pages. MathML is an XML vocabulary, so it must be well formed and valid according to the specification. You can find out more about MathML at `http://www.w3.org/Math/`.

While the W3C MathML group was developing the specification, the group realized it actually had two distinct goals. There was a need for a vocabulary that could represent both how mathematic equations were displayed, as well as the meaning of a mathematic equation. The group divided MathML into two types of encoding: presentation and content.

Presentation MathML conveys the notation and structure of mathematical formulas, while Content MathML communicates meaning without being concerned about notation. You can use either or both of these elements, depending on your task, but be aware that each has some web browser limitations.

Firefox supports Presentation MathML, as MathML is part of Mozilla's layout engine. The derived browsers Netscape, Galeon, and Kmeleon also include Presentation MathML, as does the W3C browser Amaya. Internet Explorer 6 supports MathML using plugins such as the free MathPlayer (`http://www.dessci.com/en/products/mathplayer/`) and techexplorer (`http://www.integretechpub.com/techexplorer/`). You can't use MathML within Opera.

Presentation MathML

Presentation MathML provides control over the display of mathematic notation in a web page. Thirty presentation elements and around 50 attributes allow you to encode mathematical formulas. Presentation MathML tries to map each presentation element to an element.

To start, Presentation MathML divides a formula into vertical rows using `<mrow>` elements. This basic element is used as a wrapper. Rows may contain other nested rows. Each `<mrow>` element usually has a combination of mathematical numbers (`<mn>`), mathematical identifiers (`<mi>`), and mathematical operators (`<mo>`).

This example represents $10 + (x \times y)^4$:

```
<?xml version="1.0" encoding="ISO-8859-1"?>
<!DOCTYPE math PUBLIC "-//W3C//DTD MathML 2.0//EN"
"http://www.w3.org/TR/MathML2/dtd/mathml2.dtd">
<math xmlns="http://www.w3.org/1998/Math/MathML">
 <mrow>
   <mn>10</mn>
   <mo>+</mo>
   <msup>
```

```
      <mfenced>
        <mrow>
          <mi>x</mi>
          <mo>*</mo>
          <mi>y</mi>
        </mrow>
      </mfenced>
      <mn>4</mn>
    </msup>
  </mrow>
</math>
```

In the preceding document, you start with an XML declaration, adding the DOCTYPE declaration for MathML and including the <math> document element. The document includes a default namespace for the MathML vocabulary:

```
<?xml version="1.0" encoding="ISO-8859-1"?>
<!DOCTYPE math PUBLIC "-//W3C//DTD MathML 2.0//EN"
"http://www.w3.org/TR/MathML2/dtd/mathml2.dtd">
<math xmlns="http://www.w3.org/1998/Math/MathML">
```

Next, the document includes an <mrow> element, which represents the horizontal row of the equation. The row begins with the number 10 and includes a mathematical additional operator +:

```
<mrow>
  <mn>10</mn>
  <mo>+</mo>
```

It then includes an <msup>, or mathematical superscript, section. This section allows the display of exponents and the <mn> element before the closing </msup> element indicates that the contents are raised to the power of 4.

The <msup> element includes an <mfenced> element, which corresponds to the use of brackets in a mathematical equation. Within the brackets, the equation multiplies x by y:

```
<msup>
  <mfenced>
    <mrow>
      <mi>x</mi>
      <mo>*</mo>
      <mi>y</mi>
    </mrow>
  </mfenced>
  <mn>4</mn>
</msup>
```

You'll find this document saved as `mathml_presentation.mml` with the code download resources. I also could have saved it with a `.xml` file extension. Figure 3-6 shows the effect of opening this document in Firefox 1.5.

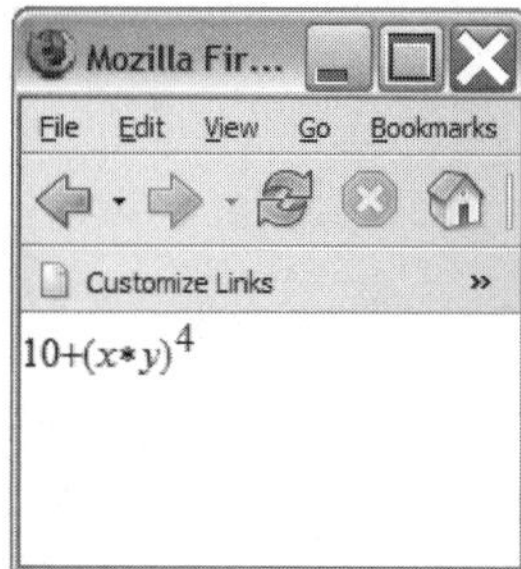

Figure 3-6. *A Presentation MathML document displayed in Firefox 1.5*

■ **Note** Firefox may prompt you to install some additional fonts from `http://www.mozilla.org/projects/mathml/fonts/`. Installing these fonts ensures that Firefox can render all mathematical symbols in your MathML document correctly.

If you try to view this document in a browser that doesn't support MathML, such as Opera 8.5, you'll see something similar to the image shown in Figure 3-7.

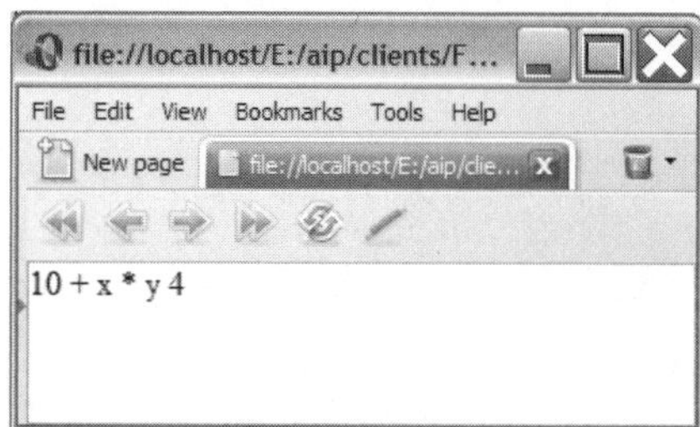

Figure 3-7. *A Presentation MathML document displayed in Opera 8.51*

Notice that the browser doesn't render the markup correctly. It doesn't insert the parentheses or raise the exponent. Essentially, it ignores all of the MathML elements and displays only the text within the XML document.

You can find a slightly more advanced example in the file `quadratic_equation_presentation.mml`. You need to install the Firefox MathML-enabled fonts in order to see the square root sign rendered correctly, as shown in Figure 3-8.

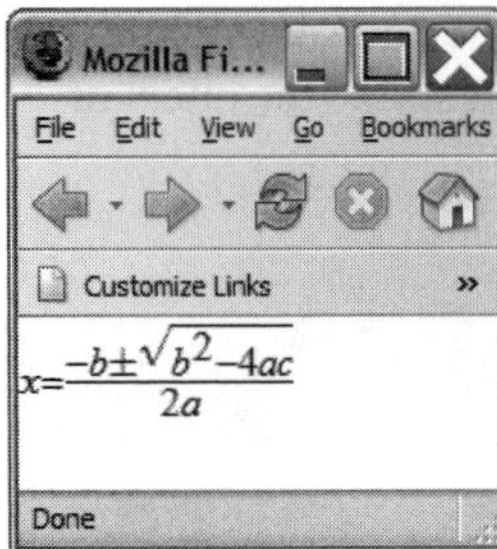

Figure 3-8. *Firefox showing a more complicated MathML page*

Content MathML

Content MathML allows you to be very explicit about the order of operations and primary equation representation. Content markup has around 100 elements and 12 attributes.

Content MathML documents begin in the same way as Presentation MathML documents. They also contain `<mrow>` elements to separate the lines of the equation. However, Content MathML elements don't use the `<mo>` element for mathematical operators. Instead, they use the `<apply>` element and specific operator and function elements. This becomes clearer when you look at the same example written in Content MathML:

```
<?xml version="1.0" encoding="ISO-8859-1"?>
<!DOCTYPE math PUBLIC "-//W3C//DTD MathML 2.0//EN"
"http://www.w3.org/TR/MathML2/dtd/mathml2.dtd">
<math xmlns="http://www.w3.org/1998/Math/MathML">
  <mrow>
    <apply>
      <plus/>
      <ci>10</ci>
      <apply>
        <power/>
        <apply>
          <times/>
          <ci>x</ci>
          <ci>y</ci>
        </apply>
        <cn>4</cn>
        </apply>
    </apply>
  </mrow>
</math>
```

You can find the document saved as `mathml_content.mml` with your resources. Let's walk through the example.

The document starts with an XML declaration, a DTD reference, and the document root, including the MathML namespace. Then, like the Presentation XML example, you include an <mrow> element:

```
<?xml version="1.0" encoding="ISO-8859-1"?>
<!DOCTYPE math PUBLIC "-//W3C//DTD MathML 2.0//EN"
"http://www.w3.org/TR/MathML2/dtd/mathml2.dtd">
<math xmlns="http://www.w3.org/1998/Math/MathML">
  <mrow>
```

From here on, the similarity ends. The example uses the <apply> element with <plus/> to include the addition operator with the value 10:

```
<apply>
  <plus/>
  <ci>10</ci>
```

Another <apply> element surrounds the <power/> element, and the value of 4 is indicated immediately before the corresponding closing element:

```
<cn>4</cn>
```

The x × y section is contained within a third <apply> block that uses the <times/> element to indicate multiplication:

```
<apply>
  <times/>
  <ci>x</ci>
  <ci>y</ci>
</apply>
```

The differences are obvious. Instead of <mi> and <mn> elements, the vocabulary uses <ci> and <cn>. There is no need for the <mfenced> element because you can be specific about the order of operations by using the <apply> element.

In the preceding example, all of the operators use postfix notation. In postfix notation, you indicate the operation first and then follow that by the operand(s). Some MathML functions use postfix notation, and some don't. For a complete listing, see http://www.w3.org/TR/MathML2/appendixf.html.

You can't view this document in the web browser because that's not the purpose of Content MathML. Instead, it's supposed to be processed by a MathML engine, which may also perform the calculation. Most web browsers simply ignore all of the elements and only display the text, as you saw in the earlier Opera example.

Scalable Vector Graphics

SVG was developed so that designers could represent two-dimensional graphics using an XML vocabulary. Just as MathML provides a detailed model to represent mathematical notation, SVG allows for the display of graphics with a high level of detail and accuracy. Again, because SVG is an XML vocabulary, it must follow the rules of XML. You can find out more about SVG at http://www.w3.org/Graphics/SVG/.

SVG has wide acceptance and support with many available viewers and editors. Both Firefox 1.5 and Opera 8 support SVG in some form, as does Amaya. For other browsers, you need to use plugins such as Adobe's SVG Viewer to view SVG documents. You can download the Adobe SVG Viewer plugin from `http://www.adobe.com/svg/`.

You can find the current SVG specification version 1.1 at `http://www.w3.org/TR/SVG11/`. The SVG 1.2 specification is currently under development.

You can break down SVG into three parts:

- Vector graphic shapes
- Images
- Text

Let's look at each of these in more detail.

Vector Graphic Shapes

Vector graphics allow you to describe an image by listing the shapes involved. In a way, they provide instructions for creating the shapes. This is in contrast to *bitmap* or *raster* graphics, which describe the image one pixel at a time. Because you store vector graphics as a set of instructions, these images are often much smaller than their raster-based counterparts.

In SVG, you can represent vector graphics using either basic shape commands or by specifying a list of points called a *path*. You can also group objects and make complex objects out of more simple ones.

To get an idea about how you can work with shapes, let's look at an SVG document that describes a basic rectangle:

```
<?xml version="1.0"?>
<!DOCTYPE svg PUBLIC "-//W3C//DTD SVG 1.1//EN"
"http://www.w3.org/Graphics/SVG/1.1/DTD/svg11.dtd">
<svg width="12cm" height="4cm" viewBox="0 0 1200 400"
xmlns="http://www.w3.org/2000/svg">
  <desc>A simple rectangle with a red border</desc>
  <rect x="10"
        y="10"
        width="200"
        height="200"
        fill="none"
        stroke="red"
        stroke-width="10"/>
</svg>
```

This file is saved as `svg_rectangle.svg`. Opening it in an SVG viewer or SVG native browser shows something similar to the image in Figure 3-9.

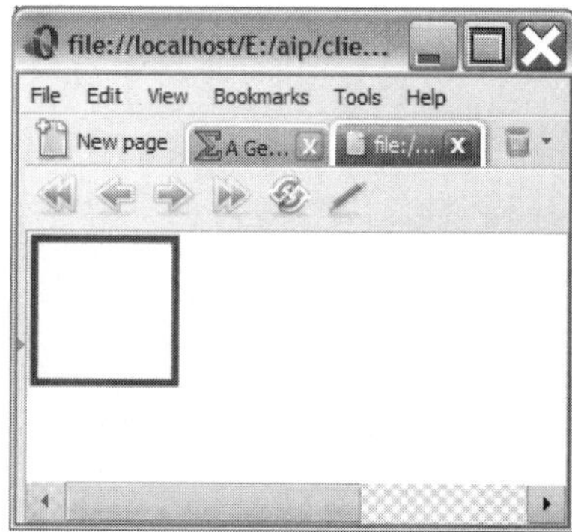

Figure 3-9. *A simple SVG document displayed in Opera 8.51*

The document starts with an XML and DOCTYPE declaration and includes a document element called <svg>. Notice that the document element includes a reference to the SVG namespace, as well as attributes determining the size:

```
<?xml version="1.0"?>
<!DOCTYPE svg PUBLIC "-//W3C//DTD SVG 1.1//EN"
"http://www.w3.org/Graphics/SVG/1.1/DTD/svg11.dtd">
<svg width="12cm" height="4cm" viewBox="0 0 1200 400"
xmlns="http://www.w3.org/2000/svg">
```

In addition to creating basic shapes, SVG allows you to add complex fill patterns and other effects, as you can see in this example:

```
<?xml version="1.0"?>
<!DOCTYPE svg PUBLIC "-//W3C//DTD SVG 1.1//EN"
"http://www.w3.org/Graphics/SVG/1.1/DTD/svg11.dtd">
<svg width="12cm" height="4cm" viewBox="0 0 1200 400"
xmlns="http://www.w3.org/2000/svg">
  <desc>A simple rectangle with a red border and a gradient fill</desc>
  <g>
    <defs>
      <linearGradient id="RedGradient" gradientUnits="objectBoundingBox">
        <stop offset="0%" stop-color="#F00" />
        <stop offset="100%" stop-color="#FFF" />
      </linearGradient>
    </defs>
    <rect x="10"
          y="10"
          width="200"
          height="200"
          fill="url(#RedGradient)"
          stroke="red"
          stroke-width="10"/>
  </g>
</svg>
```

I've saved this document as svg_rectangle_fill.svg. When viewed in an appropriate viewer, it appears as shown in Figure 3-10.

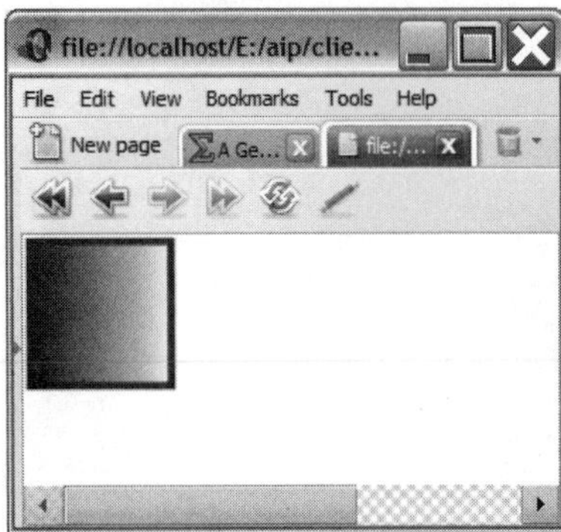

Figure 3-10. *A shape with a fill shown in Opera 8.51*

This example creates a linear gradient in the <g> graphic object element called RedGradient:

```
<linearGradient id="RedGradient" gradientUnits="objectBoundingBox">
  <stop offset="0%" stop-color="#F00" />
  <stop offset="100%" stop-color="#FFF" />
</linearGradient>
```

The rectangle element then specifies that you should use the RedGradient fill element:

```
<rect x="10"
    y="10"
    width="200"
    height="200"
    fill="url(#RedGradient)"
    stroke="red"
    stroke-width="10"/>
```

The SVG 1.1 specification allows you to create the following basic shapes: <rect>, <circle>, <ellipse>, <line>, <polyline>, and <polygon>.

Images

You also can include raster graphics in an SVG page. You might need to do this if you want to include an image of a person or landscape, or any other photo-realistic image, that you can't represent adequately as a vector drawing.

Including images in SVG is very simple:

```
<?xml version="1.0"?>
<!DOCTYPE svg PUBLIC "-//W3C//DTD SVG 1.1//EN"
"http://www.w3.org/Graphics/SVG/1.1/DTD/svg11.dtd">
<svg width="282px" height="187px" viewBox="0 0 282 187"
```

```
    xmlns="http://www.w3.org/2000/svg" xmlns:xlink="http://www.w3.org/1999/xlink">
  <desc>This SVG document contains lions.jpg</desc>
  <image x="0"
         y="0"
         width="282px"
         height="187px"
         xlink:href="lions.jpg">
    <title>Two lions</title>
  </image>
</svg>
```

This file is saved as `lions.svg`. Figure 3-11 shows how it renders in Firefox.

Figure 3-11. *An SVG page showing an image of lions*

The markup is self-explanatory. You can control how the image is displayed by changing the attributes in the SVG document. It's important to realize that the image isn't converted to a vector graphic. Instead, it maintains its original raster format and is drawn to the SVG display.

Text

In addition to creating basic shapes and including images, SVG documents can represent text. This example creates text that has a color gradient outline:

```
<?xml version="1.0" encoding="UTF-8"?>
<!DOCTYPE svg PUBLIC "-//W3C//DTD SVG 1.1//EN"
"http://www.w3.org/Graphics/SVG/1.1/DTD/svg11-flat-20030114.dtd">
<svg width="20cm" height="4cm" viewBox="0 0 400 400"
xmlns="http://www.w3.org/2000/svg">
  <desc>This SVG document contains rainbow text</desc>
  <g>
    <defs>
      <linearGradient id="RedBlueGradient" gradientUnits="objectBoundingBox">
        <stop offset="0%" stop-color="#F00" />
```

```
      <stop offset="100%" stop-color="#00F" />
    </linearGradient>
  </defs>
  <text x="-600"
        y="200"
        font-size="128"
        fill="white"
        stroke="url(#RedBlueGradient)"
        stroke-width="5">
    SVG creates gradient text!
  </text>
 </g>
</svg>
```

This file appears as svg_gradienttext.svg with your resources. Figure 3-12 shows how it appears when open in an SVG viewer.

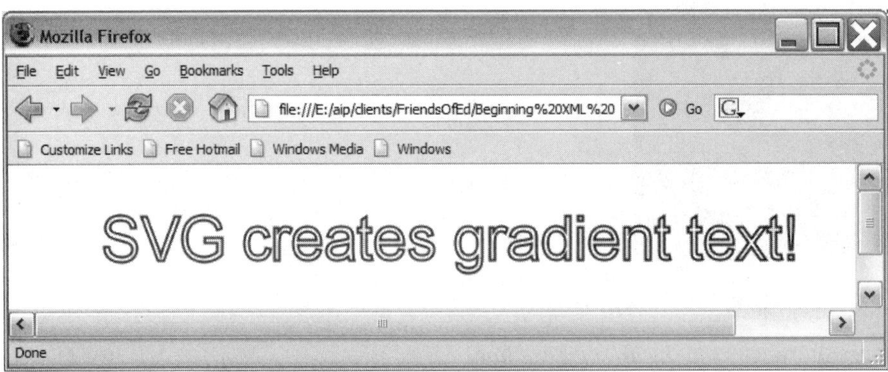

Figure 3-12. *Gradient text created with an SVG document*

The simple examples you've seen so far are only the beginning of what you can achieve with SVG. Let's move on to a more complicated example involving animation.

Putting It Together

SVG allows you to create animations, and in the next example, I'll create an animation for the imaginary "Mars Travel" web site. The completed file is saved as marstravel.svg with your resources. Note that you won't be able to view the page with Mozilla unless you use a plugin. Mozilla's native support doesn't extend to SVG animations.

The page starts with declarations:

```
<?xml version="1.0" encoding="UTF-8"?>
<!DOCTYPE svg PUBLIC "-//W3C//DTD SVG 1.1//EN"
"http://www.w3.org/Graphics/SVG/1.1/DTD/svg11-flat-20030114.dtd">
<svg width="16cm" height="9cm" viewBox="0 0 1000 600"
  xmlns="http://www.w3.org/2000/svg" xmlns:xlink="http://www.w3.org/1999/xlink">
  <desc>Mars Travel introduction</desc>
```

These declarations add the XML and DOCTYPE declarations and set the size of the drawing. I've used the <desc> element to add a description for the page.

In the next step, I've added an image for the background. Make sure that you save the resource file, mars.jpg, in the same location as the svg file:

```
<image x="650" y="100" width="250" height="250" xlink:href="mars.jpg"/>
```

The first animation occurs in the next section of the SVG document:

```
<rect width="300" height="100" fill="rgb(200,200,200)"
  fill-opacity="0.25">
  <animate attributeName="y" attributeType="XML" from="500" to="-100"
  dur="4s" repeatCount="indefinite" fill="freeze" />
</rect>
```

The lines create a <rect> object and fill it with a medium-gray color. The fill-opacity is set to 0.25. This attribute accepts values between 0 (completely transparent) and 1 (completely opaque).

The block also includes an <animate> element that modifies the y attribute from the value 500 to the value -100. This moves the block in an up-and-down motion.

The element specifies that the animation lasts for four seconds with the dur attribute and that it repeats indefinitely using repeatCount="indefinite". The fill="freeze" attribute specifies that the fill doesn't change during the animation.

In this example, I've made the effect more interesting by adding six more moving <rect> objects that cross one another:

```
<rect width="300" height="400" fill="rgb(200,200,200)" fill-opacity="0.5">
  <animate attributeName="y" attributeType="XML" from="600" to="-400"
  dur="14s" repeatCount="indefinite" fill="freeze" />
</rect>
<rect width="300" height="14" fill="rgb(200,200,200)" fill-opacity="0.25">
  <animate attributeName="y" attributeType="XML" from="600" to="-40"
  dur="3s" repeatCount="indefinite" fill="freeze" />
</rect>
<rect width="300" height="4" fill="rgb(200,200,200)" fill-opacity="0.75">
  <animate attributeName="y" attributeType="XML" from="500" to="-4"
  dur="2s" repeatCount="indefinite" fill="freeze" />
</rect>
  <rect width="300" height="300" fill="rgb(200,200,200)" fill-opacity="0.75">
  <animate attributeName="y" attributeType="XML" from="-300" to="500"
  dur="8s" repeatCount="indefinite" fill="freeze" />
</rect>
<rect width="300" height="14" fill="rgb(200,200,200)" fill-opacity="0.75">
  <animate attributeName="y" attributeType="XML" from="-90" to="510"
  dur="3s" repeatCount="indefinite" fill="freeze" />
</rect>
<rect width="300" height="4" fill="rgb(200,200,200)" fill-opacity="0.75">
  <animate attributeName="y" attributeType="XML" from="-100" to="500"
  dur="2s" repeatCount="indefinite" fill="freeze" />
</rect>
```

The rectangles are partly transparent, so they produce some interesting effects as they overlap. If you test the document now, you'll see something similar to the screen shot shown in Figure 3-13.

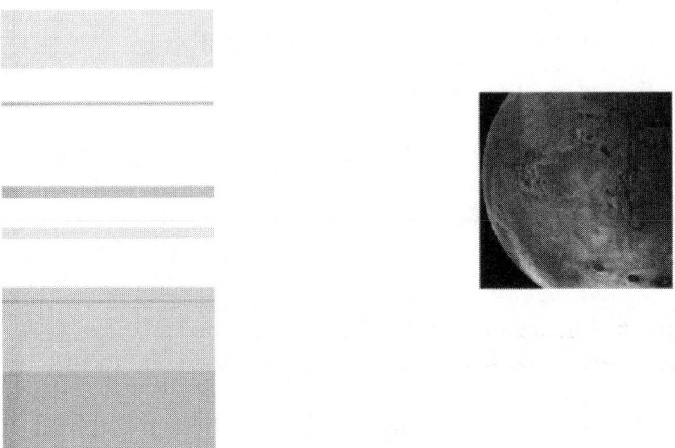

Figure 3-13. *The SVG animation so far*

The next block of code adds some text and vertical separators:

```
<!-- Default text -->
<text x="295" y="575" text-anchor="end">Scalable Vector Graphics</text>
<text x="295" y="590" text-anchor="end">by Mars Travel</text>
<!-- Separator -->
<line x1="300" y1="0" x2="300" y2="600" stroke-width="2" stroke="gray"/>
<line x1="305" y1="0" x2="305" y2="600" stroke-width="1" stroke="gray"/>
```

The `<text>` element has the attribute `text-anchor` set to `end`. This is the equivalent of aligning the text to the right. If the SVG viewer you're using has right-to-left reading enabled, the SVG aligns the text to the left. In either case, it aligns it to the "end" of the area.

The following line animates the title of the site so that it flies in from the right side:

```
<text x="1000" y="200" font-size="32" font-style="italic" font-weight="bold"
font-family="verdana" fill="#C65B2E">
  <animate attributeName="x" attributeType="XML" begin="0s" dur="2s"
  fill="freeze" from="1000" to="340"/>
  Mars Travel
</text>
```

The `<text>` element lists the text properties and also includes the `<animate>` element so that the text moves in from the right. It takes two seconds for the text to arrive at its final position.

The next code block adds some more text that enters after the “Mars Travel” text:

```
<text x="1000" y="224" font-size="24" font-style="italic" font-weight="bold"
font-family="verdana" fill="#C65B2E" >
  <animate attributeName="x" attributeType="XML" begin="2.5s" dur="2s"
  fill="freeze" from="1000" to="340" />
  Out of this world!
</text>
```

Finally, the page completes with a <text> element and closing <svg> tag. The text is linked so that users can visit the rest of the web site:

```
  <a xlink:href="http://www.apress.com/">
    <text x="750" y="467" fill="#C65B2E" font-weight="bold"
    font-family="verdana" font-size="24">ENTER >>></text>
  </a>
</svg>
```

This completes the SVG page. When you view it, you should see an animated version of the screen shot shown in Figure 3-14.

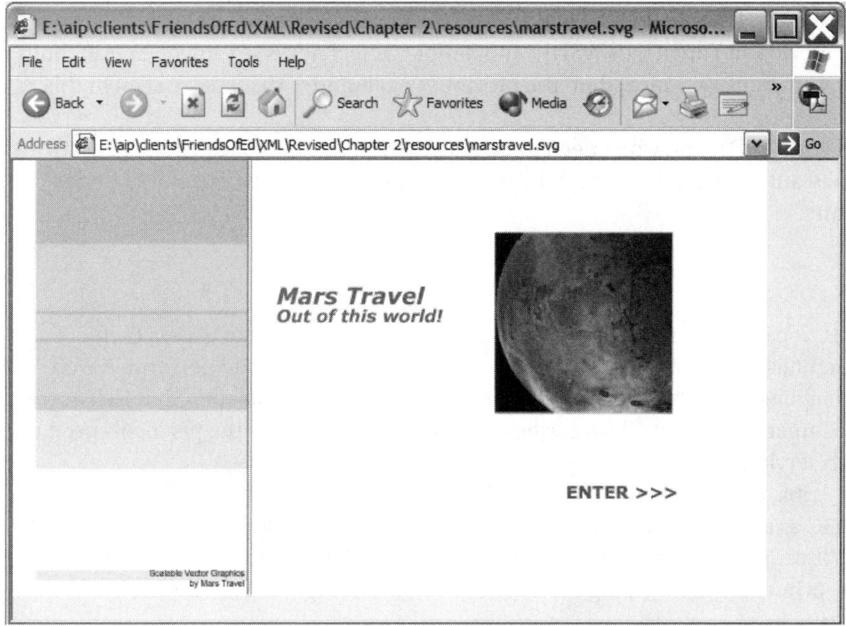

Figure 3-14. *The completed SVG animation*

Figure 3-14 shows the page displayed in Internet Explorer; I can view the SVG file in this browser because I have the Adobe SVG Viewer plugin installed. You could also view the page using the native SVG support in Opera 8.5 or in any other browser that has an SVG plugin installed. You should probably provide an alternative image for viewers who don't have this plugin or an appropriate browser.

Even though this SVG introduction is graphically rich, it isn't inaccessible to people with disabilities. As you've seen, SVG documents can include the `<desc>` element, which provides an accessible text-based description of the document.

Let's move on to two more XML vocabularies that you can use with Web services: WSDL and SOAP.

Web Services

Web services allow organizations to use the Internet to provide information to the public through XML documents. You can see examples of web services at Amazon and Google, where developers can interact with live information from the databases of both companies.

You have a number of different choices for working with web services, but all deliver their content in an XML document. When someone receives this information, it's called "consuming" a web service.

In this section, you'll briefly look at two of the XML vocabularies that impact the area: Web Services Description Language (WSDL) and Simple Object Access Protocol (SOAP). Both of these sections are more technical than the previous vocabularies that you've seen in this chapter.

Let's begin with WSDL. You won't need to be able to write this language yourself, as it's usually generated automatically. However, I'll explain the WSDL file, as it's useful to understand its structure.

WSDL

WSDL is an XML vocabulary that describes web services and how you can access them. A WSDL document lists the operations or functions that a web service can perform. A web programming language usually carries out these operations in an application that isn't accessible to the consumer. The WSDL file describes the data types as well as the protocols used to address the web service.

Microsoft, Ariba, and IBM jointly developed WSDL. They submitted the WSDL 1.1 specification to the W3C as a note. The W3C accepted the note, which you can see at `http://www.w3.org/TR/wsdl`. The W3C is currently working on the WSDL 2.0 recommendation. You can see the primer for the working draft at `http://www.w3.org/TR/2004/WD-wsdl20-primer-20041221/`.

You normally don't write the WSDL file yourself using XML tools. Instead, your web services toolkit usually generates the file automatically. However, understanding the structure of the WSDL document can be useful.

Understanding WSDL Document Structure

WSDL files are stored in locations that are accessible via the web. Anyone consuming the web service accesses these files. For example, you can find the Google web search WSDL at http://api.google.com/GoogleSearch.wsdl.

A WSDL document starts with an optional XML declaration and contains the <types>, <message>, <binding>, and <service> elements. The following code block shows the file structure of a WSDL file:

```
<?xml version="1.0" encoding="utf-8" ?>
<definitions>
  <types>
    <!-- datatype definitions -->
  </types>
  <message>
    <!-- message definitions -->
  </message>
  <portType>
    <operation>
      <!-- operation definitions -->
    </operation>
  </portType>
  <binding>
    <!-- binding definitions -->
  </binding>
..<service>
..</service>
</definitions>
```

Table 3-1 explains each of the sections.

Table 3-1. *The Major Elements Within a WSDL File*

Element	Explanation
<definitions>	Provides the root element for the WSDL document and contains the other elements
<types>	Defines the data types used by the web service
<message>	Describes the messages used when the web service is consumed
<portType>	Combines messages to create the library of operations available from the web service
<operation>	Defines the operations that the web service can carry out
<binding>	Lists the communication protocols that a user can use to consume the web service and the implementation of the web service
<service>	Defines the address for invoking the web service—usually a URL to a SOAP service

Defining Web Service Data Types

When someone consumes a web service, the service receives the request, queries an application, and sends an XML document containing the results in response. In order to use the web service, the consumer must know how to phrase the request as well as the format for the returned information. It's crucial to understand the data types used by the web service.

The WSDL document defines the data types for both the inputs to and the outputs from the web service. These might equate to the data types listed in the XML schema recommendation, or they could be more complicated, user-defined data types.

If you're only using W3C built-in simple data types, the WSDL file doesn't include the <types> element. The XML schema namespace appears in the <definitions> element and references data types in the <message> elements:

```
xmlns:xsd="http://www.w3.org/2001/XMLSchema"
```

Custom data type definitions appear in the <types> element. The WSDL file can use XML schema declarations or any alternative schema system for defining these data types:

```
<types>
  <schema xmlns="http://www.w3.org/2001/XMLSchema"
  xmlns:wsdl="http://schemas.xmlsoap.org/wsdl/">
    <!-- schema declarations here -->
..</schema>
</types>
```

Mapping Data Types to Messages

A consumer calls the web service and provides inputs. These inputs map to <message> elements. Each message has <part> elements that refer to each of the inputs received:

```
<message name="mName">
  <part name="mInputName" type=" mInputNameType"/>
</message>
```

The types referred to in the <message> elements must come from one of the schema namespaces within the document. If the type refers to the simple built-in data types from the XML schema recommendation, the element includes a reference to the XML schema namespace:

```
<message name="mName">
  <part name="mNameIO" type="xsd:string"/>
</message>
```

Listing Web Service Operations

The most important element in the WSDL document is the <portType> element. This element defines all of the operations that are available through the web service. The <portType> element is like a library of all of the available operations.

The <portType> element contains <operation> elements that have <input> and <output> elements. Inputs pass to an application for processing. The outputs are the responses received from the application that are passed to the consumer:

```
<portType name="ptName">
  <operation name="oName">
    <input message="oNameRequest"/>
    <output message="oNameResponse"/>
  </operation>
</portType>
```

The <message> elements define the inputs and outputs. They are normally prefixed with the current document's namespace.

A web service can carry out four types of operations. The most common is the *request-response* type. In this type, the web service receives a request from a consumer and supplies a response. A web service can also carry out a *one-way* operation, where a message is received but no response is returned. In this case, the operation has an <input> element.

The other options are *solicit-response*, where the web service sends a message and then receives a response. It is the opposite of a one-way operation. The operation has an <output> element followed by an <input> element. You can also specify a <fault> element. The final option is *notification*, where the service sends a message and only has an <output> element.

Mapping to a Protocol

The <portType> element contains all of the operations for a web service. Bindings specify which transport protocol each portType uses. Transport protocols include HTTP POST, HTTP GET, and SOAP. You can specify more than one transport protocol for each portType. Each binding has a name and associated type that associates with a portType.

If you're using SOAP 1.1, WSDL 1.1 includes details specific to SOAP. The binding specifies a <soap:binding> element, which indicates that the binding will use SOAP. This element requires style and transport attributes. The style attribute can take values of rpc or document.

Document style specifies an XML document call style. Both the request and response messages are XML documents. rpc style uses a wrapper element for both the request and response XML documents.

The transport attribute indicates how to transport the SOAP messages. It uses values such as

```
http://schemas.xmlsoap.org/soap/http
http://schemas.xmlsoap.org/soap/smtp
```

The following example specifies a SOAP 1.1 transport mechanism over HTTP using an rpc interaction:

```
<binding name="bName" type="bType">
  <soap:binding style="rpc"
  transport="http://schemas.xmlsoap.org/soap/http"/>
  <!-- declarations-->
  </soap:binding>
</binding>
```

The web service binds each operation using the following format. The operation name corresponds with the operation defined earlier in the <portType> element. The soapAction attribute shows the destination URI including a folder, if necessary:

```
<soap:operation name="oName" soapAction="URI">
  <input>
    <soap:body use="literal"/>
  </input>
  <output>
    <soap:body use="literal"/>
  </output>
</soap:operation>
```

You can also specify an optional SOAP encoding for each operation.

Specifying Processing Software

The <service> element shows where to process the requested operation. The service has a name attribute and a child <port> element. The <port> element specifies a portType for binding. The <port> element also has a name attribute.

If you're using SOAP, the <soap:address> element specifies the location of the processing application:

```
<service name="sName">
  <port binding="portTypeName" name="pName">
    <soap:address
    location="URI/>
  </port>
</service>
```

The file can also include a <documentation> element as a child of <service> to provide a human-readable description of the service.

Viewing a Sample WSDL Document

The concepts behind a WSDL file are easier to understand with an example. The following example shows a simple fictitious WSDL document:

```
<?xml version="1.0" encoding="utf-8" ?>
<definitions name="Author"
targetNamespace="http://www.apress.com/wsdl/Authors.wsdl
xmlns:tns="http://www.apress.com/wsdl/Authors.wsdl"
xmlns="http://schemas.xmlsoap.org/wsdl/"
xmlns:xsd="http://www.w3.org/2001/XMLSchema">
  <message name="getAuthorRequest">
    <part name="book" type="xsd:string"/>
  </message>
  <message name="getAuthorResponse">
    <part name="author" type="xsd:string"/>
  </message>
  <portType name="authorRequest">
```

```
    <operation name="getAuthor">
      <input message="tns:getAuthorRequest"/>
      <output message="tns:getAuthorResponse"/>
    </operation>
  </portType>
  <binding name="authorSOAPBinding" type="tns:authorRequest">
    <soap:binding style="rpc"
    transport="http://schemas.xmlsoap.org/soap/http"/>
    <operation name="getAuthor">
      <soap:operation
      soapAction="http://www.apresscom/getAuthor"/>
        <input>
          <soap:body use="literal"/>
        </input>
        <output>
          <soap:body use="literal"/>
        </output>
    </operation>
  </binding>
  <service name="authorSOAPService">
    <port binding="tns:authorSOAPBinding" name="Author_Port">
      <soap:address
      location="http://www.apress.com:8080/soap/servlet/rpcrouter/">
    </port>
  </service>
</definitions>
```

Notice that this WSDL file contains a number of namespaces:

```
<?xml version="1.0" encoding="utf-8" ?>
<definitions name="Author"
targetNamespace="http://www.apress.com/wsdl/Authors.wsdl
xmlns:tns="http://www.apress.com/wsdl/Authors.wsdl"
xmlns="http://schemas.xmlsoap.org/wsdl/"
xmlns:xsd="http://www.w3.org/2001/XMLSchema">
```

The `targetNamespace` in the document element allows the document to reference itself. It uses a prefix of `tns` for the namespace. The document element includes the default WSDL namespace `http://schemas.xmlsoap.org/wsdl/` as well as a reference to the XML schema namespace `http://www.w3.org/2001/XMLSchema`.

The WSDL document includes two `<message>` elements—one request and one response. The data types are the built-in `xsd:string` types:

```
<message name="getAuthorRequest">
  <part name="book" type="xsd:string"/>
</message>
<message name="getAuthorResponse">
  <part name="author" type="xsd:string"/>
</message>
```

The <portType> contains a single operation called getAuthor. The getAuthor operation has both input and output messages, which correspond to the string <message> elements:

```
<portType name="authorRequest">
  <operation name="getAuthor">
    <input message="tns:getAuthorRequest"/>
    <output message="tns:getAuthorResponse"/>
  </operation>
</portType>
```

The binding specifies the SOAP 1.1 protocol over HTTP using the rpc style:

```
<binding name="authorSOAPBinding" type="tns:authorRequest">
  <soap:binding style="rpc"
  transport="http://schemas.xmlsoap.org/soap/http"/>
  <operation name="getAuthor">
    <soap:operation soapAction="http://www.apress.com/getAuthor"/>
      <input>
        <soap:body use="literal"/>
      </input>
      <output>
        <soap:body use="literal"/>
      </output>
  </operation>
</binding>
```

The application addressed by the web service is located at http://www.apress.com:8080/soap/servlet/rpcrouter/:

```
<service name="authorSOAPService">
  <port binding="tns:authorSOAPBinding" name="Author_Port">
    <soap:address
    location="http://www.apress.com:8080/soap/servlet/rpcrouter/">
  </port>
</service>
```

You're not likely to have to write WSDL documents yourself, but understanding how they work can be useful. You can see an example of a more complicated WSDL file at http://soap.amazon.com/schemas2/AmazonWebServices.wsdl.

The next section explains the SOAP protocol, one of the most popular ways to consume a web service.

SOAP

SOAP is another XML vocabulary that works with web services. You can send SOAP messages using HTTP and even email.

When consuming a SOAP web service, the consumer sends a SOAP message to a receiver, who acts upon it in some way. For example, the SOAP message could contain a method name for a remote procedure call. The receiver could run the method on a web application and return the results to the sender.

In the simplest situation, the SOAP message involves a message between two points: the sender and the receiver. The number of messages could increase if the receiver has to send back another SOAP message to clarify the original request. A further SOAP message would then be required to respond to the clarification request. You also can send a SOAP message via an intermediary who acts before sending the message to the receiver.

The SOAP 1.2 primer is available on the W3C web site at `http://www.w3.org/TR/2003/REC-soap12-part0-20030624/`. You also can see the messaging framework at `http://www.w3.org/TR/2003/REC-soap12-part1-20030624/` and the adjuncts at `http://www.w3.org/TR/2003/REC-soap12-part2-20030624/`. The "SOAP Version 1.2 Specification Assertions and Test Collection" document is available at `http://www.w3.org/TR/2003/REC-soap12-testcollection-20030624/`.

Creating a SOAP Message

SOAP messages are XML documents that conform to the SOAP schema. Because SOAP is an XML vocabulary, a SOAP document must be well formed. A SOAP message can optionally include an XML declaration, but it can't contain a DTD or processing instructions.

The document element of a SOAP message is the `<Envelope>` element. It encloses all other elements in the message and must contain a reference to the `soap-envelope` namespace:

```
<?xml version='1.0' ?>
<env:Envelope xmlns:env="http://www.w3.org/2003/05/soap-envelope">
```

This namespace refers to the SOAP 1.2 specification. If the SOAP processor receiving the message expects a SOAP 1.1 message, it generates an error. You should match the namespace and SOAP version. For SOAP 1.1, use

```
<env:Envelope xmlns:env="http://schemas.xmlsoap.org/soap/envelope/">
```

Each SOAP message is different. It includes the parameters that are required for the operation. You can include a schema for the SOAP message so that you ensure that the contents are valid. A schema allows both the sender and the receiver to understand the format for the request and response. You can see the schema for a SOAP 1.2 message at `http://www.w3.org/2003/05/soap-envelope/`.

Understanding the Contents of a SOAP Message

SOAP messages have the following format:

- The root `<Envelope>` element identifies the message as a SOAP message.
- The `<Body>` element contains the content for the end destination.
- The `<Header>` and `<Fault>` elements are optional.

The following code shows the structure of a SOAP message:

```
<?xml version='1.0' ?>
<env:Envelope xmlns:env="http://www.w3.org/2003/05/soap-envelope">
  <env:Header>
    <!-- Optional header information -->
  </env:Header>
```

```
  <env:Body>
    <!-- Body information -->
    <env:Fault>
      <!-- Optional fault information -->
    </env:Fault>
..</env:Body>
</env:Envelope>
```

Explaining SOAP Headers

The SOAP <Header> element includes information additional to that required by the SOAP receiver. It's optional, but if it's present, it must appear directly after the <Envelope> element.

The header often includes machine-generated information such as dates and times and unique session identifiers. Any child element within a <Header> element must be qualified with a namespace.

You can include the mustUnderstand attribute in a header to require that the receiver must be able to interpret the header:

```
<env:Header>
  <e:Element xmlns:e="http://www.apress.com"
  env:mustUnderstand="True">
    <!--Element content-->
  </e:Element>
</env:Header>
```

You can also use a value of 1:

```
<e:Element xmlns:e="http://www.apress.com" env:mustUnderstand="1">
```

The processor can only process the message if it understands all elements where the value of the mustUnderstand attribute is True. If it doesn't, it returns an error message and ignores the rest of the SOAP message.

A SOAP message may pass through other points on the way to its final destination. The intermediate points may need to act on some of the headers in the message. You use the actor attribute to address the element to an intermediary:

```
<env:Header>
  <e:Element xmlns:t="http://www.apress.com"
  env:mustUnderstand="True"
  env:actor="http://www.apress.com/wsxml/">
</env:Header>
```

Understanding the SOAP Body

The <Body> element contains the information intended for the final destination. Any information contained in this element is mandatory. Child elements of the <Body> element can include a namespace declaration.

The information contained in the body must be well formed and must conform to the WSDL for the web service. In other words, the information must reference the operations set out in the WSDL. The following code shows a sample `<Body>` element:

```
<env:Body>
  <b:getAuthor xmlns:b="http://www.apress.com/bookauthor">
    <b:book>Beginning XML with DOM and Ajax</b:book>
  </b:getAuthor>
</env:Body>
```

In this fictitious example, the `<Body>` element makes a `getAuthor` request. This request takes one parameter `<book>`. In the example, you request the author details for the book `Beginning XML with DOM and Ajax`. The namespace `http://www.apress.com/bookdetails` qualifies the `getAuthor` request.

The body of the returned information might look something like this:

```
<env:Body>
  <b:getAuthorResponse xmlns:b="http://www.apress.com/
  bookauthor">
    <b:Author>Sas Jacobs</b:Author>
  </b:getAuthorResponse>
</env:Body>
```

Examining the Fault Element

The optional `<Fault>` element provides information on faults that occurred when the message was processed. If present, it must contain two elements: `<Code>` and `<Reason>`. It can also contain an optional `<Detail>` element:

```
<env:Envelope>
  <env:Body>
    <env:Fault>
      <env:Code>
        <env:Value>Value here</env:Value>
      </env:Code>
      <env:Reason>
        <env:Text xml:lang="en-US">Error reason here</env:Text>
      </env:Reason>
    </env:Fault>
  </env:Body>
</env:Envelope>
```

If there is a fault, the web service sends a fault message instead of a response. A SOAP processor can't return both a response and a fault.

Explaining SOAP Encoding

You can include an optional <encodingStyle> element in your SOAP message. For SOAP 1.2, use the following:

```
<?xml version='1.0' ?>
<env:Envelope xmlns:env="http://www.w3.org/2003/05/soap-envelope">
xmlns:enc="http://www.w3.org/2003/05/soap-encoding/"
env:encodingStyle="http://www.w3.org/2003/05/soap-encoding">
```

You use the following format for SOAP 1.1:

```
<?xml version='1.0' ?>
<env:Envelope xmlns:env="http://www.w3.org/2003/05/soap-envelope">
xmlns:enc=" http://schemas.xmlsoap.org/soap/encoding/"
env:encodingStyle=" http://schemas.xmlsoap.org/soap/encoding/">
```

The namespaces include definitions for the data types that you can use with SOAP encoding.

Let's summarize:

- The WSDL vocabulary describes web services and their operations.
- WSDL isn't a W3C recommendation; rather, it was developed by Microsoft, Ariba, and IBM.
- A WSDL file is usually generated automatically rather than being written by a human.
- SOAP is an XML vocabulary that allows someone to consume a web service.
- There are different versions of SOAP. At the time of writing, the latest is version 1.2.
- SOAP messages request and receive information from web services.

We'll finish this chapter by looking at some of the other web XML vocabularies.

Other Web Vocabularies

I've given you a brief introduction to some of the most popular web vocabularies: XHTML, MathML, SVG, WSDL, and SOAP. These vocabularies are only the tip of the iceberg, and new vocabularies appear regularly. In this section, I'll list some additional web vocabularies and provide a brief description of their use.

RSS and News Feeds

Really Simple Syndication or RDF Site Summary (RSS), commonly used in news feeds, is like a web service that works specifically with news. Companies such as The Associated Press (AP) and United Press International (UPI) make international stories available via RSS. You can find news feeds for each of them at `http://www.newsisfree.com/syndicate.php`. Smaller web sites can also provide news in this way.

There are many different versions of the RSS specification. The current version is RSS 3, and you can find out more about at `http://www.rss3.org/main.html`.

VoiceXML

VoiceXML is a W3C recommendation designed to represent aural communications on the web. VoiceXML includes support for voice-synthesizing software, digitized audio, and command-and-response conversations, among others.

The VoiceXML vocabulary is surprisingly easy to understand:

```
<?xml version="1.0"?>
<vxml version="2.0" xmlns="http://www.w3.org/2001/vxml">
  <form>
    <field name="gender">
      <prompt>Are you female or male?</prompt>
      <grammar src="gender.grxml" type="application/srgs+xml"/>
    </field>
    <block>
      <submit next="gender.asp"/>
    </block>
  </form>
</vxml>
```

Using grammar documents to specify the expected responses to a user's input, you can quickly create verbal forms to interact with users. You can find out more about VoiceXML at `http://www.w3.org/Voice/`.

SMIL

SMIL (Synchronized Multimedia Integration Language) is an XML vocabulary for authoring interactive multimedia presentations. The acronym, pronounced *smile*, is a W3C recommendation. You can find out more at `http://www.w3.org/AudioVideo/`.

Like VoiceXML, SMIL is a relatively easy vocabulary to understand. It allows you to describe the layout of items on the screen, as well as the timing and synchronization of items in the presentation.

SMIL documents can support the following media types: images, video, audio, animation, text, and textstream. You need a SMIL player or Internet Explorer 6 for Windows to be able to view your presentations.

Database Output Formats

Although database formats aren't explicitly web vocabularies, you may encounter them in your development. Some popular formats include

- Microsoft Access
- Microsoft SQL Server
- Oracle XML DB
- IBM Informix
- IBM DB2 Universal Database
- Sybase

Each of these formats is different, but stylesheets are available that can handle the conversion from one type of database to another. Most of these databases have the ability to export their data directly as XML. Additionally, some tools can extract the information and format it as XML. I'll show you examples of using XML with databases in Chapters 12 and 13.

Summary

This chapter presented an introduction to several XML vocabularies. I examined XHTML, the primary vocabulary in use on the web today. I also discussed SVG, MathML, and vocabularies involved with web services, along with some other, less well-known vocabularies.

In the chapters that follow, you'll learn how to use some of the common vocabularies of XML, and learn how they work together to create XML applications.

CHAPTER 4

Client-Side XML

In Chapters 1, 2, and 3, you looked at XML and saw its application in some specific web vocabularies. The next section of the book deals with XML on the client-side—in the web browser and desktop environment. XML is well supported in the major web browsers, and most browsers have adopted the World Wide Web Consortium (W3C) standards in their implementations of XML.

In this chapter, I'll show you the different ways that you can use XML in web browsers. I'll also talk about Adobe (formerly Macromedia) Flash and finish with a summary of the different client/server architectures that may apply in XML applications.

Why Use Client-Side XML?

To start with, it's important to understand why you might want to work with XML on the client side. There are two reasons:

- To reduce the amount of traffic between the server and client
- To pass on more of the page-processing responsibility to the client

Let's examine the first reason. If you reduce the amount of data flowing between the client and server, you'll provide for a better user experience. By removing some of the client/server communication, the browsing experience is faster, as the users aren't waiting for server responses. Client-side XML also allows users to download XML in the background or as an asynchronous task. If the data has been loaded already, the users won't perceive a lag when interacting with the page.

A second advantage of using XML on the client is that the server can pass on more of the page-processing responsibility. This reduces the web server load and should also enhance the user experience. For example, an XML application could use a stylesheet to display an XML document in the browser rather than using a server-side page to extract and format content.

Before getting started with client-side processing, it's important to add one caution: Browser support is inconsistent in areas such as Extensible Stylesheet Language Transformations (XSLT), so be aware of this when designing client-side XML solutions.

So how can you work with XML on the client?

Working with XML Content Client-Side

As you've seen in the previous chapters, XML is a language for marking up data. On the client, XML applications are likely to adopt one of the following approaches:

- Display XML content in the browser using Cascading Style Sheets (CSS) and XSLT stylesheets.
- Manipulate XML documents in the browser using Document Object Model (DOM), XSLT, and scripting languages such as JavaScript and VBScript.
- Display and manipulate XML documents using Flash and ActionScript.

I'll examine each of these approaches in turn.

Styling Content in a Browser

The purpose of an XML document is to mark up information. Stylesheets separate the content of an XML document from its layout. XSLT and CSS play slightly different roles in this process.

XSLT uses one XML document to generate another. It transforms a source XML tree into a destination XML tree. In the case of a web browser, the XSLT stylesheet uses elements in the XML document to generate XHTML. The XSLT stylesheet creates the XHTML elements by matching specific parts of the original XML document.

CSS adds styling to the transformed elements. Although CSS can style an XML document directly, it can't transform the document, as you'll see in Chapter 5. While XSLT can also add styling, that's not its main function. Figure 4-1 illustrates this relationship.

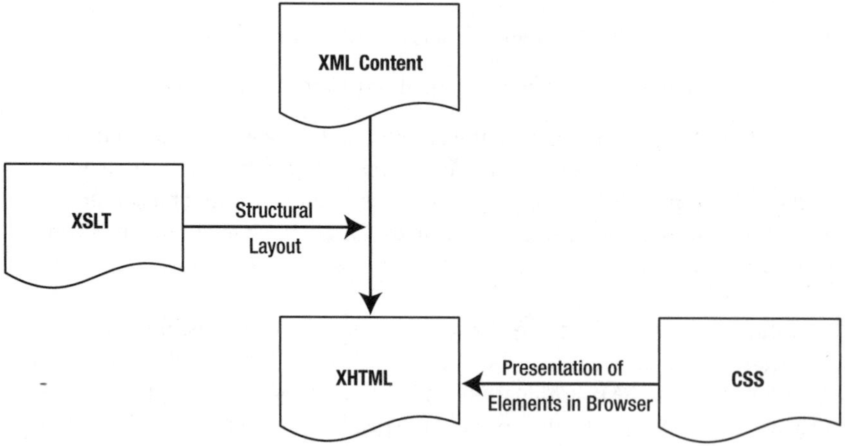

Figure 4-1. *The process of styling with an XML document*

By applying different CSS stylesheets to the same transformed XML document, you can repackage the content for a range of purposes. For example, you can use one stylesheet for a web browser display and another for a mobile phone. This gives the most flexibility to the presentation layer.

Manipulating XML Content in a Browser

Client-side code can use XML documents as a data source. JavaScript allows you to work with client-side XML to generate dynamic XHTML content. This provides an alternative to writing server-side pages that access external content, or storing large amounts of data within the client-side code in arrays.

Using XML as an external data source allows you to keep the content separate from the presentation layer. It also allows you to update the data without reloading the web page.

As an example, an XML document could provide information about the structure of a web site, and the application could use it to build a dynamic navigation system. Figure 4-2 shows how the server and client might work together to generate such a menu system.

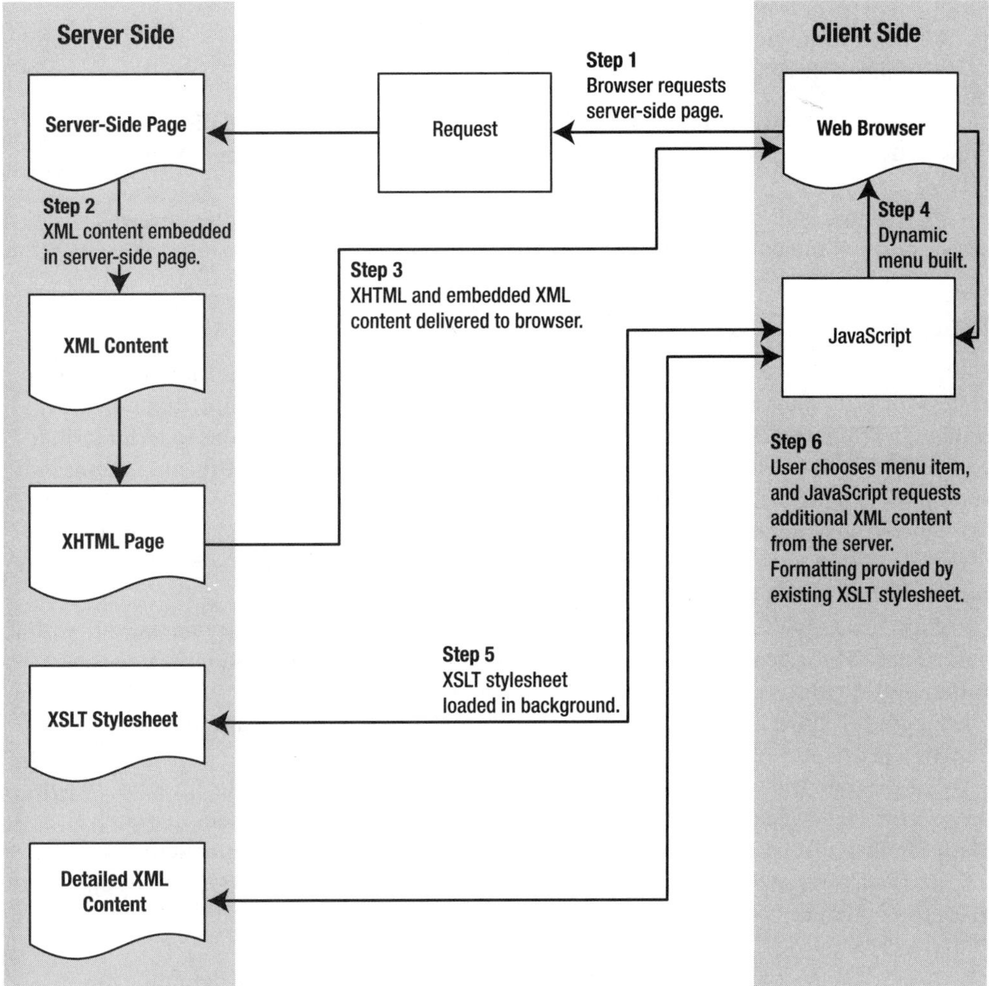

Figure 4-2. *Client and server involvement in the manipulation of XML content*

I'll explain this process:

1. When a browser requests a web page, a server-side scripting language such as Visual C# .NET (C#), Visual Basic .NET (VB .NET), or PHP can generate XHTML content.
2. The server-side logic can also include embedded XML content (a data island) within the XHTML page.
3. The XHTML page, including the XML data, is returned to the browser.
4. After loading, client-side code can access the XML within the data island and use it to generate dynamic XHTML content.
5. At the same time, you can load an XSLT stylesheet in the background.
6. When the user chooses an option from the dynamic menu, the page returns the appropriate XML data.

The XSLT stylesheet can transform the XML content into XHTML and display it in the browser. You'll learn more about this approach in the section, "Transforming XML into XHTML."

Flash movies offer an alternative to XHTML pages, as they can run either in a web browser or as standalone desktop applications.

Working with XML in Flash

Flash includes a range of tools for working with XML content. It doesn't provide support for XSLT transformations, but it does include a scripting language, ActionScript, that provides similar XML functionality to that provided by JavaScript. Flash also contains tools for styling content. Versions of Flash from MX 2004 upward include user-interface (UI) components that you can bind directly to XML content.

Further advantages of Flash are that it's not tied to a web browser, and it runs in a variety of devices. Flash can generate standalone content that runs independently, and Flash Lite 2.0 for mobile phones allows for the inclusion of XML content.

Flash includes a number of prebuilt components. Some of these components work with data such as XML documents. Other UI components provide functionality similar to that within XHTML forms.

Figure 4-3 shows how Flash might work with XML content. You'll learn more about Flash and XML in Chapter 10.

The diagram shows that Flash can work with XML content in two different ways. In both approaches, Flash receives an XML document and parses it into a document tree (step 1). Flash can then display the content within a Flash movie (step 4) using ActionScript. As an alternative, Flash can bind the XML content to prebuilt components (step 2). At this point, Flash can optionally format the data as part of the binding process (step 3) before displaying it within a Flash movie (step 4).

Steven Webster's article, "Choosing Between XML, Web Services, and Remoting for Rich Internet Applications" at `http://www.macromedia.com/devnet/flash/articles/ria_dataservices.html`, provides a good coverage of working with XML in Flash. I'll also talk about Flash in more detail in Chapter 10.

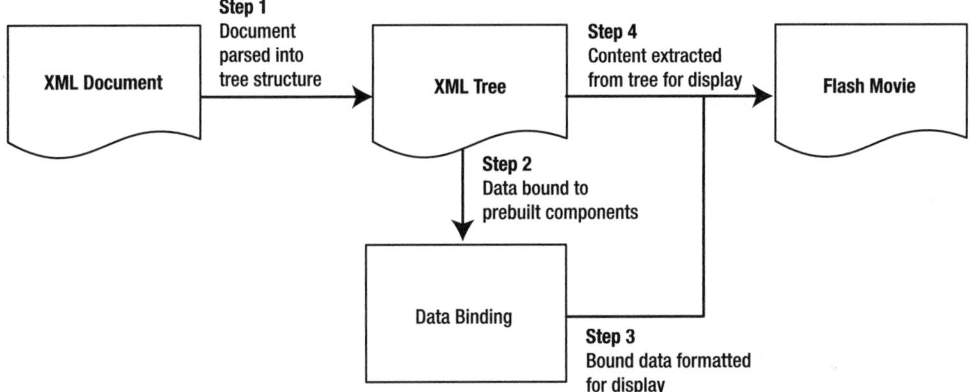

Figure 4-3. *Working with XML content in Flash*

Now that you understand the ways in which you can work with XML on the client, it's time to look at XML support in the most common web browsers.

Examining XML Support in Major Browsers

XML support can include the display of raw XML and conformity with

- The W3C DOM
- XML Schema Definition (XSD) Language
- XSLT

Before discussing browser support, let's have a quick refresher about these concepts and look at some pertinent points.

Understanding the W3C DOM

A DOM represents a document as a series of related objects. The HTML DOM provides an application programming interface (API) for addressing parts of a web document. If you've worked with JavaScript, you may have used the HTML DOM to access specific elements within an XHTML document. For example, you can find the title of an XHTML document with `document.title` or count the number of images on a page using `document.images.length`. If you've created DHTML, you've addressed the issue of browser incompatibility.

The W3C has released a recommendation that provides for three different levels of DOM support, numbered 1 to 3, respectively. The higher the DOM level, the larger the feature set that is supported. The W3C refers to the early Netscape Navigator 3 and Microsoft Internet Explorer (IE) 3 DOMs as Level 0. You can find out more at `http://www.w3.org/DOM/`.

DOM is also separated into different sections: Core, XML, and HTML. The HTML DOM extends some of the Core functionality. Because it extends this functionality, it's compatible with earlier DOM implementations.

The W3C DOM treats data as a tree of nodes, where each node has properties and methods. While DOM theoretically has a wider scope than XML documents, most of the implementations have been concerned with XML and XHTML. The recommendation is platform- and programming-language-independent. This means that, once you've learned one implementation, you'll be able to apply the same constructs with different languages.

Rather than go into detail in this short section, I'll examine DOM scripting fully in Chapter 8. In that chapter, I'll use JavaScript to manipulate DOM, and you'll work through several examples.

Understanding the XML Schema Definition Language

Schemas specify the rules for creating valid documents within a given XML vocabulary. XML schemas are one class of schema developed by the W3C. XML schemas address some of the shortcomings in Document Type Definitions (DTDs). One area addressed is the ability of the XML schema language to define complex relationships and data types within an XML document.

Understanding XSLT

XSLT is an XML vocabulary that is concerned with transforming one XML document tree into another. I'll look at this topic in more detail in Chapters 6 and 7.

The sections that follow will look at XML support in these major web browsers:

- Microsoft Internet Explorer 6
- Mozilla Firefox 1.5
- Netscape 8
- Opera 8.5

These are the current browser versions at the time of writing.

I'll cover the display of raw XML in each browser and the XML parser used by each browser, and I'll show you how the browser determines XML content. I'll also look at any XML functionality specific to the browser. Note that the forthcoming release of Opera 9 includes support for XSLT, which isn't present in the current version.

Microsoft Internet Explorer

Microsoft included XML support in early releases of the IE browser with MSXML, formerly known as the Microsoft XML Parser. MSXML is available as a DLL, in different versions.

Examining the MSXML Parser

Internet Explorer has included MSXML since version 4 of the browser. The parser provides a fairly complete implementation of most of the major W3C XML standards. In general, the more recent versions of IE provide better compliance with standards.

MSXML provides support for DOM, XML schema, and XSLT. MSXML also supports other proprietary and non-W3C standards, such as Simple API for XML (SAX).

MSXML is not a validating parser. If an XML document specifies a schema or DTD, IE isn't able to validate the document instance. For more details on MSXML, visit `http://msdn.microsoft.com/xml/` and browse to the MSXML SDK documentation.

W3C DOM Support

Microsoft has supported DOM Level 1 since MSXML version 2.0. Version 1.0 supported a Microsoft derivative of DOM, which is very similar to, but not fully compliant with, the W3C DOM Level 1.

W3C XSD

MSXML began to support the W3C XSD recommendation from version 4. MSXML 3 supported XML-Data Reduced (XDR) schemas, but this approach has since been deprecated. MSXML 6 removes support for XDR altogether.

XSLT

IE 6 offers support for XSLT 1.0 and XPath 1.0. At the time of writing, XSLT 2.0 is a candidate recommendation from the W3C, along with XPath 2.0.

MSXML Versions

IE 6 ships with version 3 of MSXML, but you can also download the component separately to upgrade to a later version. You may also have a later version if you've installed other software that requires its MSXML.

At the time of writing, the most recent version is MSXML 6, and it ships with SQL Server 2005. The state of different versions is a little confusing. It seems that Windows Vista will include MSXML 6 when released, so presumably MSXML 6 will also be distributed with IE 7. MSXML 5 was included with Microsoft Office 2003 and wasn't available as a separate download.

MSXML 6 includes support for

- XML 1.0 (DOM and SAX2 APIs)
- XML schema 1.0
- XPath 1.0
- XSLT 1.0

The most common versions of MSXML are likely to be 4 and 3 at the time of writing, so this book will focus on using them.

You can use JavaScript to determine which parser is installed. You'll find out more about this in Chapter 8. Table 4-1 shows the versions of MSXML that shipped with the various versions of IE.

Table 4-1. *IE and MSXML Versions*

Internet Explorer Version	MSXML Version
4.0	1.0
4.01 Service Pack 1 (SP1)	2.0
5.0	2.0a
5.0b	2.0b
5.01	2.5a
5.01 SP1	2.5 SP1
5.5	2.5 SP1
6	3

At the time of writing, no versions of Internet Explorer ship with MSXML 4.0 or higher.

Viewing Raw XML in IE

When IE opens an XML document, it checks first for a stylesheet processing instruction. If IE finds a stylesheet, it applies the stylesheet to transform the document. If no such processing instruction exists, IE displays the raw data in a collapsible tree structure, using its own default stylesheet.

To show you how IE displays raw XML, I'll use the `dvd.xml` file from Chapter 1. You can find this with the resources available for download from the Source Code area of the Apress web site (`http://www.apress.com`). The document follows:

```
<?xml version="1.0" encoding="UTF-8"?>
<!-- This XML document describes a DVD library -->
<library>
  <DVD id="1">
    <title>Breakfast at Tiffany's</title>
    <format>Movie</format>
    <genre>Classic</genre>
  </DVD>
  <DVD id="2">
    <title>Contact</title>
    <format>Movie</format>
    <genre>Science fiction</genre>
  </DVD>
  <DVD id="3">
    <title>Little Britain</title>
    <format>TV Series</format>
    <genre>Comedy</genre>
  </DVD>
</library>
```

Figure 4-4 shows how this XML appears when opened in IE.

Figure 4-4. *The dvd.xml document displayed in Internet Explorer*

The document displays in a tree view complete with + and - signs that you can click to open and close branches of the tree. MSXML includes a default stylesheet that IE applies when no processing instruction exists in the XML document.

■ Tip Choose View ➤ Source from the menu to see the raw source of the XML file.

You can see the default MSXML stylesheet by entering the following addresses into the browser:

- For MSXML 4, use the address `res://msxml.dll/defaultss.xsl`.
- For MSXML 3, use the address `res://msxml3.dll/defaultss.xsl`.
- For MSXML 2, use the address `res://msxml2.dll/defaultss.xsl`.

Figure 4-5 shows the MSXML 4 default stylesheet.

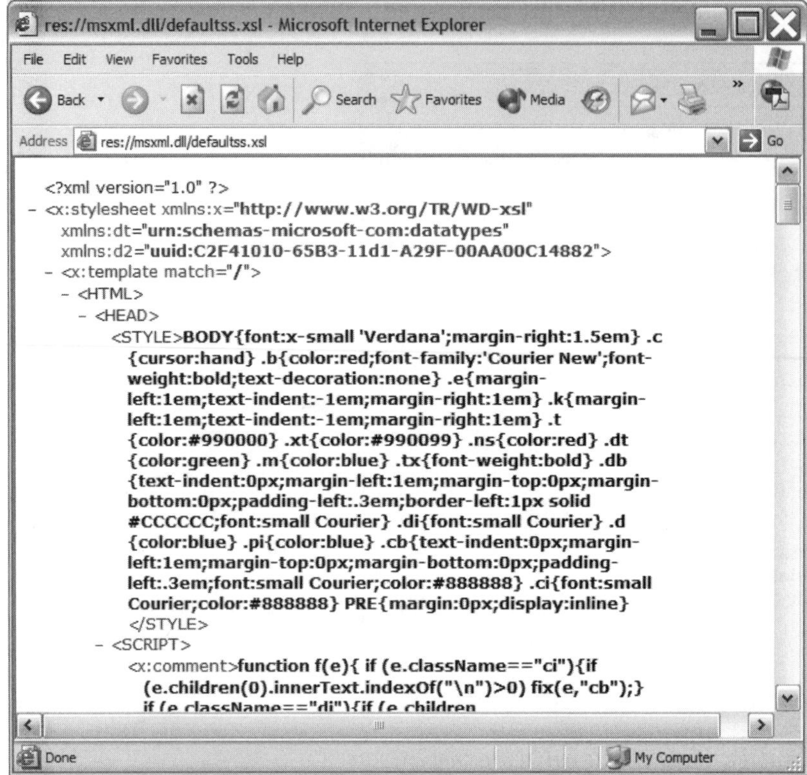

Figure 4-5. *The default stylesheet for MSXML 4*

The content might be a little hard to understand, but it provides an elegant way of formatting raw XML data. If you want to use this stylesheet in your own applications, you can't save it directly from the browser. Instead, you can copy the content and remove the + and - signs.

Determining XML Content

IE takes into account different factors to determine whether it's dealing with an XML document. If the file is loaded from the local file system, IE looks first at the file extension to see if it's a known type. Failing this, it looks for an `<?xml?>` declaration at the top of the file.

When the file is loaded from a remote server using HTTP or FTP, the browser looks to the Multipurpose Internet Mail Extensions (MIME) content type sent by the server to determine the file type. If it's unable to do this, it looks for an `<?xml?>` declaration in the document. When IE determines that the document is of the type XML based on the declaration, it still displays the appropriate MIME type in the document properties box.

Once IE determines that it's dealing with XML content, it parses the document and checks that it is well formed. If the document isn't well formed, IE displays an error message, as shown in Figure 4-6.

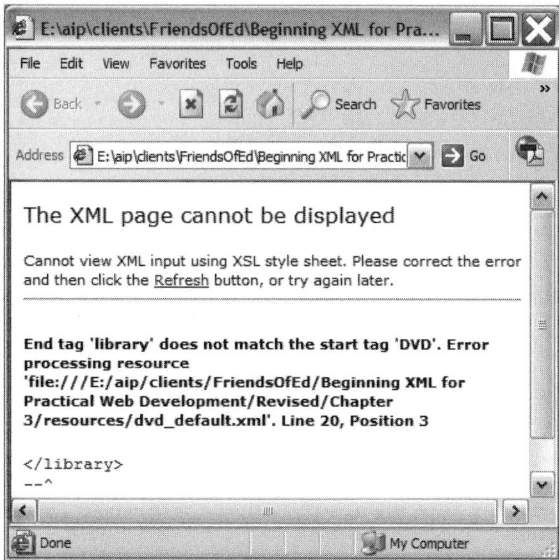

Figure 4-6. *Internet Explorer 6 showing an error message*

Using Proprietary XML Functionality in IE

IE includes the following proprietary features:

- XML data islands
- XML data binding
- XMLHTTP object

I'll discuss these in a little more detail.

XML Data Islands

JavaScript allows you to manipulate XML on the client side. IE includes proprietary functionality that loads XML into script-accessible variables when the page first loads. Microsoft calls this functionality *XML data islands*, as they are *islands* of data within a *sea* of XHTML. Be aware that MSXML no longer supports this technology.

You can include content within an XHTML page by using the proprietary `<xml>` element. You can either add the content inline

```
<xml id="dvd1">
  <DVD id="1">
    <title>Breakfast at Tiffany's</title>
    <format>Movie</format>
    <genre>Classic</genre>
    </DVD>
</xml>
```

or by referencing a URL

```
<xml id="dvd" src="dvd.xml"/>
```

You can then use JavaScript to access the data by using the XML DOM.

The resource file dvd_island.htm includes XML data islands:

```
<?xml version="1.0" encoding="UTF-8"?>
<!DOCTYPE html PUBLIC "-//W3C//DTD XHTML 1.0 Strict//EN"
"http://www.w3.org/TR/xhtml1/DTD/xhtml1-strict.dtd">
<html xmlns="http://www.w3.org/1999/xhtml">
  <head></head>
  <body>
    <p>This page contains XML data islands</p>
    <p>
      <a href="JavaScript: alert(document.all.dvd1.XMLDocument.xml)">View DVD 1</a>
      <br />
      <a href="JavaScript: alert(document.all.dvd2.XMLDocument.xml)">View DVD 2</a>
      <br />
      <a href="JavaScript: alert(document.all.dvd3.XMLDocument.xml)">View DVD 3</a>
    </p>
    <xml id="dvd1">
      <DVD id="1">
        <title>Breakfast at Tiffany's</title>
        <format>Movie</format>
        <genre>Classic</genre>
      </DVD>
    </xml>
    <xml id="dvd2">
      <DVD id="2">
        <title>Contact</title>
        <format>Movie</format>
        <genre>Science fiction</genre>
      </DVD>
    </xml>
    <xml id="dvd3">
      <DVD id="3">
        <title>Little Britain</title>
        <format>TV Series</format>
        <genre>Comedy</genre>
      </DVD>
    </xml>
  </body>
</html>
```

Each data island has a unique id, and you can use JavaScript and the XML DOM to access the XML content:

```
<a href="JavaScript: alert(document.all.dvd1.XMLDocument.xml)">View DVD 1</a>
```

Figure 4-7 shows what happens when you click this link in IE.

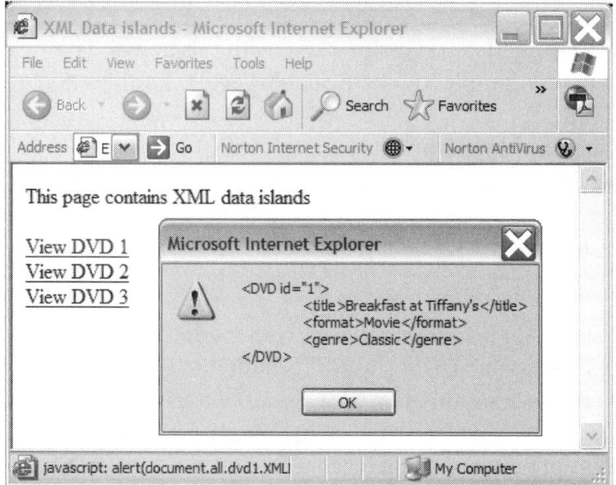

Figure 4-7. *XML data island content displayed in IE*

XML Data Binding

IE allows you to bind XML data islands to Dynamic HTML (DHTML) elements. After binding, you can view or even update the data.

XML HTTP Object

The XMLHTTP object has been included with MSXML since version 1. The object requests data over HTTP. MSXML 6 no longer supports XMLHTTP10.

The following JavaScript code shows how easy it is to retrieve data from the server:

```
var oXMLHTTP = new ActiveXObject("Microsoft.XMLHTTP");
oXMLHTTP.Open ("GET", "http://www.microsoft.com/", false );
oXMLHTTP.SetRequestHeader ("Content-type", "text/html");
oXMLHTTP.Send();
alert(oXMLHTTP.responsetext);
```

You can find this file saved as `xmlHTTP.htm` with your resources, if you want to test it yourself. After IE 5 implemented this functionality, other browser creators followed suit. Similar functionality is available within Mozilla 1.0+, Safari, and Opera 8+. You'll learn more about this in Chapter 9.

Now that you've seen how IE works with XML, it's time to look at support in Firefox and Netscape.

Mozilla

Mozilla is the basis for both the Netscape and Firefox browsers, so the XML functionality discussed in this section applies to both browsers.

Examining the Expat Parser

Most of Mozilla's XML functionality is based around a core XML parser called Expat. Expat is tightly integrated with the Mozilla engine, so all Mozilla versions ship with this parser. The parser supports XSLT stylesheets, namespaces, simple XLinks, Scalable Vector Graphics (SVG), and Mathematical Markup Language (MathML).

Expat 1.2 is also available for separate download from `http://www.jclark.com/xml/expat.html`. At the time of writing, Expat 2.0 is in development and can be downloaded from `http://expat.sourceforge.net/`.

W3C DOM Support

Mozilla provides complete support for the W3C XML DOM to Level 2, with additional support for some DOM Level 3 elements. Unlike IE, Mozilla's DOM support is built into the browser, making it very easy to work with a DOM representation of an XML document using JavaScript. Because DOM is a standardized interface, once you create the DOM objects, you can use the same code to manipulate them, regardless of browser. You'll discover more about this in Chapter 8.

W3C XSD

Expat is a nonvalidating parser, so Mozilla cannot validate an XML document using an XML schema or DTD.

XSLT

Mozilla can perform XSLT transformations in much the same way as IE. It relies on a module called TransforMiiX, which you can also use as a standalone processor.

Viewing Raw XML in Mozilla

Both Netscape 8 and Firefox 1.5 add formatting to display raw XML content in much the same way as IE. Figure 4-8 shows an XML document opened within Firefox.

Determining XML Content

Mozilla is more particular than IE in determining what is and isn't XML. Regardless of the source of the document, Mozilla tries to use the MIME type to determine content type. On platforms with no native MIME support, such as Windows, it uses the file extension.

Unlike IE, Mozilla doesn't look at the content of the file in making the determination. Mozilla treats unknown file types as `text/plain`, even though they may contain XML content. Mozilla checks that XML documents are well formed, and it displays an error in the browser if this isn't the case.

Mozilla also generates an error when it detects white space above the XML declaration. This is the correct behavior according to the specification. However, IE is not as strict about enforcing this requirement.

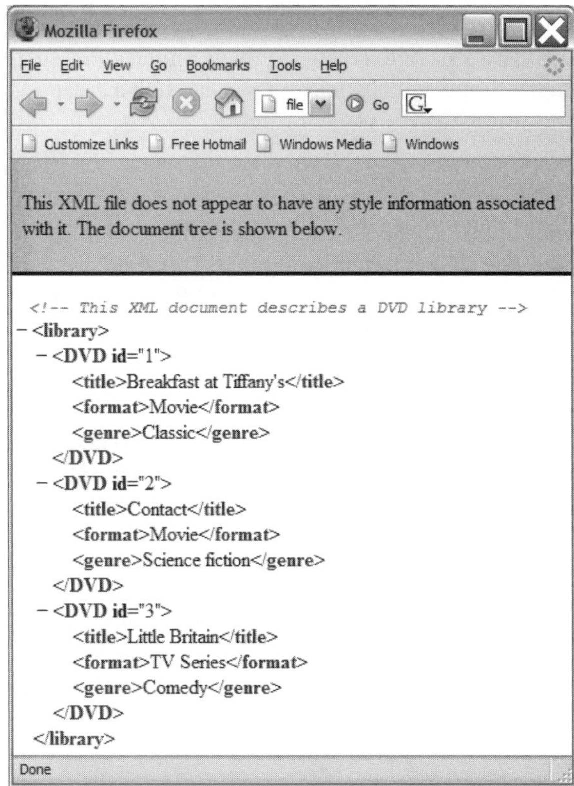

Figure 4-8. *Raw XML content displayed in Firefox 1.5*

Using Proprietary Functionality in Mozilla

Mozilla adheres to W3C recommendations and as such, it doesn't have much proprietary functionality. Like IE, though, it does have native support for XMLHTTP and data islands. Mozilla also supports XML Binding Language (XBL) and XML User Interface Language (XUL).

The Mozilla XML Extras project includes support for Simple Object Access Protocol (SOAP), Web Services Description Language (WSDL), MathML, Resource Description Framework (RDF), and SVG. In the future, Mozilla plans to provide full XLink and XPointer support.

Let's look a little more closely at XBL and XUL.

XUL

XUL (pronounced *zool* and rhymes with *cool*) is a proprietary language created by Mozilla that describes Mozilla user interfaces. You can use XUL to create interfaces containing elements such as form controls, toolbars, and menus. The advantage is that it provides a simple way to define user interface widgets.

You might use XUL to add functionality to Mozilla or to create complete applications such as Firefox and Thunderbird. XUL is beyond the scope of this book, but you can find a great introduction to it at `http://developer.mozilla.org/en/docs/XUL_Tutorial`.

XBL

XBL works with XUL to describe the behavior of XUL widgets. Again, Mozilla developed XBL and submitted it as a note to the W3C. It provides similar functionality to IE XML data binding, combined with IE DHTML behaviors. You can find out more about XBL at `http://developer.mozilla.org/en/docs/XUL_Tutorial:Introduction_to_XBL`.

Native SVG Support

Chapter 3 introduced you to SVG. The latest version of Firefox, 1.5, includes native SVG for most of the SVG 1.1 recommendation. It doesn't include support for filters, SVG-defined fonts, and declarative animations. Netscape 8 doesn't offer SVG support.

Opera

Opera has supported XML since version 4, but it doesn't yet have the same level of support offered by the other major browsers. At the time of writing, the next release, 9.0, plans to increase XML support.

Examining the Expat Parser

Like Mozilla, Opera also makes use of the Expat open source parser.

W3C DOM Support

Opera 8 has full support of XML DOM 2.

XSLT

Opera 8.5 has no support for XSLT stylesheets, though it's planned for the forthcoming release of Opera 9. You must apply XSLT stylesheet transformations on the server side if you're targeting Opera.

Viewing Raw XML in Opera

Opera ignores the XML tags within a document and displays only the content from the elements, in accordance with the recommendation. Figure 4-9 shows how the XML document `dvd.xml`, displays in Opera. Opera treats all elements as inline and renders all text in the same font.

Figure 4-9. *Raw XML content displayed in Opera 8.5*

You can see the content within the XML document by choosing View ➤ Source.

Determining XML Content

Opera uses the content type followed by the file extension to determine whether a file contains XML content. In addition, Opera looks at the first line of the file for an XML declaration.

Opera also checks whether an XML document is well formed. As with the other browsers, Opera generates a parser error if it loads a document that is not well formed. However, unlike the other browsers, Opera displays the part of the XML file that it successfully parsed prior to reaching the error.

Using Proprietary Functionality in Opera

Opera doesn't offer much in terms of proprietary XML tools. However, it offers native support for some XML vocabularies: native SVG 1.1 Tiny and native WML.

Native SVG 1.1 Tiny Support

Opera has native support for SVG 1.1 Tiny, a subset of the SVG recommendation suitable for cell phones. This means that Opera natively supports SVG opacity, font handling, and animation.

Native WML Support

WML is a vocabulary of XML used to mark up documents for display in mobile phone-based browsers. Opera supports most of WML 1.3 and WML 2.0, and Opera is the only major browser to offer support of WML natively.

Adobe (Formerly Macromedia) Flash

Flash provides another option for the display and manipulation of XML content. Since version 5, Flash has been able to parse XML documents into a tree. Flash uses an internal XML class that is similar to, but not fully compliant with, the W3C DOM. One advantage of Flash movies is that they can display in a web browser or within standalone applications. You can find out more about Flash and XML in Chapter 10.

The Le@rning Federation project provides a good example of using XML with Flash. This project is an initiative of the governments of Australia, the Australian states, and New Zealand. You can find out more about the project at `http://www.thelearningfederation.edu.au/`.

The aim of the project is to provide online content for students and teachers through learning objects. A high proportion of the learning objects available use Flash and XML for portability and platform independence. You can find examples of learning objects at `http://www.thelearningfederation.edu.au/tlf2/showMe.asp?nodeID=242#groups`. Figure 4-10 shows one learning object.

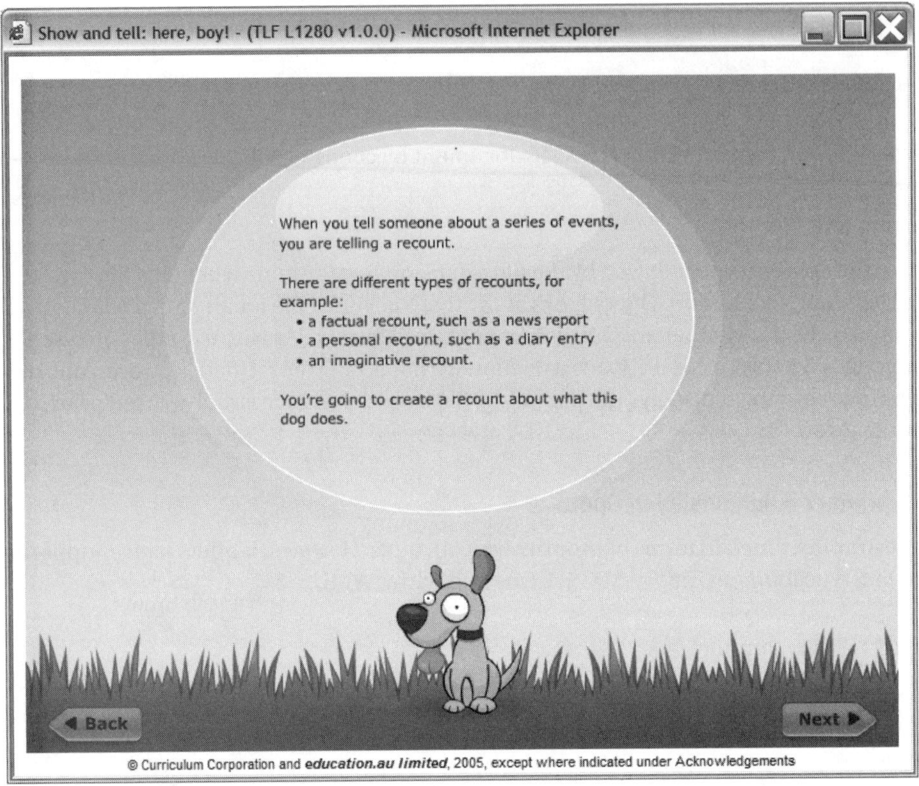

Figure 4-10. *A Flash movie displaying XML content*

Now that I've covered the range of client-side options available for working with XML data, let's examine when client-side processing is appropriate.

Choosing Between Client and Server

It's important to decide whether an XML application should use client-side XML, server-side XML, or some combination of the two types of processing. So far, you've seen several clients that can work with XML content. In Chapters 5 to 10, you'll look at client-side communication in more detail. Chapters 11 to 13 will examine server-side applications.

In this section, I'll cover different approaches for client-side and server-side interactions in XML applications.

Using Client-Side XML

At the beginning of this chapter, you saw that the main benefits of working with XML on the client were a reduction of traffic between server and client, and a reduction in server-side load. Let's examine these concepts more closely with an example.

Suppose you need to display a list of properties that are for sale on a web site. Using XHTML and server-side processing, you could

- Load a list of the property addresses and allow users to drill down to view the details of each property on a separate page
- List all details of every property in a list on a single page

The second approach isn't practical. If you need to display a large number of properties, the page will be very long and will take a long time to download. You will also have a hard time locating information.

In the first approach, viewing the details of a new property requests information from the server, which reloads the interface to display those details. Even if you need only a small amount of information, you'll still need to refresh the page and load additional content from the server each time. Separating the content from the interface saves server traffic and download times each time you want to view another property.

One solution is to use XML on the client side. The server downloads the interface once, when you first load the page. Each time you request further property details, you can download the new content to the client, transform and style the XML into the desired format, and insert the styled content into the cached interface.

The only problem with this approach is that the application can only run in a client that has the appropriate level of XML support. If the content is served within a web browser, you need to be careful, because the level of support differs greatly between the major players. For example, Opera versions 8 and below don't support XSLT.

Using Server-Side XML

One solution might be to process the XML on the server instead. Using server-side processing can avoid any of the specific browser issues. However, as discussed, this means users place more load on the server with more frequent trips to request information. Unless you're dealing with a particularly data-intensive application, this isn't likely to overshadow the advantages of the server-side approach. I'll discuss this in more detail in Chapters 11 to 13, where you'll see some approaches to using server-side XML.

There are three broad approaches to using XML in web browser applications:

- Using XML on the server side only and sending XHTML to the web browser
- Transforming the XML into XHTML for delivery to the browser
- Serving XML to the web browser and manipulating it with client-side scripting

I'll look at each of these approaches in the following sections. I'll examine Flash as a special case in Chapter 10.

Using XML Within a Dynamic Web Page

In this approach, the application processes XML using a server-side scripting language, such as C#, VB .NET, PHP, or JavaServer Pages (JSP), and presents the end result to the browser as XHTML. The browser can then style the content using server-side languages that provide DOM or SAX support, allowing the application to process XML content easily.

Transforming XML into XHTML

The second approach is to generate XML and use XSLT to transform it into XHTML for presentation on the browser. You can apply the XSLT stylesheet transformation on either the server or client, depending on the browser capabilities. If the browser has XSLT support, the transformation occurs there; otherwise, it takes place on the server. Once generated, the application can style the XHTML in the browser using CSS. Figure 4-11 shows the workflow involved in this approach.

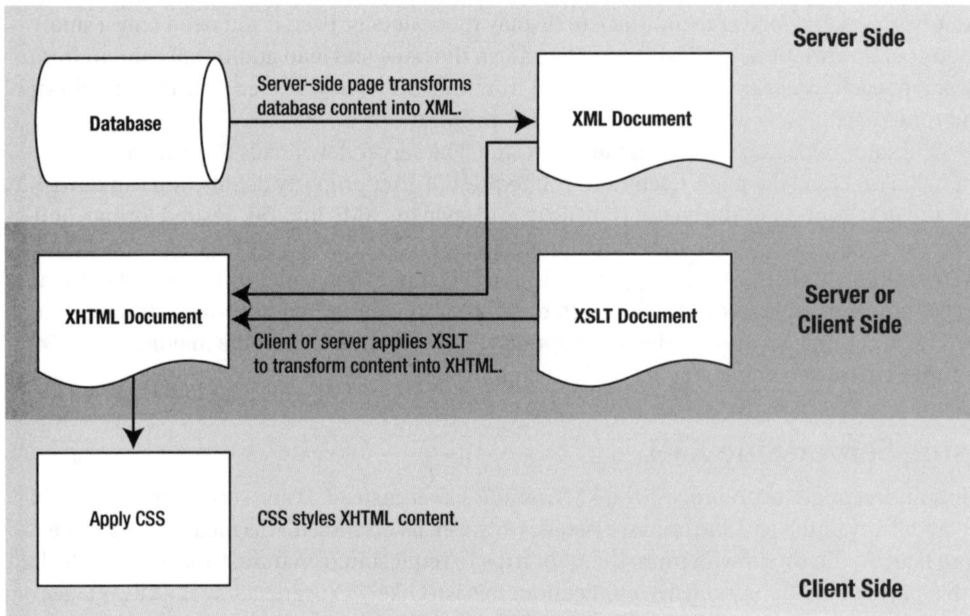

Figure 4-11. *The process of transforming XML into XHTML*

This architecture involves the following steps:

1. Generate XML on the server.
2. Transform the XML content into XHTML on either the server or client.
3. Style the XHTML with CSS.

I'll explain each step in a little more detail.

Generating XML on the Server

The first step is much like building a dynamic web page, except that instead of generating XHTML, the application generates XML. The structure of the XML depends on the data source and the application.

Transforming the XML Content into XHTML

In the second stage, the application determines where the transformation should take place and transforms the data. The result of the transformation is an XHTML document that contains CSS references.

If the client has the capability to transform the data, it should apply the stylesheet at that point to reduce the load on the server. However, this determination must be made on the server, so that you can apply a server-side transformation if necessary.

If you're using XSLT to access a small amount of content from a larger XML document, the overhead of sending the XML to the browser may be more than the time saved in client-side processing. It may make more sense to transform the content on the server and deliver XHTML to the browser.

Another alternative is to combine both server-side and client-side transformations. The server-side transform selects the content and delivers XML to the client. The client then performs another transformation to generate the final XHTML.

Styling the XHTML with CSS

Once the browser receives the XHTML content, it is styled with CSS either through a linked external stylesheet or through embedded or inline CSS declarations. The result is a styled XHTML page.

Advantages and Disadvantages

Transforming XML into XHTML is a useful approach because it offers the following advantages compared with traditional XHTML-based dynamic web pages:

- The application separates the data, layout, and styling of pages quite rigidly.
- Separating styling provides more manageability for web applications. This type of architecture can be easily adapted to a server farm environment.
- The application can target different platforms with the same server-side code. For example, the same content can be presented on web and mobile-phone browsers by applying a different XSLT stylesheet for each device.
- The same application can be used for multiple purposes. For example, stylesheets could transform application-specific XML into a format suitable for sharing with business partners. They could then "browse" the transformed XML with a corporate system, allowing both parties to interact without making major changes to either system.

Bear in mind that if you apply XSLT transformations on the server side, the server must carry out additional processing. Through this process, you may lose gains arising from reduced server traffic.

You can implement this type of architecture either by building your own framework or by relying on existing tools. Some of the existing tools include

- Apache AxKit: `http://www.axkit.org/`
- Apache Cocoon Project: `http://cocoon.apache.org/`
- PolarLake Integration Suite: `http://www.polarlake.com/en/html/products/integration/index.shtml`
- Visual Net Server: `http://www.visualnetserver.com/`

In addition, web servers such as Adobe (formerly Macromedia) ColdFusion (`http://www.macromedia.com/software/coldfusion/`) and Microsoft Internet Information Services (IIS) (`http://www.microsoft.com/WindowsServer2003/iis/default.mspx`) offer good XML application tools.

Serving XML to Client-Side Code

In this approach, the browser receives the XML content as data embedded within the client-side code. You can use this approach to build dynamic pages that don't have to make a round-trip to the server for additional processing. The application makes XML data available to client-side code by

- Loading XML into a DOM variable using the browser's proprietary DOM `load` method.
- Using the XMLHTTP Request objects in IE, Mozilla, and Opera. This option is the core technology behind an approach called Asynchronous JavaScript and XML (AJAX) that you'll learn about in Chapter 9.
- Using XML-aware client-side development tools such as Flash.
- Working with XML data islands.

Serving XML directly to the client reduces the number of round-trips to the server. Without XML, the application would have to make a call to the server each time to request new content, which has the potential to slow down the user experience.

Summary

In this chapter, you've examined the XML support available in current versions of the major browsers. You've seen the different ways that you can process XML in a web browser, including some advanced functionality offered by IE. I've also shown you three different approaches to using XML in web applications.

Chapters 5 to 10 examine how to implement the areas that you've examined in this chapter. Chapter 5 looks at styling XML documents with CSS, and Chapters 6 and 7 cover XSLT in detail. Chapter 8 looks more closely at scripting in the browser, while Chapter 9 examines one browser scripting approach, called Ajax. In Chapter 10, I'll introduce you to Flash as an alternative method for working with XML.

CHAPTER 5

Displaying XML Using CSS

You're probably familiar with Cascading Style Sheets (CSS) and using CSS declarations to style your XHTML pages. As you've already seen, stylesheets are very helpful for separating the content of an XHTML page from its presentation. They also allow you to be more efficient in managing web sites, because you can update styles across multiple pages by editing a single stylesheet.

In this chapter, you'll learn about CSS and see how you can use it to style XML documents. I'll start with an introduction to CSS and show you how it styles XHTML documents. This will help to clarify the terms and roles of CSS and show you what's possible.

You'll then work through examples that style XML documents with CSS. This process will show you some of the limitations and the special considerations when styling with CSS. I'll discuss issues such as adding links, including images, adding content before or after elements, and displaying attribute content. All of these areas require special CSS techniques.

CSS styling of XML provides some special challenges. With XHTML, a web browser understands the meaning of each of the elements and can display them accordingly. For example, a web browser understands how to render an `<a>` or `<table>` tag when it appears in an XHTML page. If the same tag appears in an XML document, there is no intrinsic meaning, so a browser cannot make any assumptions about how to render the element.

This chapter will

- Summarize how CSS works with XHTML
- Style XML documents with CSS
- Use CSS selectors with XML
- Discuss the CSS box model and the positioning schemes
- Lay out tabular XML data with CSS
- Link XML documents
- Add images to XML documents
- Add text to XML documents from the stylesheet
- Use attribute values from XML documents

Within the chapter, I'll mention which browsers support each approach. I tested these examples with Internet Explorer (IE) 6, Netscape 8, Firefox 1.5, Amaya 9.1, and Opera 8.51. Therefore, when I mention that something isn't supported in a web browser, I'm referring to these versions. I've also included support for the Macintosh IE and Safari web browsers where possible. As with the previous chapters, you can download the resources for this chapter from the Source Code area of the Apress web site (`http://www.apress.com`).

Let's start with a quick recap of CSS.

Introduction to CSS

Since the early days of printing, stylesheets have provided instructions about which font family and size to use when printing a document. You can use CSS to provide styling information for web documents. A CSS stylesheet is effectively a text document saved with the `.css` extension.

Why CSS?

When you include presentation elements within an XHTML page, the content can easily get lost within the style or presentation rules. The following benefits arise from separating the content from the style and using a stylesheet to indicate how a document can be presented visually:

- A single stylesheet can alter the appearance of multiple pages, meaning that you don't need to edit each individual page to make changes.
- Different stylesheets offer alternative views of the same content.
- The content is simpler to author and interpret because it doesn't include presentation information.
- Web pages load more quickly because a stylesheet is downloaded once and cached. You can then reuse it throughout the site. The pages themselves are smaller because they no longer contain styling information.

A CSS document contains style rules that apply to the elements of a target document, indicating how the content of those elements should be rendered in a web browser.

CSS Rules

CSS is based on rules that govern how the content of an element or set of elements should be displayed. You'll see how to specify which elements to style a little later when I discuss the CSS selectors.

Here's an example of a CSS rule:

```
h1 {color:# 2B57A1;}
```

The rule is split into two parts: the selector (`h1`) and the declaration (`color:# 2B57A1`). The selector shows which element or elements the declaration should apply to while the declaration determines how the element(s) should be styled. In this example, all `<h1>` elements have been specified, but selectors can be more sophisticated, as you'll see later.

The declaration has two components: a property and a value, separated by a colon. The property is the visual property that you want to change within the selected element(s). In this example, I've set the `color` property, which sets the foreground or text color of the heading. The value of the property is `#2B57A1`, a blue color. The rule ends with a semicolon.

■Tip A CSS declaration can consist of several property-value pairs, and each property-value pair within a rule must be separated with a semicolon. If you forget the semicolon, property-value pairs that appear afterwards will be ignored. While you don't have to add a semicolon at the end of a single declaration, it's good practice in case you want to add more declarations afterwards.

CSS supports a system of inheritance. Once you declare a rule for an element, it applies to all child elements as well. If you set a rule specifying the `color` for the `<body>`, all child elements will inherit that color, including `<p>`, `<h1>`, `<h2>`, and `<h3>` elements. The exception here is links, which a web browser often overrides. You may have to include a separate rule for the `<a>` element.

This is one of the reasons for the name *cascading* stylesheets. The CSS declarations flow down the element tree. Another reason for the name is that you can use rules from several stylesheets by importing one into another or importing multiple stylesheets into the same XHTML file. In addition, the rules apply in a cascading order. An inline declaration overrides a declaration embedded in the `<head>` section of a page, which overrides an external stylesheet.

The following example shows a single rule containing multiple declarations. This means that the rule applies to several elements at the same time:

```
h1, h2, h3 {color:# 2B57A1;
            font-family:Verdana, Arial, sans-serif;
            font-weight:bold;}
```

Commas separate the element names in the selector:

```
h1, h2, h3
```

Here, semicolons separate several properties for these elements, and all properties appear between curly braces:

```
{color:# 2B57A1;
font-family:Verdana, Arial, sans-serif;
font-weight:bold;}
```

If you want the `<h3>` element to appear in italics as well, you can add an additional rule:

```
h3 {font-style:italic;}
```

By declaring the common properties together, you can avoid repeating all the other property-value pairs when declaring the `<h3>` element individually. Rules declared individually have a higher level of precedence in the cascade. For example, if you add a `font-weight:normal` declaration in the rule for `<h3>`, it will override the `bold` declaration in the preceding rule.

You can find a list of CSS2 properties at `http://www.w3.org/TR/REC-CSS2/propidx.html`. Many web sites explain how these properties are applied within stylesheets.

> **CSS VERSIONS**
>
> At the time of writing, there are two CSS recommendations: CSS1 and CSS2. The CSS2.1 specification is in working-draft stage. The revision adds requested features and corrects errors in the CSS2 specification. CSS3, also under development, provides a modularized approach to CSS; each of the modules are at various stages of development.
>
> The CSS1 features are mostly supported by IE 6, Netscape 6+, and Opera 6+ on Windows, and by IE 5+, Netscape 6+, and Opera 5+ on Macintosh. Support for CSS2 is patchier, as you'll see throughout this chapter, despite being made a World Wide Web Consortium (W3C) recommendation in May 1998.

Styling XHTML Documents with CSS

As you saw in Chapter 3, XHTML is the reformulation of HTML using XML syntax. XHTML version 1.1 is modular, meaning that web-enabled devices can choose to support modules of XHTML, such as the tables or forms module. This makes it easier to create sites for new devices, such as phones and Internet-enabled refrigerators.

I covered how to construct XHTML in Chapter 3. I'll start this chapter by constructing a CSS stylesheet. Figure 5-1 shows the page that you'll create.

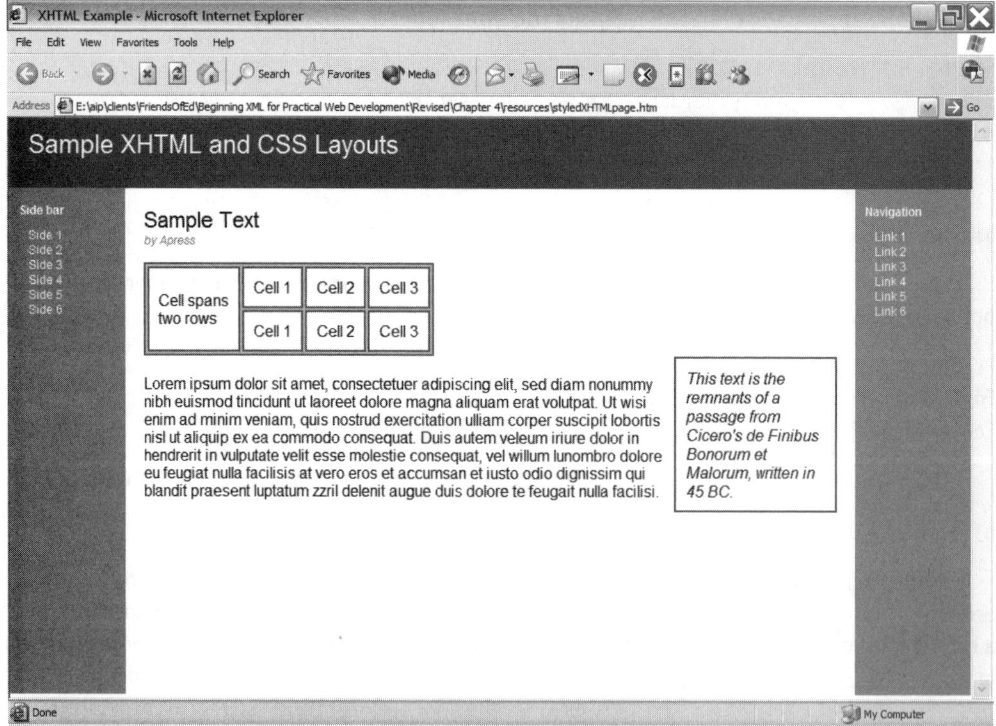

Figure 5-1. *The XHTML page that you'll create*

Without the stylesheet, Figure 5-2 shows that the document looks entirely different.

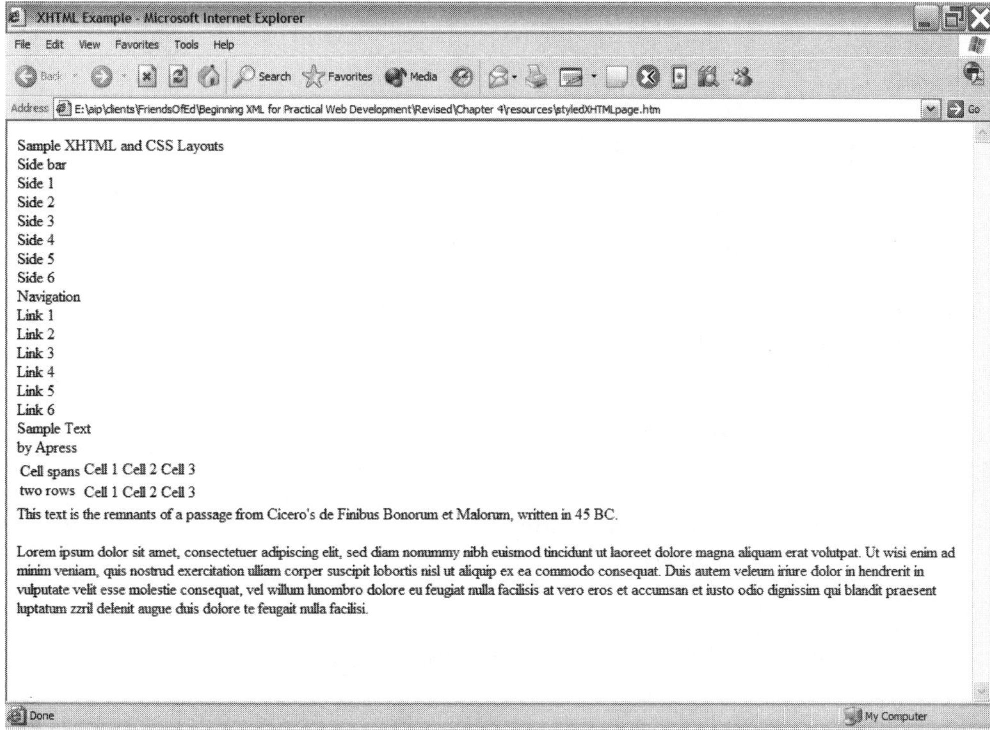

Figure 5-2. *The XHTML page without CSS styling*

As a precursor to constructing a CSS stylesheet for an XHTML document, you need to remove all styling from that document. What remains should be only content and structural tags. You'll then use CSS to position the elements instead of relying on tables.

The style declarations are stored in an external stylesheet that links to the XHTML document with the `<link>` element. You could also include the style rules inside the XHTML document using a `<style>` element within the `<head>` element, or by adding a `style` attribute to each element. However, storing the declarations in a single external document makes it easier to maintain and apply the style rules.

The file `styledXHTMLpage.htm`, which appears below, contains the styled content:

```
<!DOCTYPE html PUBLIC "-//W3C//DTD XHTML 1.0 Transitional//EN"
"DTD/xhtml1-transitional.dtd">
<html xmlns="http://www.w3.org/1999/xhtml">
  <head>
    <title>XHTML Example</title>
    <link rel="Stylesheet" href="styledXHTML.css" type="text/css" media="screen" />
  </head>
  <body>
    <div class="header">Sample XHTML and CSS Layouts</div>
    <div class="contents">
```

```
      <div class="sideBarHead">Side bar</div>
      <div class="item">Side 1</div>
      <div class="item">Side 2</div>
      <div class="item">Side 3</div>
      <div class="item">Side 4</div>
      <div class="item">Side 5</div>
      <div class="item">Side 6</div>
    </div>
    <div class="navigation">
      <div class="sideBarHead">Navigation</div>
      <div class="item">Link 1</div>
      <div class="item">Link 2</div>
      <div class="item">Link 3</div>
      <div class="item">Link 4</div>
      <div class="item">Link 5</div>
      <div class="item">Link 6</div>
    </div>
    <div class="page">
      <div class="title">Sample Text</div>
      <div class="credit">by Apress</div>
      <table>
        <tr>
          <td rowspan="2">Cell spans<br />two rows</td>
          <td>Cell 1</td>
          <td>Cell 2</td>
          <td>Cell 3</td>
        </tr>
        <tr>
          <td>Cell 1</td>
          <td>Cell 2</td>
          <td>Cell 3</td>
        </tr>
      </table>
      <div class="pullQuote">
        This text is the remnants of a passage from Cicero's de
        Finibus Bonorum et Malorum, written in 45 BC.
      </div>
      <p>Lorem ipsum dolor sit amet, consectetuer adipiscing elit, sed diam nonummy
      nibh euismod tincidunt ut laoreet dolore magna aliquam erat volutpat. Ut wisi
      enim ad minim veniam, quis nostrud exercitation ulliam corper suscipit
      lobortis nisl ut aliquip ex ea commodo consequat. Duis autem veleum iriure
      dolor in hendrerit in vulputate velit esse molestie consequat, vel willum
      lunombro dolore eu feugiat nulla facilisis at vero eros et accumsan et iusto
      odio dignissim qui blandit praesent luptatum zzril delenit augue duis dolore
      te feugait nulla facilisi. </p>
    </div>
  </body>
</html>
```

The document uses the stylesheet `styledXHTML.css`, which you can find with the downloaded resources. If you're not familiar with some of the content in this example, don't worry. Ill cover it in depth in the "Layout of XML with CSS" section later in this chapter. I'll also show you how to choose which elements to style.

The `styledXHTML.css` stylesheet follows:

```
body, p, td {
  color: #000000;
  background-color: #FFFFFF;
  font-family: Arial, Hevetica, sans-serif;
}
table, td {
  padding: 10px;
  border-style: solid;
  border-width: 2px;
}
table {background-color: #CCCCCC;}
td {background-color: #FFFFFF;}
p {padding-bottom:20px;}
.header {
  position: absolute;
  top: 0px;
  bottom: auto;
  left: 0px;
  z-index: 100;
  width: 100%;
  height: 60px;
  padding-top: 10px;
  padding-left: 20px;
  font-size: 26px;
  font-family: Arial, Hevetica, sans-serif;
  color: #FFFFFF;
  background-color: #2B57A1;
}
.contents, .navigation {
  width: 100px;
  height: 500px;
  font-size:14px;
  font-family: Arial, Helvetica, sans-serif;
  color: #FFFFFF;
  background-color: #7299D9;
  padding: 10px;
}
.contents {
  position: absolute;
  left: 0px;
  top:60px;
}
```

```
.navigation {
  position: absolute;
  right: 0px;
  top: 60px;
  padding-left: 10px;
}
.sideBarHead {
  font-size: 12px;
  font-weight: bold;
  padding-top: 15px;
  padding-bottom:10px;
}
.item {font-size: 12px;
    padding-left: 10px;
}
.page {
  width: auto;
  background-color: #FFFFFF;
  padding-top: 75px;
  padding-left: 10px;
  padding-right: 10px;
  padding-bottom: 10px;
  margin-left: 120px;
  margin-right: 120px;
}
.title {font-size:22px;}
.credit {
  font-size: 12px;
  font-style: italic;
  color: #999999;
  padding-bottom: 15px;
}
.pullQuote {
  float: right;
  width: 20%;
  background-color: #FFFFFF;
  font-style: italic;
  border: solid 2px #2B57A1;
  padding: 10px;
  margin:10px:
}
```

You can see from the range of declarations that it's possible to style XHTML elements in many different ways. The stylesheet governs the positioning of elements, padding, borders, fonts, and colors.

There are a few things to note before moving on. The example uses CSS positioning instead of tables for the header and sidebars. Separating the content of the document from the layout rules makes the page easier to edit. You should only use tables for presenting tabular data.

The XHTML document includes structural elements, such as a `rowspan` attribute within a table cell. It also separates each block within the document into separate `<div>` tags. A `<div>` element is a handy container for content within a document.

The most important point from the exercise relates to the role played by the web browser. While XHTML is HTML reformulated in XML syntax, there is a difference between XHTML and other XML vocabularies. A web browser already understands XHTML elements and knows how they should be rendered. For example, when a web browser comes across a `<table>` element, it understands how to represent the `<tr>` and `<td>` tags. It knows that the `rowspan` attribute indicates how many rows a table cell should span.

Other XML vocabularies don't offer the same advantages. Unless you're working with a specialized viewer, a web browser or other processor can't derive the display meaning attached to each element. You must be a lot more careful when constructing stylesheets for XML documents.

Styling XML Documents with CSS

You've looked at a styling example with XHTML, so now let's see what happens when you display content from an XML vocabulary that is unfamiliar to the web browser. For instance, you might want to display a custom XML document created from a database, or you could be dealing with a vocabulary that is specific to one of your trading partners. The web browser can't display the content without help. One option is to control the display with CSS.

Because XML elements represent content without any attached presentation cues, you must address the following questions:

- How can you control layout without the use of tables?
- How can you link the CSS stylesheet to the XML document?
- How can you present tabular data in XML?
- How do you include links to other documents?
- How can you display images in our XML documents?

As you style the document, some other issues will arise, including

- The extent to which you can reorder the elements so that they are presented in a different sequence to their order in the original XML document
- Whether you can add content that isn't in the original XML document, such as headers and other fixed text elements
- The display of attribute content, since many XML files contain important data you may wish to view

You can see that styling XML documents with CSS raises many issues. Let's start by attaching a CSS stylesheet to an XML document, so you can see how to render XML in a web browser.

Attaching the Stylesheet

When working with XML vocabularies other than XHTML, you can't include the styling rules inside the document. Instead, you must use a standalone stylesheet.

XML documents can link a stylesheet using a processing instruction:

```
<?xml-stylesheet type="text/css" href="styles.css"?>
```

You can't use the <link> element, because it's specific to XHTML. Instead, you can only rely on constructs common to all XML documents.

The processing instruction must include an href attribute that indicates the location of the stylesheet. It must also include a type attribute indicating the Multipurpose Internet Mail Extensions (MIME) type of the stylesheet. In the example, the value is text/css. If you're displaying the XML document in a user agent that doesn't understand the stylesheet type—for example, a non-CSS-aware mobile phone—it will not need to download the stylesheet.

The processing instruction can also take a number of optional attributes. The title attribute specifies the name of the stylesheet. You can also specify the intended media for viewing the document. Values include screen, as well as aural, braille, handheld, and tv. Probably the most common value is screen, which targets color computer monitors.

The charset attribute indicates the character set used, and alternate indicates whether the stylesheet is the preferred stylesheet. It can take the values yes or no; if a value isn't supplied, the default is no.

You can refer to multiple CSS stylesheets by adding a processing instruction for each stylesheet. You can also add processing instructions to include an Extensible Stylesheet Language Transformations (XSLT) stylesheet; I'll discuss this topic in Chapters 6 and 7.

Let's start by looking at the selectors.

Selectors

It's important to understand the role of selectors in CSS. As you'll recall, selectors indicate where the rule should apply. From your work with CSS and XHTML, you may be familiar with the selectors shown in Table 5-1.

Table 5-1. *CSS Selector Types*

Selector Type	Example	Description
Universal	*	A wildcard, which matches all element types in the document.
Type	body, myElement	Matches all element types specified in the comma-delimited list. In this case, it matches all <body> and <myElement> elements.
Class	.myClass	Matches elements with a class attribute whose value appears after the dot or period. In this case, elements with the attribute class="myClass" match. Note that this only applies to XHTML, not XML.

Selector Type	Example	Description
ID	`#myID`	Matches an element with an `id` attribute whose value appears after the hash (`#`) sign. In this case, the selector matches elements with the attribute `id="myID"`. This selector type is of limited use with XML.
Descendant	`body myElement`	Matches an element type that is a descendant of another. In this case, it matches `<myElement>` elements that are contained in `<body>` elements. The `<myElement>` elements don't need to exist directly within the `<body>` element. Rather, they can exist inside another element, such as `<p>` or `<table>`.
Child	`body > myElement`	Matches an element type that is a direct child of another. In this case, it matches `<myElement>` elements that are direct children of `<body>` elements.
Adjacent sibling	`myElement1 + myElement2`	Matches an element type that is the next sibling of another. Here, it matches `<myElement2>` elements that have the same parent as a `<myElement1>` element but appear immediately after the `<myElement1>` element.

You'll also learn about a set of selectors called *attribute selectors* in the "Using Attributes in Selectors" section.

The class selector only works in XHTML documents, because the browser already knows the meaning of the `class` attribute for these vocabularies. Even if your XML document contains a `class` attribute, the browser won't associate it with the class selector.

Similarly, the `ID` selector only works with attributes of `ID` type. While the browser understands this for XHTML elements, other XML vocabularies need to specify that an `id` attribute is of type `ID` in a DTD or XML schema. Since a web browser isn't forced to validate content, it can't reliably determine when an attribute is of type `ID`. Therefore, neither the class nor `ID` selectors are suitable for use in styling XML documents.

Layout of XML with CSS

Even though tables aren't recommended for XHTML document layout, a large number of sites still use this technique. You can't use this structure to present XML documents, because no predefined `<table>` structure is available within a web browser. You need to control the layout of all XML elements using CSS.

Before you can start styling XML documents, it's important to understand that CSS operates on a box model when rendering a page.

Understanding the W3C Box Model

When displaying a document, CSS treats each element in the document as a rectangular box. Each box is made up of four components: content surrounded by padding, a border, and margins, as shown in Figure 5-3.

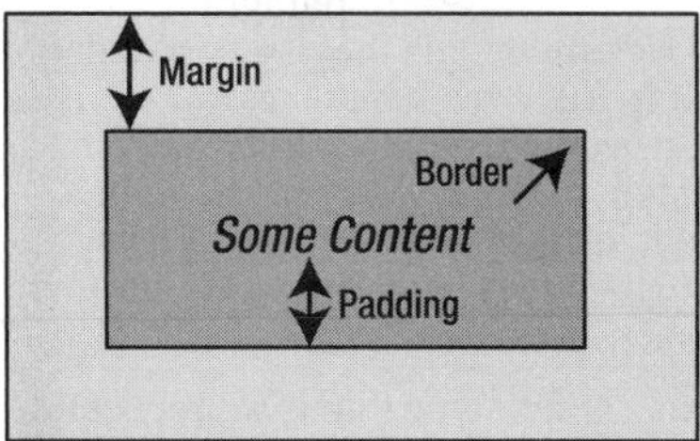

Figure 5-3. *The CSS box model*

The margins around the box are transparent. You can apply styles to the borders around the box to change the line style, thickness, and color. The area inside the border includes content surrounded by padding.

CSS specifies a default width of zero for the margin, border, and padding. You can specify different values with the `width` and `height` properties, but when you do this, you're actually setting the width and height of the content area. The margin, border, and padding are additional and can be broken down into four areas: top, bottom, left, and right.

Each box can contain other boxes, which correspond to nested elements. CSS recognizes two types of boxes: block and inline. In XHTML, you create block boxes with block-level elements such as `<p>`, `<div>`, `h1>`, and `<table>`, while you create inline boxes with tags such as `<em>` and `<span>`. Block boxes automatically include space, while inline boxes don't. This means that inline boxes can flow together.

When styling XML with CSS, all elements are inline by default. You need to identify the block-level elements by setting the `display` property value to `block`. You can also set the `display` attribute to `inline` for the inline elements.

BROWSERS AND THE BOX MODEL

This section describes the W3C box model, but some browsers support a different box model. In the alternative box model, the width is the space between borders, including the margin, padding, and border. By default, IE and Opera use the alternative box model, while Firefox follows the W3C standard.

You can change the box model to the W3C standard by including the strict DOCTYPE declaration. If you do this, IE 6 and Opera 7+ will adopt the W3C box model described here.

The following line indicates a paragraph in XHTML:

```
<p>Here is some text, <em>and a reference</em>,
then <strong>some emphasized text</strong>.</p>
```

The web browser knows that a paragraph should be displayed as a block, and the italicized and emboldened text should be displayed inline, flowing within the text in the paragraph. You can rewrite the content using the following XML:

```
<paragraph>Here is some text, <reference>and a reference,</reference>
 then <important>some emphasized text</important>. </paragraph>
```

To make it display in the same way, set the `display` property for each element as follows:

```
paragraph {
  display: block;
  padding: 10px;
}

reference {
  display: inline;
  font-style: italic;
}
important {
  display: inline;
  font-weight: bold;
}
```

You can also set the `display` property to `none` to prevent a box from being created. This tells the browser to behave as if neither the element nor any child elements exist. Even if a child element declares the `display` value, the content will not appear.

Let's look at an example where a block-level element, like the paragraph in the last example, acts as a container for other boxes. You can find the XML document saved as `boxes.xml` and the corresponding CSS file saved as `boxes.css`. Here's the XML document:

```
<?xml version="1.0" encoding="UTF-8"?>
<?xml-stylesheet type="text/css" href="boxes.css"?>
<page>
  <pageNumber>Page 1</pageNumber>
  <paragraph>
    Here is some text,
    <reference>and a reference,</reference>
    then
    <important>some important text</important>.
  </paragraph>
  <paragraph>
    Here is more text,
    <reference>another reference,</reference>
```

```
    and
    <important>more important text</important>.
  </paragraph>
</page>
```

The XML document uses the <page>, <pageNumber>, <paragraph>, <reference>, and <important> tags to describe the content. The stylesheet follows:

```
paragraph {
  display:block;
  padding-top:10px;
  border:solid 1px #A3A3A3;
  padding: 10px;
  margin: 20px;
}

reference {
  display:inline;
  font-style:italic;
  color:#CC3333;
  background-color: #E6E6E6;
}

important {
  display:inline;
  font-weight:bold;
  color:#990000;
  border:solid 1px #990000;
}

page {
  display:block;
  border:solid 2px #000000;
  padding: 10px;
  margin:10px;
}
pageNumber {
  display:block;
  padding:5px;
  border:solid 2px #336699;
  width: 60px;
  margin-bottom: 20px;
}
```

Notice that the stylesheet includes borders, margins, and padding. I've used the shorthand notation for describing borders.

When you view the XML document in a web browser, you'll see something similar to the image shown in Figure 5-4.

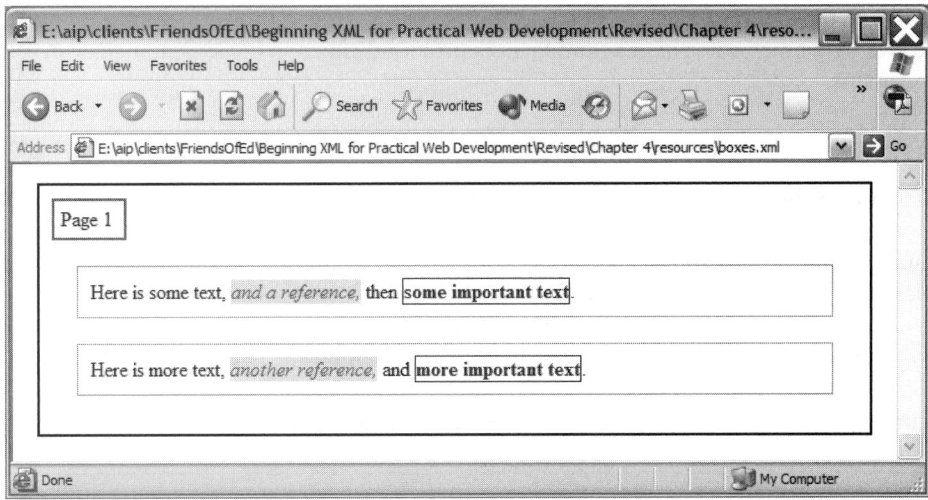

Figure 5-4. *The XML document styled with CSS*

To simplify positioning in CSS, block boxes only contain all inline boxes or all block boxes. If you include inline boxes with block boxes, the inline boxes will be treated as block boxes. An anonymous block created around the inline box simplifies the positioning process. The net result is that even if you set the `display` property on the `<pageNumber>` element to `inline`, it will behave like a block because of the anonymous box created as a container.

It's important to understand how boxes work so you can position them correctly.

Positioning in CSS

As I mentioned at the beginning of this section, you need to understand the W3C box model before you start positioning content using CSS. If you know that each element is displayed as a box, the process of layout becomes a case of deciding whether to use an inline or block box and where to position it on the page.

CSS2 has three types of positioning: normal, floating, and absolute. It also contains some subtypes, such as relative and fixed. Table 5-2 summarizes the different positioning options.

Table 5-2. *Positioning Types in CSS*

Type	Explanation
Normal	The default type. Block boxes flow from top to bottom, while inline boxes flow from left to right.
Relative	A subtype of normal positioning, where a box is offset to the left, right, top, or bottom from its container.
Floating	A box floats to the left or right, and other content flows around.
Absolute	A box is positioned at a specified top and/or left position from its container.
Fixed	A subtype of absolute positioning, where the container is always the browser window.

I'll discuss the difference between each of these types, as well as browser support for each type. Be aware that the choice of positioning has a profound effect on the appearance of an XML document.

Normal Flow

Normal flow is the default type of positioning. In this scheme, block boxes flow from the top to the bottom of the page, starting at the top of their containing block, while inline boxes flow horizontally from left to right. The containing block may be the browser window or another block element.

To see how this works, I've reworked the previous example to include a `<document>` element and a repeated `<page>` element. The files for this example are `boxes2.xml` and `boxes2.css`.

Figure 5-5 shows how the new XML document appears in a web browser.

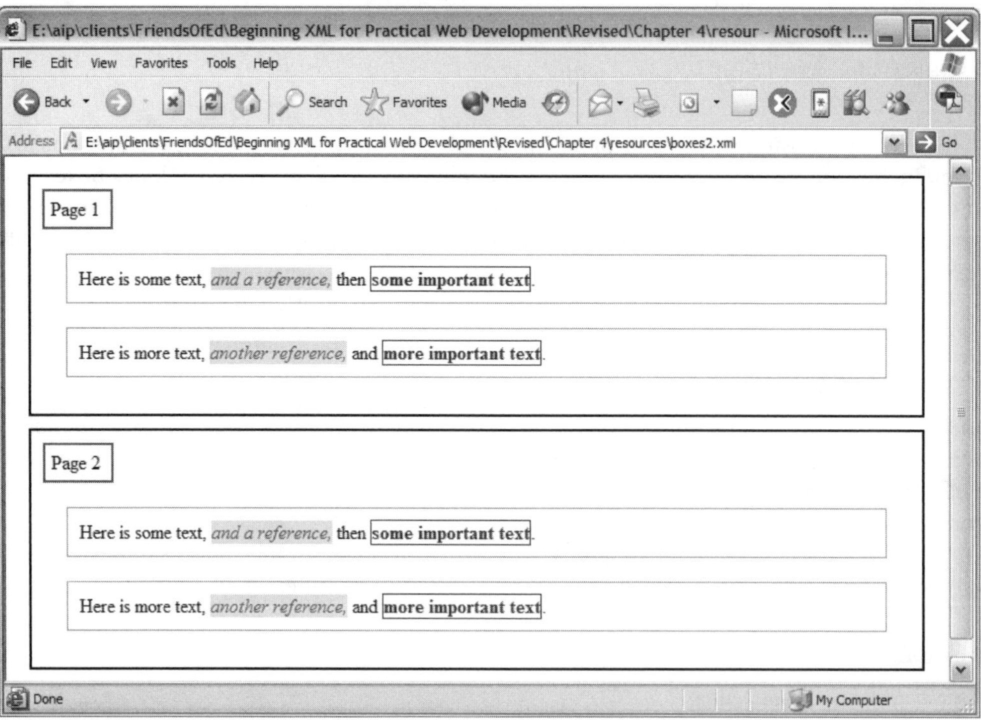

Figure 5-5. *The revised XML with a <document> element*

You can see that the document contains two pages, with the second appearing beneath the first. The paragraphs flow from top to bottom within each page. The inline elements `<reference>` and `<important>` flow with the normal text from left to right.

Inline boxes are wrapped as needed, moving down to a new line when the available width is exceeded. Vertical margins of boxes collapse in the normal flow. Instead of adding the bottom margin of a block box to the top margin of the following block box, only the larger of the two values is used. Horizontal margins, however, never collapse.

Relative Positioning

Relative positioning also falls under the "normal" category. This type of positioning renders the page according to normal flow, but then offsets the box by a given amount. A nice way to demonstrate this is by creating subscript or superscript text.

A `position` property with a value of `relative` indicates that a box should be relatively positioned. You can use `left`, `right`, `top`, and `bottom` to specify the offset values. In this example, you'll add a footnote to the reference:

```
footnote {
  position:relative;
  top:3px;
  font-size:10px;
  display:inline;
  font-weight:bold;
}
```

Note that you've specified a `top` offset to push the box downward. You can find the new files saved as `boxes3.xml` and `boxes3.css`.

■ **Tip** You should only specify one of either the left or right offset, or the top or bottom offset. If you specify both the left and right, or top and bottom, you'll need to make sure that one is the absolute negative of the other (e.g., `top:3px; bottom:-3px;`); otherwise, the offset will be ignored.

Figure 5-6 shows the effect of adding a footnote element to the XML file.

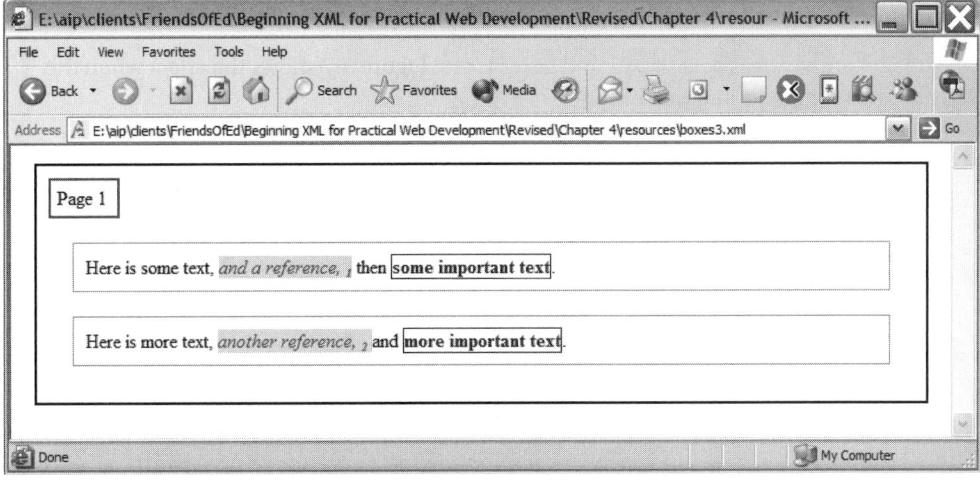

Figure 5-6. *The XML file with a relatively positioned <footnote> element*

Relative Positioning and Overlapping Boxes

When using relative positioning, you need to be careful not to overlap boxes inadvertently. Overlapping happens if you choose an offset that's too large for the surrounding elements. The effect is that one box appears on top of another.

■ **Note** If you specify relative offset values that conflict with a `width` or `height` setting for a block-level box, web browsers and other display devices will ignore them.

While an overlapping effect can be interesting, it also has some pitfalls. Unless you set either a `background-color` or `image` for the box, it will be transparent by default. This means that when text overlaps, you may end up with an unreadable mess.

The CSS specification doesn't say which element should appear on top when relatively positioned elements overlap. Hence, there may be rendering differences between browsers.

In the following example, the `<important>` element has a `relative` position `75` pixels from the right-hand side of where it would have appeared under normal flow. The example also sets `background-color`, so you can see the effect:

```
important {
  position:relative;
  background-color:#FFFFFF;
  right:75px;
  display:inline;
  font-weight:bold;
  color:#990000;
  border:solid 1px #990000;
}
```

The files are saved as `boxes4.xml` and `boxes4.css`. Figure 5-7 shows the effect when the XML document appears in a web browser.

The `<important>` element masks some of the content in the `<reference>` element.

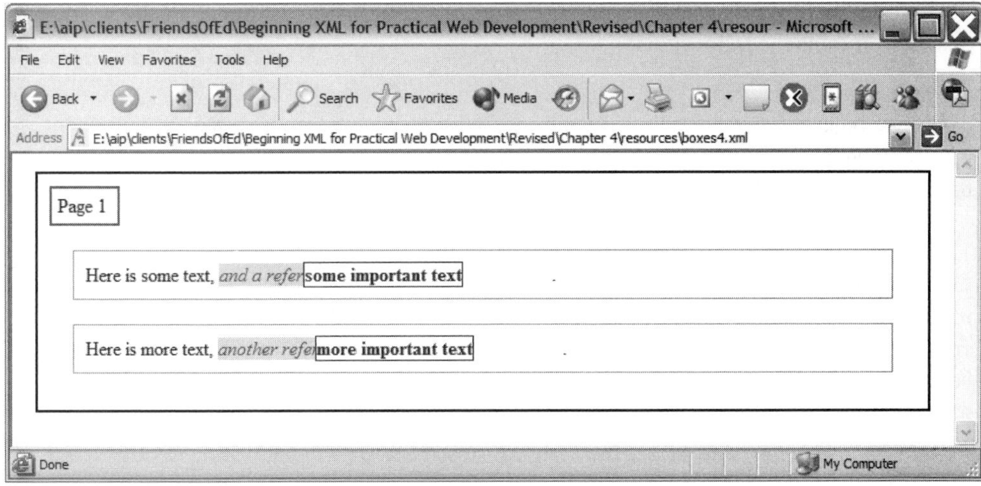

Figure 5-7. *Unintended overlapping resulting from relative positioning*

Floating

If you choose the positioning type `float`, you'll create a floating box. Other content will flow around the box. You can set the `float` property to either `left` or `right`. Floating boxes are treated as block boxes, even if you define them specifically as inline elements.

Positioning with `float` doesn't have the vertical margins collapsed above or below it, unlike normal flow. Instead, the box is aligned with the top of the containing box. Horizontally, it is shifted as far to the left or right of the containing box as is possible.

When you use this type of positioning, you should also set a `width` property indicating how wide the element should be within the containing box. If you don't do this, the floating box will automatically take up 100 percent of the width of the containing box. Because it takes up the maximum space, nothing can flow around it, and it will appear like a nonfloating block-level element.

The next example includes a `<pullQuote>` element. This element floats to the right, taking up 20 percent of the width of its container element. The XML follows:

```
<page>
  <pullQuote>
    The remnants of a passage from Cicero's de Finibus Bonorum et Malorum.
  </pullQuote>
  <paragraph>Lorem ipsum dolor sit amet, consectetuer adipiscing elit, sed diam
   nonummy nibh euismod tincidunt ut laoreet dolore magna aliquam erat volutpat. Ut
   wisi enim ad minim veniam, quis nostrud exercitation ulliam corper suscipit
   lobortis nisl ut aliquip ex ea commodo consequat. Duis autem veleum iriure dolor
   in hendrerit in vulputate velit esse molestie consequat, vel willum lunombro
   dolore eu feugiat nulla facilisis at vero eros et accumsan et iusto odio
   dignissim qui blandit praesent luptatum zzril delenit augue duis dolore te
   feugait nulla facilisi.
  </paragraph>
</page>
```

This document is saved as boxes5.xml, along with boxes5.css, the new stylesheet. The stylesheet contains the following code:

```
paragraph {
  display:block;
  padding:10px;
  border:solid 2px #A3A3A3;
}
pullQuote {
  float:right;
  width:20%;
  font-style:italic;
  border:solid 1px #CCCCCC;
  padding:10px;
  margin:10px:
}
```

Figure 5-8 shows how the floating element appears within a web browser.

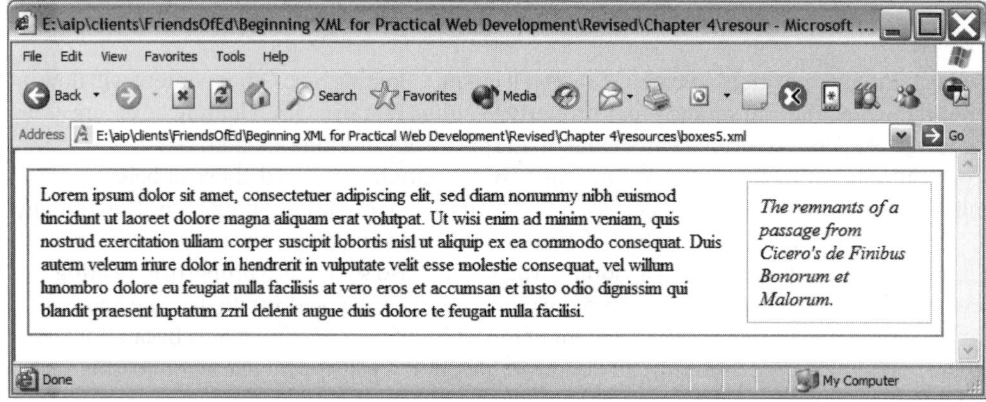

Figure 5-8. *A floating element*

One interesting thing to point out here is that it doesn't matter whether the <pullQuote> element appears before or after the <paragraph> element—it will still display in the same position within the browser. You can use this technique to present the contents of an XML document in a different sequence from the one it follows within the XML source.

Overlapping Floating Boxes

As with relatively positioned boxes, you must be careful about overlapping floating boxes. A floating box can overlap block-level boxes that are in normal flow mode. Figure 5-9 illustrates this point.

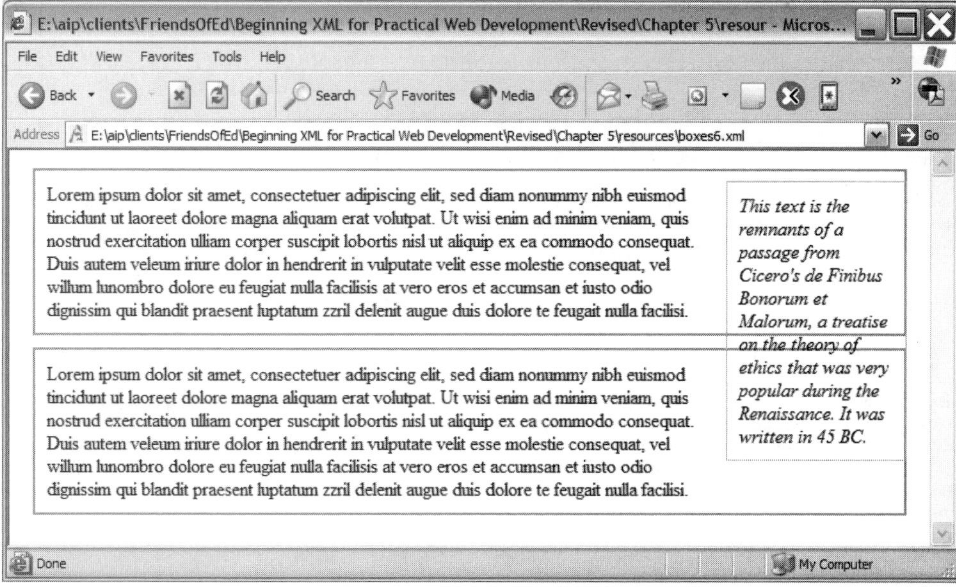

Figure 5-9. *Floating boxes can overlap, causing an unexpected effect.*

This example adds another `<paragraph>` element and increases the text in the `<pullQuote>` element. You can see the effect is not attractive. The `<pullQuote>` overlaps the second `<paragraph>` element. Even if you add another layer of nesting in the XML document, the effect will be the same. The files used in the example are saved as `boxes6.xml` and `boxes6.css`.

You can stop the `<pullQuote>` element from overlapping the second paragraph by using the `clear` property within the second `<paragraph>` element. However, you must be able to distinguish the second paragraph from the first, so change the element name to `<paragraph2>`. Then you can add an appropriate declaration to the CSS file:

```
paragraph2 {
  clear:right;
}
```

The `clear` property indicates which side(s) of an element's box must not be adjacent to an earlier floating box. The property can take the values `left`, `right`, `both`, `none`, or `inherit`.

The example files are saved as `boxes7.xml` and `boxes7.css`. Figure 5-10 shows the effect of these changes. Note that I've also added a white background to the `<pullQuote>` element.

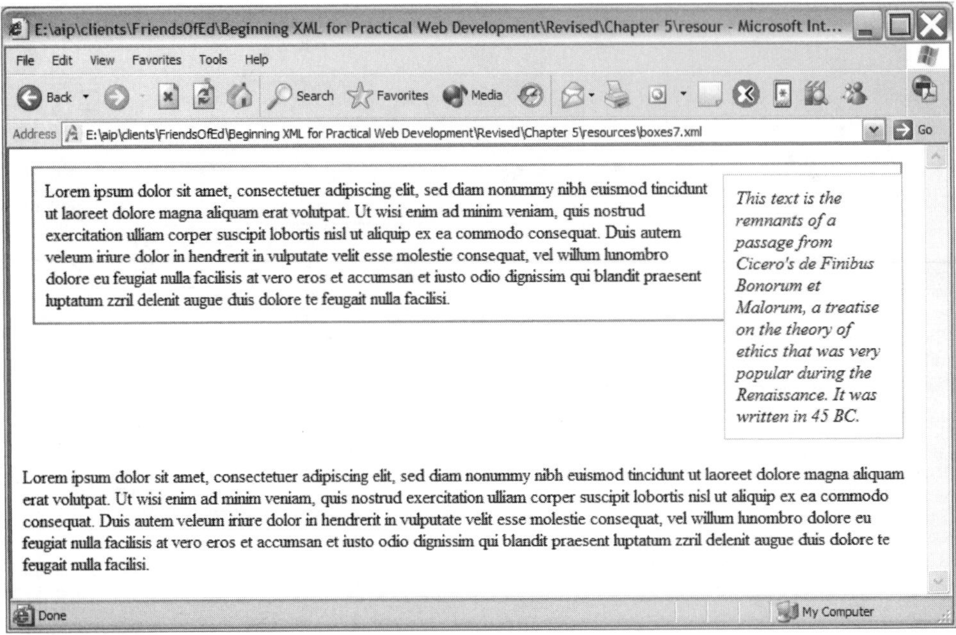

Figure 5-10. *Adding the clear property spaces the pull-quote correctly.*

Multiple Floating Boxes

There may be times when you want to position two floating boxes next to each other horizontally. Let's explore this with another example, where you have a page containing two elements, `<history>` and `<pullQuote>`, that will be represented by floating boxes. The page also contains a `<paragraph>` element in normal flow. The files are saved as `boxes8.xml` and `boxes8.css`.

The structure of the XML document follows:

```
<page>
  <history>This text is the remnants of ...</history>
  <pullQuote>This text became the standard dummy text  ...</pullQuote>
  <paragraph>Lorem ipsum dolor sit amet ...</paragraph>
</page>
```

Both the <history> and <pullQuote> elements share the following style:

```
pullQuote,history {
  float:right;
  width:20%;
  font-style:italic;
  border:solid 1px #CCCCCC;
  padding:10px;
  margin:10px;
  background-color: #FFFFFF;
}
```

Figure 5-11 shows the result.

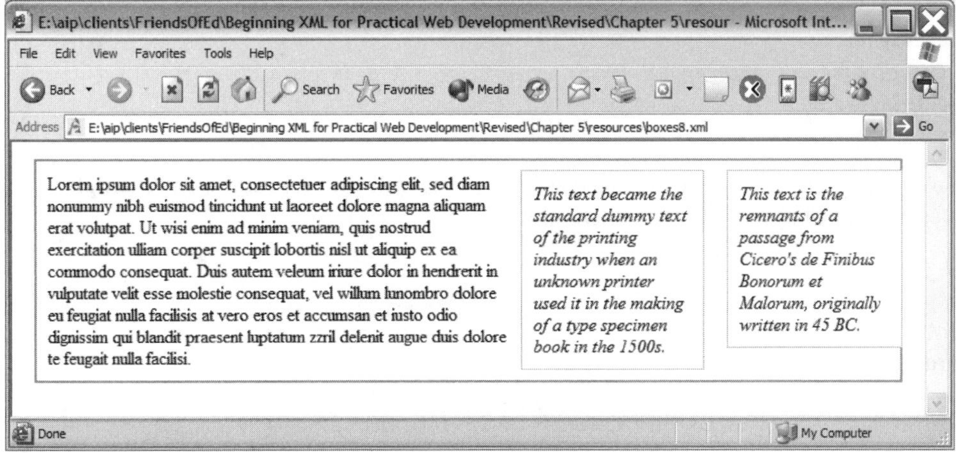

Figure 5-11. *The XML document showing two floating elements*

The floating boxes appear in the opposite order to the way they're listed in the XML document. The <pullQuote> appears first, followed by the <history> element. This occurs because both elements are aligned from the right, so the element that appears first is closest to the right. If you want them to appear the other way around, you would have to alter the XML source.

If there weren't enough space for both floating elements to appear next to each other, the later element would display beneath the element that occurs first in the document. You'll get a similar effect if there isn't enough space to float the element within the container.

By default, the height of the floating box is determined by its content. You can add `width` and `height` properties to override the default presentation.

Absolute Positioning

In absolute positioning, the `position` property has a value of `absolute`, and elements are completely removed from the normal flow. Absolutely positioned elements are always treated as block-level elements and are positioned within their containing block using offset values for the properties `left`, `top`, `right`, and `bottom`. Be aware that absolute positioning can cause problems in some browsers.

This example includes a containing block-level element called `<facingPages>`. The element contains `<pageLeft>` and `<pageRight>` elements positioned next to each other. These elements contain a single `<paragraph>` element, as shown in the following structure:

```
<facingPages>
  <pageLeft>
    <paragraph>...</paragraph>
  </pageLeft>
  <pageRight>
    <paragraph>...</paragraph>
  </pageRight>
</facingPages>
```

You can find the complete file saved as `boxes9.xml` with your resources. The example applies the following styles to these elements:

```
facingPages {
  display:block;
  width:90%;
  border:solid 4px #000000;
  padding: 10px;
  margin:10px;
}
pageLeft {
  position:absolute;
  top:10px;
  right:auto;
  bottom:auto;
  left:10px;
  width:40%;
  border:solid 2px #000000;
  padding: 10px;
  margin:10px;
}
pageRight {
  position:absolute;
  top:10px;
```

```
    right:10px;
    bottom:auto;
    left:auto;
    width:40%;
    width:40%;
    border:solid 2px #000000;
    padding: 10px;
    margin:10px;
}
paragraph {
    display:block;
    padding-top:10px;
    border:solid 2px #CCCCCC;
    padding: 10px;
    margin:10px:
}
```

The stylesheet is saved as `boxes9.css`.

Figure 5-12 shows that viewing this XML document produces some unexpected results.

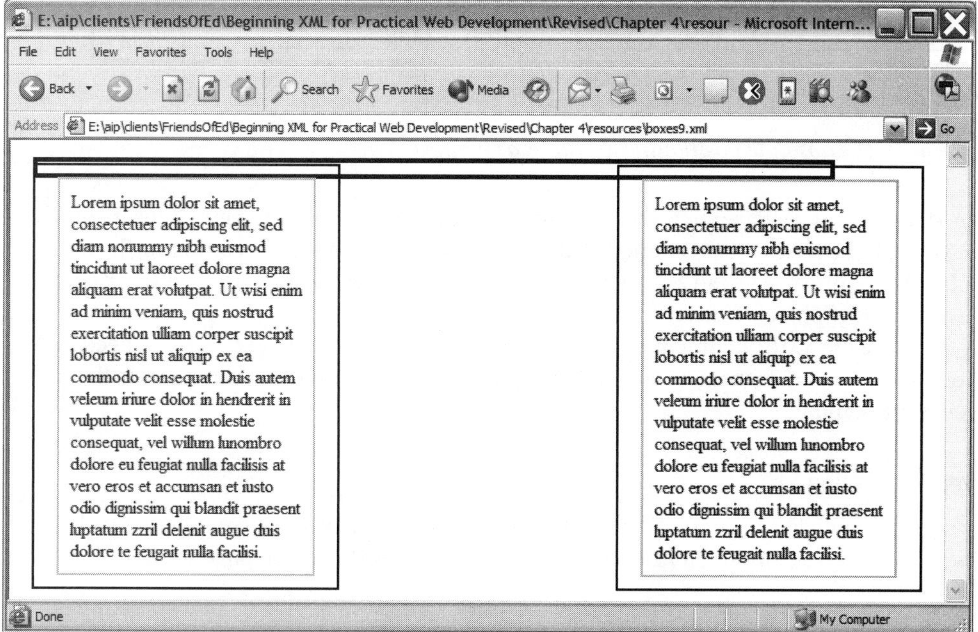

Figure 5-12. *Absolute positioning causes some unexpected results.*

Even if you test the page in Firefox 1.5 or Opera 8.51, you will see something similar. The only browser to render the positioning as expected is Netscape 8, as shown in Figure 5-13.

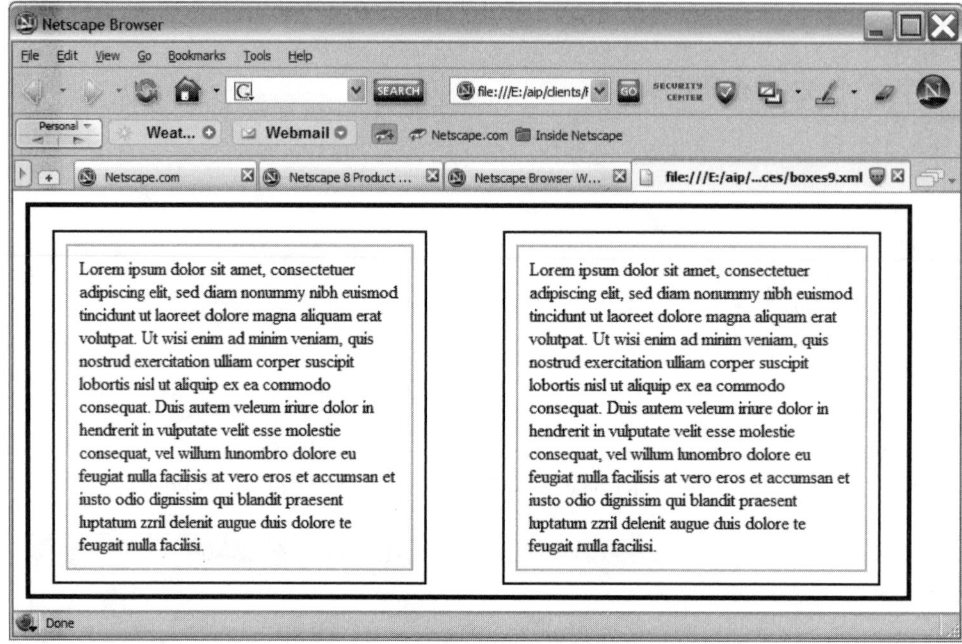

Figure 5-13. *The absolute positioning example, as it appears in Netscape 8*

The previous exercise shows that nesting absolutely positioned elements causes some problems. If the boxes are positioned so that the browser window is the containing box, the problems disappear. As soon as you introduce a container, such as the `<facingPages>` element, the rendering problems start.

Because the XML document must be well formed, this causes a dilemma. You need to have a document element such as `<facingPages>`. The only alternative is not to style the document element.

Fixed Positioning

Fixed positioning is a special subset of absolute positioning, where the containing block is always the browser window. A fixed element doesn't move when a web page scrolls.

■ **Note** Netscape 6.1+, and Opera 6+ support fixed positioning. IE 5+ and Safari for Mac also support fixed positioning. IE 6 for Windows and Netscape 6 only support fixed backgrounds, via the background-attachment property, which produces a similar effect, but only for images.

Let's work through an example of fixed positioning. The file `boxes10.xml` contains the following structure:

```
<document>
  <title>...</title>
  <pullQuote>...</pullQuote>
  <paragraph>...</paragraph>
</document>
```

The XML document uses the stylesheet `boxes10.css`:

```
title{
  position:fixed;
  height: 50px;
  width: 100%;
  color: #FFFFFF;
  font-size: 30px;
  font-weight: bold;
  background-color: #000000;
}
paragraph {
  display:block;
  padding:10px;
  border:solid 2px #A3A3A3;
  margin: 10px;

}
pullQuote {
  float:right;
  width:20%;
  font-style:italic;
  border:solid 1px #CCCCCC;
  padding:10px;
  margin:10px;
  background-color: #FFFFFF;
}
```

Notice that the `<title>` element uses the property `position:fixed`. Figure 5-14 shows what happens when you test this example in Firefox 1.5.

The `<title>` element appears on top of the other elements. This example doesn't work in IE 6 or earlier on Windows, or in Opera 6 or above. In IE 6, the fixed content appears on top of the other content and doesn't overlap. In Opera, the fixed content doesn't display.

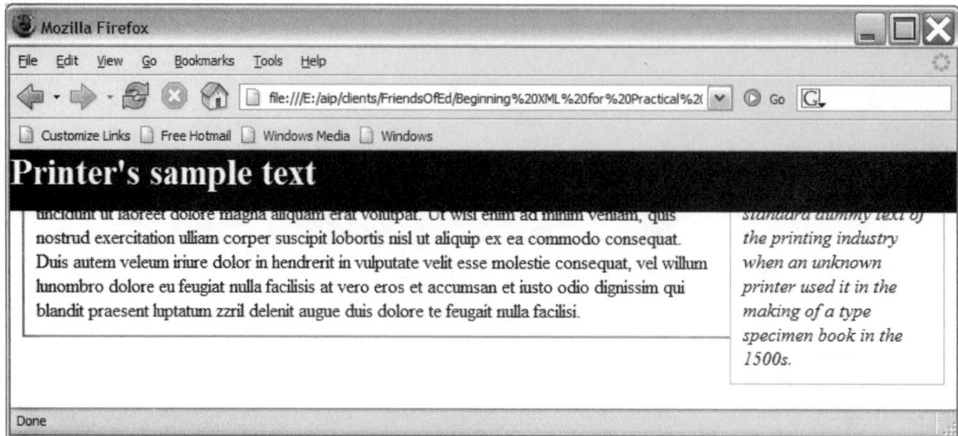

Figure 5-14. *Fixed content appears on top of the other elements in the XML document.*

Overlapping in Absolutely Positioned Elements

Where absolutely positioned elements overlap other elements, they will appear in the same order in which they occur in the document unless you specify a stacking order. You can specify the order using the `z-index` property. Assign a number to the `z-index` property that indicates the order for the element. The higher the number, the closer to the top of the stacking order the element appears. The element with the highest number appears on top.

This example uses the same elements as in the previous example. However, this time, the XML document is styled with absolute positioning, and the stacking order is set by including the `z-index` property.

The XML document is saved as `boxes11.xml`, and the stylesheet `boxes11.css` has been applied:

```
title{
  display:block;
  position: absolute;
  top:5px;
  left: 5px;
  color: #FFFFFF;
  font-size: 30px;
  font-weight: bold;
  background-color: #000000;
  z-index: 5;
 }
paragraph {
  display:block;
  position: absolute;
  top:20px;
```

```
  left: 10px;
  padding:10px;
  border:solid 2px #A3A3A3;
  margin: 10px;
  background-color: #FFFFFF;
}
pullQuote {
  display:block;
  position: absolute;
  top:80px;
  left: 360px;
  font-weight:bold;
  text-align: center;
  border:solid 2px #CCCCCC;
  padding:10px;
  background-color: #EBEBEB;
  z-index: 10;
}
```

This stylesheet uses a `z-index` property to dictate the stacking order of each of the elements. Because the `<pullQuote>` element has the highest `z-index` value (`10`), it appears on top of all other elements. The `<title>` element has a lower `z-index` value (`5`), but it still appears above the `<paragraph>` element, which has no `z-index` property assigned.

Figure 5-15 shows how this XML document appears within IE 6.

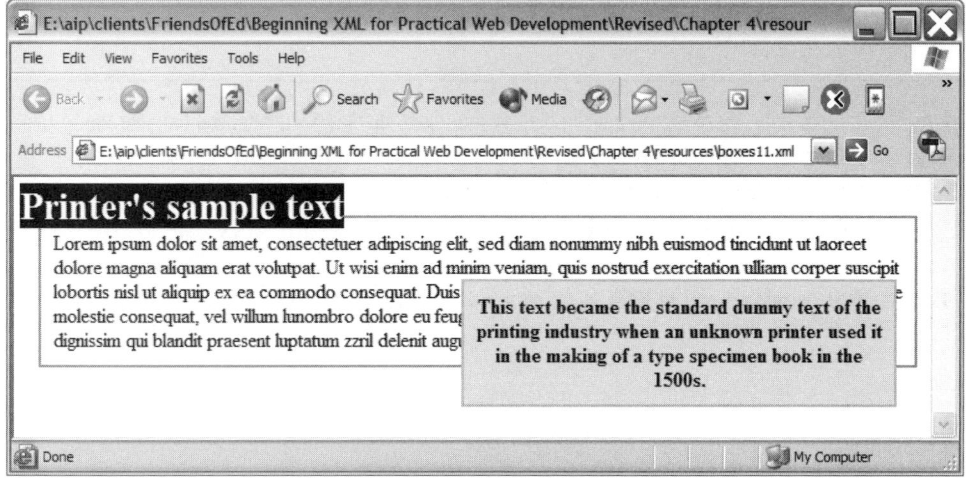

Figure 5-15. *An XML document with a stacking order*

Because you didn't add a style declaration to the document element, the absolute positioning works as expected.

Displaying Tabular Data

As you've seen, there are three schemes for positioning elements: normal flow, floating boxes, and absolutely positioned boxes. Within those groups, there are two subgroups: relative positioning, which changes the positioning of a box relative to its normal flow, and fixed positioning, which fixes the position of a box according to the browser window.

You can create sophisticated layouts for XML content using CSS. The previous examples used CSS to display blocks of text. However, it's common for XML documents to contain tabular data, so you need some additional techniques in order to display this correctly.

Working with Display Properties

Tabular data is easy to display in XHTML, as you can use the `<table>` and associated elements. Web browsers understand that they need to display these elements in a particular way. The first problem that you face when dealing with tabular data in XML is that there is no equivalent to the XHTML `<table>` tag to deal with display.

CSS provides a box model for positioning data. Because you don't often know in advance how many rows and columns will be contained within tabular XML data, it's not appropriate to style this content with absolute positioning. Instead, you need a different technique.

You can use some special values for the `display` property that are designed specifically for laying out tabular data. These values are `display:table`, which indicates that an element's content represents a table; `display:table-row`, which indicates that an element's content represents a table row; `display:table-cell`, which indicates that an element's content represents a table cell; and `display:table-caption`, which indicates that an element's content represents a table caption. The use of these values is evident. They correspond to the XHTML tags `<table>`, `<tr>`, `<td>`, and `<caption>`.

■ **Tip** As with tabular data, there are no built-in display models to display XML lists. You can use the `display:list-item` declaration in the same way as I've described `display:table` in this section. This property is buggy on IE 5+ for Macintosh, but it works with Safari.

Let's work through a sample XML document, which, as you can see, uses element names similar to those within XHTML:

```
<document>
  <table>
    <tableRow>
      <tableCell>Cell 1</tableCell>
      <tableCell>Cell 2</tableCell>
      <tableCell>Cell 3</tableCell>
```

```
    </tableRow>
    <tableRow>
      <tableCell>Cell 4</tableCell>
      <tableCell>Cell 5</tableCell>
      <tableCell>Cell 6</tableCell>
    </tableRow>
  </table>
  <tableCaption>Table caption</tableCaption>
</document>
```

This document is saved as `tabularData.xml` with your resources.

You can present the XML content with the following stylesheet, saved as `tabularData.css`:

```
document {
  color:#000000;
  display:block;
  background-color:#FFFFFF;
  border:solid 2px #000000;
  padding:10px;
  margin:10px;
}
table {
  display:table;
  background-color:#CCCCCC;
  border:solid 2px #000000;
  padding:30px;
}
tableRow {
  display:table-row;
}
tableCell {
  display:table-cell;
  background-color:#FFFFFF;
  border:solid 1px #CCCCCC;
  padding:10px;
}
tableCaption {
  display: table-caption;
}
```

The stylesheet uses the table display properties to render the elements. However, you must be very careful about which browser you use to display this XML document. Figure 5-16 shows the document displayed within Firefox 1.5. IE won't display the example correctly.

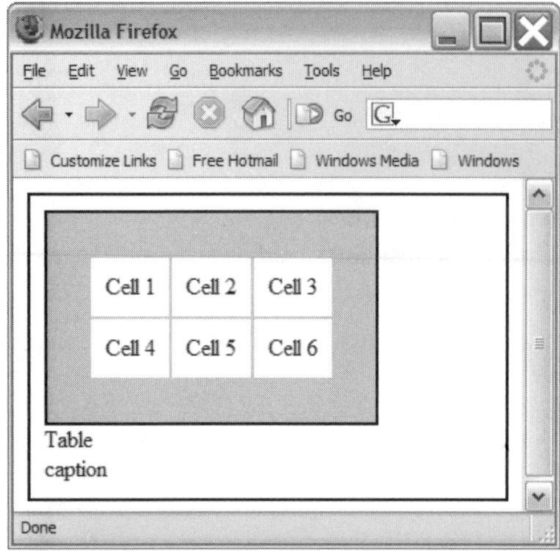

Figure 5-16. *An XML document styled to display a tabular layout*

Note that you can't assign margins, padding, borders, or background color to a `table-row`. A `table-row` works like a group for the cells it contains. A `table-cell` won't respond to margins, although you can set its `background-color` and `padding` properties.

Bear in mind that this approach is buggy on IE 5+ for Macintosh, but it works in Safari. However, Safari puts each `table-cell` on its own row if it isn't enclosed by a `table-row`.

Using these declarations works well when you have an XML document structure that corresponds with a table layout. This solution may not be available for other types of XML documents, and you may have to use a different solution, such as floating elements.

Working with Floating Elements

An alternative way of displaying tabular data is to use floating elements. Let's work through an XML document where the contents that need to display in table cells have different names. For example, the XML document could provide personnel information, and each table row may consist of elements such as `<name>`, `<personnelID>`, and `<extension>`:

```
<personnel>
  <allPeople>
    <person>
      <name>Fred Smith</name>
      <personnelID>123</personnelID>
      <extension>999</extension>
    </person>
    <person>
      <name>Mandy Jones</name>
      <personnelID>124</personnelID>
```

```
      <extension>997</extension>
    </person>
  </allPeople>
</personnel>
```

The file is saved as `tabularDataFloat.xml`. The example displays this XML document with the following stylesheet, `tabularDataFloat.css`:

```
personnel {
  color:#000000;
  display:block;
  background-color:#FFFFFF;
  border:solid 2px #000000;
  padding:10px;
  margin:10px;
}
allPeople {
  display:block;
  background-color:#FFFFFF;
  border:solid 2px #000000;
  padding:10px;
}
person {
  display:block;
  width:80%;
  height:40px;
  background-color:#CCCCCC;
  border:solid 2px #000000;
  padding:10px;
  margin:10px;
}
name {
  float:left;
  width:25%;
  background-color:#FFFFFF;
  border:solid 2px #000000;
  padding:10px;
}
personnelID, extension {
  float:left;
  width:25%;
  background-color:#FFFFFF;
  border:solid 2px #000000;
  padding:10px;
  margin-left:10px;
}
```

You can see that the elements that translate to table cells have set the `float` property. Figure 5-17 shows the result when you view the XML document in a web browser. It displays correctly in IE, Opera, Firefox, and Netscape.

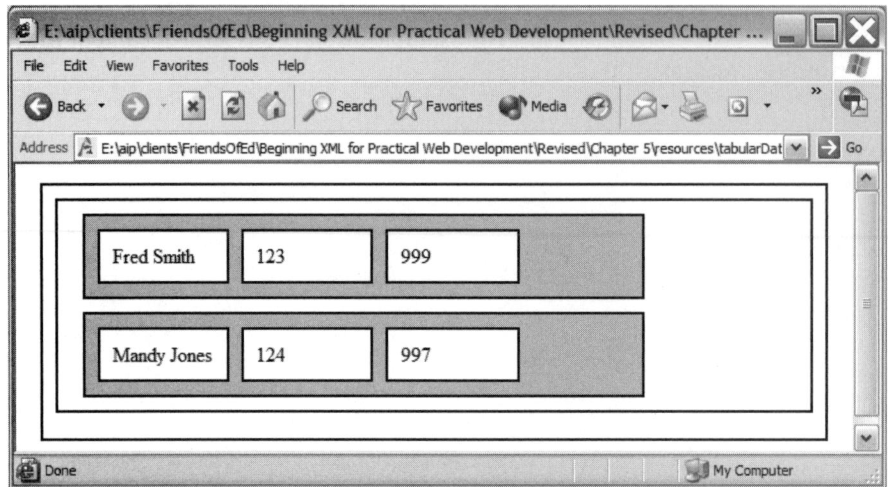

Figure 5-17. *Displaying tabular XML data using floating elements*

If you shade the rows, as in this example, you have to set the height of the rows so that the cells fit within them; otherwise, you'll see an offset where the cell is larger than the row.

To use this method, you need to know the number of columns in the table so that you can set the cell and row widths correctly. If you don't do this, you may run into problems, such as cells wrapping across multiple rows.

Table Row Spans

The only way to achieve the equivalent of a `rowspan` or `colspan` attribute in XHTML is to use additional floating elements. The structure that you use depends heavily on the structure of your XML document. I'll leave you to experiment to see what effects you can achieve.

■ **Tip** The use of the `float` property with a value of `right` is helpful in displaying the table cells in an order different from that in the original XML document.

Linking Between Displayed XML Documents

The simplicity of hyperlinks is undoubtedly one of the reasons for the success of the web. Web browsers understand and can interpret the meaning of an `<a>` tag. XML has no equivalent to this tag. If you style XML documents with CSS, you need a way to indicate that an element is a link. The CSS specifications don't address this topic.

As you saw in Chapter 2, the W3C XLink recommendation (`http://www.w3.org/TR/xlink`) addresses linking within and between XML documents. Support for XLink in web browsers, however, is far from uniform. Netscape 8 and Firefox 1.5 support simple XLinks. IE 6 does not support XLink at all.

The ability to link between XML documents is vital if you use CSS to display your XML documents in web browsers. You won't be able to explore XLinks in IE or Opera, but let's see what you can achieve in Netscape and Firefox.

XLink in Netscape and Firefox

In XML, you're not limited to using an `<a>` element to display links. You can use any element, providing you add the correct attributes. The support for XLink in Netscape and Firefox is fairly basic, although it's enough to replicate what you can do in XHTML. In these browsers, you can use XLink to embed a link into the document. XLinks can

- Replace the current document with the new document (i.e., normal HTML link behavior)
- Open the new document in a new window, equivalent to `target="_blank"` in XHTML
- Open a link automatically when a page loads, equivalent to an `onLoad` JavaScript event

To add an XLink, you need to include the XLink namespace declaration within the XML document:

```
xmlns:xlink="http://www.w3.org/1999/xlink"
```

The best approach is to add this to the document element, so you can create links anywhere within the XML structure.

You need to set the attributes appropriately for the element to be linked. First, you need to determine the type of link with `xlink:type`. While this attribute can accept values of `simple` or `extended`, web browsers only support simple links. Simple links offer the same functionality as XHTML links: They link from a source document to a destination.

You can determine the destination for the link with the `xlink:href` attribute. You can enter any valid URI as the value for this attribute. The `xlink:title` attribute allows you to include a human-readable title for the link. This is like the popup text that appears for an `alt` tag in an image.

The `xlink:show` attribute indicates whether the target document should appear in a new window (`new`), be embedded in the current page at this point (`embed`), or replace the contents of the window (`current`). The `embed` option only works for links to images in the supporting browsers.

The final attribute, `xlink:actuate`, allows you to specify when the link should be activated. The values include either `onRequest`, in which case the user activates the link by clicking, or `onLoad`, which activates when the page loads.

You must refer to these attributes with the `xlink:` prefix, associated with the XLink namespace. Let's work through an example that uses an element called `<link>` as a hyperlink. The link opens a linked web page in the current browser window.

You can style this link using CSS to indicate that it's a link—for example, by underlining it or changing its color to blue. The file is called link.xml, and the associated stylesheet is link.css:

```
<document xmlns:xlink="http://www.w3.org/1999/xlink">
  <page>
    <title>Linking With XLink</title>
    <paragraph>This
      <link xlink:type="simple" xlink:show="new" xlink:actuate="onRequest"
      xlink:title="Visit Apress" xlink:href="http://www.apress.com">link
      </link>
      will open in a new page.
    </paragraph>
  </page>
</document>
```

In XHTML, the equivalent would be

```
<a href="eg20c.xml" title="Visit Apress"
href="http://www.apress.com" target="_blank">link</a>
```

The stylesheet creates a link with a simple CSS rule that changes the color and text-decoration properties:

```
title{
  color: #000000;
  font-size: 30px;
  font-weight: bold;
}
paragraph {
  display:block;
  padding:10px;
  margin: 10px;
}
link {
  color: #0000FF;
  text-decoration: underline;
}
```

When you display the XML document in Firefox and click the link, a new browser window opens, displaying the link target. This is shown in Figure 5-18.

While the support for XLink in Netscape and Firefox is limited to simple links, it's definitely more advanced than in other browsers. You need a different approach for other browsers.

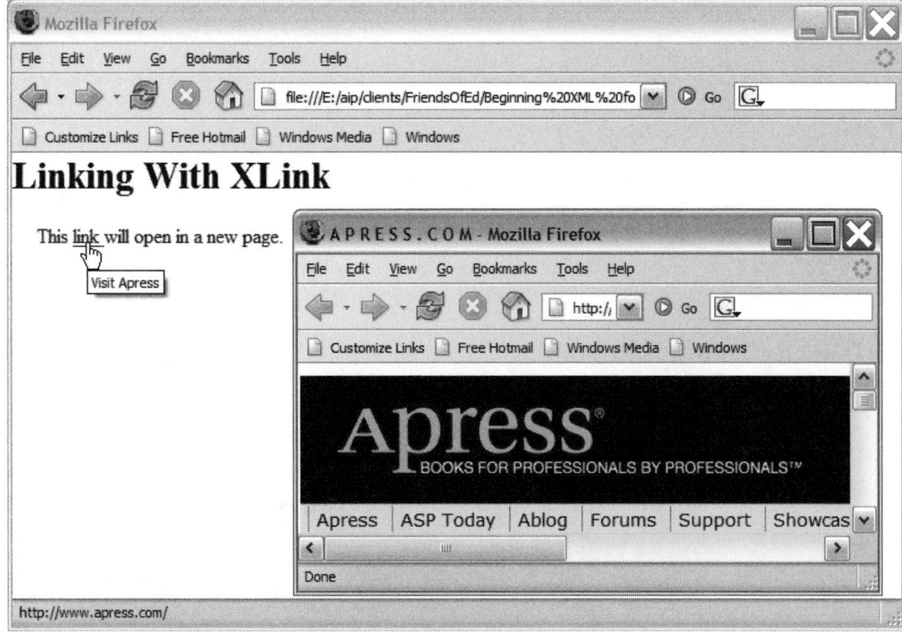

Figure 5-18. *Clicking an XLink in Firefox 1.5*

Forcing Links Using the HTML Namespace

Another trick when working with links is to embed XHTML syntax into your XML documents using the HTML namespace. When a web browser displays the XML page, the XHTML elements render appropriately. This technique works in IE and Opera. It works in Netscape 8 if you choose the "Display like Internet Explorer" option from the bottom, left-hand side of the window.

You can see this example in the file `forcedLinks.xml`:

```
<document xmlns:html="http://www.w3.org/TR/REC-html40">
  <page>
    <title>Forcing XHTML Links</title>
    <paragraph>The
    <html:a href="http://www.apress.com" target="_blank">link</html:a>
    will open in a new window.
    </paragraph>
  </page>
</document>
```

The corresponding CSS file, `forcedLinks.css`, doesn't need to contain any special content relating to the links.

Figure 5-19 shows the effect of opening this XML document in IE 6.

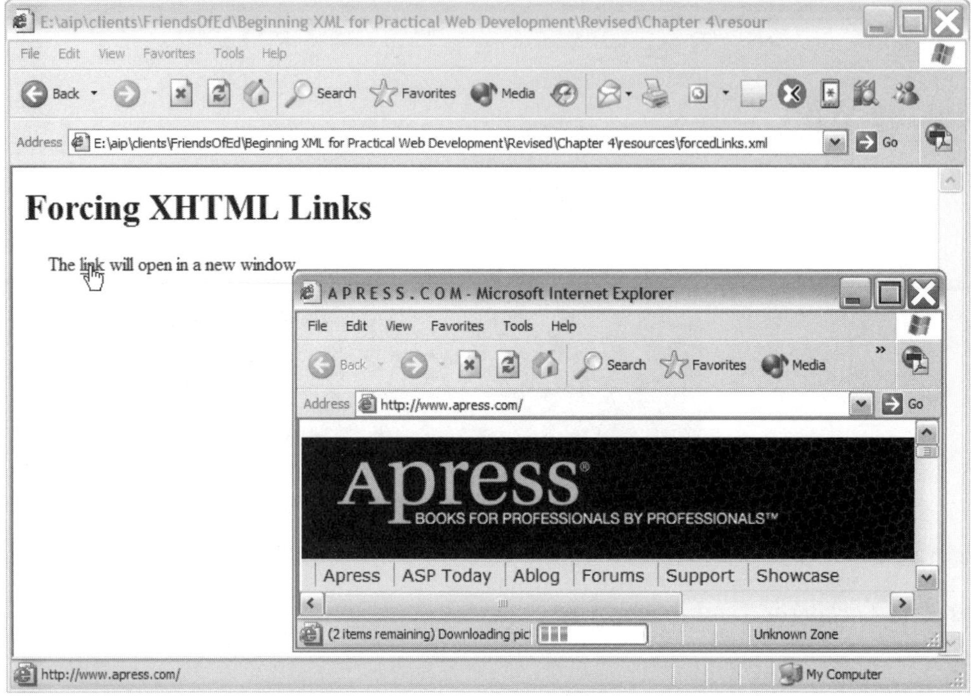

Figure 5-19. *Forcing an XHTML link in IE*

While this is a handy way of mixing HTML with XML, it's not an ideal approach, especially where there are alternatives.

The display of images is another related issue that you may face with XML documents styled with CSS.

Adding Images in XML Documents

You've just seen how to create links in XML documents, and it's not much more of a step to add images. XHTML web pages include images using a link to the image file. The page embeds the image in the document in place of the `<img>` element.

You can add an image using XLinks in both Netscape and Firefox. In other browsers, you can use the CSS `background-image` property, which I'll discuss shortly.

Adding Images with Netscape and Firefox

While you can display simple links in Netscape and Firefox using XLink, you can't currently use `xlink:show = "embed"` to embed images into your document. You can verify this with the files `linkImage.xml` and `linkImage.css`:

```
<document xmlns:xlink="http://www.w3.org/1999/xlink">
  <page>
    <title>Images With XLink</title>
    <paragraph>This
      <link xlink:type="simple" xlink:show="embed" xlink:actuate="onLoad"
      xlink:title="Lions" xlink:href="lions.jpg">link
      </link>
      should embed an image but doesn't.
    </paragraph>
  </page>
</document>
```

If you use `xlink:show = "replace"`, you can replace a document with an image or open the image in a new window:

```
<document xmlns:xlink="http://www.w3.org/1999/xlink">
  <page>
    <title>Images With XLink</title>
    <paragraph>This
      <link xlink:type="simple" xlink:show="replace" xlink:actuate="onRequest"
      xlink:title="Lions" xlink:href="lions.jpg">link
      </link>
      will replace the content with an image.
    </paragraph>
  </page>
</document>
```

You can find this example saved as `linkImage2.xml`. When you click the link, the image replaces the page content.

This option isn't very helpful, as you can't display images with the XML content. With a clever use of CSS, however, you can display an image element.

Using CSS to Add an Image

An alternative way to render an image in an XML document with CSS is to include each image within the document in its own element. You can then use the `background` or `background-image` properties in a CSS stylesheet to display the image.

The stylesheet `imageCSS.xml` includes an `<image1>` element that displays a JPEG image:

```
<document>
  <page>
    <image1 />
    <title>Adding an Image in XML</title>
    <paragraph>This page includes a lion picture.</paragraph>
  </page>
</document>
```

You must set the size of the block to match the image size. If you don't do this and the block is too large, the image will repeat. The stylesheet `imageCSS.css` uses a `background-image` property to identify the image:

```
image1 {
  display:block;
  margin:10px;
  width:282px;
  height:187px;
  background-image:url(lions.jpg)
}
```

Figure 5-20 shows the result.

Figure 5-20. *An image embedded using the background-image CSS property*

You can use this technique in all major browsers. The drawback is that it can be unwieldy if you need to include multiple images, as you'd have to include a separate element and a rule for each image.

Using CSS to Add Content

The examples you've seen so far show how to display the current content of an XML file. There are times, however, when you might need to include additional content, such as text describing table headings.

CSS2 includes the concept of pseudo-elements that allow you to add content when styling XML documents. These elements are `:before`, which inserts content before an element, and `:after`, which inserts the content afterward. Using these pseudo-elements, you can add text and images before any element in the source document. You can also use two additional pseudo-elements to add different effects to the first line or first letter of some text. These are `:first-line`, which adds special styles to the first line of the text in a selector, and `:first-letter`, which does the same to the first letter of the selector.

The syntax for all pseudo-elements is

```
selector:psuedo-element {property: value;}
```

Let's work through an example to see how these pseudo-elements might apply. The XML document, `addedContent.xml`, includes four paragraphs containing text. The elements are imaginatively called `<paragraph1>`, `<paragraph2>`, `<paragraph3>`, and `<paragraph4>`:

```
<document>
  <page>
    <paragraph1>This content is within paragraph 1</paragraph1>
    <paragraph2>This content is within paragraph 2</paragraph2>
    <paragraph3>This content is within paragraph 3</paragraph3>
    <paragraph4>This content is within paragraph 4</paragraph4>
  </page>
</document>
```

In this example, the stylesheet associates different pseudo-elements with each paragraph. The CSS required to style the first paragraph follows:

```
paragraph1:first-letter {
  float:left;
  font-size:24pt;
  font-style:italic;
  font-weight:bold;
  padding-right:4px;
}
```

Unfortunately, none of the major browsers support the `first-letter` pseudo-selector, so the page doesn't display properly.

The style declaration for the second paragraph uses the following to display the entire line in uppercase:

```
paragraph2:first-line {
  text-transform:uppercase;
  font-weight:bold;
}
```

Again, none of the major browsers support this pseudo-selector.

In the third paragraph, the stylesheet inserts some text before the paragraph. The text to be added is placed in quotes as the value of the `content` property. This time, the example works in Netscape, Firefox, and Opera:

```
paragraph3:before {
  font-weight:bold;
  text-transform:uppercase;
  content:"Text before paragraph 3 - ";
}
```

The styling for the fourth paragraph adds an image at the end of the paragraph, using `url(imageLocation)` as the value of the content property. Again, this works in Netscape, Firefox, and Opera:

```
paragraph4:after {
  content: url(lions.jpg);
}
```

Safari also supports pseudo-elements, but IE for Macintosh doesn't.

Figure 5-21 shows the effect of the styling on the `<paragraph3>` and `<paragraph4>` elements. I've excluded the first two elements from the screen shot for obvious reasons.

Figure 5-21. *It's possible to add content using pseudo-elements in CSS declarations.*

In the next section, I want to show you how to work with content from XML attributes.

Working with Attribute Content

The preceding examples all use element names as selectors for the style declarations. What happens when it comes to displaying the content stored in attributes? In this section, you'll see how to use attributes in selectors, and how to access attribute values in XML documents.

Using Attributes in Selectors

CSS2 introduced the ability to use attributes and their values as selectors for CSS rules. They can be used in the following ways:

- `myElement[myAttribute]` which matches when `<myElement>` contains an attribute called `myAttribute`.
- `myElement[myAttribute=myValue]` which matches when `<myElement>` contains an attribute called `myAttribute`, whose value is `myValue`.
- `myElement[myAttribute~=myValue]` which matches when `<myElement>` contains an attribute called `myAttribute`, whose value is a space-separated list of words, one of which is exactly the same as `myValue`.
- `myElement[myAttribute|=myValue]` which matches when `<myElement>` contains an attribute called `myAttribute`, whose value contains a hyphen-separated list of words beginning with `myValue`.

Support for this approach is limited to Netscape, Firefox, and Safari. You can't use attribute selectors in any version of IE.

You can see the source XML content in the example file `attributesCSS.xml`:

```
<document>
  <paragraph style="normal">
    Here is some text in a paragraph whose <code>style</code>
    attribute has a value of <code>normal</code>.
  </paragraph>
  <paragraph style="summary">
    Here is some text in a paragraph whose <code>style</code>
    attribute has a value of <code>summary</code>.
  </paragraph>
  <paragraph style="code foreground">
    Here is some text in a paragraph whose <code>style</code>
    attribute contains the value of <code>code</code> or <code>foreground</code>.
  </paragraph>
  <paragraph style="code-background">
    Here is some text in a paragraph whose <code>style</code>
    attribute starts with <code>code background</code>.
  </paragraph>
</document>
```

Each `<paragraph>` element has a different value for its `style` attribute. The related stylesheet, `attributesCSS.css`, shows the different ways of matching these attributes and attribute values. I've presented them in the same order that I introduced them earlier:

```
paragraph[style] {
  font-size:12px;
  color:#0000FF;
  display: block;
}
```

```
paragraph[style=summary] {
  font-style:italic;
  font-size: 16px;
}
paragraph[style~=foreground] {
  font-family:courier, serif;
  font-weight:bold;
  background-color:#CCCCCC;
}
paragraph[style|=code] {
  font-family:courier, serif;
  font-weight:bold;
  background-color:#FFFFFF;
  border-style:solid 2px #000000;
}
```

Figure 5-22 shows the effect of these selectors in Firefox 1.5.

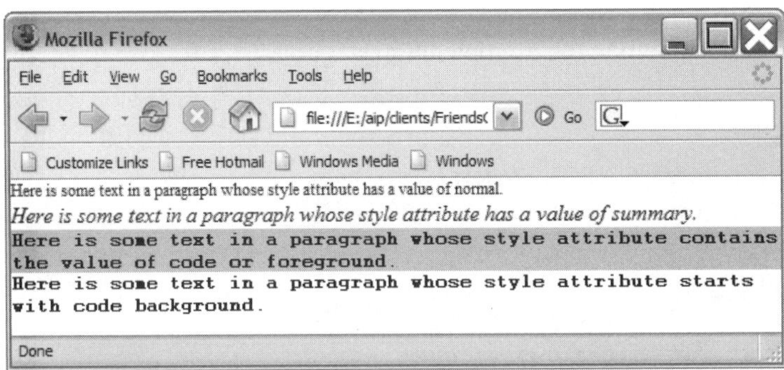

Figure 5-22. *Attribute selectors used with CSS declarations*

You can see that each paragraph changes according to the styles associated with the attribute selectors. This simple example shows you how powerful the use of attribute values can be when coupled with CSS attribute selectors. Attribute selectors could also allow you to associate images with a `background-image` property. Unfortunately, at the time of writing, neither IE nor Opera support this option.

Using Attribute Values in Documents

Another way to display attribute values is to use a trick with the `:before` and `:after` pseudo-elements. As you saw, these pseudo-elements allow a stylesheet to add text or an image before or after an element. The `:before` and `:after` pseudo-elements also allow the stylesheet to add the content of an attribute using the `content` property, with a value of `attr(attributeName)`. The `attributeName` reference is the name of the attribute whose content you want to display.

The file `attributesPsuedo.xml` contains the following content:

```
<paragraph
   keyWords="displaying, attribute, content, XML, CSS"
   xref="CSS2 Section 12.2">
   This example demonstrates how we can use the <code>:before</code> and
   <code>:after</code> pseudo classes to add attribute content to a document.
</paragraph>
```

You can use the `:before` and `:after` pseudo-elements to include the content of the attributes:

```
paragraph {
  display:block;
  background-color:#FFFFFF;
  font-family:Arial, Helvetic, sans-serif;
  padding:20px;
}
paragraph:before {
  display:block;
  background-color#CCCCCC;
  font-weight:bold;
  color:#0000FF;
  content:"Cross reference:" attr(xref);
}
paragraph:after {
  font-style:italic;
  color:#0000FF;
  content:"Key words: " attr(keyWords);
}
```

You can find this stylesheet saved as `attributesPsuedo.css`.

This approach doesn't work in IE, but Netscape, Firefox, and Opera display something similar to Figure 5-23.

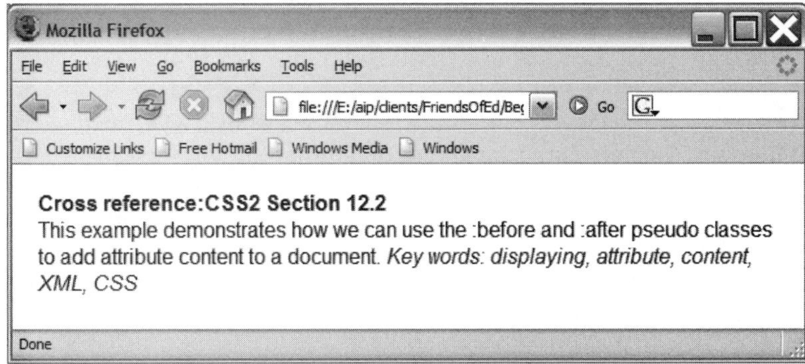

Figure 5-23. *Display attributes values using pseudo-elements*

As you can imagine, referencing attributes with pseudo-elements is very helpful for displaying content, although you're somewhat limited with this approach because:

- *You have limited formatting control over the attribute values*: While you can display the content in either a block or inline box, or change the `color`, `font-style`, and `font-weight` properties, you're not able to use the text in a structure like a table.
- *You can only present the content of two attributes in any element*: You're limited to using the `:before` and `:after` pseudo-elements.

The conclusion you should draw is that while CSS is capable of rendering XML documents, it's limited in its ability to display content from attributes.

Summary

In this chapter, you've seen many different ways to display XML content in a web browser using CSS. Because an XML document is focused on content, you can only display elements by using an associated CSS declaration for each one. This is more labor-intensive than using CSS with XHTML, where the browser already understands how to render certain structural elements, such as tables.

In this chapter, you learned how to use

- Element type selectors without `class` or `id` attributes
- The box model to display element content using three positioning schemes: normal flow, floating boxes, and absolute positioning
- CSS declarations to display tabular data
- Floating boxes to create more complex table layouts
- XLinks to create links between documents
- CSS `background` or `background-image` properties to force the display of an image in XML documents
- The `:before` and `:after` pseudo-classes to display images and text in addition to XML document content
- The `:before` and `:after` pseudo-classes to display attribute content

Despite the flexibility of CSS, it still creates limitations when used to style XML documents directly in a web browser. The most important limitation is that support for CSS2 is mixed across the major web browsers.

Other limitations include the following:

- Tabular data needs element names and structures that fit a particular model, so that you can identify data correctly.
- If you want to display elements in a different order from the XML document, you have to use one of these two options:
    - Absolute positioning, which requires that you know exactly how much data or how many elements will be displayed
    - Floating boxes, which can reorder boxes from left to right within the screen's width
- Linking via XLink currently has limited support. A workaround is to use the XHTML namespace and `<a>` tags.
- In order to display images, you must have a different element or different attribute name for each image.
- You can only display the values of two attributes per element.

Using CSS with XHTML documents allows you to separate content from styling information. It also allows you to update pages more easily, and prevents a web browser from having to download style rules more than once. While CSS is capable of presenting XML content, it doesn't provide the most flexible means of display for the layout of data and tables. Furthermore, the limited support for XLinks and images makes CSS a frustrating experience for the XML developer.

In the next two chapters, you'll see an alternative to CSS for display purposes: XSLT. XSLT provides much more flexibility in the rendering of XML content, and you can use it to structure content that you then style with CSS. XSLT also allows for dynamic manipulation of data on the client. In later chapters, you'll see examples of using XSLT on the server, so that you can deliver XHTML to browsers without them having to interpret XSLT.

CHAPTER 6

Introduction to XSLT

In this chapter and the one that follows, you'll explore Extensible Stylesheet Language Transformations (XSLT). XSLT is a World Wide Web Consortium (W3C) recommendation, and you can find out more about it at `http://www.w3.org/Style/XSL/`. The W3C has two XSLT recommendations—1.0 and 2.0. At the time of writing, XSLT 2.0 is a candidate recommendation.

You use XSLT to transform a source XML document into a different XML document, called the *results tree*. As XHTML is a vocabulary of XML, you can also use XSLT to transform XML into XHTML for display in a web browser.

In Chapter 5, you saw how to use Cascading Style Sheets (CSS) to display XML. Using CSS, the XML document can take on many style attributes to make it appear like an XHTML page. You can use some advanced CSS techniques to add additional content or to display images. However, the browser still displays an XML document.

XSLT offers an alternative approach because it generates XHTML from the XML document. You can then use CSS to apply styling. XSLT makes it much easier to add extra content compared with CSS. You can also use advanced features such as sorting and filtering.

XSLT isn't limited to producing XHTML documents. It can also convert your content into alternative formats, such as Rich Text Format (RTF) documents and comma-separated values (CSV) files for Microsoft Word and Excel. XSLT's cousin, Extensible Stylesheet Language Formatting Objects (XSL-FO), can create printed content such as that found in PDF files.

CSS and XSLT serve different purposes when working with XML. XSLT is a very powerful tool, but CSS can often be better for simple tasks. Sometimes you need to use a combination of both technologies to achieve the right outcome. This chapter will provide you with enough information so that you can decide which technology is appropriate for your needs.

In Chapters 11 to 13, you'll learn how to apply XSLT transformations server-side. In this chapter, I'll focus on client-side transformations. I'll give you an overview of XSLT and demonstrate how to style XML in the web browser. Chapter 7 will cover some more complicated applications of XSLT.

Let's start by looking at which browsers support XSLT.

Browser Support for XSLT

As you saw in Chapter 4, most recent browsers support XSLT 1.0, with the exception of Opera 8.5. At the time of writing, the forthcoming Opera 9 release is expected to support XSLT. Table 6-1 shows the support for XSLT in the most recent browser versions.

Table 6-1. *Support for XSLT in Recent Web Browsers*

Web Browser	XSLT Processor and Support
Internet Explorer (IE) 6	Microsoft XML Parser (MSXML) 3.0 (can be upgraded) supporting XSLT 1.0
Mozilla (Netscape 8 and Firefox 1.5)	TransforMiiX supporting XSLT 1.0
Opera	No support

Let's work through a series of examples so you can see how to work with XSLT. You can download the resources referred to in this chapter from the Source Code area of the Apress web site (`http://www.apress.com`). These examples work with Internet Explorer (IE) 6, Netscape 8, and Firefox 1.5. They may also work in earlier browser versions. I'll work through the following examples:

- Creating headers and footers in an XHTML page
- Creating a table of contents in an XHTML page
- Presenting an XML document
- Including images in an XML document

You'll see further examples in the next chapter. Let's start by looking at how XSLT can transform an existing XHTML document to add new information.

Using XSLT to Create Headers and Footers

Web sites commonly include repeating content such as navigation and copyright notices on all or most of the pages. Developers often use Server-Side Include (SSI) files or server-side code to generate the content. This example looks at an alternative approach and uses XSLT to add a header and footer to a simple XHTML page.

Using client-side XSLT to generate content offers the following advantages:

- You can centralize the added content to one location with a single XSLT stylesheet, making the site much easier to update.
- Users need to download the XSLT code only once for the entire site, reducing page-loading time and offering bandwidth savings.
- All transformations can occur on the client, reducing the load on the server.

This example uses the page `planets.htm`. If you open this file from your resources, you'll see that is contains the following code:

```
<html>
  <head>
  <title>A simple HTML page</title>
  <style type="text/css">
    body { font-family: Verdana, Arial, sans-serif; font-size: 12px;}
  </style>
  </head>
  <body>
  <h1>Our neighbours</h1>
  <h2>Venus</h2>
  Venus is the second planet from the sun and it has a thick layer of sulfuric
  acid clouds covering the entire planet.
  <ul>
    <li><strong>Diameter</strong> 12104 km (7505 miles)</li>
    <li><strong>Moons:</strong> 0</li>
    <li><strong>Mean temperature:</strong> 482C (900F)</li>
    <li><strong>Length of one day:</strong> 243.01 earth days</li>
    <li><strong>Length of one year:</strong> 224.7 earth days</li>
  </ul>
  <h2>Mars</h2>
    Mars is the fourth planet from the sun and is often called the red planet.
  <ul>
    <li><strong>Diameter</strong> 6796 km (4214 miles)</li>
    <li><strong>Moons:</strong> 2</li>
    <li><strong>Mean temperature:</strong> -63C (-81F)</li>
    <li><strong>Length of one day:</strong> 24.62 earth hours</li>
    <li><strong>Length of one year:</strong> 686.98 earth days</li>
  </ul>
  </body>
</html>
```

I've simplified this page to make it easier to follow. Figure 6-1 shows the page displayed within IE.

You can save this file as an XML document by adding the following XML declaration and stylesheet processing instruction:

```
<?xml version="1.0" encoding="UTF-8"?>
<?xml-stylesheet type="text/xsl" href="planets.xsl" ?>
```

The new line references the XSLT stylesheet called `planets.xsl`. You can find the changed file saved as `planets.xml` with your resources.

You saved the new page as an XML file so that you can apply an XSLT transformation. Because the document started as well-formed XHTML, the change only involved adding a declaration and changing the file extension.

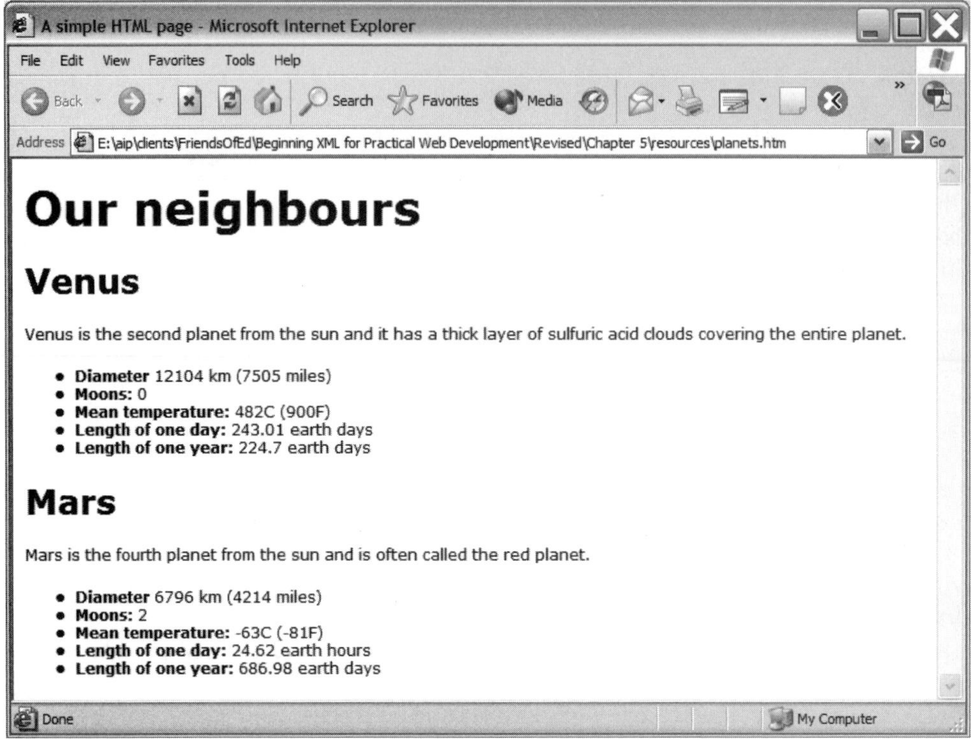

Figure 6-1. *The XHTML page planets.htm shown in IE*

Understanding XHTML, XSLT, and Namespaces

You need to be aware that an XSLT stylesheet acts on elements in the default namespace. If you include the `xmlns` attribute in the `<html>` root element, you will specify that all elements in the XML document are in the `http://www.w3.org/1999/xhtml` namespace.

In order for the stylesheet to find the XHTML elements within that namespace, you must include a namespace declaration in the stylesheet and include the namespace prefix whenever you refer to the XHTML elements. For simplicity, I haven't done this.

Creating the XSLT Stylesheet

Now that you've created the XML document, you need a stylesheet to add the header and footer information. You can achieve this with the following XSLT stylesheet, `planets.xsl`:

```
<?xml version="1.0" encoding="UTF-8"?>
<xsl:stylesheet version="1.0" xmlns:xsl="http://www.w3.org/1999/XSL/Transform">
  <xsl:output method="html" version="4.0" indent="yes"/>
  <xsl:template match="node()|@*">
    <xsl:copy>
      <xsl:apply-templates select="node()|@*"/>
    </xsl:copy>
```

```
  </xsl:template>
  <xsl:template match="html:body">
    <body>
      <p>
        <a href="http://www.nasa.gov/">Visit NASA!</a> |
        <a href="http://www.nineplanets.org/">Tour the solar system</a>
      </p>
      </table>
      <xsl:apply-templates/>
      <hr/>
      Copyright Planetary Fun 2006.
    </body>
  </xsl:template>
</xsl:stylesheet>
```

I'll work through this stylesheet in a moment. Figure 6-2 shows how the transformed page appears in IE 6. It looks the same in Firefox 1.5 and Netscape 8.

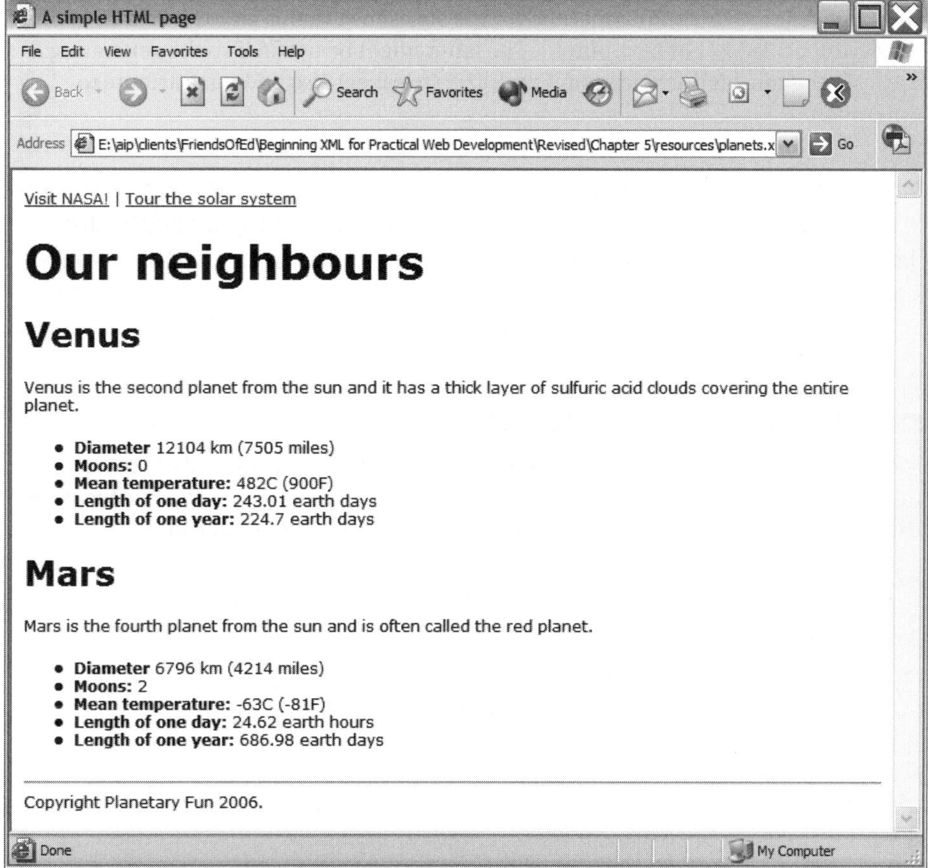

Figure 6-2. *The page planets.xml showing a header and footer*

The transformed output includes a header and footer. For simplicity, I've included only two links in the header, but you could easily add more.

Understanding the Stylesheet

Let's work through each part of the stylesheet so you can understand what's going on. The stylesheet is a well-formed XML document. It starts with an XML declaration and a stylesheet document element. It also includes an output method:

```
<?xml version="1.0" encoding="UTF-8"?>
<xsl:stylesheet version="1.0" xmlns:xsl="http://www.w3.org/1999/XSL/Transform">
  <xsl:output method="html" version="4.0" indent="yes"/>
```

You'll be familiar with the XML declaration by now. The `<stylesheet>` element specifies both the stylesheet version (1.0) and the namespaces. The first URI refers to the XSLT namespace, while the second refers to the XHTML namespace. All stylesheet declarations must start with the prefix `xsl`, while the XHTML elements need to use the `html` prefix. The web browser uses namespaces to check the elements that you refer to in the stylesheet. The browser doesn't actually load the URI indicated by the namespace.

The last line refers to the output method for the stylesheet. In this case, it's HTML 4.0. You could also have specified `xml` or `text` output. The latter might be useful if you're generating a file for use in a program such as Microsoft Excel. The stylesheet also adds an attribute to indent the content.

■ **Note** It may seem strange to specify HTML as the output method for XSLT as opposed to XML 1.0 (for XHTML). However, you need to choose this output method so that the content appears correctly in Mozilla browsers. Try changing the output method to XML 1.0 to see the effect.

Transforming the <body> Element

The purpose of the transformation is to add content at the beginning and end of the web page. The content of the page lives within the `<body>` element, so this element is the focus of the stylesheet. The `<body>` transformation appears partway down the stylesheet:

```
<xsl:template match="body">
  <body>
    <p>
      <a href="http://www.nasa.gov/">Visit NASA!</a> |
      <a href="http://www.nineplanets.org/">Tour the solar system</a>
    </p>
    <xsl:apply-templates/>
    <hr/>
    Copyright Planetary Fun 2006.
  </body>
</xsl:template>
```

The first line of this code block tells the XSLT processor to match the <body> element. The transformation applies to everything between the opening and closing <body> tags. The stylesheet achieves this with the <xsl:template> element, which specifies a template for the transformation.

The next four lines show what to insert at the start of the template, *before* the contents from the original <body> element. The stylesheet adds a paragraph with two links. The template doesn't transform the <body> tag itself, so you have to include this tag at the start of the template.

The transformation changes the starting <body> tag to

```
<body>
  <p>
    <a href="http://www.nasa.gov/">Visit NASA!</a> |
    <a href="http://www.nineplanets.org/">Tour the solar system</a>
  </p>
```

This transformation includes a header with two links.

Applying the Transformation

The following line actually applies the transformation to the <body> element:

```
<xsl:apply-templates/>
```

This line says, "Work through all of the contents of the <body> element and perform any other transformations you need to on any tags you find." In this case, you don't want to transform the rest of the <body> element. Rather, you want it to pass through unchanged. You'll see how this happens shortly.

Adding the Footer

The last lines in this code block add the footer after the unchanged <body> element:

```
    <hr/>
    Copyright Planetary Fun 2006.
  </body>
</xsl:template>
```

This creates a horizontal rule followed by the words "Copyright Planetary Fun 2006." Unfortunately, because you're outputting to HTML 4.0, the <hr/> tag transforms to <hr>. You end by closing the <xsl:template> element to tell the XSLT processor that you've finished working with the <body> element.

Transformation Without Change

When the stylesheet applies the transformation, you want the remaining document contents to remain unchanged, including the <html>, <head>, <title>, <style>, <b>, <h1>, <h2>, <ul>, and <li> elements. If you don't specify a transformation for these tags, the XSLT processor will ignore them.

WHICH TEMPLATE WILL BE APPLIED?

In XSLT 1.0, `<xslt:template>` has a priority attribute that allows you to specify which template to apply if several match a node. A higher priority indicates that the template should apply in preference to others.

If the template doesn't specify a priority, it's quite complicated to determine the order in which templates apply. Section 5.5 of the XSLT specification describes the complete process (`http://www.w3.org/TR/xslt#conflict`). In essence, the rules state that the XSLT processor should use the most specific of all matching templates. In this example, the identity template matches every node, including the `<body>` element, but because you have a specific `<body>` template, that takes precedence.

You can use the following *identity transformation* lines to pass these tags through unchanged:

```
<xsl:template match="node()|@*">
  <xsl:copy>
    <xsl:apply-templates select="node()|@*"/>
  </xsl:copy>
</xsl:template>
```

The identity transformation template leaves everything in its original state. It matches every part of the source XML document that doesn't have its own style rule and passes it through unchanged.

The identity transformation matches all nodes (`node()`) and attributes (`@*`) within the source document. When it finds a match, the rule uses `<xsl:copy>` to create an identical copy of the matching item. The `<xsl:apply-templates>` tag processes the contents of the matched item without changing them. If this were the only template within an XSLT stylesheet, it would produce a document functionally the same as the source document.

You can't use this template when the output document is substantially different from the input document. Normally, you'd use it as you've seen in this example—to pass through the unchanged content along with another simple template.

Each element or attribute in the source XML document can only be matched by one template, so you need to copy the `<body>` element to the output document rather than relying on the identity template to do it for you. Because the `<body>` template is more specific than the identity transformation template, that declaration takes precedence.

Let's move on to another example, where I'll use XSLT to repeat content from the source document using a different layout.

Creating a Table of Contents

This example creates a table of contents showing the nearest planets to us in the solar system. It shows how to generate new content automatically from existing content. Without this approach, you would have to generate the list with server-side logic or by using JavaScript to manipulate the Document Object Model (DOM) and write out the contents.

Using XSLT to generate the table of contents is useful because

- You can generate the table of contents from existing XHTML, and you don't need to use server-side logic to extract the information from a database or other data source.
- The table of contents always reflects the current page contents, and it updates when the current page changes; you'll see an example a little later in this section.
- You reduce server load because no server-side processing is required to generate the table of contents.

You can see this example in the file `planets2.xml`. If you open the file, you'll notice that the first line refers to a stylesheet called `planets2.xsl`:

```
<?xml-stylesheet type="text/xsl" href="planets2.xsl" ?>
```

The `planets2.xsl` stylesheet follows:

```
<?xml version="1.0" encoding="UTF-8"?>
<xsl:stylesheet version="1.0" xmlns:xsl="http://www.w3.org/1999/XSL/Transform">
  <xsl:output method="html" version="4.0" indent="yes"/>
  <xsl:template match="node()|@*">
    <xsl:copy>
      <xsl:apply-templates select="node()|@*"/>
    </xsl:copy>
  </xsl:template>
  <xsl:template match=" body">
    <body>
      <p>
        <a href="http://www.nasa.gov/">Visit NASA!</a> |
        <a href="http://www.nineplanets.org/">Tour the solar system</a>
      </p>
      <h2>Quick reference</h2>
      <ul>
        <xsl:for-each select=" h2">
          <li>
            <a>
              <xsl:attribute name="href">
                #<xsl:value-of select="text()"/></xsl:attribute>
              <xsl:value-of select="text()"/>
            </a>
          </li>
        </xsl:for-each>
      </ul>
      <xsl:apply-templates/>
      <hr/>
      Copyright Planetary Fun 2006.
    </body>
  </xsl:template>
  <xsl:template match="h2">
```

```
      <a>
        <xsl:attribute name="name"><xsl:value-of select="text()"/></xsl:attribute>
        <h2>
          <xsl:apply-templates/>
        </h2>
      </a>
    </xsl:template>
  </xsl:stylesheet>
```

Figure 6-3 shows how `planets2.xml` appears in IE.

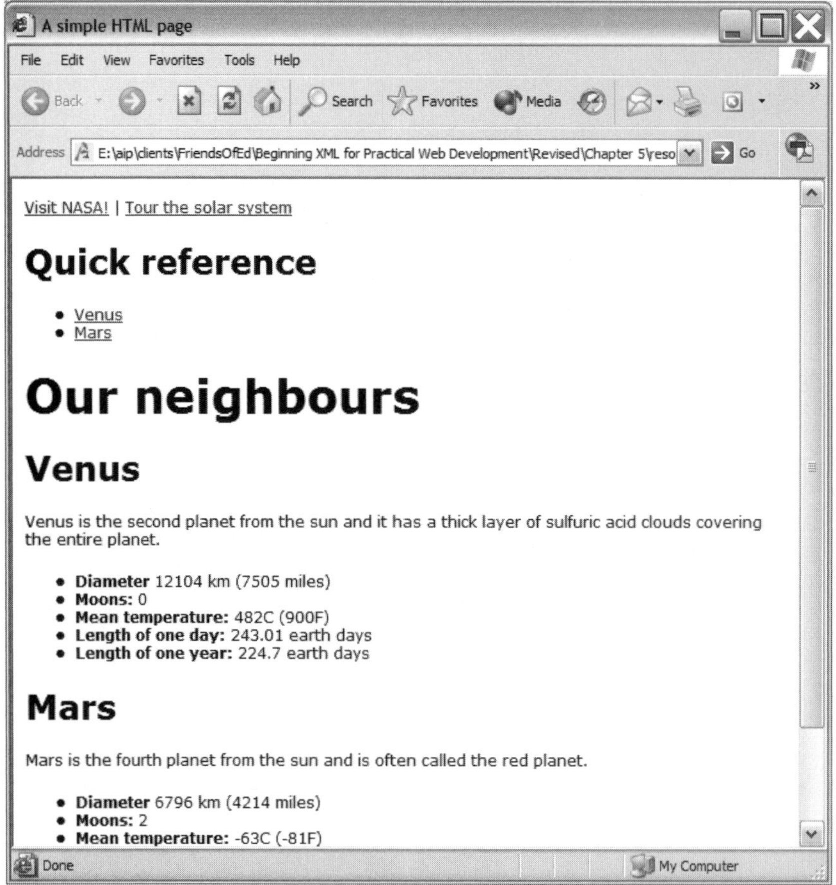

Figure 6-3. *The page planets2.xml showing a simple table of contents*

You can see a “Quick reference” section at the top of the page with links to each of the sections below.

Selecting Each Planet with <xsl:for-each>

The beginning lines of planets2.xsl are the same as in the previous example. The first change to the stylesheet is in the header template. The new lines appear in bold:

```
<xsl:template match="body">
  <body>
    <p>
      <a href="http://www.nasa.gov/">Visit NASA!</a> |
      <a href="http://www.nineplanets.org/">Tour the solar system</a>
    </p>
    <h2>Quick reference</h2>
    <ul>
      <xsl:for-each select="html:h2">
        <li>
          <a>
            <xsl:attribute name="href">
              #<xsl:value-of select="text()"/></xsl:attribute>
            <xsl:value-of select="text()"/>
          </a>
        </li>
      </xsl:for-each>
    </ul>
```

The added lines create a heading for the table of contents and start an unordered list. The stylesheet loops through each of the <h2> elements in the <body> element. The content from each <h2> element—the name of the planet—provides the name for the anchor. It also supplies the text for each list item:

```
<xsl:for-each select="h2">
  <li>
    <a>
      <xsl:attribute name="href">
        #<xsl:value-of select="text()"/></xsl:attribute>
      <xsl:value-of select="text()"/>
    </a>
  </li>
</xsl:for-each>
```

To explain it in a bit more detail, each time the template finds an <h2> element in the body of the page, it outputs an <li> tag. After that, it creates an <a> tag. Then the template uses xsl:attribute to add an attribute to the <a> tag called href, and it sets the value of the attribute to be a hash symbol (#) followed by whatever content is in the <h2> tag (text()). Finally, the template closes the href attribute. So, if the <h2> tag contains the text "Venus," the template outputs the following <a> tag:

```
<a href="Venus">
```

The text content of the <h2> tag also provides the text between the <a> and </a> tags, and the template finishes with a closing </a> tag. Finally, it closes the <li> element and ends the loop with </xsl:for-each>. Again, looking at the Venus heading, the template creates the following transformed XHTML:

```
<a href="Venus">Venus</a>
```

When the template finishes the loop, it adds a closing </ul> tag.

The complete block of links generated by the XSLT stylesheet follows:

```
<h2>Quick reference</h2>
<ul>
  <li><a href="#Venus">Venus</a></li>
  <li><a href="#Mars">Mars</a></li>
</ul>
```

Adding a New Planet

You can see the flexibility of this transformation if you add another planet to the list. The planets3.xml file contains information on three planets. The new item follows:

```
<h2>Mercury</h2>
Mercury is the closest planet to the sun.
<ul>
  <li><strong>Diameter</strong> 4879 km (3025 miles)</li>
  <li><strong>Moons:</strong> 0</li>
  <li><strong>Mean temperature:</strong> 179C (354F)</li>
  <li><strong>Length of one day:</strong> 58.65 earth days</li>
  <li><strong>Length of one year:</strong> 87.87 earth days</li>
</ul>
```

Figure 6-4 shows the effect on the table of contents within planets3.xml.

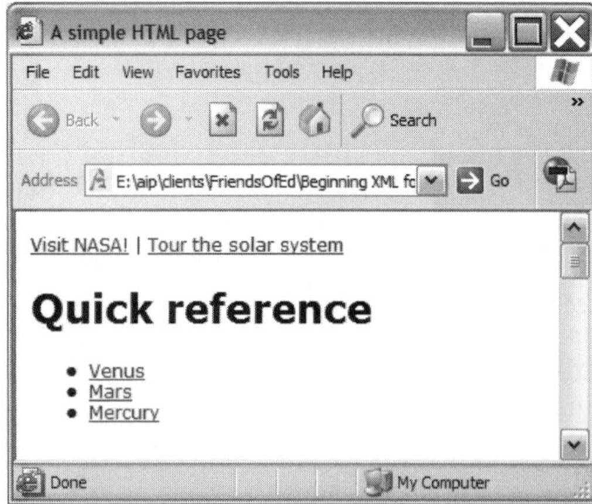

Figure 6-4. *The page planets3.xml showing an additional link in the table of contents*

The preceding new block of code creates the table of contents links. The stylesheet still has to add anchors to the relevant headings in the XHTML document. It contains another template to transform the <h2> elements:

```
<xsl:template match=" h2">
  <a>
    <xsl:attribute name="name"><xsl:value-of select="text()"/></xsl:attribute>
    <h2>
      <xsl:apply-templates/>
    </h2>
  </a>
</xsl:template>
```

This transformation works in much the same way as the last. It takes the text within an <h2> element and adds it to the name attribute of an <a> element, producing something similar to

```
<a name="Venus">Venus</a>
```

In this example, the stylesheet generates new content from an existing XML (XHTML) document. When you update the contents of the XML document, the additional content also updates.

The first two examples work with a specific XML vocabulary, XHTML. Let's move on to an example that works with a more generic XML document.

Presenting XML with XSLT

So far, you've used XSLT with an XHTML document saved as XML. The document already contained structural elements such as <ul>, <li>, and <strong> tags. You didn't need to use the XSLT stylesheet to lay out the XML document content.

A more flexible approach would be to remove all structural elements from the source document. You could use a scripting language such as Visual C# .NET (C#), Visual Basic .NET (VB .NET), PHP, or JavaServer Pages (JSP) to create the XHTML page from the XML document. However, a better approach is to transform the XML document with an XSLT stylesheet and generate an XHTML page. Doing this provides the following benefits:

- The source XML document only contains data and doesn't concern itself with layout elements. You can then reuse and repurpose this source document easily in XHTML and other formats.
- You can alter the layout and design of the content without changing the underlying XML document.
- You can easily use the same XML document for different purposes, such as within mobile devices and other enterprise-level systems.
- The bandwidth savings are potentially greater than in the previous examples, as all design and layout rules for the web site are downloaded to the client once.

Moving from XHTML to XML

Let's change the planets.xml document to remove all structural elements. You can find this version of the data in the resource file planets4.xml:

```
<?xml version="1.0" encoding="UTF-8"?>
<?xml-stylesheet type="text/xsl" href="planets4.xsl" ?>
<neighbours>
  <planet name="Venus">
    <description>
      Venus is the second planet from the sun and it has a thick layer of sulfuric
      acid clouds covering the entire planet.
    </description>
    <diameter> 12104 km (7505 miles)</diameter>
    <moons> 0</moons>
    <meanTemp> 482C (900F)</meanTemp>
    <oneDay> 243.01 earth days</oneDay>
    <oneYear> 224.7 earth days</oneYear>
  </planet>
  <planet name="Mars">
    <description>
      Mars is the fourth planet from the sun and is often called the red planet.
    </description>
    <diameter> 6796 km (4214 miles)</diameter>
    <moons> 2</moons>
    <meanTemp> -63C (-81F)</meanTemp>
    <oneDay> 24.62 earth hours</oneDay>
    <oneYear> 686.98 earth days</oneYear>
  </planet>
</neighbours>
```

This document is much simpler than the earlier XHTML example. It contains data that is marked up by descriptive tag names. The document is self-describing because you can understand the structure and content from the element names.

Styling the XML with XSLT

You'll notice that the revised XML document refers to a stylesheet called planets4.xsl. This stylesheet transforms the XML file into XHTML by adding the appropriate structural elements:

```
<?xml version="1.0" encoding="UTF-8"?>
<xsl:stylesheet version="1.0" xmlns:xsl="http://www.w3.org/1999/XSL/Transform">
  <xsl:output method="html" version="4.0" indent="yes"/>
  <xsl:template match="/">
    <xsl:apply-templates/>
  </xsl:template>
  <xsl:template match="text()"/>
  <xsl:template match="neighbours">
    <html>
```

```
      <head>
        <title>A simple HTML page</title>
        <style type="text/css">
          body { font-family: Verdana, Arial, sans-serif; font-size: 12px;}
      </style>
      </head>
      <body>
        <div style="border: solid thin black; width: 105px; padding: 2px;">
        <p>
        <a href="http://www.nasa.gov/">Visit NASA!</a> |
        <a href="http://www.nineplanets.org/">Tour the solar system</a>
      </p>
        <h1>Our neighbours</h1>
        <xsl:apply-templates/>
        <hr/>
        Copyright Planetary Fun 2006.
    </body>
    </html>
  </xsl:template>
  <xsl:template match="planet">
    <h2><xsl:value-of select="@name"/></h2>
    <xsl:value-of select="description/text()"/>
    <ul><xsl:apply-templates/></ul>
  </xsl:template>
  <xsl:template match="diameter">
    <li><strong>Diameter: </strong><xsl:value-of select="text()"/></li>
  </xsl:template>
  <xsl:template match="moons">
    <li><strong>Moons: </strong><xsl:value-of select="text()"/></li>
  </xsl:template>
  <xsl:template match="meanTemp">
    <li><strong>Mean temperature: </strong><xsl:value-of select="text()"/></li>
  </xsl:template>
  <xsl:template match="oneDay">
    <li><strong>Length of one day: </strong><xsl:value-of select="text()"/></li>
  </xsl:template>
  <xsl:template match="oneYear">
    <li><strong>Length of one year: </strong><xsl:value-of select="text()"/></li>
  </xsl:template>
</xsl:stylesheet>
```

If you view the transformed document in a web browser, it looks much the same as in the previous example. The stylesheet also contains similar elements to those included in the previous examples, with a couple of differences.

Because the XML file isn't really XHTML, there is no XHTML namespace reference in the `<xsl:stylesheet>` element. This means that you don't need to preface any element names with a namespace prefix. Because the XML document isn't using the XHTML vocabulary, you're free to use any appropriate element names. Now, instead of matching a <body> element, the stylesheet looks for the <neighbours> element:

```
<xsl:template match="neighbours">
```

You'll notice that the transformation has to include all of the XHTML elements required to make up the web page. The XSLT stylesheet specifically mentions the <html>, <head>, and <body> elements. Note that I haven't included other XHTML declarations for simplicity.

The stylesheet matches the <planet> element and uses the name attribute to generate the subheadings:

```
<xsl:template match="planet">
  <h2><xsl:value-of select="@name"/></h2>
  <xsl:value-of select="description/text()"/>
  <ul><xsl:apply-templates/></ul>
</xsl:template>
```

The XPath location @name finds the name attribute within the context of the <planet> element. When the transformation is applied, it produces

```
<h2>Venus</h2>
```

The description/text() XPath expression selects the text within the <description> element. Because the <xsl:value-of> element is within the context of the <planet> element, the template only accesses <description> elements that are children of the <planet> element. If there were any, the XSLT processor would ignore other <description> elements within the document.

The <xsl:apply-templates /> statement tells the XSLT processor to apply any templates to the contents of the <planet> element. This affects the <diameter>, <moons>, <meanTemp>, <oneDay>, and <oneYear> elements. However, because the stylesheet also defines individual templates for these tags, these more specific transformations apply. For example, the <diameter> transformation follows:

```
<xsl:template match="diameter">
  <li><strong>Diameter: </strong><xsl:value-of select="text()"/></li>
</xsl:template>
```

Because the stylesheet specifies a template for each child element, the child elements all appear within the transformed document.

Removing Content with XSLT

It's very easy to exclude source content from the transformed output. If you don't specify a template for an element, the XSLT processor will ignore it, providing you don't include the identity transformation in the stylesheet. This example doesn't include the identity transformation, so the transformed content relies entirely on the templates listed in the stylesheet.

You may have noticed that the stylesheet includes the following template:

```
<xsl:template match="text()"/>
```

XSLT has a built-in rule for text, which specifies that any text in the source XML document should pass through unchanged unless otherwise specified. The equivalent of the rule is

```
<xsl:template match="text()">
  <xsl:value-of select="."/>
</xsl:template>
```

Writing your own rule overrides this built-in rule. This stops the text from passing through automatically and gives you control over when and how the text appears in the document. If you want to see the effect of the rule, remove it from the stylesheet and reload the XML document.

Understanding the Role of XPath in XSLT

I've mentioned XPath a couple of times in the preceding sections. For example, the following line includes an XPath expression, shown in bold:

```
<xsl:value-of select="description/text()"/>
```

This expression refers to the text child within the `<description>` element. The expression is evaluated against the current node. In this case, this XPath statement appears within the following block:

```
<xsl:template match="planet">
</xsl:template>
```

The XPath expression is evaluated against the `<planet>` context. In other words, the template finds the text child within the `<description>` element that is within the `<planet>` element.

XSLT uses XPath expressions inside the `match` and `select` attributes of many elements. These expressions allow the stylesheet to select nodes from the source document. XPath expressions consist of a path, a nodetest, and a predicate:

```
/axis::nodetest[predicate]
```

The path navigates through the nodes within the source XML document. The nodetest identifies which node(s) to select, and the optional predicate applies a filter to the selection. You can also write a shorthand form of XPath statements. For example, the following expression includes a shorthand statement:

```
<xsl:value-of select="@name"/>
```

To select the `name` attribute with XPath, the expression can use the `@` character followed by the name of the attribute, which in this case is `name`.

Adding a predicate offers a lot of power to XPath statements, as you can apply filters to selected nodes. For example, you can locate information on the planet Venus using

```
<xsl:template match="planet[@name='Venus']" />
```

You can also combine conditions using `and` and `or`:

```
<xsl:template match="planet[@name='Venus' or @name= 'Mars']">
```

This XPath expression finds all nodes where the `name` attribute of the `<planet>` element is `Venus` or `Mars`.

You can also match specific elements using a position within the collection of nodes:

```
<xsl:template match="planet[1]" >
```

This example matches the first `<planet>` element within the document.

XPath expressions can specify the parents for elements by adding them to the path with a forward-slash character (/):

```
<xsl:template match="neighbours/planet">
```

In this case, the `<planet>` elements are children of a `<neighbours>` element. The expression won't select other `<planet>` elements with different parents. You could specify an indirect relationship using

```
<xsl:template match="neighbours//planet">
```

The XPath recommendation is much more complicated than you've seen here, and you can find the complete document at `http://www.w3.org/TR/xpath`. It contains many more options, including a range of functions such as `substring`, `count`, and `contains` that I'll discuss more in Chapter 7. You'll also see more examples of XPath in the remaining examples within this chapter.

In the previous chapter, you added images to an XML document using CSS. This was a difficult process, so you'll be glad to know that this is much easier to achieve using XSLT.

Including Images

In this example, you'll use XSLT to include external images in the transformed page. The example uses the files `planets5.xml` and `planets5.xsl` from your resources. This stylesheet is almost the same as the last one, except for some changes to the `<planet>` template. The new lines appear in bold:

```
<xsl:template match="planet">
  <img width="100" height="100">
  <xsl:attribute name="src">
      <xsl:value-of select="@name"/>.jpg
    </xsl:attribute>
  </img>
  <h2><xsl:value-of select="@name"/></h2>
  <xsl:value-of select="description/text()"/>
  <ul><xsl:apply-templates/></ul>
</xsl:template>
```

The revised template creates an `<img>` element with a predefined height and width. It also adds a `src` attribute that uses the `name` attribute of the `<planet>` element with a `.jpg` suffix. In the case of Venus, the template creates the following XHTML:

```
<img width="100" height="100" src="Venus.jpg"></img>
```

Figure 6-5 shows `planets5.xml` displayed within a web browser, complete with images.

Figure 6-5. *The page planets5.xml showing images*

Importing Templates

In the previous example, you created an entire stylesheet to change a single template. A better approach would have been to import the common declarations to the new stylesheet and write a new template to add the images.

I've taken this approach in the resource files `planets6.xml` and `planets6.xsl`. The new stylesheet imports `planets4.xsl` and adds a new `<planet>` template:

```
<?xml version="1.0" encoding="UTF-8"?>
<xsl:stylesheet version="1.0" xmlns:xsl="http://www.w3.org/1999/XSL/Transform">
  <xsl:import href="planets4.xsl" />
  <xsl:output method="html" version="4.0" indent="yes"/>
  <xsl:template match="planet">
    <img width="100" height="100">
      <xsl:attribute name="src">
        <xsl:value-of select="@name"/>.jpg
      </xsl:attribute>
    </img>
```

```
    <xsl:apply-imports />
  </xsl:template>
</xsl:stylesheet>
```

The `<xsl:import href="planets4.xsl" />` line imports all of the templates defined in `planets4.xsl`. Any declarations within the current stylesheet, `planets6.xml`, take priority over those in `planets4.xml`. Displaying the XML document within a browser results in a transformed document that looks the same as the previous example.

You can also apply the lower-priority `planet` template from the imported stylesheet. That's the purpose of the line `<xsl:apply-imports />` within the `planet` template. By applying this, you style the heading and text from the imported template and use the current template to add the image. It's a little like appending the imported template to the one in the current stylesheet. The XSLT processor applies the other templates from `planets4.xsl`.

Including Templates

I also could have used the `<xsl:include>` element to include `planets4.xsl`:

```
<xsl:include href="planets4.xsl" />
```

This alternative is equivalent to copying and pasting the included stylesheet into the main stylesheet.

The `include` directive is less powerful than importing a stylesheet, because it doesn't automatically give included templates a lower priority than the ones defined in the current stylesheet. You can also get errors if you specify the same match pattern in the current and included stylesheet. This happens because the included stylesheet is treated as if it were part of the current stylesheet, and two templates with the same pattern cause an error. As a general rule, you should only use `include` if you don't want to add more template declarations.

You've seen several examples showing how to carry out common tasks using XSLT. Without XSLT, you would need to use server-side code to achieve the same outcomes. For the advantages outlined earlier, you may want to consider working with XSLT as an alternative. If you choose this approach, you'll save a lot of time if you work with tools designed specifically for XSLT.

Tools for XSLT Development

As with XHTML, you need to test your XSLT transformations in the target web browsers. If you test your transformations in IE 6, you can download tools that allow you to view the XSLT output. The download is called "Internet Explorer Tools for Validating XML and Viewing XSLT Output," and you can find it by visiting the Microsoft Download Center at `http://www.microsoft.com/downloads/search.aspx`. I haven't included the direct link, as it's generated dynamically.

By default, the tools install in a folder called `IEXMLTLS`. You have to right-click the `.inf` files in the folder and choose `Install` before they are available in IE. After installation, right-click a transformed XML page. The context menu will show two additional options: `Validate XML` and `View XSL Output`. Choose the second option to see the transformed content, as shown in Figure 6-6.

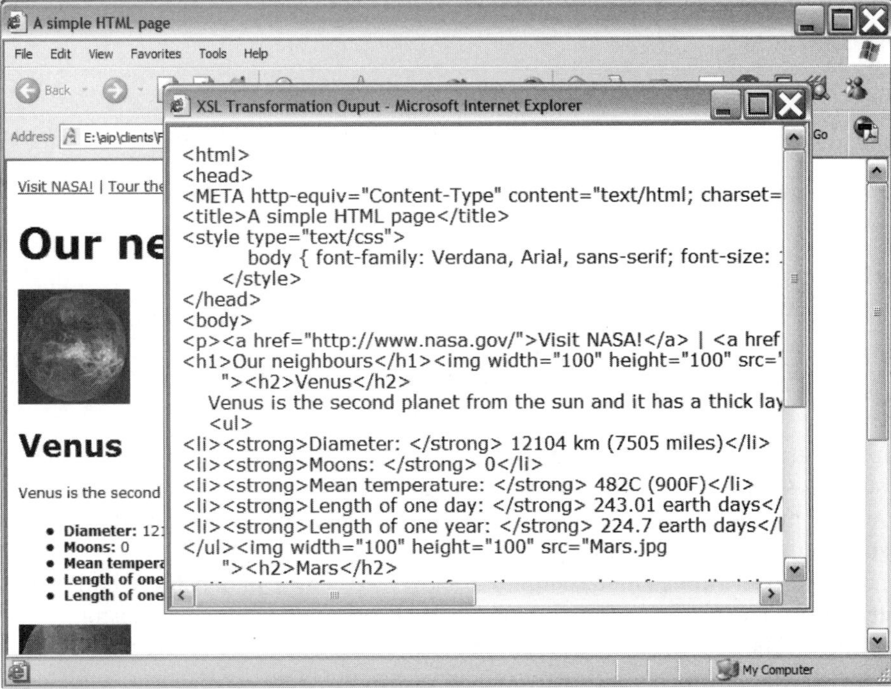

Figure 6-6. *The transformed content within IE*

If you want to view your transformed content in Mozilla, you can use the DOM Inspector. Choose `Tools` ➤ DOM Inspector, and the Inspector will open. You can drill down into the transformed structure and display the contents of any node, as shown in Figure 6-7.

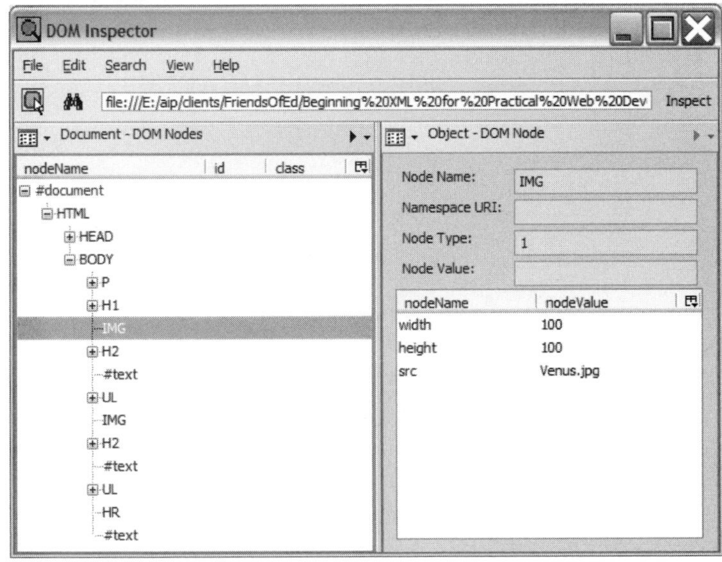

Figure 6-7. *The DOM Inspector in Firefox showing transformed content*

In addition to the browser tools, a number of commercial tools can make constructing XSLT easier. These include

- Altova's XMLSpy: `http://www.altova.com/products_ide.html`
- Stylus Studio's XSLT tools: `http://www.stylusstudio.com/xslt.html`
- Late Night Software's XSLT Tools for Macintosh: `http://www.latenightsw.com/freeware/XSLTTools/index.html`

A search in your favorite search engine will show many other tools that you can use to speed up your development time.

Summary

In this chapter, you saw how to use XSLT to transform XML documents into XHTML for display in a web browser. The transformations were applied client-side, so you didn't need to utilize server-side processing. At the time of writing, you can view these transformations in all current browser versions, excluding Opera 8.5.

The chapter worked through four examples to show you the type of transformations that are possible with XSLT. In the first example, you added a header and footer to an existing XHTML document. The next example generated a table of contents from existing XHTML elements. You saw that modifying the source document caused the table of contents to update automatically.

In the third example, you removed the XHTML vocabulary and created a more generic XML document. You applied XSLT to generate the complete XHTML for the page, including all structural elements. The last example added images to an XML document. You also saw how to import other stylesheets.

In the next chapter, I'll work through some more advanced XSLT examples. I'll also give you some tips and troubleshooting suggestions for issues that arise when transforming XML documents with XSLT.

CHAPTER 7

Advanced Client-Side XSLT Techniques

In the previous chapter, you saw some simple examples showing how to work with Extensible Stylesheet Language Transformations (XSLT) on the client side. I showed you how to apply XSLT transformations to both XHTML and XML documents, and you were able to add content and provide structure to the source document.

This chapter works through additional examples that introduce advanced XSLT techniques such as sorting and filtering. You'll work through the following examples:

- Sorting data within an XML document
- Sorting dynamically with JavaScript
- Adding extension functions to Internet Explorer (IE)
- Working with named templates
- Generating JavaScript

Most of these examples work with IE 6, Netscape 8, and Firefox 1.5 and may also work in earlier versions of these browsers. Some examples are specific to IE 6, and none of the examples work in Opera 8.5. Each example includes inline Cascading Style Sheets (CSS) declarations rather than references to external CSS files. While this is not the recommended approach for working with CSS, it makes the examples a little simpler to follow.

I'll finish the chapter with some tips for working with XSLT. By the end of the chapter, you should have a thorough understanding of XSLT and how you can apply client-side transformations in a web browser. As with the previous chapter, you can download the resources from the Source Code area of the Apress web site (`http://www.apress.com`).

Let's start by learning how to sort an XML document using XSLT.

Sorting Data Within an XML Document

In the first example for this chapter, you'll use XSLT to sort XML content within a web browser. If you didn't know how to use XSLT, you could achieve something similar using server-side code or by writing JavaScript. You may be surprised to find out how easy it is to apply sorting with XSLT.

Using XSLT provides the following benefits:

- *The* `<xsl:sort>` *element allows for different types of sorting*: You can sort on multiple levels and on a range of data types, and you can apply both ascending and descending sorts.
- *XSLT sorting is very flexible*: Any new data added to the XML document will be included automatically when using `<xsl:sort>`.
- *The XSLT stylesheet only needs to include a single line to sort content*: You'd need more code to achieve the same outcome using JavaScript arrays.

In this example, I'll include the sorting criteria in the XSLT file. The next example shows you how to apply dynamic sorting criteria using JavaScript. This example uses the resource file planets7.xml:

```
<?xml version="1.0" encoding="UTF-8"?>
<?xml-stylesheet type="text/xsl" href="planets7.xsl" ?>
<neighbours>
  <planet name="Venus">
    <description>
    Venus is the second planet from the sun and it has a thick layer of sulfuric
    acid clouds covering the entire planet.
    </description>
    <positionFromSun>2</positionFromSun>
    <diameter> 12104 km (7505 miles)</diameter>
    <moons> 0</moons>
    <meanTemp> 482C (900F)</meanTemp>
    <oneDay> 243.01 earth days</oneDay>
    <oneYear> 224.7 earth days</oneYear>
  </planet>
  <planet name="Mars">
    <description>
    Mars is the fourth planet from the sun and is often called the red planet.
    </description>
    <positionFromSun>4</positionFromSun>
    <diameter> 6796 km (4214 miles)</diameter>
    <moons> 2</moons>
    <meanTemp> -63C (-81F)</meanTemp>
    <oneDay> 24.62 earth hours</oneDay>
    <oneYear> 686.98 earth days</oneYear>
  </planet>
  <planet name="Mercury">
    <description>
    Mercury is the closest planet to the sun.
    </description>
    <positionFromSun>1</positionFromSun>
```

```
    <diameter> 4879 km (3025 miles)</diameter>
    <moons> 0</moons>
    <meanTemp> 179C (354F)</meanTemp>
    <oneDay> 58.65 earth days</oneDay>
    <oneYear> 87.87 earth days</oneYear>
  </planet>
</neighbours>
```

You'll notice that the first line of the XML document refers to a stylesheet called planets7.xsl. I've included three planets in this document and added a new element called <positionFromSun>.

In the previous chapter, you saw that it is possible to import and include stylesheets to avoid duplicating the same XSLT content in different files. I'll use the same approach in this chapter. The XHTML transformations appear within the file planetsToXHTML.xsl. You'll import this into the new stylesheet, planets7.xsl, which follows:

```
<?xml version="1.0" encoding="UTF-8"?>
<xsl:stylesheet version="1.0" xmlns:xsl="http://www.w3.org/1999/XSL/Transform">
  <xsl:import href="planetsToXHTML.xsl"/>
  <xsl:output method="html" version="4.0" indent="yes"/>
  <xsl:template match="neighbours">
    <html>
      <head>
        <title>Sorted planets</title>
        <style type="text/css">
          body { font-family: Verdana, Arial, sans-serif; font-size:12px;}
      </style>
      </head>
      <body>
        <h1>My sorted list of planets</h1>
        <xsl:apply-templates>
          <xsl:sort select=" @name" order="descending"/>
        </xsl:apply-templates>
      </body>
    </html>
  </xsl:template>
</xsl:stylesheet>
```

The stylesheet starts by importing the planetsToXHTML.xsl stylesheet. This stylesheet determines the display of the planets in the same way as the examples did in the previous chapter. The imported templates apply to elements that don't include a higher-priority match in the current stylesheet. As the stylesheet only matches the document element <neighbours>, it won't override the other declarations from the imported stylesheet. However, the <neighbours> template from the imported stylesheet is ignored, so you have to include the <head>, <body>, and <child> elements within this template.

Figure 7-1 shows planets7.xml displayed in IE.

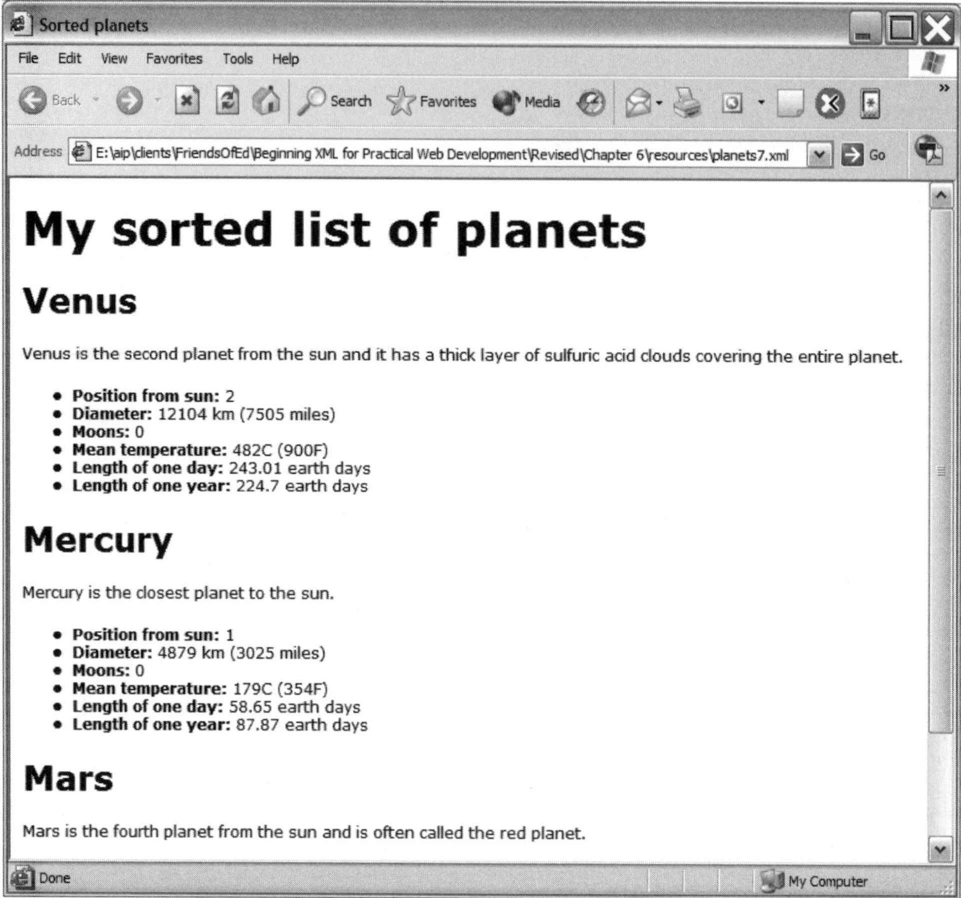

Figure 7-1. *The planets7.xml page shown in IE*

The transformation shows the planets sorted into descending alphabetical order. The stylesheet achieves this with the following line:

```
<xsl:sort select="@name" order="descending"/>
```

The `<xsl:sort>` element is applied within the `<neighbours>` element. The sorting applies to the element's children—in this case, `<planet>` elements. It finds the `name` attribute and displays each child element in descending order. You can also specify `ascending` order, which is the default if you omit the `order` attribute.

You could also sort the planets in order of their position from the sun. You can see this in the files `planets8.xml` and `planets8.xsl`. The new stylesheet includes the following sort line:

```
<xsl:sort select="positionFromSun/text()" order="ascending"/>
```

Opening the new XML file in a browser shows something similar to Figure 7-2.

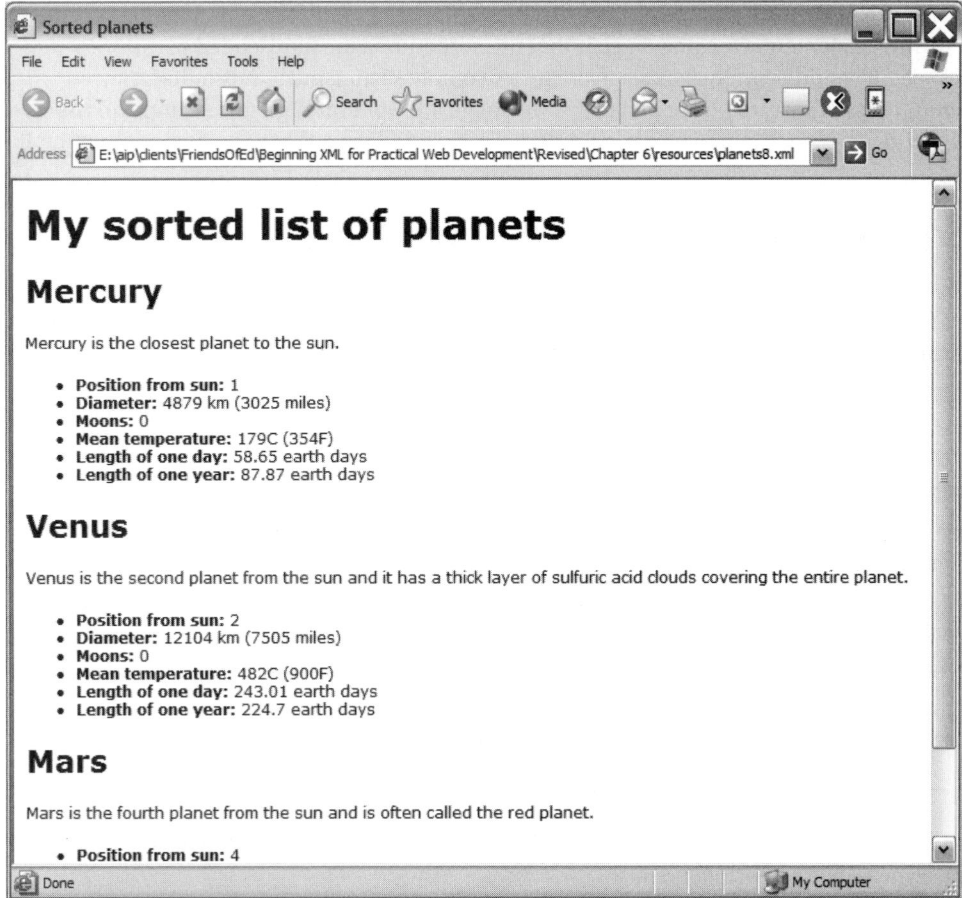

Figure 7-2. *The planets8.xml page showing a different sort order in IE*

This time, the planets display in order of their position from the sun. The sort is based on the `text()` contents within the `<positionFromSun>` child element of the `<planet>` elements. As this approach uses a text sort, you'd experience problems if you were trying to display more than 10 planets. In that case, the stylesheet could specify a numeric data type.

Stylesheets can also sort by part of the text within an element. For example, to sort in order of mean temperature from lowest to highest, a stylesheet would use the following code:

```
<xsl:sort select="substring-before(meanTemp/text(), 'C')" data-type="number"/>
```

This line uses the XPath function `substring-before` to extract all text from the `<meanTemp>` element before the `C` character. The line also specifies that the data type of the sort is `number`. Applying this sort puts the planets in order from coldest to warmest, and you can see the files `planets9.xml` and `planets9.xsl` for this example.

This example shows how easy it is to apply sorting to a complete element or part of the text within an element. One drawback is that the sort criteria are hard-coded in the XSLT stylesheet. It would be more flexible to create a dynamic sorting mechanism that allowed different types of sorts to be applied to the web page. I'll work through this example in the next section.

Sorting Dynamically with JavaScript

In this section, I'll use JavaScript to create a more dynamic sorting mechanism for the XML data. You could achieve the same outcome using server-side code to apply dynamic sorting. However, this increases the server load because you would have to reload the page with each new sort.

■ **Note** JavaScript, developed originally by Netscape, is a client-side scripting language for use with web pages. It is often used to add interactivity to a page. Because JavaScript is a client-side language, it adheres to client-side security restrictions. For example, you can't use JavaScript to create external files on the server. One use for JavaScript is to interact with XML and XHTML documents, and you'll see examples of this in the next chapter.

Dynamic sorting on the client with JavaScript and XSLT is good because:

- JavaScript can alter the sort settings and reapply the new sort transformation.
- Using JavaScript to modify the sort criteria is easier than storing the data in client-side arrays and reordering them.
- Using a client-side solution removes the overhead and processing time that would be required if using a server-side solution.

The web page needs to use slightly different JavaScript to achieve dynamic sorting for IE 6 compared with Mozilla. IE uses ActiveX controls to load and transform stylesheets, whereas Mozilla uses the TransforMiiX XSLT processor. The code in this exercise is for IE 6 only. In Chapter 8, I'll show you a JavaScript library that supports both IE and Mozilla.

This example uses the files `planets10.xml` and `planets10.xsl`. The new stylesheet follows:

```
<?xml version="1.0" encoding="UTF-8"?>
<xsl:stylesheet version="1.0" xmlns:xsl="http://www.w3.org/1999/XSL/Transform">
  <xsl:template match="neighbours">
    <table border="1">
      <tr>
        <th>Name</th>
        <th>Position from sun</th>
        <th>Diameter</th>
        <th>Moons</th>
        <th>Mean temp</th>
```

```
      </tr>
      <xsl:apply-templates>
        <xsl:sort select="@name" order="ascending"/>
      </xsl:apply-templates>
    </table>
  </xsl:template>
  <xsl:template match="planet">
    <tr><td><xsl:value-of select="@name"/></td><xsl:apply-templates/></tr>
  </xsl:template>
  <xsl:template match="positionFromSun">
    <td><xsl:value-of select="text()"/></td>
  </xsl:template>
  <xsl:template match="diameter">
    <td><xsl:value-of select="text()"/></td>
  </xsl:template>
  <xsl:template match="moons">
    <td><xsl:value-of select="text()"/></td>
  </xsl:template>
  <xsl:template match="meanTemp">
    <td><xsl:value-of select="text()"/></td>
  </xsl:template>
  <xsl:template match="text()"/>
</xsl:stylesheet>
```

The stylesheet creates a page containing a table. The stylesheet matches the <neighbours> element in the XML document to create the <table> tags and headings. At the same time, it applies ascending alphabetic sorting into planet-name order:

```
<xsl:template match="neighbours">
  <table border="1">
    <tr>
      <th>Name</th>
      <th>Position from sun</th>
      <th>Diameter</th>
      <th>Moons</th>
      <th>Mean temp</th>
    </tr>
    <xsl:apply-templates>
      <xsl:sort select="@name" order="ascending"/>
    </xsl:apply-templates>
  </table>
</xsl:template>
```

The details of each planet are displayed in a template that matches the <planet> element:

```
<xsl:template match="planet">
  <tr><td><xsl:value-of select="@name"/></td><xsl:apply-templates/></tr>
</xsl:template>
```

Templates match individual child elements to display their details in the table:

```
  <xsl:template match="positionFromSun">
    <td><xsl:value-of select="text()"/></td>
  </xsl:template>
  <xsl:template match="diameter">
    <td><xsl:value-of select="text()"/></td>
  </xsl:template>
  <xsl:template match="moons">
    <td><xsl:value-of select="text()"/></td>
  </xsl:template>
  <xsl:template match="meanTemp">
    <td><xsl:value-of select="text()"/></td>
  </xsl:template>
  <xsl:template match="text()"/>
</xsl:stylesheet>
```

Figure 7-3 shows how the table appears in IE.

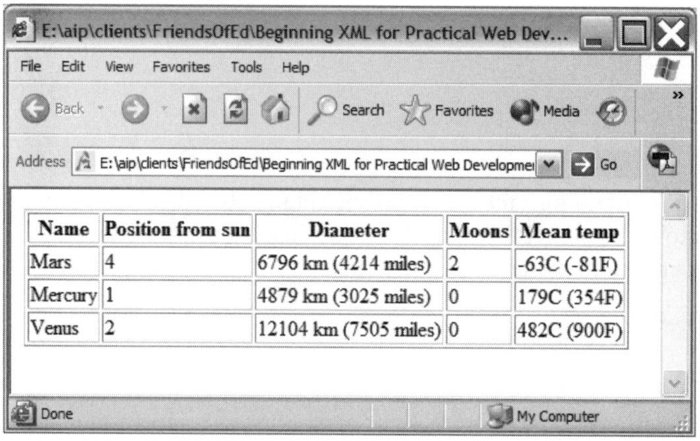
E:\aip\clients\FriendsOfEd\Beginning XML for Practical Web Dev...
File Edit View Favorites Tools Help
Back
Search
Favorites
Media
Address
E:\aip\clients\FriendsOfEd\Beginning XML for Practical Web Developme
Go
Name | Position from sun | Diameter | Moons | Mean temp
Mars | 4 | 6796 km (4214 miles) | 2 | -63C (-81F)
Mercury | 1 | 4879 km (3025 miles) | 0 | 179C (354F)
Venus | 2 | 12104 km (7505 miles) | 0 | 482C (900F)
Done
My Computer

Figure 7-3. *The planets' table displayed in IE*

You might notice that the `<neighbours>` template purposely doesn't include `<html>`, `<head>`, and `<body>` elements. That's because the example will load the XML document and apply the XSLT stylesheet in a separate XHTML document. The XHTML page will display the result of the transformation in a `<div>` element. It will also add buttons that allow the user to sort the table using JavaScript. You can find this code in the new XHTML page, `sortingPlanets10.htm`:

```
<html>
  <head>
    <style>
      body {font-family: verdana, arial, sans-serif; }
      td {padding: 4px; font-size: 12px;}
    </style>
```

```
    <script language="JavaScript">
      var xmlfile = "planets10.xml";
      var xslfile = "planets10.xsl";
      var xml, xsl;
      function init() {
        xml = loadDocumentIE(xmlfile);
        xsl = loadDocumentIE(xslfile);
        doTransform();
      }
      function loadDocumentIE(filename) {
        var xmldocument = new ActiveXObject("Microsoft.XMLDOM");
        xmldocument.async = false;
        xmldocument.load(filename);
        return xmldocument;
      }
      function doTransform() {
        document.getElementById("sortoutput").innerHTML = xml.transformNode(xsl);
      }
      function orderBy(select, dataType) {
        xsl = loadDocumentIE(xslfile);
        var sortItem = xsl.getElementsByTagName("xsl:sort")[0];
        sortItem.setAttribute("select", select);
        sortItem.setAttribute("data-type", dataType);
        doTransform();
      }
  </script>
  </head>
  <body onLoad="init();">
    <h1>Table of planet information</h1>
    <div id="sortoutput">Sort output goes here</div>
    <form>
      <input type="button" onClick="orderBy('@name', 'text');"
      value="Order by name" />
      <input type="button" onClick="orderBy('positionFromSun/text()', 'number');"
      value="Order by position from the sun" />
      <input type="button" onClick="orderBy('substring-before(meanTemp/text(),➥
      \'C\');', 'number')" value="Order by mean temp" />
    </form>
  </body>
</html>
```

The code seems complicated, but I'll work through it in more detail shortly.

Open the file `sortingPlanets10.htm` in IE 6, and you should see the table of XML data, as well as three buttons. Click the buttons to sort the table. Figure 7-4 shows the page.

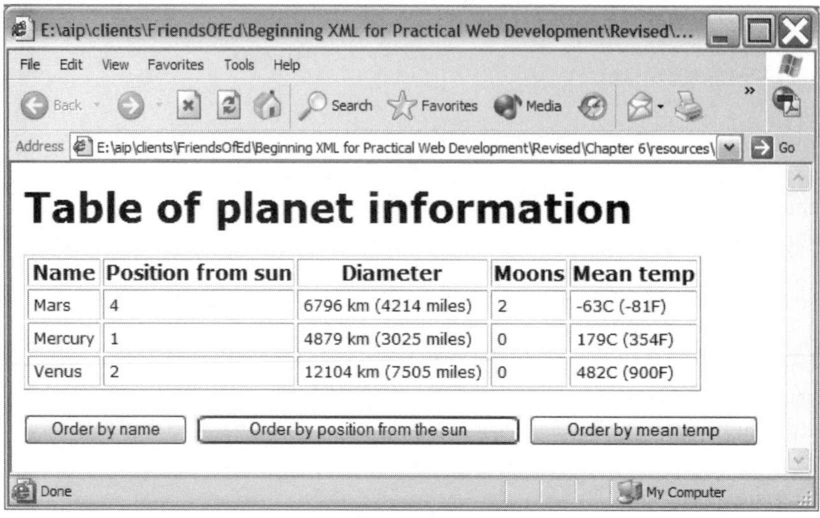

Figure 7-4. *The sortingPlanets10.htm page displayed in IE*

Let's work our way through the contents of `sortingPlanets10.htm`. The page starts with some declarations and an opening `<script>` tag:

```
<html>
  <head>
    <style>
      body {font-family: verdana, arial, sans-serif; }
      td {padding: 4px; font-size: 12px;}
    </style>
    <script language="JavaScript">
```

I'll come back to the JavaScript content.

The remainder of the page consists of layout information:

```
  <body onLoad="init();">
    <h1>Table of planet information</h1>
    <div id="sortoutput">Sort output goes here</div>
    <form>
      <input type="button" onClick="orderBy('@name', 'text');"
      value="Order by name" />
      <input type="button" onClick="orderBy('positionFromSun/text()', 'number');"
      value="Order by position from the sun" />
      <input type="button" onClick="orderBy('substring-before(meanTemp/text(),➥
      \'C\')', 'number');" value="Order by mean temp" />
    </form>
  </body>
</html>
```

The <body> section includes a header, a <div> container for the transformed content, and a form. The form contains buttons that you can click to change the sort order. Shortly, you'll see the JavaScript that powers those buttons.

The <body> declaration includes an onLoad event handler:

```
<body onLoad="init();">
```

When the page loads, the onLoad event handler triggers the init() function, which follows:

```
function init() {
  xml = loadDocumentIE(xmlfile);
  xsl = loadDocumentIE(xslfile);
  doTransform();
}
```

The init() function calls the loadDocumentIE() function twice, loading both the XML document and the XSLT stylesheet. The function calls pass the variables xmlfile and xslfile. Those variables were defined at the beginning of the script block in the <head> section of the page:

```
var xmlfile = "planets10.xml";
var xslfile = "planets10.xsl";
```

The loadDocumentIE() loads the XML and XSLT documents:

```
function loadDocumentIE(filename) {
  var xmldocument = new ActiveXObject("Microsoft.XMLDOM");
  xmldocument.async = false;
  xmldocument.load(filename);
  return xmldocument;
}
```

The function creates an instance of the XML parser (Microsoft.XMLDOM) and references it with the variable xmldocument. The code sets the async property of the xmldocument variable to false so that the file loads synchronously—in other words, the function waits until the external XML document has finished loading before proceeding. The function finishes by using the load() method to load the specified XML document into the xmldocument variable. It returns the XML document.

The loadDocumentIE() function is called with both the XML document and XSLT stylesheet. This function can load the stylesheet because, after all, it's an XML document.

After the init() function loads both documents, it calls the doTransform() function. This function applies the XSL transformation to the XML document:

```
function doTransform() {
  document.getElementById("sortoutput").innerHTML = xml.transformNode(xsl);
}
```

The doTransform() function uses the transformNode() method of the XML parser to apply an XSLT transformation. The code passes the xsl variable to this method to specify which stylesheet to use. After the transformation, the code displays the results in the innerHTML of the sortoutput (<div>) element.

Note Because the transformation is applied using JavaScript and the XML parser, planets10.xml doesn't need to include a stylesheet reference to planets10.xsl. However, I've included the reference within the XML document so you can test the transformation in a browser.

The XHTML page includes three buttons that you can click to sort the table. Clicking a button calls the orderBy() function. Each button passes the sort criteria in the function call. This includes the sorted element, as well as the type of sort to apply:

```
<input type="button" onClick="orderBy('@name', 'text');" value="Order by name" />
<input type="button" onClick="orderBy('positionFromSun/text()', 'number');"
  value="Order by position from the sun" />
<input type="button" onClick="orderBy('substring-before(meanTemp/text(), \'C\')',➥
  'number');" value="Order by mean temp" />
```

The orderBy() function follows:

```
function orderBy(select, dataType) {
  xsl = loadDocumentIE(xslfile);
  var sortItem = xsl.getElementsByTagName("xsl:sort")[0];
  sortItem.setAttribute("select", select);
  sortItem.setAttribute("data-type", dataType);
  doTransform();
}
```

The orderBy() function receives the element to sort on and its data type as parameters. The code uses these parameters to modify the XSLT stylesheet dynamically. When you click a button, the orderBy()function reloads planets10.xsl. This is required because IE makes the loaded stylesheet read-only after applying the transformation. Reloading the document allows the JavaScript to read the XSLT stylesheet again.

The code identifies the <xsl:sort> element in the stylesheet by using the getElementsByTagName() method:

```
var sortItem = xsl.getElementsByTagName("xsl:sort")[0];
```

This method returns any <xsl:sort> elements in the document. The code selects the first element by specifying index 0.

The code then sets the values of the select and datatype attributes of the <xsl:sort> element to those passed into the function. When you click the second button

```
<input type="button" onClick="orderBy('positionFromSun/text()', 'number')"
  value="Order by position from the sun" />
```

the code dynamically alters the <xsl:sort> element as follows:

```
<xsl:apply-templates>
  <xsl:sort select="positionFromSun/text()" data-type="number" order="ascending"/>
</xsl:apply-templates>
```

Finally, the code calls doTransform() to apply the altered transformation and update the sortoutput (<div>) element.

In this example, Document Object Model (DOM) scripting manipulates the elements in the stylesheet. This example touched briefly on the subject, and I'll explain it more fully in the next two chapters. In this XHTML page, JavaScript rewrote a portion of the stylesheet dynamically. You could totally rewrite the stylesheet using this method.

Caution If you have Windows XP with Service Pack 2 installed, you will run into security problems if you try to use this method to access XML files located in a different domain from the web page.

Adding Extension Functions (Internet Explorer)

If you've worked as a web developer for some time, you probably remember the days of version 3 and 4 browsers. At that time, the HTML standard wasn't consistently applied between Netscape and IE. Each browser manufacturer added nonstandard HTML tags, and there were differences in the application of existing standards. The result was that some sites had to be written in two versions—one for Netscape and one for IE.

Because of this, the XSLT specification defines a standard method of extending XSLT using extension functions and extension elements. In this example, you'll see how to create extension functions to display specific text in uppercase. I won't examine extension elements, as Microsoft XML Parser (MSXML) 3 doesn't support them. However, you could use an extension element to change the value of a variable while the stylesheet is loading.

You can use extension functions to write specific functionality. These functions are written in languages other than XSLT and are best suited to tasks such as text manipulation and disk access. They are particularly useful for quarantined environments such as intranets, where you can rely on a standard operating environment and web browser.

Although most server-side processors support extension functions, only IE supports client-side extension functions. This example only works in IE and not the Mozilla-based browsers.

In this example, I'll create JavaScript extension functions to work with the text in the <description> element. The example will capitalize the planet's name wherever it appears in the description. This is the same type of technique that you could use to highlight search terms within search results.

Unlike XSLT, JavaScript supports regular expressions. This allows you to specify any case for the planet's name. This example uses the resource files planets11.xml and planets11.xsl. The new stylesheet follows. I'll explain it in detail shortly:

```
<?xml version="1.0" encoding="UTF-8"?>
<xsl:stylesheet version="1.0" xmlns:xsl=http://www.w3.org/1999/XSL/Transform
  xmlns:msxsl="urn:schemas-microsoft-com:xslt"
  xmlns:user="http://www.apress.com/namespace" extension-element-prefixes="msxsl">
  <xsl:import href="planetsToXHTML.xsl"/>
  <xsl:output method="html" version="4.0" indent="yes"/>
  <msxsl:script language="JScript" implements-prefix="user">
    <![CDATA[
      function capitalizeMatchingText(fullText, highlightText) {
        var reg = new RegExp(highlightText, "gi");
        var splitList = fullText.split(reg);
        return splitList.join(highlightText.toUpperCase());
      }
    ]]>
  </msxsl:script>
  <xsl:template match="planet">
    <h2>
      <xsl:value-of select="@name"/>
    </h2>
    <xsl:value-of select= ➥
    "user:capitalizeMatchingText(string(description/text()),string(@name))"/>
    <ul>
      <xsl:apply-templates/>
    </ul>
  </xsl:template>
  <xsl:template match="neighbours">
    <html>
      <head>
        <title>A simple HTML page</title>
        <style type="text/css">
          body { font-family: Verdana, Arial, sans-serif; font-size: 12px; }
      </style>
      </head>
      <body>
        <xsl:apply-templates/>
      </body>
    </html>
  </xsl:template>
</xsl:stylesheet>
```

Figure 7-5 shows how this page appears in IE.

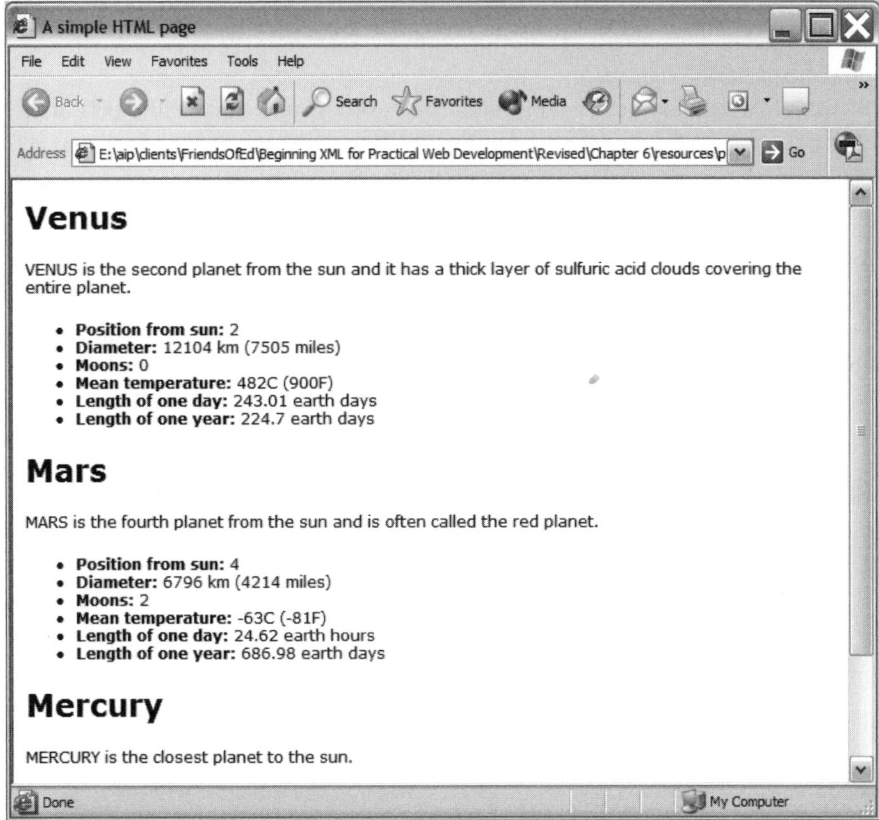

Figure 7-5. *The planets11.xml page displayed in IE*

You'll notice that instances of the planet name appear capitalized in the description.

We'll work through the code in this example in the next section. One immediate difference from the previous examples is the use of multiple namespaces. It's important to understand a little more about why these are important when working with extension functions.

Understanding More About Namespaces

Namespaces are an important concept when working with XML documents. You'll recall from earlier in the book that namespaces allow you to associate elements with a specific XML vocabulary. If you need a refresher on namespaces, you might want to reread Chapter 2.

As I mentioned, the stylesheet in this example includes two new namespace declarations. Including these namespaces allows extension functions to be added to the stylesheet:

```
<xsl:stylesheet version="1.0"
  xmlns:xsl=http://www.w3.org/1999/XSL/Transform
  xmlns:msxsl="urn:schemas-microsoft-com:xslt"
  xmlns:user="http://www.apress.com/namespace"
  extension-element-prefixes="msxsl">
```

The declarations associate the msxsl namespace with the urn:schemas-microsoft-com:xslt URI. This URI is defined by Microsoft and tells the XSLT processor to make Microsoft extension functions available to the stylesheet.

When you want to use elements from this namespace, you'll prefix them with msxsl in the stylesheet. The prefix msxsl is the convention for IE extensions; however, the text itself isn't significant. You could use any other prefix, providing that you use it consistently.

The second of the new namespace declarations defines the user prefix. This prefix will apply to extension functions. By convention, this namespace should be a URI referencing the organization. In this case, I've referred to an Apress URI—http://www.apress.com/namespace.

The URI might contain a web page describing the functions available within the namespace. However, there is no requirement for this to happen. The uniqueness of the URI is what is important here. You're not bound to use the prefix user and could use any other valid text.

The <xsl:stylesheet> element also includes the attribute

```
extension-element-prefixes="msxsl"
```

This attribute prevents the extension namespace msxsl from being included as output in the transformed document.

Because the declaration includes the msxsl namespace, the <msxsl:script> element is available to the stylesheet. This allows the stylesheet to include a script block containing extension functions.

```
<msxsl:script language="JScript" implements-prefix="user">
```

Notice that the <msxsl> element can specify the language for the script—in this case, JScript. The implements-prefix="user" attribute shows that the stylesheet will prefix the extension functions with the text user.

■ **Note** JScript is the Microsoft implementation of JavaScript, used with IE.

Once the stylesheet includes these namespaces, it can include extension functions within the <msxsl:script> element.

Adding Extension Functions to the Stylesheet

The stylesheet imports the standard stylesheet planetsToXHTML.xsl and sets the output method:

```
<xsl:import href="planetsToXHTML.xsl"/>
<xsl:output method="html" version="4.0" indent="yes"/>
```

The extension functions are then included in the `<msxml:script>` element. As I mentioned earlier, the `implements-prefix` attribute specifies that the word `user` will prefix any extension functions:

```
<msxsl:script language="JScript" implements-prefix="user">
  <![CDATA[
    function capitalizeMatchingText(fullText, highlightText) {
      var reg = new RegExp(highlightText, "gi");
      var splitList = fullText.split(reg);
      return splitList.join(highlightText.toUpperCase());
    }
  ]]>
  </msxsl:script>
```

You'll notice that a `CDATA` block encloses the extension function. This is necessary because the function includes the < and > characters. As an alternative, I could have used the HTML entities `<` or `>`, but using a `CDATA` block makes the code easier to read.

The `capitalizeMatchingText()`function takes two text strings—the full text to modify (`fullText`) and the phrase to style (`highlightText`). If the second string appears within the first, the function replaces the second with a capitalized version. The switch `gi` in the `RegExp` object specifies that the function will ignore the case of the `highlightText` string (`i`)and that it will do a global search (`g`) for all occurrences of the pattern. If you call the `capitalizeMatchingText()` function with the following parameters

```
capitalizeMatchingText("xml is great","Xml")
```

the function will return

```
XML is great
```

having changed the first word from lowercase to uppercase.

Although the current stylesheet imports the `planetsToXHTML.xsl` stylesheet, it redefines the `<planet>` element template to call the new JavaScript function with the following code:

```
<xsl:value-of select= ➥
  "user:capitalizeMatchingText(string(description/text()),string(@name))"/>
```

The line passes two arguments to the function: the text within the `<description>` element and the `name` attribute of the planet. The `<xsl:value-of>` element works with the return value from the `capitalizeMatchingText()` function.

Note that the code uses the XPath `string()` function to cast the values into text strings. If it didn't do this, it would have to convert these values into strings within the `capitalizeMatchingText()` function instead.

The resource files `planets12.xml` and `planets12.xsl` show the effect of calling a different function, `wrapMatchingText()`:

```
<msxsl:script language="JScript" implements-prefix="user">
  <![CDATA[
    function wrapMatchingText(fullText, highlightText) {
      var reg = new RegExp(highlightText, "gi");
      var splitList = fullText.split(reg);
      return splitList.join("<span class='planetname'>"+highlightText+"</span>");
    }
  ]]>
</msxsl:script>
```

Instead of capitalizing the text, this function encloses it with a `<span>` tag. This tag includes a CSS class declaration. Calling the function with the parameters

```
wrapMatchingText("xml is great","Xml")
```

returns

```
<span class='planetname'>xml</span> is great".
```

Because the stylesheet generates XML output, the `<xsl:value of>` is a little different in the stylesheet:

```
<xsl:value-of disable-output-escaping="yes"
  select="user:wrapMatchingText(string(description/text()),string(@name))"/>
```

This time, the stylesheet sets the `disable-output-escaping` attribute value to `yes` because it is generating `<span>` elements. If the stylesheet left out the attribute, the angle brackets would be converted to the entities `<` and `>`. The `<span>` tags would then display on the page as text rather than being interpreted as XHTML elements.

The stylesheet `planets12.xsl` also includes the following CSS class declaration:

```
.planetname {background-color: #FFFF00; font-weight:bold;➥
  border: 1px solid #000000; padding: 2px;}
```

Figure 7-6 shows the transformed content using the new function. The highlight appears in a yellow color within the description, which may not be obvious from the screen shot.

GENERATING NEW XHTML TAGS

The approach shown in `planets12.xsl` is one way to generate new XHTML tags within a transformation. Although this method appears to be easy, you should use it with caution because it's easy to create documents that aren't well formed.

In Chapter 8, I'll show you how you can use the DOM to generate XML nodes rather than creating them as text. Generating XML through the DOM guarantees that the resulting content will be well formed.

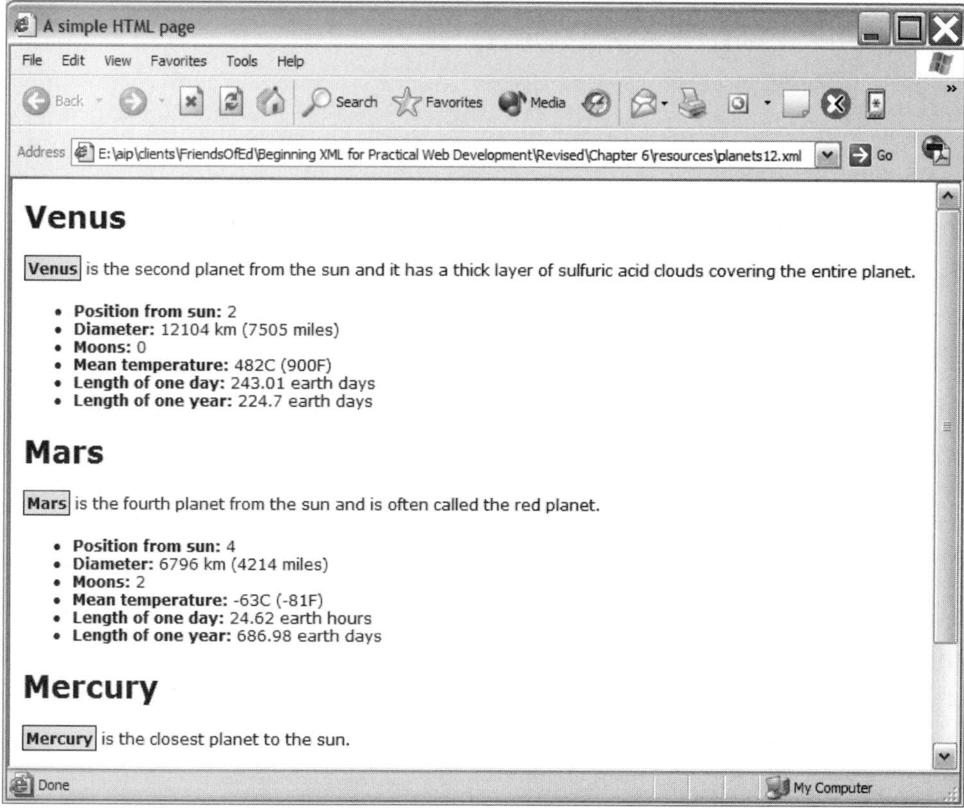

Figure 7-6. *The planets12.xml page displayed in IE*

Providing Support for Browsers Other Than IE

It would be convenient to use the same stylesheet for browsers that support extension functions and provide alternative output for other browsers. You can do this by using the `<xsl:choose>` element. This element allows you to select from one of a range of alternatives. This example checks to see if the extension function exists and calls a different transformation if necessary.

You can find this example within the files `planets13.xml` and `planets13.xsl`. The `<planet>` template from the stylesheet follows, with new lines shown in bold:

```
<xsl:template match="planet">
  <h2>
    <xsl:value-of select="@name"/>
  </h2>
  <xsl:choose>
    <xsl:when test="function-available('user:wrapMatchingText')">
      <xsl:value-of disable-output-escaping="yes"➥
      select="user:wrapMatchingText(string(description/text()),string(@name))"/>
    </xsl:when>
```

```
    <xsl:otherwise>
      <xsl:value-of select="description/text()"/>
    </xsl:otherwise>
  </xsl:choose>
  <ul>
    <xsl:apply-templates/>
  </ul>
</xsl:template>
```

The <xsl:choose> block provides *if, then, else* functionality to the stylesheet. It checks if the wrapMatchingText() function is available using a function-available test. If the function exists, the stylesheet calls it as before. However, if the function is unavailable, as in a non-IE browser, the stylesheet outputs the text from within the <description> element with no processing. Figure 7-7 shows how the page appears within both IE 6 and Firefox 1.5.

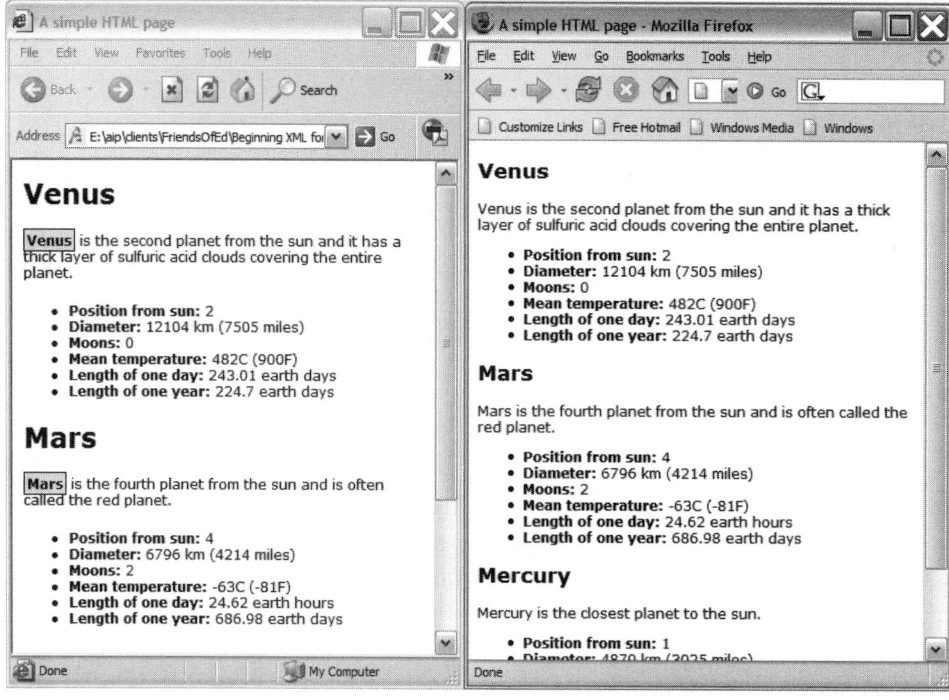

Figure 7-7. *The planets13.xml page displayed in both IE 6 and Firefox 1.5*

Working with Named Templates

Typically, in an XML-driven web site, you create a master XSLT file for the whole site and import it into other XSLT stylesheets. This manages consistency within the site, and allows for flexibility within individual sections.

The previous example imported the <planet> element template from the master stylesheet planetsToXHTML.xsl. The stylesheet duplicated the contents from the master stylesheet within planets12.xsl and planets13.xsl and edited them to introduce changes. This causes a problem if you then need to change the master stylesheet. You'd have to update the copied section each time. Using this approach would make it difficult to maintain and keep stylesheets consistent.

An alternative is to introduce a named template into the master stylesheet. You can see this approach in planets14.xml, planetsToXHTMLNamed.xsl, and planets14.xsl. The master stylesheet planetsToXHTMLNamed.xsl includes a named template. It follows with the changed lines shown in bold:

```
<?xml version="1.0" encoding="UTF-8"?>
<xsl:stylesheet version="1.0" xmlns:xsl="http://www.w3.org/1999/XSL/Transform">
  <xsl:output method="html" version="4.0" indent="yes"/>
  <xsl:template match="text()"/>
  <xsl:template match="neighbours">
    <html>
      <head>
        <title>A simple HTML page</title>
        <style type="text/css">
          <xsl:call-template name="css" />
      </style>
      </head>
      <body>
        <p>
          <a href="http://www.nasa.gov/">Visit NASA!</a> |
          <a href="http://www.nineplanets.org/">Tour the solar system</a>
        </p>
        <h1>Our neighbours</h1>
        <xsl:apply-templates/>
        <hr/>
        Copyright Planetary Fun 2006.
    </body>
    </html>
  </xsl:template>
  <xsl:template name="css">
    body {font-family: Verdana, Arial, sans-serif; font-size: 12px;}
  </xsl:template>
  <xsl:template match="planet">
    <h2><xsl:value-of select="@name"/></h2>
    <xsl:value-of select="description/text()"/>
    <ul><xsl:apply-templates/></ul>
  </xsl:template>
  <xsl:template match="positionFromSun">
    <li><strong>Position from sun: </strong><xsl:value-of select="text()"/></li>
  </xsl:template>
  <xsl:template match="diameter">
    <li><strong>Diameter: </strong><xsl:value-of select="text()"/></li>
```

```
  </xsl:template>
  <xsl:template match="moons">
    <li><strong>Moons: </strong><xsl:value-of select="text()"/></li>
  </xsl:template>
  <xsl:template match="meanTemp">
    <li><strong>Mean temperature: </strong><xsl:value-of select="text()"/></li>
  </xsl:template>
  <xsl:template match="oneDay">
    <li><strong>Length of one day: </strong><xsl:value-of select="text()"/></li>
  </xsl:template>
  <xsl:template match="oneYear">
    <li><strong>Length of one year: </strong><xsl:value-of select="text()"/></li>
  </xsl:template>
</xsl:stylesheet>
```

Instead of making style declarations within the `<style>` element, the stylesheet makes a call to a named template:

```
<xsl:call-template name="css" />
```

The stylesheet also includes the template `css`:

```
<xsl:template name="css">
  body { font-family: Verdana, Arial, sans-serif; font-size: 12px; }
</xsl:template>
```

When the stylesheet processor reaches the `<xsl:call-template>` tag, it searches through all available templates to find one with a matching name. It then acts upon this template. If it can't find one, the processor will throw an error. The processor will first look through all templates in the current stylesheet and then through parent stylesheets. Bear in mind, though, that you can't import named templates.

Named templates are ideal for reducing duplicated code in stylesheets. You can easily override a named template in the current stylesheet with a further declaration using the same template name:

```
<xsl:template name="css">
  body {font-family: Verdana, Arial, sans-serif; font-size: 12px;}
  .planetname {background-color: #FFFF00; font-weight:bold; ➥
  border: 1px solid #000000; padding: 2px;}
</xsl:template>
```

If you view the `planets13.xml` document in a web browser, you won't be able to see the effect of changing the code structure. The page will render as it did previously.

The `xsl:call-template` element is a very powerful XSLT tool. You can pass parameters into a template and treat it very much like a JavaScript function with arguments. You can also use it in recursive functions. I won't cover these aspects in this book, so you may wish to explore these features further yourself.

Generating JavaScript with XSLT

In the examples so far, you've used XSLT to generate XHTML for display in a web browser. You can also use XSLT to generate output such as JavaScript. This might be useful to create web pages that are more dynamic. It also provides an alternative to using extension functions.

You can find the examples from this section in `planets14.xml` and `planets14.xsl`. Be aware that you can only apply this stylesheet in IE. The new stylesheet follows:

```
<?xml version="1.0" encoding="UTF-8"?>
<xsl:stylesheet version="1.0" xmlns:xsl="http://www.w3.org/1999/XSL/Transform">
  <xsl:param name="planetName">Please select a planet</xsl:param>
  <xsl:output method="html" version="4.0" indent="no"/>
  <xsl:template match="neighbours">
    <html>
      <head>
        <title>A simple HTML page with JavaScript</title>
        <style>
      body {font-family: Verdana, Arial, sans-serif; font-size: 12px;}
    </style>
    <script language="JavaScript">
      var planetList = new Array();
      <xsl:apply-templates mode="js"/>
      function displayPlanet(name) {
        if (name!="<xsl:value-of select="$planetName"/>") {
          var w = window.open("","planetpopup", "resizable,width=400,height=300");
          w.document.open();
          w.document.write(planetList[name]);
          w.document.close();
        }
      }
    </script>
      </head>
      <body>
        <form>
        Select your planet:
        <select onChange="displayPlanet(this.options[selectedIndex].text)">
            <option>
              <xsl:value-of select="$planetName"/>
            </option>
            <xsl:apply-templates/>
          </select>
        </form>
      </body>
    </html>
  </xsl:template>
  <xsl:template match="planet" mode="js">
    planetList["<xsl:value-of select="@name"/>"]= ➥
      '<xsl:apply-templates select="." mode="onelinehtml"/>';
```

```
  </xsl:template>
  <xsl:template match="planet" mode="onelinehtml">
    <img src="{@name}.jpg" width="100" height="100"/>
    <h2><xsl:value-of select="@name"/></h2>
    <p>
      <xsl:value-of select="normalize-space(description/text())"/>
      <br/>
      <xsl:text><hr/>Copyright Planetary Fun 2006.</xsl:text>
    </p>
  </xsl:template>
  <xsl:template match="planet">
    <option><xsl:value-of select="@name"/></option>
  </xsl:template>
</xsl:stylesheet>
```

Figure 7-8 shows what happens when you view the `planets14.xml` page in IE 6 and choose a planet from the drop-down list.

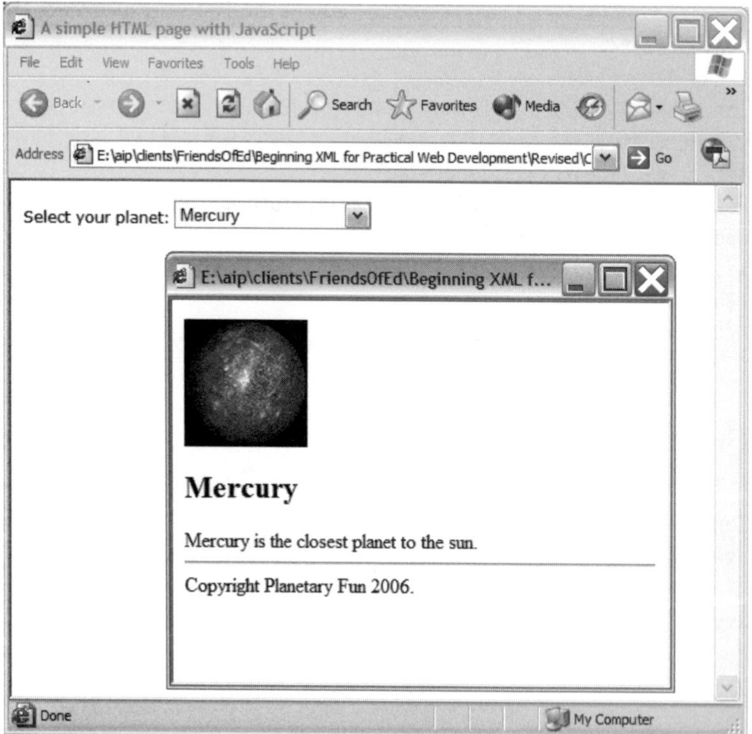

Figure 7-8. *The planets14.xml page displayed in IE*

You'll notice that the transformed content creates a list of planets in a drop-down list. When the user selects a planet from the list, a pop-up window appears showing an image and the planet's description.

Let's work through the new stylesheet to see how to achieve this effect.

Understanding XSLT Parameters

The stylesheet starts as normal with an XML declaration and an `<xsl:stylesheet>` element. The first change to the stylesheet is the introduction of a new element, `<xsl:param>`:

```
<xsl:param name="planetName">Please select a planet</xsl:param>
```

The new element is an XSLT parameter. This parameter allows the stylesheet to generate repeating content during the transformation. In this case, it defines a parameter called `planetName` that will be used as a placeholder in the drop-down list of planets. The parameter starts with the text `Please select a planet`. The stylesheet will add the other planets to the list using XSLT. The user will then be able to select any planet contained within the XML document.

You can access the value in the parameter using an `<xsl:value-of>` element and referring to the parameter name `$planetName`:

```
<xsl:value-of select="$planetName"/>
```

You'll see this a little later in the stylesheet.

As the parameter is defined at the top level of the stylesheet, it is a global parameter. Stylesheet processors can address global parameters from outside of the stylesheet. You can use JavaScript to set the parameter values.

Understanding White Space and Modes

The next line of the stylesheet sets the output for the stylesheet:

```
<xsl:output method="html" version="4.0" indent="no"/>
```

The stylesheet sets output to `html` version `4.0` for Mozilla compatibility. In previous examples, you saw the `indent` attribute set to `yes`; however, in this case, the `<xsl:output>` element sets it to `no`.

The `indent="no"` attribute allows the stylesheet to remove white space. If you don't include the declaration, the output will be indented by default to improve readability. Web browsers normally ignore white space, so it makes no difference when you output XHTML. However, white space can cause serious problems when working with JavaScript. A common problem is new line characters appearing in the middle of strings.

The stylesheet includes a template for the `<neighbours>` element. In addition to the `<head>` section and style declarations, the template creates the following JavaScript section:

```
<script language="JavaScript">
  var planetList = new Array();
  <xsl:apply-templates mode="js"/>
  function displayPlanet(name) {
    if (name!="<xsl:value-of select="$planetName"/>") {
      var w = window.open("","planetpopup", "resizable,width=400,height=300");
      w.document.open();
      w.document.write(planetList[name]);
      w.document.close();
    }
  }
</script>
```

I'll work through this JavaScript code block in detail a little later.

However, you should note that the code block starts by creating a JavaScript array called planetList:

```
<script language="JavaScript">
  var planetList = new Array();
```

This array will store XHTML strings relating to the planets from the XML document.

The next line

```
<xsl:apply-templates mode="js" />
```

applies templates to all elements within the current <neighbours> tag, where they have the matching mode attribute of js. If you look through the stylesheet, you'll see different <planet> templates that use the mode attribute. This attribute allows the stylesheet to apply different templates to the same content.

The stylesheet contains only one template for the <planet> elements with the mode value of js:

```
<xsl:template match="planet" mode="js">
  planetList["<xsl:value-of select="@name"/>"]= ➥
    '<xsl:apply-templates select="." mode="onelinehtml"/>';
</xsl:template>
```

This template generates JavaScript content for the planetList array.

The js mode template adds an entry to the planetList array for each <planet> element. The array key is the planet name, and the value comes from the <planets> template in onelinehtml mode. You'll see this template in the next section.

Incidentally, this example also includes a default <planet> template that doesn't have a mode attribute. The default template produces a list of options for the <select> element:

```
<xsl:template match="planet">
  <option><xsl:value-of select="@name"/></option>
</xsl:template>
```

This template will display the select box on the page.

■ **Note** The mode names don't come from a predetermined list. You can choose any mode name for your templates. This example uses descriptive names that indicate the purpose of each template.

You can see what's added to the JavaScript array by working through the onelinehtml template.

Working Through the onelinehtml Template

The onelinehtml template sets the value for each of the array items in planetList:

```
<xsl:template match="planet" mode="onelinehtml">
  <img src="{@name}.jpg" width="100" height="100"/>
  <h2><xsl:value-of select="@name"/></h2>
  <p>
    <xsl:value-of select="normalize-space(description/text())"/>
    <br/>
    <hr/>
    <xsl:text>Copyright Planetary Fun 2006.</xsl:text>
  </p>
</xsl:template>
```

This template creates an XHTML string that you'll ultimately display in the pop-up window.

The src attribute of the <img> tag comes from the name attribute. The stylesheet assumes that all images are named the same way—using the planet name and a .jpeg suffix. The @name expression is interpreted as XPath, as it appears within braces { }. This provides a quicker way to write an attribute value compared with the method shown in Chapter 6:

```
<xsl:attribute name="src">
  <xsl:value-of select="@name"/>.jpg
</xsl:attribute>
```

The <p> element contains an <xsl:value-of> element with the normalize-space function. This function strips leading and trailing white-space characters and converts multiple white-space characters to a single space. The effect is that new line characters are removed from the <description> element in the source XML document.

The template ends with an <xsl:text> element that contains the copyright text. This element writes literal text in the output, preserving white space that appears inside the element.

XSLT stylesheets ignore white space between two elements that don't contain text—for example,
<hr/>. White space between an element and text is significant. So the white space between the following two lines is significant:

```
<p><xsl:value-of select="normalize-space(description/text())"/><br /><hr/>
Copyright 2002 DinosaurOrg
```

The <xsl:text> element wraps the copyright text, so there are no spaces between tags and text:

```
<p><xsl:value-of select="normalize-space(description/text())"/><br/><hr/>
  <xsl:text>Copyright Planetary Fun 2006.</xsl:text>
</p>
```

Now, you can be sure that the output produced by the onelinehtml mode <planet> template won't contain white space and, therefore, won't generate JavaScript errors.

In the case of the planet Venus, the onelinehtml template generates the following output:

```
<img src="Venus.jpg" width="100" height="100">
<h2>Venus</h2>
<p>Venus is the second planet from the sun and it has a thick layer of sulfuric
acid clouds covering the entire planet.<br><hr>Copyright Planetary Fun 2006.</p>
```

This content appears within the planetList JavaScript array, as shown:

```
planetList["Venus"]= '<img src="Venus.jpg" width="100" height="100">➥
  <h2>Venus</h2><p>Venus is the second planet from the sun and it has a thick ➥
  layer of sulfuric acid clouds covering the entire planet.<br><hr>➥
  Copyright Planetary Fun 2006.</p>';
```

The code generates one array element for each planet, each containing XHTML content to display in the pop-up window.

Finishing Off the Page

The preceding section shows the effect of applying the js mode template with this line:

```
<xsl:apply-templates mode="js"/>
```

Remember, this line appears within the <script> block at the top of the page.

After the JavaScript code block uses the js template to add the XHTML for each planet to the planetList array, it defines a JavaScript function, displayPlanet(). The function uses the parameter defined earlier and refers to it using the variable $planetName:

```
function displayPlanet(name) {
  if (name!="<xsl:value-of select="$planetName"/>") {
    var w = window.open("","planetpopup", "resizable,width=400,height=300");
    w.document.open();
    w.document.write(planetList[name]);
    w.document.close();
  }
}
```

When the XSLT processor applies the XSLT stylesheet, the first line of this function transforms to

```
if (name!=" Please select a planet") {
```

In other words, the function only proceeds if the user has selected a planet. The code then creates the pop-up window

```
var w = window.open("","planetpopup", "resizable,width=400,height=300");
```

and writes the XHTML details from the planetList array to the document:

```
    w.document.open();
    w.document.write(planetList[name]);
    w.document.close();
  }
}
```

After the JavaScript function, the neighbours template creates the remainder of the XHTML page:

```
<body>
  <form>
    Select your planet:
    <select onChange="displayPlanet(this.options[selectedIndex].text)">
      <option>
        <xsl:value-of select="$planetName"/>
      </option>
      <xsl:apply-templates/>
    </select>
  </form>
</body>
```

The page consists of a form that includes a select box populated with the planet names. The `<xsl:apply-templates />` element calls the default `<planet>` template, which doesn't specify a mode. The default template creates the `<option>` elements for the `<select>` form element and uses the planetName parameter. You saw the XHTML file created by this stylesheet in Figure 7-8.

This example shows you how you can use a variety of XSLT techniques to create powerful and dynamic transformations. However, so far, this example will only work in IE. In the next section, we'll remedy this problem.

Generating JavaScript in Mozilla

The stylesheet that you saw in the previous example won't work properly in Mozilla because of a subtle difference between the way that IE and Mozilla treat the XSLT output. IE serializes the XML/XSLT output and reparses it as XHTML. Mozilla generates the XHTML tree directly.

In XHTML, a `<script>` element can't contain other elements, such as the `<img>` and `<p>` tags that the stylesheet generates from the onelinehtml template. Because IE creates the XSLT output as text and reparses it as HTML, this doesn't cause a problem.

However, using this approach in Mozilla generates JavaScript errors. Including the `<img>` and `<p>` tags in a `<script>` element isn't legal in XHTML, so the tags are ignored. The planetList[] array entry isn't populated correctly, generating a JavaScript error. You can avoid this problem by using CDATA sections and changing the way that the JavaScript function populates the array.

You can find the solution in the files planets15.xml and planets15.xsl. The amended js template follows:

```
<xsl:template match="planet" mode="js">
  planetList["<xsl:value-of select="@name"/>"]= ➥
    '<xsl:value-of select="@name"/>|<xsl:value-of select=➥
    "normalize-space(description/text())"/>';
</xsl:template>
```

The array is populated with two values separated by a pipe (|) character. The code needs to do this because it can't pass XHTML elements directly into the JavaScript array. Instead, it passes two concatenated values.

The displayPlanet() function looks quite different because it uses JavaScript to compose the XHTML tags and write them to the document:

```
function displayPlanet(name) {
  if (name!="<xsl:value-of select="$planetName"/>") {
    var w = window.open("","planetpopup", "resizable,width=400,height=300");
    var docContents = '';
    var contentArray = planetList[name].split("|");
    w.document.open();
    docContents = '<![CDATA[<img src="]]>'+ contentArray[0] + ➥
      '<![CDATA[.jpg" width="100" height="100" /><h2>]]>';
    docContents += contentArray[0];
    docContents += '<![CDATA[</h2><p>]]>';
    docContents += contentArray[1];
    docContents += '<![CDATA[<hr/>Copyright Planetary Fun 2006.</xsl:text></p>]]>';
    w.document.write (docContents)
    w.document.close();
  }
}
```

The function receives a parameter, name, that contains both the name and description of the planet, separated by a pipe (|) character. The built-in JavaScript split() function converts the string into an array called contentArray(). The first element contains the name, while the second element contains the description. The code can then write each part of the array separately to the document using document.write().

The fixed text, including XHTML elements, is wrapped in CDATA blocks and concatenated with the array content to produce output. It's a little clumsy but, when you test it, you'll find that the approach works in both IE 6 and Mozilla.

You've seen several examples showing some more advanced uses of XSLT. Now it's time to look at some tips and common troubleshooting approaches.

XSLT Tips and Troubleshooting

In this section, I want to introduce some tips for working with XSLT stylesheets. I'll also cover some techniques that you can use to troubleshoot problems that arise.

Dealing with White Space

White space is one area that can cause many headaches for new XSLT developers. If you generate only XHTML output, it's not likely to cause too many problems. As you saw with the previous example, once you start generating JavaScript, you can run into some nasty issues.

Common problems include too much white space from indenting, white space in the source document, or white space in the stylesheet. In the earlier examples, you set the indent attribute in the <xsl:output> element to yes:

```
<xsl:output method="html" version="4.0" indent="yes"/>
```

This makes it easier to read through the output from the transformation. Figure 7-9 shows the same file in IE 6, with indenting turned on (on the left) and off (on the right). The example on the left is much easier for a human to read.

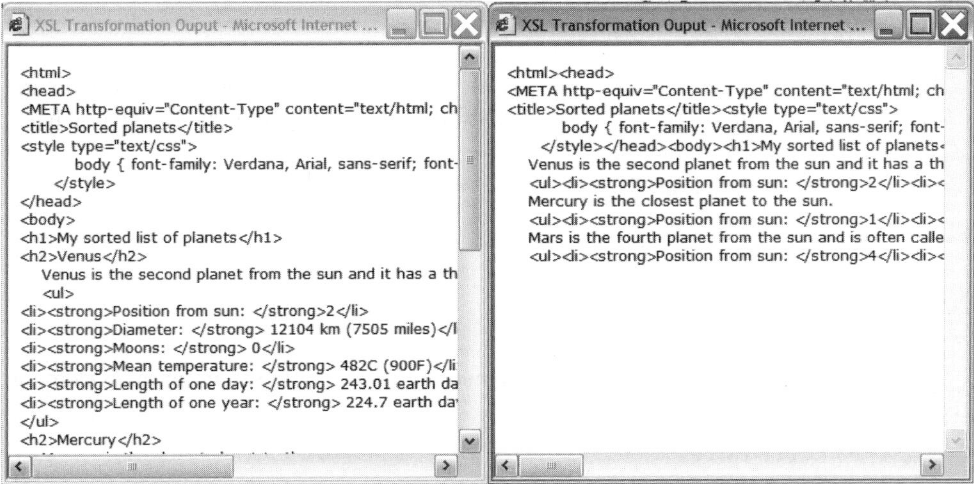

Figure 7-9. *The planets14.xml page displayed in IE*

When applying XSLT stylesheets in a web browser, indenting output can cause problems for generated JavaScript. In this case, make sure you set the value of the `indent` attribute to `no`:

```
<xsl:output indent="no"/>
```

This benefits server-side XSLT as well. Because you include less white space, the generated files are smaller.

As you saw in the previous example, you can deal with white space in the source document using the `normalize-space()` function. This function removes leading and trailing spaces, and it compresses internal white space to a single space character. You saw this within the following line:

```
<xsl:value-of select="normalize-space(description/text())"/>
```

You can also use the top-level `<xsl:strip-space>` element to strip out white-space-only nodes from elements in the source document. You can apply this to all elements with this line:

```
<xsl:strip-space elements="*" />
```

Be aware that `<xsl:strip-space>` acts on nodes that only contain white space, not nodes that include text as well as white space. The opposite is the `<xsl:preserve-space>` element, which allows you to preserve white space within a document.

As you saw in the previous example, dealing with white space in a stylesheet requires an understanding of what happens when an XSLT processor generates output. The processor removes all text nodes containing only white space, unless they're within an `<xsl:text>` element.

You can use an empty <xsl:text/> element to split text with a mixture of white space and characters into two separate text nodes:

```
<xsl:template match="planet">
  <xsl:text/>Name: <xsl:value-of select="@name"/>
</xsl:template>
```

If the stylesheet doesn't include the <xsl:text/> element, it will create white space before the text Name. Instead, the <xsl:text> element splits the white space from the text so that it is ignored. Only the text Name remains.

The <xsl:text> element also preserves white space:

```
<xsl:template match="/">
  <br/><xsl:text>
</xsl:text>
</xsl:template>
```

In this code block, using the <xsl:text> element forces a new line after the <br/> element. You could also use the entity for a new line:

```
<xsl:text>&#10;</xsl:text>
```

You can read the full details of how XSLT deals with white space at http://www.w3.org/TR/xslt#strip.

Using HTML Entities in XSLT

In XHTML, you've probably used named entities such as © and   to represent characters that don't appear on all keyboards. However, in XML, the only entities that are defined are < (<), > (>), & (&), " ("), and ' ('). You have to use the numeric form for all other entities in XML. For example, the entity & represents the ampersand (&) character.

One way to get around this is to reference entity declarations in your stylesheet:

```
<!DOCTYPE doc [
<!ENTITY e SYSTEM "entity-URI">
]>
```

Replace entity-URI with the URI for the entities that you want to include. You can then use them within your stylesheet using the normal syntax. You can find the XHTML entity definitions at http://www.w3.org/2003/entities/.

However, Mozilla does not support external entities. You can define all of the entities within the stylesheet, but that could significantly increase the size of each stylesheet. In this case, you should probably use the numeric values.

Checking Browser Type

One common role for JavaScript developers is determining the browser type of the site viewer. In XSLT 1.0 browsers, you can achieve something similar by using the system-property function to determine the vendor:

```
<xsl:value-of select="system-property('xsl:vendor')"/>
```

IE 6 returns `Microsoft`, whereas Mozilla and Netscape return `TransforMiiX`.

This should probably be a last resort when creating XSLT templates, because it's usually possible to write XSLT that works well in both IE and Mozilla.

Both IE 6 and Mozilla adhere closely to the XSLT 1.0 standard, but there are some small differences in interpretation. In general, Mozilla offers a more accurate XSLT representation than IE. This means that it's less forgiving of errors. If your stylesheet works in Mozilla, it will usually work in IE 6, but the reverse isn't always true.

If the stylesheet works when tested locally but doesn't work in Mozilla on a web server, the most likely problem is that the web server is not using a `text/xml` MIME type for serving the XML and XSLT pages. You'll need to change the web server configuration appropriately to counter this problem.

If no output appears from your stylesheet in Mozilla, even locally, then it may be that you're not generating what the browser considers valid XHTML. In order to display XHTML, the minimum output required is

```
<html><body>Some content</body></html>
```

If you include one of the `<html>` or `<body>` elements, the text of the document will appear without any XHTML markup. Without either element, nothing will appear.

The major difference between IE and Mozilla is the treatment of the XSLT output. As mentioned earlier, IE serializes the output and reparses it as XHTML. Mozilla generates the XHTML tree directly. You saw this difference in the last example, where you couldn't include XHTML elements within JavaScript arrays using XSLT. You can find more on Mozilla's XSLT support at `http://www.mozilla.org/projects/xslt/`.

Building on What Others Have Done

EXSLT (`http://www.exslt.org/`) is a community initiative to provide extensions for XSLT. The extensions are available in a number of modules on the web site, including common, math, functions, dates and times, strings, and regular expressions. Some extensions are written in pure XSLT, some use MSXML extensions so they work only in IE, and some are only for use server-side. Before creating your own functionality, you may be able to build on something from this site.

Understanding the Best Uses for XSLT

Once you start working with XSLT, you'll soon see that it is a detailed language in its own right. It can be very tempting to use it for every purpose in your XML/XHTML applications. However, XSLT works best when transforming structured data. XSLT is not good at transforming text within XML documents or styling content, and it doesn't handle calculations particularly well. You may find that the following solutions are more appropriate:

- For text formatting and styling, CSS 2 offers many useful tools and is more suited than XSLT.
- You can use extension functions for calculations if you're working in a single-browser environment such as an intranet.
- If you need to support both IE 6 and Mozilla, you may be able to use XSLT to generate client-side JavaScript that performs calculations.

Summary

In this chapter, you've worked through some of the more advanced features that you can use when working with client-side XSLT. You've learned to apply sorting with XSLT and use JavaScript to create a dynamic sorting mechanism.

You've also expanded XSLT functionality with extension functions in IE. You saw that stylesheets can check for the availability of extension functions and perform alternative transformations for non-IE browsers. You also used named templates to reduce code duplication in XSLT stylesheets. In the last example, you used XSLT to generate JavaScript. This example showed the different approaches to generating JavaScript in IE compared with Mozilla.

Finally, you've seen some of the tips and tricks for working with XSLT. The last piece of advice is that, although XSLT is powerful, it should only be used where appropriate. Other tools may be more useful.

In the next chapter, I'll discuss using browser scripting to work with XML documents. You'll see how you can use JavaScript to work with the XML DOM so that you can traverse and manipulate XML documents on the client side.

CHAPTER 8

Scripting in the Browser

Chapters 6 and 7 showed how to work with client-side XML. I discussed support for XML in the major web browsers and examined how to transform data using Extensible Stylesheet Language Transformations (XSLT). I briefly touched on some uses of JavaScript to work with the Document Object Model (DOM).

JavaScript provides great flexibility for working with client-side XML. In this chapter, I'll show you how to use JavaScript to work with XML content. The chapter starts by looking at the World Wide Web Consortium (W3C) XML DOM and then shows how to use it with JavaScript to manipulate XML documents.

I'll examine some of the key DOM interfaces before looking at the differences between Internet Explorer (IE) and Mozilla. You'll see one approach to managing these differences using a wrapper library, and you'll finish the chapter by applying what you've learned. During the chapter, you'll learn how to work with XML data dynamically and request content without server-side processing.

I tested the examples in Firefox 1.5 and IE 6.0. You can download the code samples from the Source Code area of the Apress web site (`http://www.apress.com`).

Let's start by learning more about the XML DOM.

The W3C XML DOM

I introduced the W3C DOM earlier in this book. The DOM represents structured documents as an object-oriented model. It creates a tree-like structure of objects that developers can use to target and manipulate parts of the document.

Vendors can implement the DOM interfaces in a language or platform of their choice. This chapter uses JavaScript to manipulate the DOM in IE and Firefox. Both of these browsers provide support for the W3C DOM, but there are some differences between the two.

INTERFACES

An interface defines the way that an object interacts with the outside world. Interfaces specify the methods and properties that are available to objects that implement those interfaces. The W3C DOM defines a set of interfaces for accessing XML programmatically. Vendors can implement these interfaces in any language or platform that is appropriate. Both Mozilla and IE implement the W3C DOM. Because they both implement the same interfaces, they share a common set of properties and methods.

The W3C DOM represents an XML document as a tree of nodes. You can see this structure using the dvd.xml document example from Chapter 1:

```
<?xml version="1.0" encoding="UTF-8"?>
<!-- This XML document describes a DVD library -->
<library>
  <DVD id="1">
    <title>Breakfast at Tiffany's</title>
    <format>Movie</format>
    <genre>Classic</genre>
  </DVD>
  <DVD id="2">
    <title>Contact</title>
    <format>Movie</format>
    <genre>Science fiction</genre>
  </DVD>
  <DVD id="3">
    <title>Little Britain</title>
    <format>TV Series</format>
    <genre>Comedy</genre>
  </DVD>
</library>
```

Figure 8-1 shows this document represented in a tree structure.

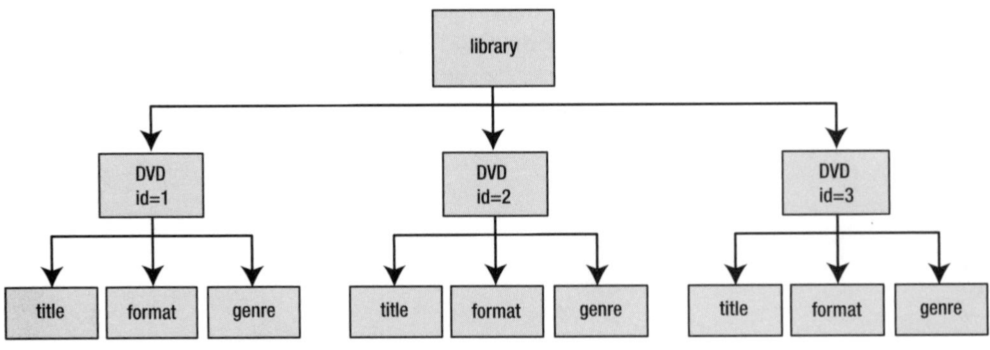

Figure 8-1. *The dvd.xml document shown as a tree structure*

The tree contains a hierarchical set of nodes of different types. At the base of the tree, the `<library>` element has a number of `<DVD>` elements. Each `<DVD>` element has `<title>`, `<format>`, and `<genre>` elements.

Let's look at how to interpret this document using DOM interfaces.

Understanding Key DOM Interfaces

The W3C XML DOM includes three levels. Level 1 focuses on XML and HTML documents. Level 2 adds stylesheet support to DOM Level 1 and provides mechanisms for applications to manipulate style information programmatically. Level 2 also supports XML namespaces and defines an event model. Level 3 builds on Level 2 to specify Document Type Definitions (DTDs) and schemas. Mozilla supports DOM Level 2 and parts of DOM Level 3, while IE 6 supports DOM Level 1.Both provide additional areas of support outside of the DOM.

The DOM Level 1 Core includes the following interfaces:

- `Document`
- `DocumentFragment`
- `DocumentType`
- `EntityReference`
- `Element`
- `Attr`
- `ProcessingInstruction`
- `Comment`
- `Text`
- `CDATASection`
- `Entity`
- `Notation`
- `Node`
- `NodeList`
- `NamedNodeMap`

You can find out more about these interfaces at `http://www.w3.org/TR/1998/REC-DOM-Level-1-19981001/level-one-core.html#ID-1590626201`. Each of these interfaces has other member interfaces. You can think of these interfaces as objects within the JavaScript code that you'll write.

In the next section, I'll work through the following interfaces:

- Document
- Node
- NodeList
- NamedNodeMap

Understanding the Document Interface

The Document interface represents the entire document and is the parent for the rest of the object model. The document object hosts the Document interface. This interface is the root of the document tree.

The interface also contains a number of factory methods that create new objects. You can use these methods to add new elements, text nodes, and attributes using code. Factory methods create content within the Document interface.

The Document interface includes the following members:

- documentElement
- createElement()
- createTextNode()
- createAttribute()
- getElementsByTagName()

You can find out more about the Document interface at http://www.w3.org/TR/1998/REC-DOM-Level-1-19981001/level-one-core.html#i-Document.

documentElement

The documentElement attribute provides direct access to the root element of the XML document:

```
var docRoot = oDocument.documentElement;
```

In an XHTML document, this is the <html> element. The documentElement references an Element object, which is a type of Node object.

createElement(tagName)

The createElement()method is a factory method used to create an Element. It requires a tag name. The method creates an element with the specified tag name:

```
oDocument.createElement("eName");
```

When this method creates a new element, it doesn't have any position in the document tree. You still need to add it, usually using the appendChild() method:

```
oDocument.documentElement.appendChild(oDocument.createElement("DVD"));
```

The preceding code creates a <DVD> element and appends it to the root element of the document. Note that the code refers to the document oDocument when it uses the createElement() method.

There are a number of similar create methods, including createTextNode() and createAttribute().

createTextNode(value)

The createTextNode()factory method creates text nodes containing the passed-in value. This is equivalent to adding text inside an element or attribute, because a text node is the child. You can use the method in the following way:

```
oElement = oDocument.createElement("title");
oElement.appendChild(oDocument.createTextNode("Splash");
oDocument.documentElement.appendChild(oElement);
```

This code creates the following element:

```
<title>Splash</title>
```

createAttribute(attrName)

You can use the createAttribute() factory method to create Attr (attribute) objects. The value of an attribute appears within a text node inside that attribute, so you can use a similar approach to the one used to add a value to an Element. You can also use the value property to set the value of the text node in the attribute:

```
oAttribute = oDocument.createAttribute("ID");
oAttribute.value = "4";
oNamedNodeMap = oDocument.documentElement.attributes;
namedNodeMap.setNamedItem(oAttribute);
```

This code sample creates an attribute with the value 4. The code then inserts it into the attributes collection of an element by calling the setNamedItem() method on a NamedNodeMap. You'll learn a little more about the NamedNodeMap shortly.

These other factory methods create the remaining node types:

- createCDATASection()
- createComment()
- createDocumentFragment()
- createEntityReference()
- createProcessingInstruction()

You can find these methods detailed in the DOM Level 1 reference at http://www.w3.org/TR/1998/REC-DOM-Level-1-19981001/level-one-core.html.

getElementsByTagName(tagName)

The `getElementsByTagName()` method returns all matching elements as a `NodeList`. The method requires a string, which is the name of tags to identify. Note that the method doesn't return attributes with the specified name:

```
oDocument.getElementsByTagName('title');
```

This line returns a collection of elements called `<title>`. Note that in XML, the tag name is case-sensitive.

Understanding the Node Interface

The `Node` interface represents a single node in the document tree. It is the fundamental building block in the DOM representation of XML data.

Different types of `Node` objects share some common methods and properties. All nodes have the `childNodes` property, even if they don't have children. The `Node` object includes many different properties and methods. I'll cover the following:

- `attributes`
- `parentNode`
- `childNodes`
- `firstChild`
- `lastChild`
- `previousSibling`
- `nextSibling`
- `nodeName`
- `nodeType`
- `hasChildNodes()`
- `appendChild()`
- `cloneNode()`
- `insertBefore()`
- `removeChild()`
- `replaceChild()`

Figure 8-2 shows the relationship between the most important `Node` properties.

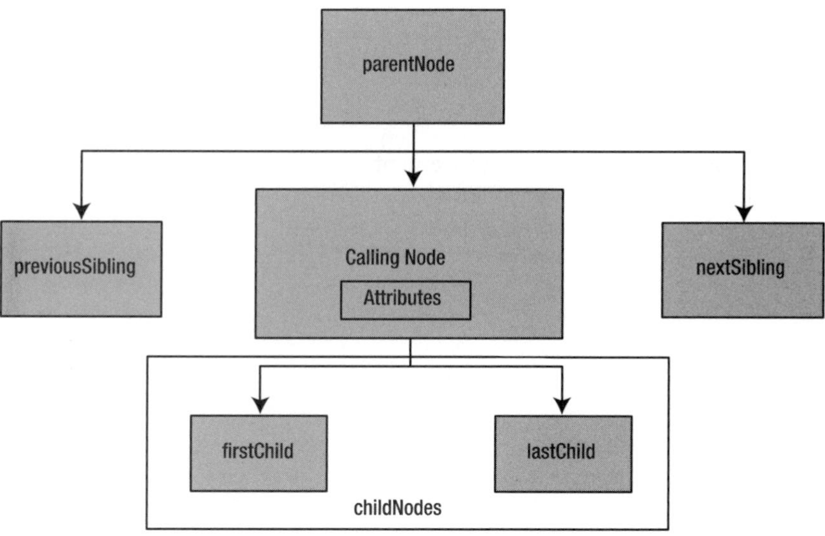

Figure 8-2. *Important Node properties and relationships*

attributes

The `attributes` property returns a `NamedNodeMap` that contains all of the attributes of an `Element` node:

```
oDocument.documentElement.firstChild.attributes;
```

The previous line returns the attributes of the first child of the `documentElement` of an XML document. This property returns `null` for other types of nodes.

parentNode

The `parentNode` property returns the parent of the current node:

```
oDocument.getElementsByTagName('title')[0].parentNode;
```

The preceding line finds the parent of the first `<title>` element.

Most nodes have parents, except for the `Document` itself, a `DocumentFragment`, and an `Attr` (attribute) node. Nodes without parents return `null`. Notice that an attribute is not the child of the node in which it resides. The node just created doesn't get a parent until you insert it into the document tree.

childNodes

The `childNodes` property returns a `NodeList` that contains all of this node's child nodes:

```
oDocument.getElementsByTagName('title')[0].childNodes
```

This line finds the children of the first `<title>` element.
The following element types can contain children:

- `Attr`
- `Document`
- `DocumentFragment`
- `Element`
- `Entity`
- `EntityReference`

Note that the text inside an attribute is a child node of that attribute.

firstChild and lastChild

These two properties return the first and last nodes in the `childNodes` collection for the current node. You can use `firstChild` with `nextSibling` to iterate through the `childNodes` `NodeList`:

```
for(var n = oDocument.documentElement.firstChild; n != null; n = n.nextSibling){
  alert(n.nodeName);
}
```

previousSibling and nextSibling

These properties return the previous and next nodes that share the same parent as the current node:

```
oDocument.documentElement.lastChild.previousSibling;
```

This line returns the second-to-last child of the `documentElement`.

nodeName

The `nodeName` property returns the name of the current node. It is a read-only property. In the following node

```
<DVD id="4"/>
```

the `nodeName` property returns `DVD`.

nodeValue

The nodeValue property returns the content of the current node. For an element, this is null, but for an attribute or text node, the property returns the attribute value or text content:

```
oDocument.getElementsByTagName('title')[0].firstChild.nodeValue;
```

The preceding example finds the text within the first <title> element. Note that the text is actually within the first child of this element.

nodeType

The nodeType property provides information about the type of the current node. Table 8-1 overleaf shows information about each node type.

hasChildNodes()

This method returns a Boolean value indicating whether the current node has child nodes:

```
oDocument.getElementsByTagName('title')[0].hasChildNodes;
```

The method is useful when recursively navigating through the document tree.

appendChild(newChild)

The appendChild()method adds a new child to the end of the list of child nodes for the current node. You need to create the node before it is appended:

```
oNewNode = oDocument.createElement("title");
oDocument.documentElement.appendChild(oNewNode);
```

cloneNode(deep)

This method clones an existing node, making a copy of all attributes and their values. It has a Boolean parameter deep that determines whether to clone recursively:

```
oDocument.getElementsByTagName('title')[0].cloneNode(true);
```

The method returns the cloned node without a parent. You still need to append it within the document.

insertBefore(newChild, refChild)

The insertBefore()method inserts a new child node before an existing child node:

```
var oOldNode = oDocument.getElementsByTagName('title')[0];
oNewNode = oDocument.createElement("title");
oDocument.documentElement.insertBefore(oNewNode, oOldNode);
```

If refChild is null, the child is inserted as the last child. If the new node already exists in the tree, the method removes it from the original position.

Table 8-1. *Node Types*

Constant	Value	Description	Example	Child Of	Child Node Types	Notes
NODE_ELEMENT	1	An Element node	**<DVD/>**	Document, DocumentFragment, EntityReference, Element	Element, Text, Comment, ProcessingInstruction, CDATA, EntityReference	Represents an element within a document. nodeValue returns null.
ATTRIBUTE_NODE	2	An Attr (attribute) node	<DVD **id="1"**/>	None	Text, EntityReference	Represents an attribute. Has both a nodeValue and nodeName. Attributes are not children of the elements they describe, so parentNode, previousSibling, and nextSibling return null.
TEXT_NODE	3	A Text node	<title>**Splash**</title>	Attribute, DocumentFragment, Element, EntityReference	None	Represents the text content of an Element or Attr.
CDATA_SECTION_NODE	4	A CDATASection node	**<![CDATA[<strong>Strong text</strong>]]>**	DocumentFragment, EntityReference, Element	None	Escapes blocks of text containing markup.
ENTITY_REFERENCE_NODE	5	An EntityReference node	**&**	Attribute, DocumentFragment, Element, EntityReference	Element, ProcessingInstruction, Comment, Text, CDATASection, EntityReference	Indicates where the content of an entity should be included.

Continued

Table 8-1. *Continued*

Constant	Value	Description	Example	Child Of	Child Node Types	Notes
ENTITY_NODE	6	An Entity node	**<!ENTITY ...>**	DocumentType	Anything representing the expanded entity (Text, EntityReference)	The entity within a document.
PROCESSING_ INSTRUCTION_NODE	7	A ProcessingInstruction node	**<?xml-stylesheet type="text/xsl" href="a.xslt"?>**	Document, DocumentFragment, Element, EntityReference	None	
COMMENT_NODE	8	A Comment node	**<!--This is a comment-->**	Document, DocumentFragment, Element, EntityReference	None	
DOCUMENT_NODE	9	A Document node		None	Element (maximum of one), ProcessingInstruction, Comment, DocumentType	Represents the root of the document tree.
DOCUMENT_ TYPE_NODE	10	A DocumentType node	**<!DOCTYPE>**	Document	Notation, Entity	Provides an interface to the list of entities that are defined for the document.
DOCUMENT_ FRAGMENT_NODE	11	A DocumentFragment node		None	Element, ProcessingInstruction, Comment, Text, CDATASection, EntityReference	Associates a node or subtree with a document without being contained in the document.
NOTATION_NODE	12	A Notation node	**<!NOTATION ...>**	DocumentType	None	Represents a notation declared in the DTD.

removeChild(oldChild)

The removeChild() method removes the old child parameter from the current node's childNodes collection. It returns a reference to the removed node:

```
oCurrentNode = oDocument.documentElement;
oOldNode = oCurrentNode.removeNode(oCurrentNode.lastChild);
```

This code removes the last child of the current node.

replaceChild(newChild, oldChild)

This method replaces a child of the current node with a new child. It returns the replaced child. The following code creates a new node and uses replaceChild to replace the last child element:

```
oNewNode = oDocument.createElement("title");
oRootNode = oDocument.documentElement;
oOldNode = oRootNode.replaceChild(oRootNode.lastChild,oNewNode);
```

Understanding the NodeList Interface

The NodeList interface deals with an ordered collection of nodes. Each node in the collection is indexed, starting with 0. You saw earlier that the childNodes property returns a NodeList. You need to be familiar with the length property and item() method.

length

The length read-only property indicates the length of the NodeList.

item (index)

The item() method takes an index argument and returns the node at that index from the NodeList:

```
for (var i=0; i < oDocument.documentElement.childNodes.length; i++) {
  alert(oDocument.documentElement.childNodes.item(i).nodeName);
}
```

This code block uses a for loop to iterate through the childNodes collection of documentElement. It pops up an alert box showing the nodeName of each node in that collection.

You can also use shorthand syntax to access the list of nodes:

```
alert(oDocument.documentElement.childNodes[i].nodeName);
```

Understanding the NamedNodeMap Interface

The NamedNodeMap interface reflects a collection of nodes that you can access by name or index. The collection is not held in any particular order, and you can use the interface to add and delete nodes from within the collection.

NamedNodeMap is most commonly associated with the collection of attributes within a node. A NamedNodeMap is also returned for collections of entities and notations. You can't use NamedNodeMap with the childNodes collection.

NamedNodeMap has the same members as NodeList. In addition, it has the following members:

- getNamedItem()
- removeNamedItem()
- setNamedItem()

getNamedItem(name)

The getNamedItem() method retrieves a node by name using the name string parameter:

```
oDocument.documentElement.lastChild.attributes.getNamedItem("id");
```

removeNamedItem(name)

This method uses the name argument to determine which node to remove. The method returns the removed node:

```
oDocument.documentElement.lastChild.attributes.removeNamedItem("id");
```

setNamedItem(newNode)

The setNamedItem()method takes a Node as a parameter and adds it to the end of the NamedNodeMap:

```
var idAttr = oDocument.documentElement.firstChild.attributes.removeNamedItem("id");
oDocument.documentElement.lastChild.attributes.setNamedItem("id");
```

The preceding code removes the id attribute from the first child and adds it to the attributes collection of the last child element. You must ensure that the node you're inserting is of the correct type.

■ **Caution** NodeList and NamedNodeMap are live objects. This means that changes made to the list are reflected immediately. Therefore, you should be very careful when making changes to the list while inside a loop iterating through that list.

For example, if your loop has an exit condition that relies on reaching the end of the list, adding new nodes will increase the length of the list. You'll never exit the loop because you'll never get to the end of the list. The length updates continually as the NodeList grows.

Examining Extra Functionality in MSXML

Microsoft XML Parser (MSXML) 3, which ships with IE 6, provides some additional properties and methods that you can use with the DOM interfaces discussed previously. You'll see examples of some of these additions later, as well as how to create similar functionality in Mozilla.

Let's start by looking at extensions to the `Document` and `Node` interfaces:

Additions to the MSXML Document Interface

MSXML includes the following additions to the `Document` interface:

- `load()`
- `loadXML()`
- `readystate`
- `onreadystatechange()`

load(url)

The `load()` method loads XML content from the `URL` argument:

```
oDocument.load("dvd.xml");
```

The loading happens asynchronously, which means that the method returns immediately and the parser loads the XML. As the content loads, it changes the value of the `readystate` property and raises the `onreadystatechange` event.

The `load()` method is also part of the DOM Level 3 Save and Load module. Mozilla supports both this method and the `async` property from DOM Level 3.

loadXML(xml)

The `loadXML()`method loads XML string data into a `Document` object. When called, it loads asynchronously. The method is useful for using string manipulation to create XML in JavaScript. The following line loads some simple XML content into a `DOM Document` from a string:

```
oDocument.loadXML('<?xml version="1.0"?><library/>');
```

readyState

The `readyState` property is read-only and indicates the state of a loaded document. Table 8-2 summarizes the values for this property and their meaning.

Table 8-2. *readyState Property Values*

Constant	Value	Description
LOADING	1	Indicates that the loading process has started and the data is being retrieved.
LOADED	2	Indicates that the data has been retrieved and that the parser is parsing the XML document. At this point, the object model is not available.
INTERACTIVE	3	Indicates that some data has been parsed, and the object model is available on a partial data set. At this stage, the object model is read-only.
COMPLETED	4	Indicates that the loading process is finished. Doesn't indicate whether the document was successfully loaded.

onreadystatechange

This event fires every time the `readyState` property changes. You can use it to assign a handler for the event:

```
oDocument.onreadystatechange = processXML;
```

MSXML Node Interface Additions

MSXML includes the following additions to the `Node` interface:

- `xml`
- `nextNode()`
- `selectNodes()`
- `selectSingleNode()`
- `transformNode()`
- `transformNodeToObject()`

xml

The `xml` property is a read-only property that returns the serialized contents of a node. In other words, it converts the raw XML into a text format:

```
var strXML = oDocument.xml;
```

nextNode()

This method returns the next node in the node collection:

```
oDocument.getElementsByTagName('title')[0].nextNode();
```

The method will return the first node if no previous node has been selected. You can use the `reset()` method to return to the starting point.

selectNodes(patternString)

The `selectNodes()` method creates a `NodeList` of all nodes that match the specified XPath expression:

```
oDocument.selectNodes("DVD/title");
```

If no match is made, the method returns `null`.

selectSingleNode(patternString)

This method works in the same way as the `selectNodes()` method, except that it selects the first matching node:

```
oDocument.selectSingleNode("DVD/title");
```

transformNode(styleSheet)

The `transformNode()` method performs XSLT transformations on the current node and returns the result of the transformation as a string. This method takes a `stylesheet` argument, which is a `DOM Document` containing the XSLT stylesheet:

```
oDocument.transformNode(oXSLT);
```

transformNodeToObject(styleSheet, OutputDOM)

The `transformNodeToObject()` method is very similar to the previous method. The difference is that it fills the `OutputDOM` document with the result of the transformation:

```
oDocument.transformNodeToObject(oXSLT, oTransDocument);
```

XMLHttpRequest ActiveX Object

MSXML also includes an ActiveX object called the `XMLHttpRequest` object. This object provides a mechanism for content to be loaded from the server and is at the heart of an approach called Asynchronous JavaScript and XML (Ajax). Mozilla and Opera offer native support for this object, and you'll find out more about both the object and Ajax in Chapter 9.

Browser Support for the W3C DOM

Now that you've seen the interfaces available in the W3C DOM, let's examine how you can use JavaScript to work with XML data stored in a DOM Document on the client. You can create a DOM Document using an ActiveX object in IE.

You can use the following code to create an instance of the MSXML parser:

```
var oDocument =new ActiveXObject("Microsoft.XMLDOM");
```

Bear in mind that different versions of IE use different ActiveX objects. Mozilla creates a document using this line:

```
var oDocument =document.implementation.createDocument("", "", null);
```

These lines are just the start of the differences between the two major browsers.

Given that the DOM implementations in MSXML and Mozilla aren't completely compatible, you need to be careful to develop client-side code suitable for both browsers. You could write code that branches to accommodate each different approach. However, a better solution is to use a wrapper to allow both browsers to exhibit the same JavaScript behaviors. This book includes the xDOM wrapper, written specifically for this chapter.

Using the xDOM Wrapper

xDOM is a JavaScript library that makes it easier to write cross-browser JavaScript code for client-side manipulation of the DOM. You can find the library in the files xDOM.js and browserDetect.js with your resources.

The wrapper needs to use a common method to create documents. It also needs to be able to provide a mechanism for Mozilla to deal with MSXML-specific methods and properties and the application of XSLT stylesheets on the client side.

Table 8-3 summarizes the functions available in xDOM.js.

Table 8-3. *Functions Available in xDOM.js*

Function Name	Description	Public
xDOM.createDOMDocument()	This is the main function in xDOM. It creates a DOM Document.	Yes
_Moz_Document_loadXML(strXML)	An implementation of loadXML() for the Mozilla DOM. You add a method to the Mozilla DOM to call this function.	No
_Moz_Document_load(strURL)	Replaces the Mozilla DOM load() method. You override the existing method on the Mozilla DOM to call this function.	No
document_onload()	A local event handler used to call fireOnLoad() when the document is loaded in Mozilla.	No
fireOnLoad(oDOMDocument)	Checks for a parser error and changes the readyState if required.	No

Continued

Table 8-3. *Continued*

Function Name	Description	Public
`_Moz_node_transformNode (oStylesheetDOM)`	An implementation of the `transformNode()` method for the Mozilla DOM. You add a method to the Mozilla DOM to call this function.	No
`_Moz_node_transformNodeToObject (oStylesheetDOM,oOutputDOM)`	An implementation of the `transformNodeToObject()` method for the Mozilla DOM. You add a method to the Mozilla DOM to call this function.	No
`_Moz_Node_getXML()`	An implementation of the `xml` property for the Mozilla DOM. You add a property to the Mozilla DOM to call this function.	No
`updateReadyState(oDOMDocument, intReadyState)`	Changes the `readyState` property to the DOM and calls the added `onreadystatechange()` event handler if there is one.	No

■ **Note** The xDOM library uses the "Ultimate JavaScript Client Sniffer Version 3.03" created by Netscape Communications. This is included in the code directory (as `browserDetect.js`), along with `xDOM.js`. You need to include both of these JavaScript files to use xDOM.

xDOM Walkthrough

This section walks through the `xDOM.js` file and describes the code therein. If you aren't interested in the details of the xDOM wrapper, please feel free to skip ahead to the "Using JavaScript with the DOM" section.

The code starts by declaring global variables that library functions will use. The most important line follows:

```
var arrMSXMLProgIDs = ["MSXML4.DOMDocument", "MSXML3.DOMDocument", ➥
  "MSXML2.DOMDocument", "MSXML.DOMDocument", "Microsoft.XmlDom"];
```

This line creates an array of strings that contain the ProgIDs for creating different versions of the MSXML `DOMDocument` object.

The next step initializes the wrapper. The method used depends on the browser version.

Initializing in IE

For IE, the initialization code determines which version of MSXML a user has available on his or her machine by iterating through the `arrMSXMLProgIDs` array:

```
if (is_ie) {
  var blnSuccess = false;
  for (var i=0; i < arrMSXMLProgIDs.length && !blnSuccess; i++) {
    try {
      var oDOMDocument = new ActiveXObject(arrMSXMLProgIDs[i]);
      strMSXMLProgID = arrMSXMLProgIDs[i];
      blnSuccess = true;
    } catch (oException) {
    }
  }
  if (!blnSuccess  ){
     blnFailed = true;
     strFailedReason = "No suitable MSXML library on machine.";
  }
}
```

Initializing in Mozilla

The Mozilla initialization code is slightly more complicated. It makes use of JavaScript prototypes, which allow you to add methods or properties to objects at run-time. In this case, the code adds methods that mimic the way that MSXML behaves:

```
Document.prototype.__load__ = Document.prototype.load;
Document.prototype.load = _Moz_Document_load;
```

Note that `_Moz_Document_load` is a function that the wrapper declares later.

The preceding code replaces the default `load` method in the Mozilla DOM with a new method, `_Moz_Document_load()`. It keeps a reference to the default method by first assigning it to a prototype of a different name, `Document.prototype.__load__`. The wrapper must do this because it still needs to call the original method from within the new method. From an object-oriented perspective, this is like overriding a method and then calling that method on the super/parent class within the new method implementation.The wrapper also declares a new event handler called `onreadystatechange`:

```
Document.prototype.onreadystatechange = null;
```

The wrapper initially assigns the event handler a `null` value. Later, the wrapper attaches code that runs when the event fires.

The final prototype declares a `Getter` method to get the value of a variable:

```
Node.prototype.__defineGetter__("xml", _Moz_Node_getXML);
```

A `Getter` method appears as a property to the end user, but is implemented as a function. You don't need a corresponding `Setter` method because the `xml` property is read-only.

xDOM.createDocument() Method

The `xDOM.createDOMDocument()` is the only method that you call with JavaScript—in other words, it's a public method. This method determines which browser is being used and creates a `DOMDocument` object using the appropriate method for that browser.

The method also attaches an event handler to the Mozilla `load` event so that you can raise this event in the same way as in IE:

```
xDOM.createDOMDocument = function() {
  var oOutDOMDocument = null;
  if (is_gecko) {
    oOutDOMDocument = document.implementation.createDocument("", "", null);
    oOutDOMDocument.addEventListener("load", document_onload, false);
  } else if (is_ie) {
    oOutDOMDocument = new ActiveXObject(strMSXMLProgID);
    oOutDOMDocument.preserveWhite space = true;
  }
  return oOutDOMDocument;
}
```

Private xDOM Library Functions

The remainder of the library file contains the implementations of the prototypes that you declared earlier. You can look through these to see how Mozilla natively handles some of its more advanced XML features.

The first method implemented is the Mozilla version of the MSXML `loadXML()` method. This uses the `XMLParser` object that is included in the Mozilla `XMLExtras` library. This library ships with all Mozilla installations:

```
function _Moz_Document_loadXML(strXML) {
  updateReadyState(this, 1);
  var oDOMParser = new DOMParser();
  var oDOM = oDOMParser.parseFromString(strXML, "text/xml");
    while (this.hasChildNodes())
      this.removeChild(this.lastChild);
    for (var i=0; i < oDOM.childNodes.length; i++) {
      var oImportNode = this.importNode(oDOM.childNodes[i], true);
      this.appendChild(oImportNode);
    }
  fireOnLoad(this);
}
```

This method copies the nodes from the newly parsed DOM.

The Moz_Document_load() overrides the Mozilla load() method. This allows the wrapper to include code for firing the MSXML equivalent events:

```
function _Moz_Document_load(strURL) {
  this.parseError = 0;
  updateReadyState(this, 1);
  try {
    this.__load__(strURL);
  } catch (oException) {
    this.parseError = -1;
  }
  updateReadyState(this, 4);
}
```

The updateReadyState() function is a helper method that sets the readyState property and fires the necessary events:

```
function updateReadyState(oDOMDocument, intReadyState) {
  oDOMDocument.readyState = intReadyState;
  if (oDOMDocument.onreadystatechange != null && ➥
      typeof DOMDocument.onreadystatechange == "function")
    oDOMDocument.onreadystatechange();
}
```

The two functions that deal with XSLT are very similar. The only difference is that one of them serializes the result to a string, and the other returns the processed result as a DOMDocument object. Both functions allow the Mozilla XSLTProcessor object to mimic XSLT transformations in MSXML:

```
function _Moz_node_transformNode(oStylesheetDOM) {
  var oXSLTProcessor = new XSLTProcessor();
  var oOutDOM = document.implementation.createDocument("","",null);
  oXSLTProcessor.transformDocument( this, oStylesheetDOM, oOutDOM, null);
  return (new XMLSerializer()).serializeToString(oOutDOM);
}
```

Some of the extra functions in the wrapper aren't included in this brief walkthrough. You can look through the code if you want to explore further.

WHY EXTEND MOZILLA?

Given that the Mozilla implementation is more standards-compliant, you may be wondering why you're using a JavaScript wrapper that makes Mozilla work like IE. MSXML is a separate library from IE, so it's not possible to extend it with JavaScript prototypes. IE was the first browser to support XML and is still the most popular web browser. By replicating the behavior of IE, you can use the large number of IE-specific examples available on the Internet in your own projects more easily.

xDOM Caveats

There are some important points to note when using xDOM. The first is that the wrapper cannot check the version of XSLT supported by the `DOM Document` you create. If you need to support much older browsers, you may need to load a different XSLT document based on the version of MSXML installed. You can do this by looking at the value of the `strMSXMLProgID` variable initialized when the xDOM library loads.

The xDOM library doesn't allow the free threaded version of the MSXML `DOM Document` to be created. The free threaded version is most important when running code on the server side. The object uses a different threading model to interact with the operating system, and this is important when there are multiple requests for the `DOMDocument` at the same time, as in server-side applications.

The xDOM wrapper doesn't provide a complete solution to the differences between MSXML and Mozilla. You still need to test your application rigorously in all browser versions that you're targeting. I checked xDOM with IE 6.0 and Mozilla 1.0.

So far, you've seen some of the theory behind scripting the DOM. Now it's time to look at how to apply this code in some examples.

Using JavaScript with the DOM

Let's use JavaScript to work with the xDOM library in a test web page. You can find this page, `test.htm`, with your resources. It contains code that shows you how to perform many simple XML tasks using the xDOM library.

Figure 8-3 shows `test.htm` displayed in Firefox 1.5.

The test page contains a series of `<div>` elements that illustrate the following:

- Creating a `DOM Document`
- Loading XML from a URL
- Checking that XML is well-formed and has loaded successfully
- Applying an XSLT transformation
- Iterating through the DOM
- Iterating through elements
- Iterating through attributes
- Loading XML from a string variable
- Adding nodes to the document
- Removing and replacing nodes in the document

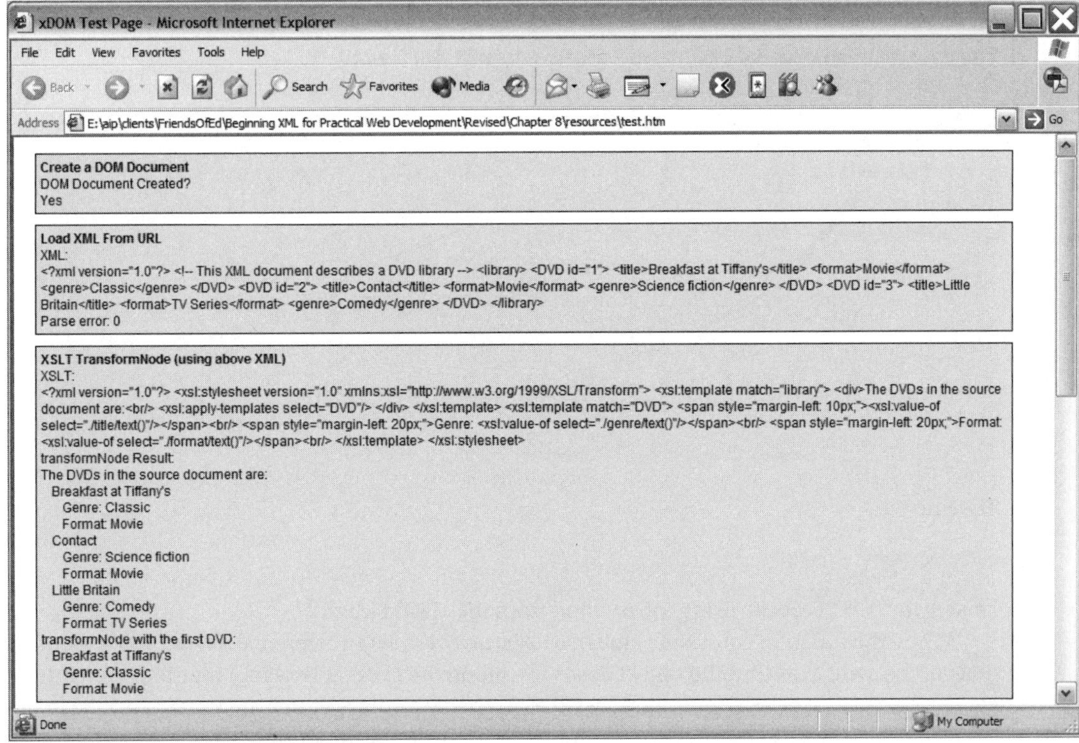

Figure 8-3. *The test.htm page displayed in IE*

■ **Note** The test page uses the xDOM library to write cross-browser code. Apart from creating the `DOM Document`, all of this code in `test.htm` works correctly in IE. However, in Mozilla, the xDOM library manages several of the function calls. You can find out how to carry out the tasks natively in Mozilla by looking at the "Initializing in Mozilla" section earlier in this chapter.

Let's work through each section of the `test.htm` page so you can see how the code works. The resource file contains several comments that aren't included in the code that follows.

Creating DOM Document Objects and Loading XML

To start, you need to create a `DOMDocument` object so that you can work with the external XML text. When `test.htm` loads, it calls the `runTest()` function. The `runTest()` function starts by calling the `doCreateDOMDocument()` function.

Creating a DOMDocument Object

The doCreateDOMDocument() function creates the DOM Document:

```
function doCreateDOMDocument() {
  var oDOMDocument;
  var oElement;
  try {
    oDOMDocument = xDOM.createDOMDocument();
    oElement = oDOMDocument.createElement("DVD");
    document.getElementById("divCreateDOMDocument").innerHTML = "Yes";
  }
  catch (oException) {
    document.getElementById("divCreateDOMDocument").innerHTML = "No";
  }
}
```

The line

```
oDOMDocument = xDOM.createDOMDocument();
```

creates the DOM Document using the method from the xDOM library.

When the function runs, the value of oDOMDocument is set to reference a new DOMDocument object. The code tests that the object exists by calling the createElement() method. Using the getElementById() method with the innerHTML property displays either the value Yes or No in the web page. Figure 8-4 shows the resulting output from this function.

Create a DOM Document
DOM Document Created?
Yes

Figure 8-4. *The DOM Document is created successfully.*

Loading XML from a URL

Once the DOMDocument object exists, you can use it to load DVD.xml by calling the doLoadXMLFromURL() function:

```
function doLoadXMLFromURL() {
  oXMLFromURL = xDOM.createDOMDocument();
  oXMLFromURL.onreadystatechange = onLoad_LoadXMLFromURL;
  oXMLFromURL.load("DVD.xml");
}
```

The function creates a DOM Document, sets the onreadystatechange handler, and loads the XML document. Figure 8-5 shows how the JavaScript processing occurs.

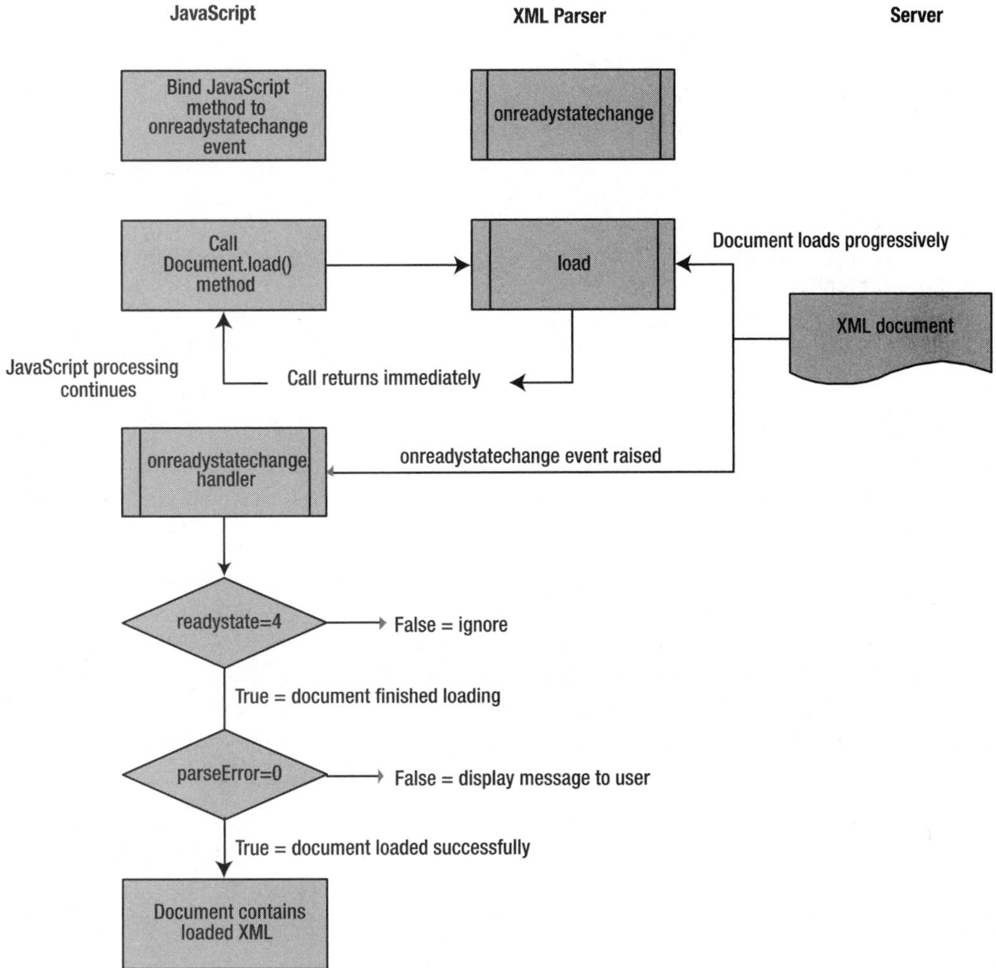

Figure 8-5. *Asynchronous loading of XML document*

The doLoadXMLFromURL() function sets the onreadystatechange handler to the onLoad_LoadXMLFromURL() function. It then calls the load() method to load the file DVD.xml asynchronously. The load() function call returns immediately while the XML document loads in the background. This allows other JavaScript processing to continue while the XML document loads.

The `onreadystatechange` event handler function determines when the XML file has finished loading so it can be processed:

```
function onLoad_LoadXMLFromURL() {
  if (oXMLFromURL.readyState == 4) {
    var strXML = doReplace(oXMLFromURL.xml);
    document.getElementById("divXMLFromURLRawXML").innerHTML = strXML;
    document.getElementById("divXMLFromURLParseError").innerHTML = ➥
      oXMLFromURL.parseError;
    oXSLT=xDOM.createDOMDocument();
    oXSLT.onreadystatechange = onLoad_XSLtdOM;
    oXSLT.load("test.xslt");
    doIterationExample();
    doGetAttributesExample();
  }
}
```

The `onreadystatechange` event is raised each time the `readyState` property changes. The document is completely loaded when `readyState` is equal to `4`. When the document loads, the code shows the XML content in the `divXMLFromURLRawXML` element. It also displays the value of `parseError`.

■Note When the browser loads an invalid XML file, the loading process completes successfully and `readyState` equals `4`. Because of this, the code needs to include an additional check of the `parseError` property of the `DOM Document` to see the outcome of the load. The `test.htm` document includes an example of loading a document that is not well formed.

Figure 8-6 shows the appearance of the test page when the XML file loads successfully.

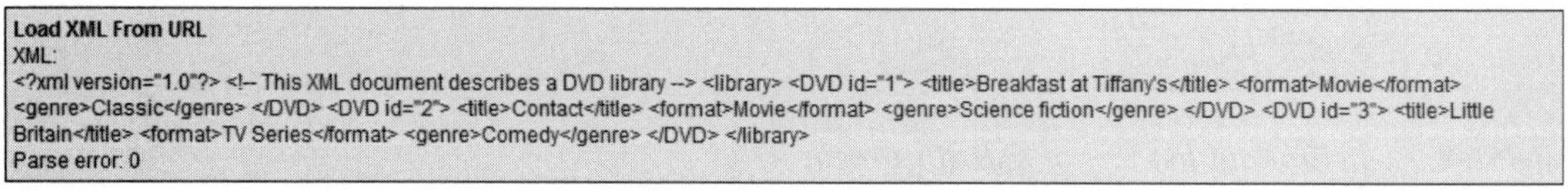

Load XML From URL
XML:
<?xml version="1.0"?> <!-- This XML document describes a DVD library --> <library> <DVD id="1"> <title>Breakfast at Tiffany's</title> <format>Movie</format> <genre>Classic</genre> </DVD> <DVD id="2"> <title>Contact</title> <format>Movie</format> <genre>Science fiction</genre> </DVD> <DVD id="3"> <title>Little Britain</title> <format>TV Series</format> <genre>Comedy</genre> </DVD> </library>
Parse error: 0

Figure 8-6. *Displaying the loaded XML document*

Figure 8-7 shows what happens in Firefox when you load a document that isn't well formed.

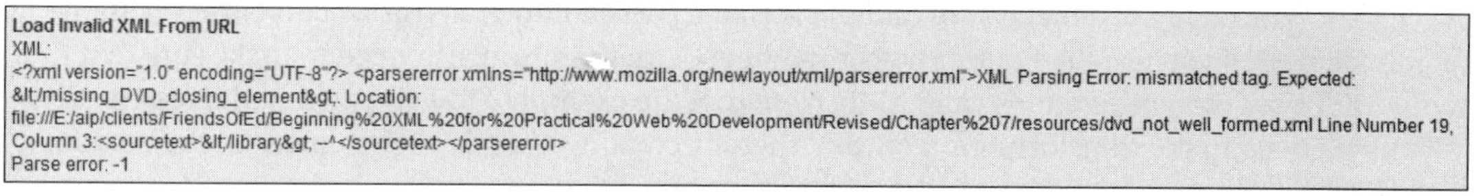

```
Load Invalid XML From URL
XML:
<?xml version="1.0" encoding="UTF-8"?> <parsererror xmlns="http://www.mozilla.org/newlayout/xml/parsererror.xml">XML Parsing Error: mismatched tag. Expected:
&lt;/missing_DVD_closing_element&gt;. Location:
file:///E:/aip/clients/FriendsOfEd/Beginning%20XML%20for%20Practical%20Web%20Development/Revised/Chapter%207/resources/dvd_not_well_formed.xml Line Number 19,
Column 3:<sourcetext>&lt;/library&gt; --^</sourcetext></parsererror>
Parse error: -1
```

Figure 8-7. *An XML document that isn't well formed displayed in Firefox*

IE acts a little differently from Mozilla, as it won't display any XML content from a document that is not well formed. In IE, you wouldn't see any XML output at all.

XSLT Manipulation

In Chapters 6 and 7, I worked through XSLT transformation techniques that allowed you to generate XHTML content from XML. MSXML includes the methods `transformNode()` and `transformNodeToObject()`. As these methods aren't available in Mozilla, they've been added to the xDOM library. The `transformNode()` method returns the transformed content as a string, whereas `transformNodeToObject()` populates the `DOMDocument` object passed as a parameter.

The MSXML `transformNodeToObject()` method can send the results to an `IStream`, which can stream information into Microsoft components. However, because this is Microsoft-specific, xDOM doesn't support the feature.

Applying Stylesheets to Documents

The test page contains an example that uses `transformNode()` and `transformNodeToObject()`:

```
function onLoad_XSLtdOM() {
  if (oXSLT.readyState == 4) {
    var strOutput;
    var oOutput = xDOM.createDOMDocument();
    strOutput = oXMLFromURL.transformNode(oXSLT);
    oXMLFromURL.transformNodeToObject(oXSLT,oOutput);
    document.getElementById("divTransformNodeXSLT").innerHTML = ➥
      doReplace(oXSLT.xml);
    document.getElementById("divTransformNodeResult").innerHTML = strOutput;
    strOutput = oXMLFromURL.getElementsByTagName("DVD")[1].transformNode(oXSLT);
    document.getElementById("divTransformNodePartOfTree").innerHTML = strOutput;
  }
}
```

The code must make sure that the variable passed into `transformNodeToObject()` is initialized. If you use the `transformNodeToObject()` method, you also need to make sure that the XSLT stylesheet generates valid XML. Note that the example XSLT file, `test.xslt`, uses a `<div>` tag to wrap the transformation output, thereby creating a single root element in the transformation.

Figure 8-8 shows the XSLT document and the transformation resulting from `test.xslt`. It also shows a single node transformation.

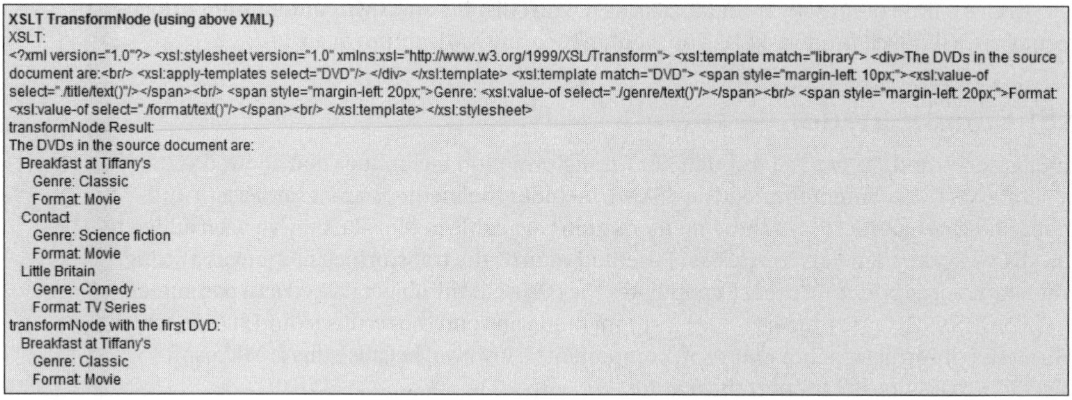

```
XSLT TransformNode (using above XML)
XSLT:
<?xml version="1.0"?> <xsl:stylesheet version="1.0" xmlns:xsl="http://www.w3.org/1999/XSL/Transform"> <xsl:template match="library"> <div>The DVDs in the source document are:<br/> <xsl:apply-templates select="DVD"/> </div> </xsl:template> <xsl:template match="DVD"> <span style="margin-left: 10px;"><xsl:value-of select="./title/text()"/></span><br/> <span style="margin-left: 20px;">Genre: <xsl:value-of select="./genre/text()"/></span><br/> <span style="margin-left: 20px;">Format: <xsl:value-of select="./format/text()"/></span><br/> </xsl:template> </xsl:stylesheet>
transformNode Result:
The DVDs in the source document are:
  Breakfast at Tiffany's
    Genre: Classic
    Format: Movie
  Contact
    Genre: Science fiction
    Format: Movie
  Little Britain
    Genre: Comedy
    Format: TV Series
transformNode with the first DVD:
  Breakfast at Tiffany's
    Genre: Classic
    Format: Movie
```

Figure 8-8. *The test.xslt document and transformation*

MSXML Template and Processor Objects

MSXML includes two objects that you can use together to compile an XSLT stylesheet for several transformations. This functionality increases efficiency and is most suited to a server-side environment, where the same stylesheet runs with each page request. I won't cover these objects here, but you can find out more about the `IXSLProcessor` and `IXSLTemplate` interfaces in the MSXML documentation.

DOM Manipulation and XSLT Combined

Because the `transformNode()` methods are declared on the `Node` interface, you can combine the power of DOM iteration with XSLT by selecting a single node for transformation:

```
strOutput = oXMLFromURL.getElementsByTagName("DVD")[0].transformNode(oXSLT);
document.getElementById("divTransformNodePartOfTree").innerHTML = strOutput;
```

In this case, I've matched the first DVD element using `getElementsByTagName("DVD")[0]`. The template matches this element:

```
<DVD id="1">
  <title>Breakfast at Tiffany's</title>
  <format>Movie</format>
  <genre>Classic</genre>
</DVD>
```

Only this node is transformed.

Extracting Raw XML

One task for developers is retrieving XML content from the DOM as a string. The W3C DOM specification is silent on how to achieve this task. MSXML provides the read-only `xml` property on the `Node` interface. This returns the raw XML from a specific node as text.

xDOM provides a Mozilla version of this property. There is no specific example in the `test.htm` document, but the property is used in many of the other examples.

■ **Note** The `xml` property is provided within the `Node` interface. Because the `Document` interface inherits the `Node` interface, you can access this property on the `DOM Document` object:

The following code sets the variable `strXML` to equal the serialized contents of the `oXMLFromString` `DOM Document`:

```
var strXML = oXMLFromString.xml;
```

Manipulating the DOM

The `test.htm` document also includes examples of traversing, adding to, and editing the contents of a `DOM Document`.

Traversing a DOM Document

You can iterate through the `DOM Document` in much the same way as with other data structures such as arrays. The following example shows one way to loop through the collection of child nodes of an XML document:

```
function doIterationExample() {
  var strOutput;
  strOutput = "";
  for (var node=oXMLFromURL.documentElement.firstChild; node != null; ➥
    node = node.nextSibling) {
    strOutput = strOutput + node.nodeName + "<br/>";
  }
  document.getElementById("divIterateDOM").innerHTML = strOutput;
}
```

Figure 8-9 shows the output from this function.

Iterate Through DOM
nodeName for each node in documentElement.childNodes:
#text
DVD
#text
DVD
#text
DVD
#text

Figure 8-9. *Iterating through the nodes in an XML document*

Note that the output shows text nodes as well as the <DVD> elements. However, if you look at the XML document, you can see that no text nodes exist between these elements. Text nodes appear because the parser treats white space as text when it falls within an element. In this case, the tabs and carriage returns inside the <library> element are treated as text nodes.

This is not the default behavior for the MSXML parser. You need to tell the parser explicitly to preserve the white space nodes when you create the ActiveX object in the xDOM library:

```
oOutDOMDocument.preserveWhiteSpace = true;
```

If you don't do this, you'll see different behavior in MSXML and Mozilla, and you won't be able to write cross-browser code.

Accessing Element Values

You can access the text within elements by using the `nodeValue` property. Remember that text within an element is a child of that element. This example shows how to retrieve the title for each DVD:

```
function doGetElementsExample(){
  var strOutput;
  strOutput = "";
  var oNodeList;
  oNodeList = oXMLFromURL.documentElement.getElementsByTagName("title");
  for (var i=0; i < oNodeList.length; i++) {
    strOutput = strOutput + oNodeList[i].firstChild.nodeValue + "<br/>";
  }
  document.getElementById("divElementDOM").innerHTML = strOutput;
}
```

Figure 8-10 shows the output from this function.

Get title elements
nodeValue for each title element in the document:
Breakfast at Tiffany's
Contact
Little Britain

Figure 8-10. *Displaying the text within the elements in an XML document*

Accessing Attributes

You can access attributes within an element by name:

```
oCityNode.attributes.getNamedItem("id").firstChild.nodeValue;
```

This line retrieves the text from the first child of the id attribute node. The first child contains the text content of the attribute. The doGetAttributesExample() function shows an example:

```
function doGetAttributesExample() {
  var strOutput;
  strOutput = "";
  var oNodeList;
  oNodeList = oXMLFromURL.documentElement.getElementsByTagName("DVD");
  for (var i=0; i < oNodeList.length; i++) {
    strOutput = strOutput + oNodeList[i].attributes.getNamedItem("id").value ➥
      + "<br/>";
  }
  document.getElementById("divAttributeDOM").innerHTML = strOutput;
}
```

Figure 8-11 shows how this appears.

Get id attributes
id attribute from each DVD element in the document:
1
2
3

Figure 8-11. *Iterating through the DVD id attributes*

Loading XML from a String

Instead of loading an external XML document, you can load XML data from a string variable. As with the load() method, loading from a string variable uses an asynchronous loading process. The only difference is the following line, which uses the loadXML() method instead of load():

```
oXMLFromString.loadXML('<?xml version="1.0"?><library><DVD id="4">➥
<title>The Constant Gardener</title></DVD></library>');
```

Tip Because the XML string contains an attribute, I've used two types of quotation marks in the JavaScript line. The `loadXML()` method encloses the string XML content in a single quotation mark, while the attributes use double quotes. You could also use the quotation marks in the opposite way or escape the quotes within the `loadXML` string variable.

Adding Elements and Attributes

The `test.htm` document includes an example that adds a node to the `DOM Document`. The relevant portion of the `onLoad_LoadXMLFromString()` function follows:

```
var oElement= oXMLFromString.createElement("DVD");
var oAttribute = oXMLFromString.createAttribute("id");
oAttribute.value = "5";
oElement.attributes.setNamedItem(oAttribute);
oElement.appendChild(oXMLFromString.createTextNode("Pride and Prejudice"));
oXMLFromString.documentElement.appendChild(oElement);
```

The code starts by creating a new `<DVD>` element using `createElement()`:

```
var oElement= oXMLFromString.createElement("DVD");
```

Then the code creates an attribute called `id` with the `createAttribute()` method and sets its value to `5`:

```
var oAttribute = oXMLFromString.createAttribute("id");
oAttribute.value = "5";
```

Next, the code uses `appendChild()` to add a new text node to the element:

```
oElement.appendChild(oXMLFromString.createTextNode("Pride and Prejudice"));
```

Finally, the code appends the new element to the `documentElement` of the `DOM Document`:

```
oXMLFromString.documentElement.appendChild(oElement);
```

Figure 8-12 shows the XML string after adding the new element.

Manipulate XML String
Adding new DVD:
<?xml version="1.0"?> <library><DVD id="4"><title>The Constant Gardener</title></DVD><DVD id="5">Pride and Prejudice</DVD></library>
Removing and replacing node:
<?xml version="1.0"?> <library><DVD id="5">Pride and Prejudice</DVD></library>

Figure 8-12. *Manipulating an XML string*

Deleting and Replacing Elements

You'll notice that Figure 8-12 also includes an example of removing and replacing a node. The following code removes the new element and replaces an existing element:

```
var oRootNode = oXMLFromString.documentElement
var oOldNode = oRootNode.removeChild(oRootNode.lastChild);
oRootNode.replaceChild(oOldNode,oRootNode.firstChild);
```

These lines use the `removeChild()` method to remove the last `<DVD>` child element, which is stored in the `oOldNode` variable. The code then uses the `replaceChild()` method to replace the first `<DVD>` child element. Figure 8-12 shows the effect of the replacement.

You've seen the main aspects of using xDOM with an XML document. In the next section, let's look at an example that puts these techniques into practice.

Putting It into Practice

In this section of the chapter, I'll use the xDOM library with a real-world example. You can find the example in the `contacts` folder with the other resources for this chapter.

This example provides a simple demonstration of some of the concepts discussed in this chapter. The example relies heavily on XSLT transformations. Because both IE and Mozilla work with stylesheets in a similar way, this approach provides a cross-browser solution. It's too difficult to generate complex XHTML using DOM manipulation alone. Note that the example won't work in Opera 8.5 and below.

Understanding the Application

The application loads an XML document containing information about contacts. It uses two XSLT stylesheets to display the content in a web browser dynamically. The first stylesheet creates a link for each contact. Clicking the link displays the contact details. Figure 8-13 shows the process that I'll work through in the application.

In brief, the user requests an XHTML page that includes JavaScript. The page loads an XML document and two stylesheets. One stylesheet transforms the XML document to display a set of links. When the user clicks a link, the second stylesheet provides the details of the selected option. I'll use parameters so that the same transformation displays details for each of the links.

A key point of this application is that the user can display different contact details without the browser having to return to the server. All the relevant data is downloaded once, when the page first loads.

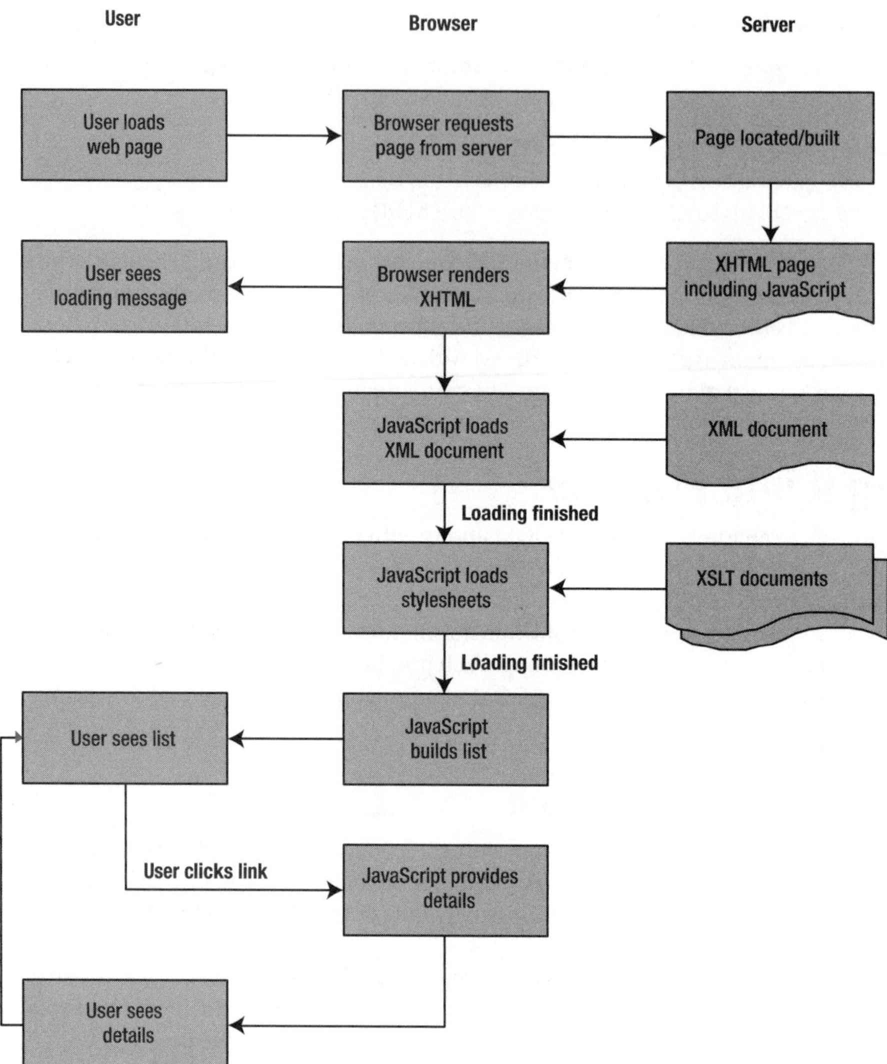

Figure 8-13. *The contacts application-processing example*

Examining the Code

Let's work through the application. First, the structure of the source XML document, `contacts.xml`, follows:

```
<?xml version="1.0" encoding="UTF-8"?>
<!-- This XML document describes a contacts list -->
<contacts>
  <person id="9407001" type="supplier">
    <first_name>John</first_name>
    <last_name>Smith</last_name>
```

```
    <company>Banana Computing</company>
    <address1>1 Fiction Street</address1>
    <address2>Imaginary Town</address2>
    <country>Strangeland</country>
    <postal_code>ABC 567</postal_code>
    <last_contact>2005-05-27</last_contact>
  </person>
</contacts>
```

Obviously, this XML file contains multiple contacts, but for brevity, I've only shown the structure of the first `<person>` element. The information is contained in a physical XML file, but it could just as easily be generated from a database with server-side code or consumed from a web service.

The `contacts_demo.htm` page starts the process with an `onload` handler in the `<body>` tag:

```
<body onLoad="runInit();">
```

The `runInit()` function checks that the xDOM library initializes successfully and calls the `doLoadXMLFromURL()` function to load the document:

```
function runInit() {
  if (blnFailed){
    alert(strFailedReason);
  }
  else {
    doLoadXMLFromURL();
  }
}
```

The `doLoadXMLFromURL()` function is similar to the code you saw in the previous section:

```
function doLoadXMLFromURL() {
  oXMLFromURL = xDOM.createDOMDocument();
  oXMLFromURL.onreadystatechange = onLoad_LoadXMLFromURL;
  oXMLFromURL.load("contacts.xml");
}
```

The function creates a `DOM Document` and sets the `onreadystatechange` handler. It then loads the `contacts.xml` file. The handler function follows:

```
function onLoad_LoadXMLFromURL() {
  if (oXMLFromURL.readyState == 4) {
    oXSLT=xDOM.createDOMDocument();
    oXSLT.onreadystatechange = onLoad_XSLTDOM;
    oXSLT.load("select.xslt");
    oXSLTDisplay=xDOM.createDOMDocument();
    oXSLTDisplay.onreadystatechange = onLoad_XSLTDOM;
    oXSLTDisplay.load("display.xslt");
  }
}
```

This function checks that readyState is equal to 4—in other words, that the XML document loads successfully. The function then loads two stylesheets, select.xslt and display.xslt, setting the onreadystatechange handlers.

The select.xslt stylesheet creates the list of links for the application:

```
<?xml version="1.0" encoding="UTF-8"?>
<xsl:stylesheet version="1.0" xmlns:xsl="http://www.w3.org/1999/XSL/Transform">
  <xsl:template match="/">
  <div>
    <xsl:apply-templates select="/contacts/person"/>
  </div>
  </xsl:template>
  <xsl:template match="person">
  <a href="javascript:showPerson({@id});">
    <xsl:value-of select="first_name"/><xsl:text> </xsl:text>
    <xsl:value-of select="last_name"/>
   </a><br/>
  </xsl:template>
</xsl:stylesheet>
```

This stylesheet creates the links in a <div> element. Each link calls the showPerson() function, passing the value of the id attribute.

The second XSLT stylesheet, display.xslt, is also very simple. However, it contains a parameter that will be used to select which person to display:

```
<?xml version="1.0" encoding="UTF-8"?>
<xsl:stylesheet version="1.0" xmlns:xsl="http://www.w3.org/1999/XSL/Transform">
<xsl:param name="personid">0</xsl:param>
  <xsl:template match="/">
    <xsl:if test="$personid > 0">
      <div>
        <xsl:apply-templates select="/contacts/person[@id=$personid]"/>
      </div>
    </xsl:if>
  </xsl:template>
  <xsl:template match="person">
    Name:
    <xsl:value-of select="first_name"/><xsl:text> </xsl:text>
    <xsl:value-of select="last_name"/><br/>
    Type: <xsl:value-of select="@type"/><br/>
    Company: <xsl:value-of select="company"/><br/>
    Address: <xsl:value-of select="address1"/>, <xsl:value-of select="address2"/>,
    <xsl:value-of select="country"/> <xsl:text> </xsl:text>
    <xsl:value-of select="postal_code"/>
  </xsl:template>
</xsl:stylesheet>
```

The value of the personid parameter is set dynamically when users choose which person's details they want to view.

After the first stylesheet loads, the transformation creates the list of links in the XHTML page. It achieves this with the onLoad_XSLTDOM() function:

```
function onLoad_XSLTDOM() {
  var strOutput;
  var oOutput = xDOM.createDOMDocument();
  if (oXSLT.readyState == 4) {
    strOutput = oXMLFromURL.transformNode(oXSLT);
    document.getElementById("contacts").innerhtml = strOutput;
  }
}
```

Note that the transformation is a nondestructive process. After the transformation is completed, the application still has the original DOMDocument object containing the XML content. Because the XML data remains intact, the code can use it again when the user clicks another link. You have effectively cached the XML data in a client-side variable.

Clicking a contact link calls the showPerson() function, passing the relevant id. The id is then passed into the display.xslt stylesheet:

```
function showPerson(intPersonID){
  var strOutput;
  for (var i=0; i < oXSLTDisplay.documentElement.childNodes.length; i++) {
    if (oXSLTDisplay.documentElement.childNodes[i].nodeName == "xsl:param") {
      oXSLTDisplay.documentElement.childNodes[i].childNodes[0].nodeValue = ➥
      intPersonID;
    }
  }
  strOutput = oXMLFromURL.transformNode(oXSLTDisplay);
  document.getElementById("displayDetails").innerHTML = strOutput;
}
```

The following lines set the value of the parameter in the XSLT stylesheet:

```
if (oXSLTDisplay.documentElement.childNodes[i].nodeName == "xsl:param") {
  oXSLTDisplay.documentElement.childNodes[i].childNodes[0].nodeValue = intPersonID;
}
```

■Note Mozilla doesn't offer specific support for parameters, so you can use the DOM to manipulate the values of the <xsl:param> element before applying the transformation.

The code applies the updated transformation and displays the result using the `innerHTML` property of the `displayDetails` `<div>` element. Figure 8-14 shows the XHTML document with a selected contact. I purposely haven't included CSS styling within this document.

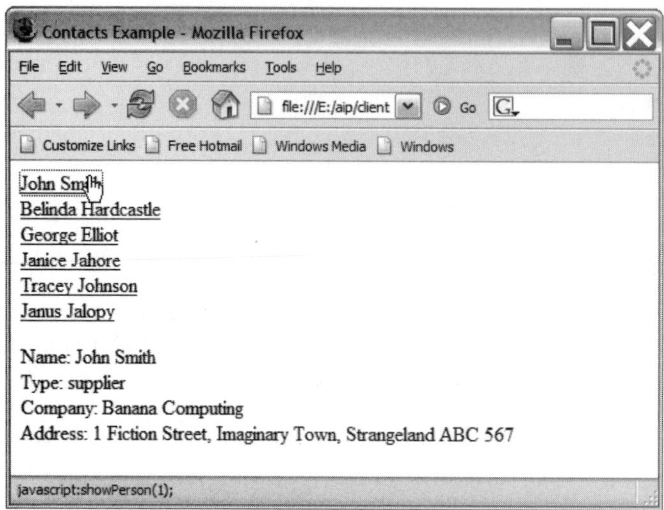

Figure 8-14. *The real-estate example*

You need to be careful when using this approach with large amounts of data. Because the application downloads all data to the client when the page first loads, you may actually download information that is never used. The user may look only for the first contact and not click the other links.

Because the list of contacts is very small, the issue doesn't arise in this example. However, if you're working with a large organization, the user could wait for a long time while the entire XML document loads. In the next section, I'll show you how to deal with situations where there is too much data to download all at once.

Dealing with Large XML Documents

If you have a large amount of XML content, it may not be efficient to download it all at once. Instead, you can send XML overview data to the client and load other data when it is requested. You may already use this approach with server-side languages.

Let's see how this works in a modified version of the contacts example. You can find this example in the `contacts_async` folder with the other resources. The example uses similar stylesheets and draws the same content. This time, each contact is stored in a single XML document, and the correct document is loaded when required.

Figure 8-15 shows the process. It is identical until the user clicks a link in the list.

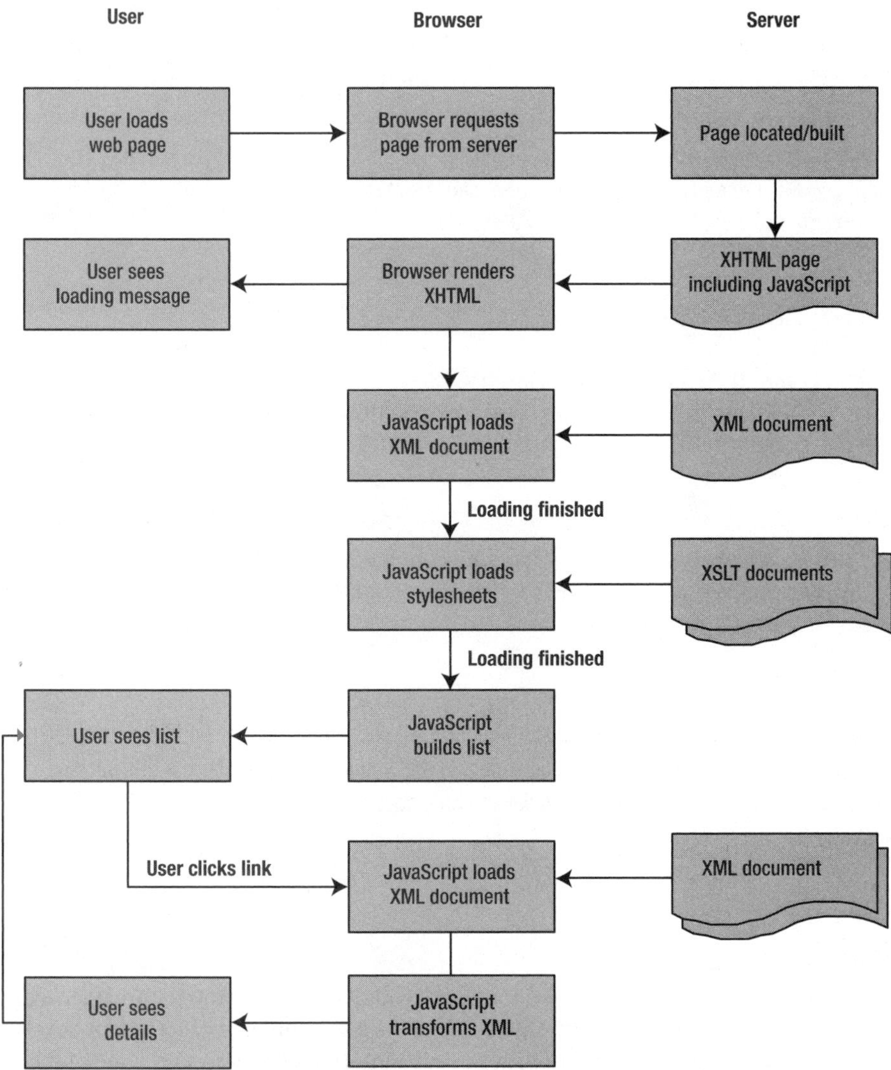

Figure 8-15. *The contacts application-processing example modified to deal with large amounts of XML*

The main difference between the two versions of this application is in the `showProperty()` function. In addition, the new version doesn't need the XSLT parameter because the `showProperty()` function loads the correct XML document from the server.

The transformation now appears in the onLoad event handler for the XML DOM, which contains the detailed data. You can load the requested data asynchronously without refreshing the page:

```
function showPerson(intPersonID){
  oXMLDetailFromURL = xDOM.createDOMDocument();
  oXMLDetailFromURL.onreadystatechange = onLoad_XMLDetail;
  oXMLDetailFromURL.load("contacts" + intPersonID + ".xml");
}

function onLoad_XMLDetail() {
  var strOutput;
  if (oXMLDetailFromURL.readyState == 4) {
    strOutput = oXMLDetailFromURL.transformNode(oXSLTDisplay);
    document.getElementById("displayDetails").innerHTML = strOutput;
  }
}
```

Testing the new application will show the same contact details as before. As with the previous example, the application caches the user interface, and the role of the server is limited to providing data for the application.

■Note This application uses a separate XML document for each contact. In the real world, it's more likely that the XML would be generated using server-side code and that you'd load a page from a URL such as `contactsXML.aspx?id=1` rather than generating several XML documents.

Summary

This chapter showed you how to use JavaScript to work with XML in the browser. You learned about the W3C XML DOM and worked through some of the key interfaces. The chapter covered the most important methods and properties of each interface. You also saw some of the MSXML-specific methods and properties.

Within the chapter, I used the xDOM wrapper to generate cross-browser JavaScript capable of working with both IE 6 and Mozilla. I used the wrapper in a real-life example to load contacts into a web page. The application used XML, XSLT, and JavaScript to include dynamic content without the need for refreshing the interface. I also extended the example to see how it might work with large amounts of XML content.

As you saw, Mozilla and IE don't offer universal support for XML and XSLT. Opera 8.5 has no XSLT support, although this is likely to change with the release of Opera 9. The use of a DOM wrapper allows you to create a cross-browser application that takes advantage of client-side XML and XSLT. In the next chapter, I'll extend this concept further and look at the Ajax approach to working with XML in the browser.

CHAPTER 9

■ ■ ■

The Ajax Approach to Browser Scripting

In the previous chapter, I showed you how to use the World Wide Web Consortium (W3C) Document Object Model (DOM) to work with XML documents in a web browser. I loaded an XML document and manipulated the structure using JavaScript and the DOM. I used the xDOM library to create cross-browser JavaScript appropriate for both Internet Explorer (IE) and Mozilla.

In this chapter, I'll show you another way to work with XML on the client—using Asynchronous JavaScript and XML (Ajax). Jesse James Garrett of Adaptive Path coined the term *Ajax*, which describes an approach to creating XML applications using XML with XHTML, Cascading Style Sheets (CSS), the DOM, JavaScript, Extensible Stylesheet Language Transformations (XSLT), and the `XMLHttpRequest` object. It is part of the Web 2.0 approach, where the request-response nature of the web is largely invisible to the end user. In Web 2.0, the user experience is much more like working with a desktop application.

Building applications with Ajax provides all of the advantages of working client-side with XML content. The application caches the interface and makes asynchronous requests for data. The user isn't waiting for pages to load from the server.

Another advantage of Ajax is that you can use the approach with most major browsers. The `XMLHttpRequest` object is available on IE for Windows, Safari on Macintosh, Mozilla, and Opera 8 and above. If you use Ajax with XSLT on the client, it's available to IE, Mozilla, and Safari. However, this is likely to change when Opera releases version 9 of its browser software.

Ajax is a mainstream approach, and you can see examples of it working in Google Suggest (`http://www.google.com/webhp?complete=1&hl=en`), Google Maps (`http://maps.google.com/`), and Flickr (`http://www.flickr.com/`).

I'll work through some examples so you can understand how to use Ajax. You can download the resources used in this chapter from the Source Code area of the Apress web site (`http://www.apress.com`).

Understanding Ajax

It's important to understand that Ajax is not a technology; rather, it's an approach to using other technologies in web applications. Ajax uses a combination of the following technologies:

- XML
- `XMLHttpRequest` object
- JavaScript
- XSLT
- XHTML
- CSS

Explaining the Role of Ajax Components

Each component within the Ajax approach has a specific role. Table 9-1 summarizes the role of each component.

Table 9-1. *The Role of the Technologies Used Within Ajax Applications*

Component	Role
XML	Stores data. You can also use other text-based data formats.
`XMLHttpRequest` object	Allows data to be retrieved asynchronously from the server.
JavaScript	Allows loading and manipulation of data.
XSLT	Transforms XML content into XHTML. May also add sorting and filtering to data.
XHTML	Generates the interface for the application.
CSS	Provides styling for the XHTML content within the application.

Figure 9-1 shows the interaction between these technologies. Start reading from the right-hand side of the diagram.

Ajax redefines the role of the server and client compared with traditional web applications. As you can see from Figure 9-1, some of the logic and the interface management move to the client. The changes can be summarized as follows:

- The role of the server changes from interface building to provision of data.
- The client loads the interface only once, when the application first starts.
- Client-side functionality persists even as content changes.
- The application can easily respond to a range of client-side events. For example, in Google Suggest, suggestions occur in response to a user entering keystrokes.
- Changes appear to occur instantaneously, providing responsiveness similar to that found in desktop applications.

You'll be familiar with most of the technologies involved within Ajax from earlier chapters in the book. The new concept here is the `XMLHttpRequest` object.

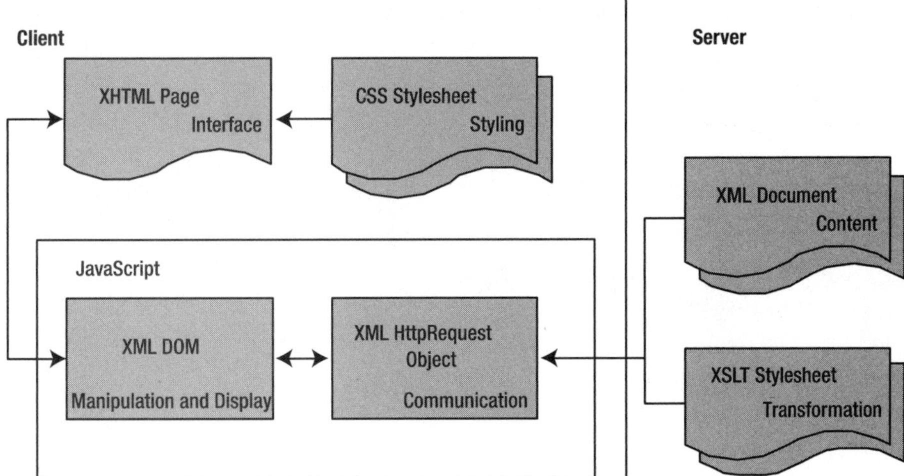

Figure 9-1. *The interaction of technologies used in Ajax*

Understanding the XMLHttpRequest Object

In the previous chapter, you saw some of the IE extensions to the XML DOM. The `XMLHttpRequest` object is another of those extensions. Luckily, other browsers, in addition to IE, support this object, although in a slightly different way. The `XMLHttpRequest` object is at the heart of the Ajax approach.

The `XMLHttpRequest` object allows web pages to request information from a server using client-side code. The object isn't limited to working with XML. In fact, it can work with any type of document.

Microsoft first implemented the `XMLHttpRequest` ActiveX object in IE 5 for Windows. Mozilla engineers implemented a native version of this functionality for Mozilla 1.0. Safari introduced the object in version 1.2.

Before I move on to some examples, it's important to understand the `XMLHttpRequest` object.

Working with the XMLHttpRequest Object

In IE, you can create the `XMLHttpRequest` ActiveX object using

```
xmlhttp = new ActiveXObject("Msxml2.XMLHTTP");
```

or

```
xmlhttp = new ActiveXObject("Microsoft.XMLHTTP");
```

depending on your MSXML version.

In Mozilla, Opera, and Safari, you need to use

```
xmlhttp = new XMLHttpRequest();
```

You can create a cross-browser version using the following code:

```
if (window.XMLHttpRequest) {
  // we have Mozilla, Opera or Safari
  xmlhttp = new XMLHttpRequest();
}
else if (window.ActiveXObject) {
  // we have IE
  try {
    xmlhttp = new ActiveXObject("Msxml2.XMLHTTP");
  } catch(e) {
    try {
      xmlhttp = new ActiveXObject("Microsoft.XMLHTTP");
    } catch(e) {
      xmlhttp = false;
    }
  }
}
```

■Tip In the Mozilla code, you may need to include a call to the `overrideMimeType()` method if you want to ensure that non-XML data is returned correctly:

```
xmlhttp.overrideMimeType('text/xml');
```

Once you create the object, you should set the `onreadystatechange` event handler before making the request. I'll cover that shortly.

When you have the object and event handler, you can make the request and optionally send data to the server:

```
xmlhttp.open("GET", "dvd.xml", true);
xmlhttp.send(null);
```

You use the `open()` method to make the request. This might be a `GET`, `POST`, or `HEAD` request, and you set the request type in the first parameter as a string value. The second parameter is the page you're requesting. In the preceding code, I've referred to a static page, but you could also request content from a server-side page.

The last parameter sets the request to be asynchronous. You should set this value to `true` or asynchronous. If you create a synchronous call, you run the risk of a server problem stopping the execution of the remainder of the page.

SECURITY

For security reasons, you can't use Ajax to request content from a domain outside of the current one. This is referred to as the Ajax sandbox. If you're running the web page on `http://www.apress.com`, you can only request from that domain.

As you're working within a sandbox, you can make server-side requests without a domain name. For example, I could request XML from a server-side file using this code:

```
xmlhttp.open("GET", "/bin/getXML.aspx", true);
```

You could also include a parameter in this method call:

```
xmlhttp.open("GET", "/bin/getXML.aspx?contactName=" + escape(cName), true);
```

The `send()` method can pass information with a request. You'll probably use it to `POST` information that filters the returned content. You send data in variable pairs:

```
xmlhttp.send('var1=val1&var2=val2&var3=val3');
```

Make sure you use `escape` to encode the values that you send. You can also use the value `null` to indicate that you're not sending variables.

If you're posting data, you need to change the MIME type of the request:

```
xmlhttp.setRequestHeader('Content-Type', 'application/x-www-form-urlencoded');
```

You can use an `onreadystatechange` event handler as I did in the previous chapter to check the value of the `readyState` property. The event handler can determine one of the following five values:

- `0`: The request is not yet initialized. This occurs before calling the `open()` method.
- `1`: The request is initialized but not sent. This occurs before calling the `send()` method.
- `2`: The request has been sent and is being processed.
- `3`: The request is being processed but hasn't been finished.
- `4`: The response is completed. You can access the information with the `responseText` or `responseXML` property.

The ready states don't work exactly the same way on each type of web browser. If you track the value of the `readyState` property, you might see different results in Safari compared with IE.

Each time the `readyState` property changes, the application calls the event handler function. The code responds when the `readyState` equals `4`, indicating that the response is complete:

```
xmlhttp.onreadystatechange = onLoad_LoadXMLHttp;
function onLoad_LoadXMLHtpp() {
  if (xmlhttp.readyState == 4) {
....//do some processing
  }
}
```

Once the readyState value reaches 4, the code needs to check that the content loaded correctly by retrieving the status code of the response. If the status code is 200, the content loaded correctly; other values indicate an error:

```
if (http_request.status == 200) {
  //success loading
  var textResponse = xmlhttp.responseText;
  var xmlDocumentResponse = xmlhttp.responseXML;
}
else {
  //error loading
}
```

You may want to add more sophisticated error handling to report error messages to the user. You can access the status error message using the statusText property.

As shown in the previous example, you can capture the response as text using the responseText property, or as an XML document object using responseXML. If you choose the latter, you can then use the DOM to traverse the document tree.

The best way to understand how the object works is to work through some simple examples. In this section, I'll work through the following examples:

- Making a HEAD request
- Displaying the contents of an XML document in the browser
- Using XMLHttpRequest with the DOM

You need to run all of these examples through a web server such as Internet Information Services (IIS). If you use IIS, you'll need to save the files to a folder within C:\InetPub\wwwroot. You can then access the examples through http://localhost/foldername. I'll start by using Ajax to make a HEAD request.

Making a HEAD Request

You can make a HEAD request to extract all or some of the headers of a document. You might use this to find the last modified date of a document or to find out its content type. You can find this example saved as getHeaders.htm. Figure 9-2 shows the headers for the document dvd.xml.

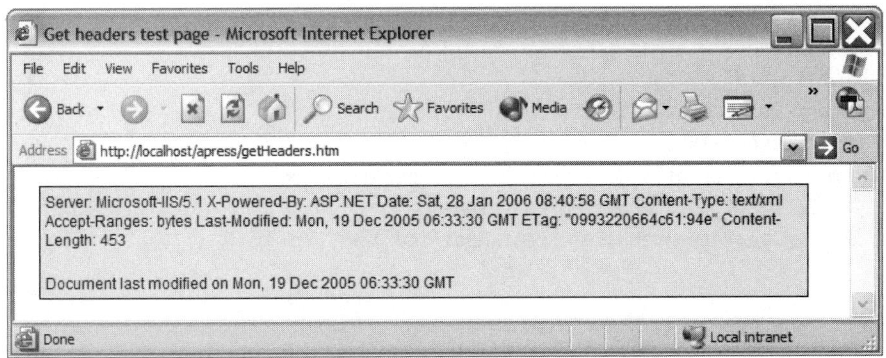

Figure 9-2. *Displaying the headers for dvd.xml using the XMLHttpRequest object*

The code to achieve this follows:

```
<html>
  <head>
  <title>Get headers test page</title>
  <style>
    //some style declarations left out for brevity
  </style>
    <script type="text/javascript">
    var xmlhttp=null;
    var toLoad = "dvd.xml";
    function getHeaders() {
      if (window.XMLHttpRequest){
        xmlhttp=new XMLHttpRequest();
      }
      else if (window.ActiveXObject){
        try {
          xmlhttp = new ActiveXObject("Msxml2.XMLHTTP");
        } catch(e) {
          try {
            xmlhttp = new ActiveXObject("Microsoft.XMLHTTP");
          } catch(e) {
            xmlhttp = false;
          }
        }
      }
      if (xmlhttp){
        xmlhttp.onreadystatechange=onReadyState;
        xmlhttp.open("HEAD", toLoad, true);
        xmlhttp.send(null);
      }
    }
```

```
    function onReadyState() {
      if (xmlhttp.readyState==4) {
        if (xmlhttp.status==200) {
          document.getElementById('divContent').innerHTML=➥
            xmlhttp.getAllResponseHeaders();
          document.getElementById('divContent').innerHTML+= ➥
            "<p>Document last modified on " + ➥
            xmlhttp.getResponseHeader("Last-Modified") + "</p>";
        }
      }
    }
  </script>
</head>
<body onload="getHeaders();">
  <div class="divStyle" id="divContent" >Loading...</div>
</body>
</html>
```

I'll walk through this code.

When the page loads, it calls the `getHeaders()` function, which creates the `XMLHttpRequest` object. After creating the object, the code sets the `onreadystatechange` handler to `onReadyState()` and makes the request . No parameters are sent with the request:

```
xmlhttp.onreadystatechange=onReadyState;
xmlhttp.open("HEAD", toLoad, true);
xmlhttp.send(null);
```

The code tests to see if the content finished loading (`readyState == 4`) and that the process doesn't return an error message (`status == 200`). When the requested page loads successfully, the code displays all response headers as well as the last modified date header:

```
document.getElementById('divContent').innerHTML=xmlhttp.getAllResponseHeaders();
document.getElementById('divContent').innerHTML+="<p>Document last modified on "➥
  + xmlhttp.getResponseHeader("Last-Modified") + "</p>";
```

Let's move on to a slightly more complicated example, where I'll show you how to load and display the contents of an XML document.

Displaying the Contents of an XML Document

In this example, I'll display the contents of an XML document in an XHTML page. Figure 9-3 shows the page `getXML.htm` loaded within a web browser. The page displays the contents of the document `dvd.xml`.

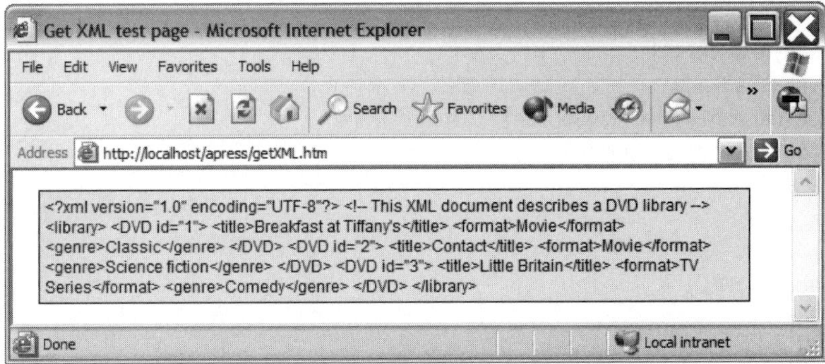
Get XML test page - Microsoft Internet Explorer
File Edit View Favorites Tools Help
Back Search Favorites Media
Address http://localhost/apress/getXML.htm
Go
<?xml version="1.0" encoding="UTF-8"?> <!-- This XML document describes a DVD library --> <library> <DVD id="1"> <title>Breakfast at Tiffany's</title> <format>Movie</format> <genre>Classic</genre> </DVD> <DVD id="2"> <title>Contact</title> <format>Movie</format> <genre>Science fiction</genre> </DVD> <DVD id="3"> <title>Little Britain</title> <format>TV Series</format> <genre>Comedy</genre> </DVD> </library>
Done
Local intranet

Figure 9-3. *Loading the dvd.xml document using the XMLHttpRequest object*

The code within the `getXML.htm` page follows:

```
<html>
  <head>
  <title>Get XML test page</title>
  <style>
    //some style declarations left out for brevity
  </style>
  <script type="text/javascript">
    var xmlhttp=null;
    var toLoad = "dvd.xml";
    function sendRequest(){
      if (window.XMLHttpRequest){
        xmlhttp=new XMLHttpRequest();
      }
      else if (window.ActiveXObject){
        try {
          xmlhttp= new ActiveXObject("Msxml2.XMLHTTP");
          } catch(e) {
          try {
            xmlhttp = new ActiveXObject("Microsoft.XMLHTTP");
            } catch(e) {
            Xmlhttp = false;
          }
        }
      }
      if (xmlhttp){
        xmlhttp.onreadystatechange=onReadyState;
        xmlhttp.open("GET", toLoad, true);
        xmlhttp.send(null);
      }
    }
```

```
    function onReadyState(){
      if (xmlhttp.readyState==4){
        if (xmlhttp.status==200) {
          document.getElementById('divContent').innerHTML➥
            =doReplace(xmlhttp.responseText);
        }
      }
    }
    function doReplace(strXML) {
      var strOut = "";
      var strL = /</g;
      var strG = />/g;
      var strAmp = /&/g;
      strOut = strXML;
      strOut = strOut.replace(strAmp, "&amp;");
      strOut = strOut.replace(strL, "&lt;");
      strOut = strOut.replace(strG, "&gt;");
      return strOut;
    }
  </script>
  </head>
  <body onload="sendRequest()">
    <div class="divStyle" id="divContent" >Loading...</div>
  </body>
</html>
```

I'll walk through the code so you can see what's happening. As with the previous example, it includes an `onload` event handler. This time, when the page loads, it calls the `sendRequest()` function, which uses the same code as in the previous example. As with the last example, no parameters are sent with the request.

The `onreadystatechange` event handler checks the `readyState` property and displays the XML content in the element `divContent`:

```
function onReadyState(){
  if (xmlhttp.readyState==4){
    document.getElementById('divContent').innerHTML➥
      =doReplace(xmlhttp.responseText);
  }
}
```

I've used the `doReplace()` function so that I can display the angle brackets using entities. You saw the result of running this page in a browser in Figure 9-3.

An alternative would be to manipulate the content using JavaScript with DOM methods. You'll see that in the next example.

Using XMLHttpRequest with the DOM

In the previous example, I used the `responseText` property to access the loaded XML as a string. I can also use `responseXML` to return an XML document that I can manipulate with DOM scripting methods. You can see the `responseXML` example in the file `getXMLDocument.htm`. Figure 9-4 shows the example in IE.

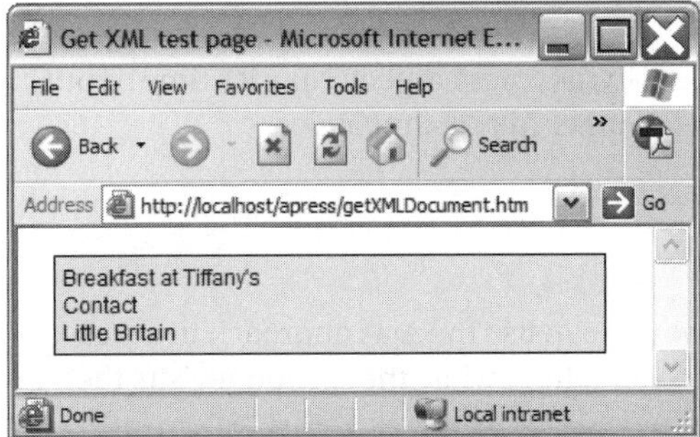

Figure 9-4. *Traversing the dvd.xml document with the XML DOM*

Here, the main difference from the previous example is in the `onReadyState` function. The changed lines appear in bold:

```
function onReadyState(){
  if (xmlhttp.readyState==4){
    if (xmlhttp.status==200) {
      xmlDoc = xmlhttp.responseXML;
      var dvdList = xmlDoc.getElementsByTagName("title");
      for (var i=0; i < dvdList.length; i++) {
        strOutput += dvdList[i].firstChild.nodeValue + "<br/>";
      }
      document.getElementById('divContent').innerHTML=strOutput;
    }
  }
}
```

The code uses the `responseXML` property of the `XMLHttpRequest` object to access the XML content of the request. It can then use the DOM to traverse the tree and extract content. In this example, I select the `<title>` elements:

```
var dvdList = xmlDoc.getElementsByTagName("title");
```

The `dvdList` variable contains an array of `<title>` elements. The code loops through the elements to concatenate the titles and display them within the `<divContent>` element:

```
for (var i=0; i < dvdList.length; i++) {
  strOutput += dvdList[i].firstChild.nodeValue + "<br/>";
}
document.getElementById('divContent').innerHTML=strOutput;
```

■ **Note** If you return XML from a server-side page, you must set the `Content-Type` header to `text/xml`. If you set it to `text/plain` or `text/html`, you'll only be able to use the `responseText` property to access the content. You also need to set the `Cache-Control` header to `no-cache`, or else the browser will cache the response and you won't see updated results.

You've seen some simple examples using the `XMLHttpRequest` object. Now it's time to put together what you've learned in this chapter with the other Ajax technologies.

Putting It Together

In this section, I'll look at two examples to see how you can use the Ajax approach in a web application. The first example applies simple form validation, while the second revisits the contacts example from the previous chapter.

Username Validation with the XMLHttpRequest Object

I'll start with a simple example that shows how to use the `XMLHttpRequest` object to validate a username in a form. When the user enters the username, I'll use the `XMLHttpRequest` object to check an XML file to see if the username is already in use. You can find this example in the `form` folder with your resources.

The file `form.htm` contains the following simple form:

```
<form>
  <p>
    Username: <input type="text" id="txtUserName" size="20" ➥
      onblur="doCheck(this.value);"/>
    <span id="invalidMessage" class="invalid"></span>
  </p>
  <p>
    Password: <input type="text" id="txtPassword" size="20"/>
  </p>
</form>
```

The form checks the username by calling the `doCheck()` function when the user leaves the field—the `onblur` event. It also contains a `<span>` element with the id `invalidMessage` that will display a message if the user enters a duplicate username.

The `doCheck()` function creates the request and loads the file `usernames.xml`:

```
function doCheck(username) {
  if (username.length > 0) {
    document.getElementById("invalidMessage").innerHTML = "";
    if (window.XMLHttpRequest){
      xmlhttp=new XMLHttpRequest();
    }
    else if (window.ActiveXObject){
```

```
      try {
        xmlhttp = new ActiveXObject("Msxml2.XMLHTTP");
      } catch(e) {
        try {
          xmlhttp = new ActiveXObject("Microsoft.XMLHTTP");
        } catch(e) {
        xmlhttp = false;
      }
    }
  }
  if (xmlhttp){
    xmlhttp.onreadystatechange=checkNames;
    xmlhttp.open("GET", "usernames.xml", true);
    xmlhttp.send(null);
    }
  }
}
```

The function first checks to see that the user has entered a username—there's no point in proceeding unless there is a username to check. It then clears any existing messages in the invalidMessage <span> element.

The doCheck() function creates the XMLHttpRequest by testing the browser support and branching to the appropriate code. If the object is created successfully, the code assigns the checkNames() function to the onreadystatechange handler. It then uses a GET request to retrieve the usernames.xml file, sending no parameters with the request.

After the XML document loads, it calls the handler function checkNames():

```
function checkNames() {
  if (xmlhttp.readyState==4){
    if (xmlhttp.status==200) {
      var enteredUserName = document.getElementById("txtUserName").value;
      var usernameList = xmlhttp.responseXML.getElementsByTagName("username");
      for (var i=0; i < usernameList.length; i++) {
        if (enteredUserName == usernameList[i].firstChild.nodeValue) {
          document.getElementById("invalidMessage").innerHTML = "Sorry this ➥
            username is already in use. Choose another."
          break;
        }
      }
    }
  }
}
```

As usual, the code checks for a readyState value of 4 to determine whether the XML document has finished loading. If so, it then checks the status of the document and looks for the entered username:

```
var enteredUserName = document.getElementById("txtUserName").value;
```

The code then retrieves all of the `<username>` nodes from the XML document:

```
var usernameList = xmlhttp.responseXML.getElementsByTagName("username");
```

Finally, the code loops through the collection of nodes and compares the value to what the user entered:

```
for (var i=0; i < usernameList.length; i++) {
  if (enteredUserName == usernameList[i].firstChild.nodeValue) {
    document.getElementById("invalidMessage").innerHTML = "Sorry this ➥
      username is already in use. Choose another."
    break;
  }
 }
```

If the code finds a match, an error message is displayed and the code breaks out of the loop. Figure 9-5 shows the error message that appears if the code detects a duplicate username.

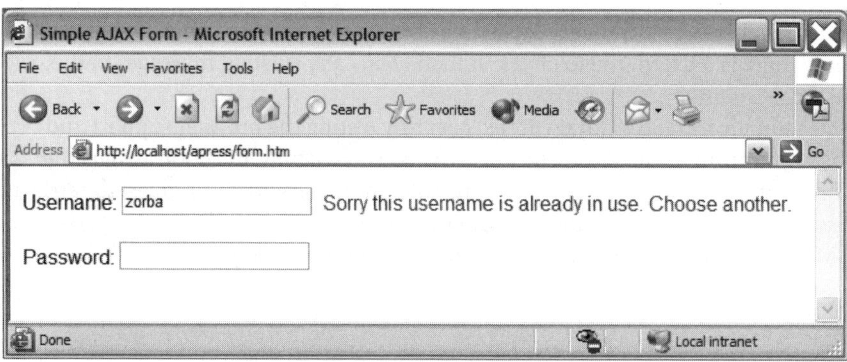

Figure 9-5. *The username validated with the XMLHttpResponse object*

The example is simplistic, but it illustrates how you can use the `XMLHttpRequest` object with DOM scripting to achieve form field validation. Notice that you can work with the `xmlhttp.responseXML` property as a `DOM Document`:

```
xmlhttp.responseXML.getElementsByTagName("username");
```

Of course, this example doesn't take into account different letter cases and doesn't provide full form functionality, so you need to adjust these factors when using the approach in a working application.

■ **Note** In the real world, a complete list of usernames could potentially create a large XML document, making it impractical for use with this approach. An alternative would be to post the username to a server-side file to check for a match.

Let's move on to a more complicated example that includes an XSLT transformation. I'll revisit the contacts address book from Chapter 8.

Contacts Address Book Using an Ajax Approach

If you remember back to Chapter 8, you might recall that I created an asynchronous version of the contacts application. I stored each contact in a separate XML document and created a summary XML document. I then loaded the contact in response to a user click.

In this example, I'll use the same XML files, but this time the `XMLHttpRequest` object will load the content. I'll then apply an XSLT transformation to generate XHTML, which will be styled with a CSS stylesheet. You can find all the files for this example in the `contact` folder. It includes the files described in Table 9-2.

Table 9-2. *Files Found in the Contact Folder*

File	Description	Notes
`contacts_AJAX_demo.htm`	The XHTML page hosting the application.	For simplicity, this page includes embedded CSS styles, although you'd normally reference an external CSS stylesheet.
`contacts_summary.xml`	An XML document containing a summary list of all contacts.	This document provides information that will be used to look up the details of each contact.
`display.xslt`	The XSLT stylesheet associated with the summary XML list.	This stylesheet sorts the summary list and generates XHTML for inclusion on the XHTML page.
`contacts1.xml - contacts6.xml`	XML documents containing details of each contact.	These XML documents are referenced after locating the contact from the summary XML list.
`details.xslt`	The XSLT stylesheet associated with the detail XML documents.	The stylesheet generates XHTML to display the details of a selected contact.

Note that this example won't work with Opera 8.5 and below because these versions don't support client-side XSLT.

Figure 9-6 shows a screen shot of the application after selecting a contact name. The styling is purposely very simple in this example.

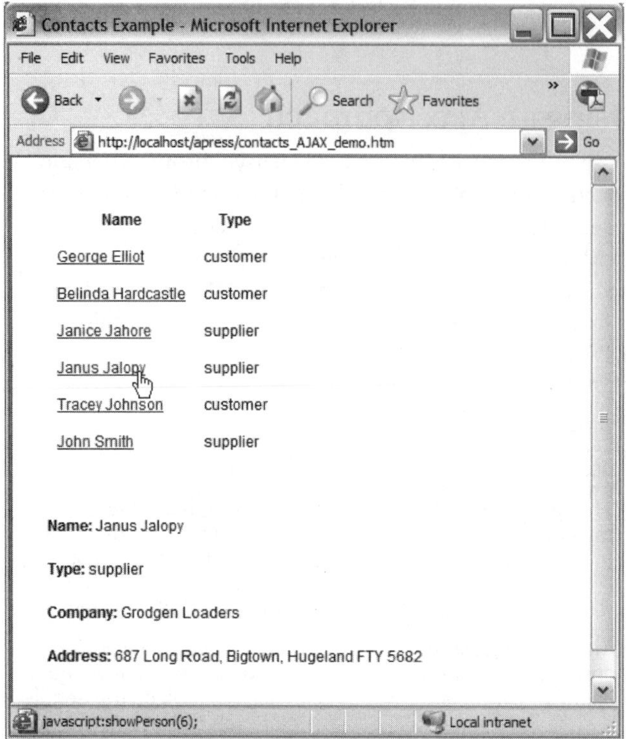

Figure 9-6. *The contacts application using the Ajax approach*

The key point about this simple application is that the content is loaded and structured from XML files without reloading the interface. In that way, the contact list mimics a desktop application. I'll work through the `contacts_AJAX_demo.htm` page so you can see how the application works.

The content of the page consists of two `<div>` elements:

```
<body onLoad="init();">
  <div id="contactDetails">Loading...</div>
  <div id="displayDetails"></div>
</body>
```

All of the work is done with JavaScript.

When the page loads, it calls the `init()` function:

```
function init() {
  sendRequest('contacts_summary.xml', 'display.xslt', xmlReady, xslReady);
}
```

This function calls the `sendRequest()` function, passing through the parameters for the XML document, stylesheet, and `XMLHttpRequest` objects:

```
function sendRequest(xmlURL, xslURL, xmlHandler, xslHandler) {
  xmlhttp = setupXMLHR();
  if (xmlhttp){
    xmlhttp.onreadystatechange=xmlHandler;
     xmlhttp.open("GET", xmlURL, true);
     xmlhttp.send(null);
   }
   xslhttp = setupXMLHR();
   if (xslhttp){
     xslhttp.onreadystatechange=xslHandler;
     xslhttp.open("GET", xslURL, true);
     xslhttp.send(null);
   }
}
```

You'll notice that the sendRequest() function uses the setupXMLHR() function to generate the XMLHttpRequest objects. This function looks very similar to the code you've seen earlier in this chapter, except that it returns an XMLHttpRequest object:

```
function setupXMLHR() {
  var request = null;
  if (window.XMLHttpRequest){
    request=new XMLHttpRequest();
  }
  else if (window.ActiveXObject){
    try {
      request = new ActiveXObject("Msxml2.XMLHTTP");
    } catch(e) {
      try {
        request = new ActiveXObject("Microsoft.XMLHTTP");
      } catch(e) {
        request = false;
      }
    }
  }
  return request;
}
```

The functions xmlReady() and xslReady() deal with the loaded XML and XSLT document. Both functions are very similar:

```
function xmlReady() {
  if (xmlhttp.readyState==4){
    if (xmlhttp.status==200) {
      xmlContacts = xmlhttp.responseXML;
      doTransform("contactDetails", xmlContacts, xslContacts);
    }
  }
}
```

```
function xslReady() {
  if (xslhttp.readyState==4){
    if (xslhttp.status==200) {
      xslContacts = xslhttp.responseXML;
      doTransform("contactDetails", xmlContacts, xslContacts);
    }
  }
}
```

They both check for a readyState value of 4 and a status of 200. When these conditions are met, both functions call the doTransform() function. The code calls the doTransform() function twice—once from the loading of the XML document and once by the XSLT document. The second call is made from the document that loads last. By that time, both documents are loaded and available for scripting.

The doTransform() function follows:

```
function doTransform(docElement, xmlDoc, xslDoc) {
  if (xmlDoc == null || xslDoc == null) return;
  if (window.ActiveXObject){
    document.getElementById(docElement).innerHTML=➥
      xmlDoc.transformNode(xslDoc);
  }
  else{
    var xsltProcessor = new XSLTProcessor();
    xsltProcessor.importStylesheet(xslDoc);
    var fragment =xsltProcessor.transformToFragment(xmlDoc,document);
    document.getElementById(docElement).innerHTML = "";
    document.getElementById(docElement).appendChild(fragment);
  }
}
```

As mentioned, the function starts by testing that both documents are loaded. If not, the function returns.

You can see straight away that there are two different stylesheet approaches for IE and Mozilla. For IE, you can use the transformNode() method, passing the XSLT stylesheet as a parameter.

In Mozilla, the code needs to create an instance of the xsltProcessor object to transform XML documents with XSLT. I can use importStylesheet() to import the XSLT document. Then, the transformToFragment() method transforms the XML document into a results tree. I can add the results tree to the document using the appendChild() method. Notice that I had to clear the element first by setting the innerHTML property to a zero-length string. If you don't do this, you'll see the old content as well as the new contact.

The stylesheet in this example is similar to the one used in the previous chapter:

```
<?xml version="1.0" encoding="UTF-8"?>
<xsl:stylesheet version="1.0" xmlns:xsl="http://www.w3.org/1999/XSL/Transform">
  <xsl:template match="/">
    <div>
      <table>
```

```
        <tr>
          <th>Name</th>
          <th>Type</th>
        </tr>
        <xsl:apply-templates select="/contacts/person">
          <xsl:sort select="last_name" order="ascending"/>
        </xsl:apply-templates>
      </table>
    </div>
  </xsl:template>
  <xsl:template match="person">
    <tr>
      <td><a href="javascript:showPerson({@id});">
        <xsl:value-of select="first_name"/><xsl:text> </xsl:text>
        <xsl:value-of select="last_name"/>
      </a></td>
      <td><xsl:value-of select="@type"/></td>
    </tr>
  </xsl:template>
</xsl:stylesheet>
```

The main difference here is that I've applied a sort order to the contacts—they are sorted by ascending last name. The example also displays the contacts in a table within a <div> element. I've linked the name so that the user can click it to display the details of the selected person.

When the user selects a person, the link calls the showPerson() function. This function receives the contact's id in the parameter intPersonID:

```
function showPerson(intPersonID) {
  var url = "contacts" + intPersonID + ".xml";
  sendRequest(url, 'details.xslt', xmlDetailsReady, xslDetailsReady);
}
```

The showPerson() function builds the XML document name and calls the sendRequest() function, passing in parameters for the new XML document and the details.xslt stylesheet. It also sets the two event handler functions. These event handlers are similar to the functions you saw earlier:

```
function xmlDetailsReady() {
  if (xmlhttp.readyState==4){
    if (xmlhttp.status==200) {
      xmlDetails = xmlhttp.responseXML;
      doTransform("displayDetails", xmlDetails, xslDetails);
    }
  }
}
function xslDetailsReady() {
  if (xslhttp.readyState==4){
    if (xslhttp.status==200) {
```

```
      xslDetails = xslhttp.responseXML;
      doTransform("displayDetails", xmlDetails, xslDetails);
    }
  }
}
```

The event handler functions call the doTransform() function, passing in the name of the display element and the two documents. The function transforms the XML details using the details.xslt stylesheet. This stylesheet is similar to the one from Chapter 8:

```
<?xml version="1.0" encoding="UTF-8"?>
<xsl:stylesheet version="1.0" xmlns:xsl="http://www.w3.org/1999/XSL/Transform">
  <xsl:template match="/">
    <div>
      <xsl:apply-templates select="/contacts/person"/>
    </div>
  </xsl:template>
  <xsl:template match="person">
    <p><span class="emphasis">Name: </span>
    <xsl:value-of select="first_name"/>
    <xsl:text> </xsl:text>
    <xsl:value-of select="last_name"/></p>
    <p><span class="emphasis">Type: </span> <xsl:value-of select="@type"/></p>
    <p><span class="emphasis">Company: </span><xsl:value-of select="company"/></p>
    <p><span class="emphasis">Address: </span> <xsl:value-of select="address1"/>,
    <xsl:value-of select="address2"/>,
    <xsl:value-of select="country"/>
    <xsl:text> </xsl:text>
    <xsl:value-of select="postal_code"/></p>
  </xsl:template>
</xsl:stylesheet>
```

Notice that I've added some structure and styling information. For example, I've included a reference to the emphasis class, which highlights the titles. As I mentioned earlier, the style declarations are embedded in the XHTML page.

In the previous two examples, I had to branch the code to respond to the differences between web browsers. An alternative is to use across-browser library.

Using Cross-Browser Libraries

As you saw in the previous section, you must address a number of cross-browser issues when writing Ajax applications. You need to create the XMLHttpRequest object using ActiveX in IE, whereas it's a native object in Mozilla and Opera. You also need to apply XSLT transformations differently depending on the browser.

Using a library is one solution to creating cross-browser Ajax applications. In this section, I'll look at the Sarissa library.

Sarissa

Sarissa is a cross-browser JavaScript library that works with XML manipulation. You can use the basic functionality with IE, Mozilla, Opera, and Safari. Bear in mind, though, that the XSLT features won't work with Opera 8.5 and below.

Sarissa uses function calls that are similar to the native `XMLHttpRequest` object:

```
var xmlhttp = new XMLHttpRequest();
xmlhttp.onreadystatechange = processXML;
xmlhttp.open("GET", "dvd.xml", true);
xmlhttp.send(null);

function processXML(){
  if(xmlhttp.readyState == 4){
    alert(xmlhttp.responseXML);
  }
}
```

It mimics the `XSLTProcessor` object to manipulate stylesheets in IE, and you can use Sarissa for other tasks such as creating a `DOM Document`:

```
var oDomDoc = Sarissa.getDomDocument();
oDomDoc.onreadystatechange = processXML;
oDomDoc.load("dvd.xml");

function processXML {
  if(oDomDoc.readyState == 4)
    alert(Sarissa.serialize(oDomDoc));
  }
}
```

To get started with Sarissa, you need to download the library from `http://sourceforge.net/projects/sarissa`. You'll see how it works by revisiting the contacts example. You can find the files in the `contacts_Sarissa` folder. I'll walk through this example so you can see how the use of the Sarissa wrapper streamlines the code.

You'll notice that the resource folder includes the `sarissa.js` and `sarissa_ieemu_xslt.js` files. The first file includes the core functionality for Sarissa, while the second provides the XSLT functionality for IE. The page `contacts_Sarissa_AJAX_demo.htm` hosts the application and includes the following lines:

```
<script type="text/javascript" src="sarissa.js"></script>
<script type="text/javascript" src="sarissa_ieemu_xslt.js"></script>
```

The first change comes in the init() function, where the code tests for the existence of Sarissa before proceeding:

```
function init() {
  if (!Sarissa) return;
  sendRequest('contacts_summary.xml', 'display.xslt', xmlReady, xslReady);
}
```

I've also changed the sendRequest() function, because I can use Sarissa to create a new XMLHttpRequest object for either IE or Mozilla:

```
function sendRequest(xmlURL, xslURL, xmlHandler, xslHandler) {
  xmlhttp = new XMLHttpRequest();
  if (xmlhttp){
    xmlhttp.onreadystatechange=xmlHandler;
    xmlhttp.open("GET", xmlURL, true);
    xmlhttp.send(null);
  }
  xslhttp = new XMLHttpRequest();
  if (xslhttp){
    xslhttp.onreadystatechange=xslHandler;
    xslhttp.open("GET", xslURL, true);
    xslhttp.send(null);
  }
}
```

The code no longer needs to call the setupXMLHR() function as in the previous example.

The onreadystatechange event handler functions don't change. In fact, the only other change in the code is in the doTransform() function. I've simplified the function because I can use the Sarissa XSLTProcessor object:

```
function doTransform(docElement, xmlDoc, xslDoc) {
  if (xmlDoc == null || xslDoc == null) return;
  var xsltProcessor = new XSLTProcessor();
  xsltProcessor.importStylesheet(xslDoc);
  var fragment =xsltProcessor.transformToDocument(xmlDoc);
  document.getElementById(docElement).innerHTML = Sarissa.serialize(fragment);
}
```

These lines create a new XSLTProcessor object and import the stylesheet. The transformtoDocument() method creates XHTML, and the Sarissa.serialize() method adds the string contents to the innerHTML property of the appropriate element.

Viewing the XHTML document in a browser shows the same results as the previous example. The difference here is that the code doesn't need to branch to deal with different browser types. It makes for a more elegant solution and wraps the code nicely. It would probably be even more elegant to remove the JavaScript from the XHTML document to an external .js file.

Sarissa is one of a range of frameworks and toolkits that can help with Ajax style applications.

Other Ajax Frameworks and Toolkits

You can use several other frameworks and toolkits to build Ajax applications, including

- Backbase
- Bindows
- Dojo
- Interactive Website Framework
- qooxdoo

Backbase

Backbase (`http://www.backbase.com`) is a commercial framework that helps you build Rich Internet Applications (RIAs). It uses the Backbase Presentation Client (BPC) Ajax JavaScript engine to provide a cross-browser framework without plugins.

Bindows

The Bindows (`http://www.bindows.net/`) framework is a commercial software development kit that operates within the browser. It provides widgets such as menus, forms, grids, sliders, and gauges.

Dojo

Dojo (`http://dojotoolkit.org`) is an open source JavaScript toolkit that includes widgets, an event model, and messaging.

Interactive Website Framework

Interactive Website Framework (`http://sourceforge.net/projects/iwf/`) provides the basis for creating Ajax-style applications, and it uses a JavaScript graphical user interface (GUI) toolkit. It includes a custom XML parser and provides a wrapper around the DOM.

qooxdoo

qooxdoo (`http://qooxdoo.sourceforge.net`) is an open source Ajax user interface library. It includes widgets and layout managers.

In addition, a number of other frameworks allow for integration with server-side languages.

Criticisms of Ajax

You've seen that Ajax can provide a powerful approach to developing web applications, but it has also been criticized for a number of reasons. These criticisms relate to the following areas:

- *Difficulties in recognizing changed data*: When received, changes in content may not be immediately obvious to the user. This is in contrast to traditional web applications where the user can see the page refreshing and infer that the content has changed.
- *Server or network impacts*: During periods of heavy load, there may be longer-than-normal delays in server or network response. Variations in server load can also mean that client-side processing doesn't run in the expected order.
- *Reduced usability*: Ajax can break the `Back` button functionality and make it impossible to bookmark application states.

The following solutions may go some way to addressing these criticisms.

Providing Visual Cues

Ajax-style applications need to provide visual cues to users to tell them what's happening to the content. While documents are loading, code can display a "loading" message. You saw this in the earlier examples.

In the examples, the code only tested for a `readyState` value of `4`. You could have tested for the other values and displayed an appropriate response for each state.

You can highlight new or changed information by using different CSS styling. You saw this in Figure 9-5 earlier in the chapter, where a validation error message displayed in red. I achieved this using the `invalid` class:

```
.invalid {
  padding: 5px;
  color: #FF0000;
}
```

I also applied the validation after entering the field details and before submitting the form to the server. Traditional web applications tend to validate all fields after the form is completed, but before it is submitted. In the case of a long form, this means that users can experience quite a delay before receiving feedback.

In traditional web applications, the alert box provides validation feedback to users. Unfortunately, alert boxes interrupt users and require them to click a button before proceeding. The appearance is fixed because alert boxes can't accept styling. Showing validation text in a `<div>` element provides a more elegant solution and doesn't interrupt the users' flow through the form.

Updating the Interface

Ajax applications can use dynamic interfaces to guide users through the application and increase usability. For example, in a shopping-cart application, adding an item may initiate a server request that needs to complete before adding more items. It may be useful to disable the `Add` button during the first server request, so that users can't add more items until the first request has completed successfully. You can use this approach to rewrite links or change the source of images dynamically to guide users through the application.

Preloading Data

One of the key points about Ajax is that it operates asynchronously. This allows the JavaScript code to process in the background while users carry out other tasks. If your application includes a lot of data, you can use asynchronous loading to your advantage. It can preload data that users may request later in the application. This can help to prevent users from waiting for content at a later point. You can also avoid downloading information that is rarely requested.

Providing Links to State and Enabling the Back Button

Ajax applications can exist in many different states, all with the same URL. This occurs because the web browser doesn't refresh and use a unique URL for each server request. Unless you specifically address this issue, users can't bookmark or link to application states.

One solution to this problem is to use the anchors in URLs to provide permanent links:

```
page.htm#location
```

You can set the value of an anchor using

```
window.location.hash = newlocation;
```

By setting a new anchor value, you can provide a unique URL that users can bookmark. You can then provide branches within your code to replicate that state if users want to enter the application at that point.

This process is a lot more complicated than it sounds. There are a number of cross-browser issues, and several articles have been written on the subject. One solution is to use the Really Simple History framework for Ajax available from `http://codinginparadise.org/weblog/2005_09_20_archive.html`. You can find an article describing the implementation at `http://www.onjava.com/pub/a/onjava/2005/10/26/ajax-handling-bookmarks-and-back-button.html`.

Ajax Best Practices and Design Principles

Ajax is a relatively new approach to developing web applications, even though its component parts have been available for some time. Despite the novelty of the approach, some best practices and design principles are starting to emerge. These include

- Minimizing server traffic
- Using standard interface methods
- Using wrappers or libraries
- Using Ajax appropriately

I'll look at each of these points.

Minimizing Server Traffic

Ajax-style applications can request content without refreshing the page. This effectively caches the user interface, increasing responsiveness to users. You'll wipe out these gains in responsiveness if you continually make server requests. It's important, therefore, to minimize the traffic between the client and server.

You can minimize traffic by loading the data asynchronously and working with local content wherever possible. Explicitly force the user to take action to trigger changes, perhaps by clicking a button or link. Create code that responds to these events, so you're not downloading content that isn't required or responding unnecessarily to user interactions.

Using Standard Interface Methods

Users are familiar with conventional methods of interacting with web applications, such as clicking buttons or links. Your Ajax applications will be more successful if you continue to use these methods. If you use alternative methods for user interaction, your users will have to learn how to use these methods. You run the risk of alienating users if these methods prove too challenging.

Using Wrappers or Libraries

To enable Ajax to operate in a cross-browser environment, create or use existing Ajax wrappers for JavaScript functionality. In this chapter, you saw how to use Sarissa with the contacts application. You also saw some other toolkits that you can use.

By using existing libraries, you can capitalize on the experience of other developers, and you won't be reinventing the wheel. You will also be able to write cleaner, more elegant code in your applications.

Using Ajax Appropriately

Ajax isn't a replacement for all other web application models. It's best suited for applications that load small amounts of content. For example, it wouldn't be appropriate to use Ajax to load full pages. First, this would slow down the page-loading process, and second, you'd lose the benefits of caching the interface.

Summary

This chapter introduced the Ajax style of creating XML applications. Ajax uses a combination of XML, the `XMLHttpRequest` object, JavaScript, XSLT, XHTML, and CSS to create responsive web applications. Because you'd seen the other technologies earlier in the book, I focused on the new `XMLHttpRequest` object in this chapter.

You saw how to use the `XMLHttpRequest` object to make server requests. You were able to display a `HEAD` request and retrieve content from an XML document. You looked at two simple examples—validating a username in a form, and creating an address-book application.

I showed how to use the Sarissa library to create cross-browser code, and I listed some of the other toolkits that may help. I finished by looking at criticisms of Ajax and some ways to address these. I also covered some of the Ajax best practices.

In the next chapter, I'm going to look at a totally different approach to working with XML on the client. You'll see how to use Flash to load and display XML content.

CHAPTER 10

Using Flash to Display XML

So far, you've seen how to work with XML data on the client side. I've looked at browser support for XML and styled and transformed content using Cascading Style Sheets (CSS) and Extensible Stylesheet Language Transformations (XSLT). I've also used the XML Document Object Model (DOM) to script XML applications in the browser with JavaScript. In the previous chapter, you learned about Ajax and used it to load XML content from the server without refreshing the page.

In this chapter, I'll look at an alternative way to work with XML on the client—by using Adobe (formerly Macromedia) Flash to provide the interface. At the time of writing, the latest version of the software is Flash 8. Flash 8 is available in two versions: Flash Basic 8 and Flash Professional 8. This chapter assumes that you have the second version.

If you're not familiar with Flash, it creates Shockwave Flash (SWF) files that are embedded as objects in a web page. I'll refer to Flash content as a *Flash movie*. Once the movie is compiled, it creates a `.swf` file for use within a web browser. Flash movies provide an alternative to using an XHTML interface to display XML content.

Flash includes a scripting language called ActionScript that is similar to JavaScript in many ways. ActionScript appeared in its current format in Flash 5 in 2000. It was called ActionScript 1.0 in Flash 6, which extended the language and added new features. ActionScript 2.0 was introduced in 2003, and this version of the language contains object-oriented features such as strict data typing, class and interface declarations, and inheritance. At the time of writing, ActionScript 3.0 is in beta-testing phase.

Since Flash 5, each version of ActionScript includes the native XML class that works with internal or external XML content. In this chapter, I'll use ActionScript 2.0 for the examples.

One of the advantages of building an interface in Flash is that you don't need to worry about cross-browser scripting. As long as the viewing browser includes the Flash Player, users can see and interact with the Flash movie. In December 2005, the Flash Player was available to 97.7 percent of web page viewers worldwide (`http://www.macromedia.com/software/player_census/flashplayer/`). Given the popularity and distribution of Flash Player, it's appropriate to rely on Flash as a mainstream technology for working with XML.

Another advantage of Flash is that it includes a number of prebuilt user interface (UI) components. These components mimic and extend the functionality available within XTHML form elements. Flash Professional also includes data components that can connect to external data sources such as XML documents and web services. They allow developers to work visually.

Flash also provides multimedia capabilities that aren't possible using XHTML alone. The most recent versions of Flash include support for sound and video.

Be aware that Flash can't validate XML content using either a Document Type Definition (DTD) or XML schema. Flash is not able to save changes to external data sources without server-side assistance. It can't apply XSLT transformations to XML content. If you need to transform content, you'll need to do that either on the server or write appropriate ActionScript code.

In this chapter, I'll explore the `XML` and `XMLNode` classes, and the `XMLConnector` component. I'll show you two approaches to including XML content in a Flash interface. Both of these methods use a request-response approach to load XML content. This means that Flash can't respond to real-time data changes without issuing another request for content. If necessary, you can use the `XMLSocket` class to work with real-time content; however, that's beyond the scope of this book.

I'll start by looking at the `XML` and `XMLNode` classes. I'll look at the `XMLConnector` component a little later in the chapter. As with the previous chapters, you can download the source files for the chapter from the Source Code area of the Apress web site (`http://www.apress.com`).

The XML Class

Flash has supported dynamic XML content since version 5. Flash 6 included XML as a native object, significantly speeding up the process of working with XML. The latest version, Flash 8, includes the `XML` and the related `XMLNode` classes for working with XML content. The `XML` class is similar to the `Document` interface in the XML DOM, while the `XMLNode` class is like the `Node` interface.

The `XML` class stores XML content in document trees in the Flash interface. The class allows you to

- Create new XML documents or document fragments
- Load external XML documents from physical files, server-side scripts, or web services
- Modify XML content
- Send XML information from Flash to a server-side script for processing

The `XML` and `XMLNode` classes allow you to traverse and manipulate XML content using properties and methods similar to those you saw in Chapter 8. Flash uses properties and methods similar to the XML DOM methods used with JavaScript. I'll start this chapter by loading an XML document using the XML class.

Loading an XML Document

The process of loading an XML document into a Flash `XML` object is very similar to loading it into a `DOM Document` object with JavaScript. The code needs to instantiate the object, set an event handler to deal with the parsed XML document tree, and then load the content. Flash includes a property that allows you to ignore white space within the XML document.

In Flash, you can write the following ActionScript 2.0 code to load an external XML document:

```
var oXML:XML = new XML();
oXML.ignoreWhite = true;
oXML.onLoad = processXML;
oXML.load("filename.xml");
```

If you load the content from a server-side file, you'll need to replace `filename.xml` with the full path to the document—e.g., `http://localhost/apress/filename.php`.

■ **Note** Flash includes a security sandbox that may impact XML documents loaded from another domain. Unless the remote domain contains a `crossdomain.xml` file granting permission, you won't be able to load the XML content. The restriction also applies to subdomains of the current domain. I'll cover this topic in more detail in the "Understanding Flash Security" section later in the chapter.

■ **Tip** You can see from the loading example that ActionScript looks very much like JavaScript. However, one advantage of ActionScript 2.0 is that it supports strict data typing. You can assign a data type when you declare an ActionScript variable by adding a colon and the data type after the declaration—e.g., `var intCounter:Number`. Although not required, it's good practice to do this so you can avoid type mismatch errors.

When Flash calls the `load` method, it parses the contents of the document into a tree and returns a value to the `onLoad` handler function, indicating whether the file loaded successfully. The following code shows how to use this value in an `onLoad` handler function:

```
function processXML(success:Boolean):Void{
  if (success) {
    //do some processing
  }
}
```

The `success` variable is Boolean and indicates if loading completed successfully. The name `success` isn't significant; you can choose any other appropriate name.

An XML document can load successfully even if it's not well formed. You can use the `status` property to determine whether Flash encountered any errors while parsing the document:

```
function processXML(success:Boolean):Void{
  if (success) {
    if (this.status == 0) {
      //no error
    }
  }
}
```

Table 10-1 shows the possible values for the `status` property.

Table 10-1. *Values for the status Property of the XML Object*

Value	Meaning
0	No error; the document parsed successfully.
-2	A CDATA section is not terminated properly.
-3	The XML declaration is not terminated properly.
-4	The DOCTYPE declaration is not terminated properly.
-5	A comment is not terminated properly.
-6	An XML element is malformed.
-7	The application is out of memory.
-8	An attribute value is not terminated properly.
-9	A start tag is not matched with an end tag.
-10	An end tag exists without a matching start tag.

Note that where a document contains more than one error, the `status` property returns the value for the first error. Even when Flash detects an error, an application may still be able to traverse all or part of the document tree.

You can see an example that loads the `dvd.xml` document into the Flash 8 file `dvd.fla`. Open `dvd.fla` in Flash 8, and compile a SWF file by using the Ctrl+Enter shortcut. Figure 10-1 shows an Output window containing the XML content from the external document.

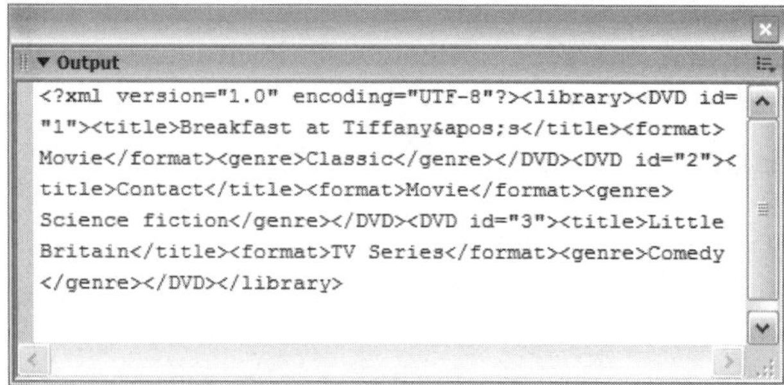
Output
<?xml version="1.0" encoding="UTF-8"?><library><DVD id=
"1"><title>Breakfast at Tiffany's</title><format>
Movie</format><genre>Classic</genre></DVD><DVD id="2"><
title>Contact</title><format>Movie</format><genre>
Science fiction</genre></DVD><DVD id="3"><title>Little
Britain</title><format>TV Series</format><genre>Comedy
</genre></DVD></library>

Figure 10-1. *Displaying XML content in Flash*

The complete ActionScript code contained within this Flash file follows:

```
var oXML:XML = new XML();
oXML.ignoreWhite = true;
oXML.onLoad = processXML;
oXML.load("dvd.xml");
```

```
function processXML(success:Boolean):Void{
  if (success){
    if (this.status ==0) {
      trace (this);
    }
  }
}
```

You can display the contents within Flash using the previous line shown in bold.

■ **Note** The `trace()` action displays content in the Output window within Flash. You won't see these messages if you test the compiled Flash movie in a web browser.

If you open the `dvd.xml` file, you'll notice that Flash loads the entire contents of the document, including the XML declaration. However, Flash removes all white space because of the `true` value assigned to the `ignoreWhite` property.

You should note the following points about loading content into Flash:

- The loading process is asynchronous, so you need to set an event handler to respond to the loaded document.
- Flash doesn't maintain a link back to the external XML document, so you need to reload it if the content changes.

Once you've loaded the document, you'll need to traverse the document tree so you can display and manipulate the contents.

Understanding the XML Class

The `XML` class represents the entire XML document and includes methods similar to the factory methods within the XML DOM. You'll remember from Chapter 8 that factory methods create new objects within the document tree. The `XML` class includes the following methods:

- `createElement()`
- `createTextNode()`
- `parseXML()`

The `XML` class includes other methods such as `addRequestHeader()`, `getBytesLoaded()`, `getBytesTotal()`, `send()`, and `sendAndLoad()` that I won't cover here for the sake of brevity.

createElement(name:String)

The `createElement()`method returns a new `XMLNode` object with the specified name:

```
var oElement:XMLNode = oXML.createElement("eName");
```

Like the XML DOM methods, using createElement() in ActionScript generates an element without a position in the document tree. You then need to position it using either the appendChild() or insertBefore() methods of the XMLNode class.

createTextNode(value:String)

The createTextNode()method returns a text node from the value argument:

```
var oTextNode:XMLNode = oXML.createTextNode("Some text");
```

Again, this node has no position in the document tree and will need to be positioned using appendChild() or insertBefore().

parseXML(value:String)

The parseXML()method parses text within the value parameter and populates an XML object:

```
var XMLString:String = "<library><dvd id="4"><title>Splash</title></library>";
var oXML:XML = new XML();
oXML.parseXML(XMLString);
```

The XML class also inherits methods and properties from the XMLNode class.

Understanding the XMLNode Class

The XMLNode class represents elements within the document tree. An XML object is made up of XMLNode objects. The XMLNode class includes the following members:

- attributes
- parentNode
- childNodes
- firstChild and lastChild
- previousSibling and nextSibling
- nodeType
- nodeName
- nodeValue
- hasChildNodes()
- appendChild()
- cloneNode()
- insertBefore()
- removeNode()

Unlike the XML DOM, ActionScript doesn't include the replaceChild() method.

Let's look at each of these methods and properties so you can understand them in more detail.

attributes

The attributes property returns an object containing all of the attributes of the specified XMLNode object:

```
oXMLNode.attributes
```

You can loop through all attributes within the XMLNode using this code:

```
for (var theAtt:String in oXMLNode.attributes) {
..//process attributes
}
```

parentNode

The parentNode property returns the XMLNode that is the parent of the current node:

```
oXMLNode.parentNode
```

Remember that attributes don't have a parent node, as they are not the children of their containing element. If the node doesn't have a parent, it returns null.

childNodes

The childNodes property returns an array of child XMLNode objects:

```
oXMLNode.childNodes
```

You can refer to a specific child node by using its position within the collection:

```
oXMLNode.childNodes[0]
```

The previous line refers to the first child node of the oXMLNode element.

You can find out how many child nodes exist within an element by using the length property:

```
oXMLNode.childNodes.length
```

This allows you to loop through the collection:

```
for (var i:Number=0; i < oXMLNode.childNodes.length; i++) {
  //do something
}
```

As text nodes don't have child nodes, this property will return undefined.

firstChild and lastChild

The firstChild and lastChild properties return the first and last XMLNode objects in the XMLNode's list of child nodes:

```
oXMLNode.firstChild
oXMLNode.lastChild
```

If there are no children, the lastChild property returns null.

Note that text nodes are always the first child of their containing element.

previousSibling and nextSibling

These properties return the previous and next XMLNode objects that share the same parent as the current XMLNode object:

```
oXMLNode.previousSibling
oXMLNode.nextSibling
```

nodeType

Unlike the XML DOM property of the same name, this property returns a value of either 1 (element node) or 3 (text node) for the specified XMLNode:

```
oXMLNode.nodeType
```

Flash doesn't support the other numeric node type indicators from the recommendation.

nodeName

The nodeName property returns the name of the current XMLNode object:

```
oXMLNode.nodeName
```

Text nodes don't have a nodeName property. XMLNodes with a nodeType of 3—i.e., text nodes—will return null.

nodeValue

The nodeValue property returns the content of the specified text node:

```
oXMLNode.firstChild.nodeValue
```

The preceding line finds the text within the oXMLNode element. Note that the text node is the firstChild of the XMLNode object.

The property returns null for an element node (nodeType = 1).

hasChildNodes()

The hasChildNodes()method returns a Boolean value that indicates whether an XMLNode object has child elements:

```
oXMLNode.hasChildNodes()
```

appendChild(newChild:XMLNode)

The appendChild()method adds a new child after the last child node of the current XMLNode object. You can use this method to append a node that you've just created:

```
oNewNode = oXML.createElement("dvd");
oXML.childNodes[0].appendChild(oNewNode);
```

You can also use the method to move an existing node to a new location.

cloneNode(deep:Boolean)

The cloneNode()method clones an existing XMLNode object. It copies all attributes within the node. Set the deep parameter to true to clone all child nodes recursively:

```
oXML.oXMLNode.cloneNode(true)
```

The method returns the cloned node without a parent. You'll need to use appendChild() or insertBefore() to locate it within the document tree.

insertBefore(newChild:XMLNode, insertPoint:XMLNode)

This method inserts a new XMLNode object before an existing XMLNode object:

```
var oOldNode:XMLNode = oXML.firstChild.childNode[1];
var oNewNode:XMLNode = oXML.createElement("dvd");
oXML.insertBefore(oNewNode, oOldNode);
```

If insertPoint is not a child of the XMLNode object, the insert will fail.

removeNode()

The removeChild()method removes the specified XMLNode. It returns nothing:

```
var nodeToRemove:XMLNode = oXML.firstChild.childNodes[2];
nodeToRemove.removeNode();
```

Loading and Displaying XML Content in Flash

In the previous section, I covered the methods and properties that are available to you when working with XML content in Flash. These will make much more sense if I work through an example.

The example file dvd2.fla shows how to load the dvd.xml file into Flash and display the details of a selected DVD in UI components. Figure 10-2 shows this movie with a selected DVD.

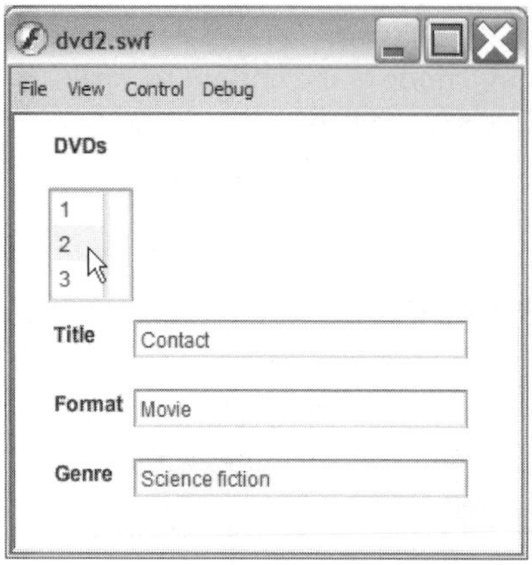

Figure 10-2. *Displaying XML content in UI components*

I'll walk through this example so you can see how to traverse the document tree. The example will also show you how to work with the UI components in Flash.

Open the `dvd2.fla` file in Flash 8, and you'll see a number of UI components on the `Stage`. If you're not familiar with Flash, clicking each component displays its name in the `Properties` panel at the bottom of the screen. Figure 10-3 shows the `Properties` panel with the `List` component selected. I can refer to a component using this name.

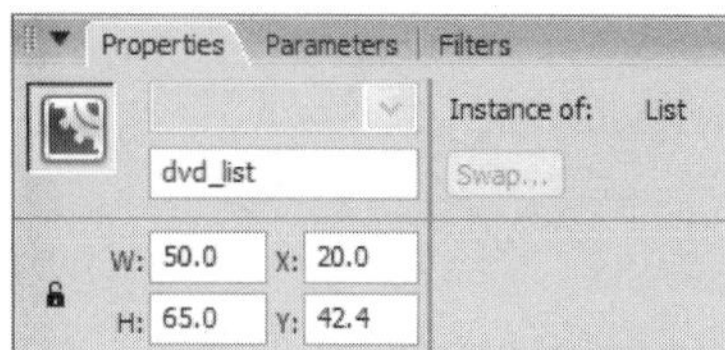

Figure 10-3. *The Properties panel showing a component instance name*

You'll also see two layers in the timeline in the top left-hand corner of the screen. Select Frame 1 of the `actions` layer, as shown in Figure 10-4.

Figure 10-4. *Selecting Frame 1 of the actions layer*

You can press the F9 shortcut key to see the actions added to this frame in the Actions panel. All of the ActionScript required to run this simple application appears on Frame 1 of this layer. I'll work through the code.

The code starts by declaring timeline variables. These are similar to variables with global scope in a JavaScript code block:

```
var rootNode:XMLNode;
var selectedDVDNode:XMLNode;
```

The rootNode variable stores a reference to the document element. In the dvd.xml file, that's the <library> element. The selectedDVDNode variable stores a reference to the DVD chosen by the user.

The next code block loads the XML document and sets the onLoad event handler:

```
var oXML:XML = new XML();
oXML.ignoreWhite = true;
oXML.onLoad = processXML;
oXML.load("dvd.xml");
```

When the dvd.xml document loads into Flash, it calls the processXML function. The function appears at the bottom of the Actions panel:

```
function processXML(success:Boolean):Void{
  if (success){
    if (this.status == 0) {
      rootNode = this.firstChild;
      loadList();
    }
  }
}
```

This function starts by testing that the XML document loaded successfully. It then checks the value of the status property to make sure that there are no errors. The remaining lines set the value of the rootNode variable to the first child of the loaded XML object, and call the loadList function:

```
rootNode = this.firstChild;
loadList();
```

Setting the rootNode variable is useful because it allows an application to access content from the XML document, without the XML declaration, from anywhere within the Flash movie.

The loadList() function loads the content into the List component:

```
function loadList():Void {
  dvd_list.removeAll();
  var dvdID:Number;
  for (var i:Number=0; i < rootNode.childNodes.length; i++) {
    dvdID = rootNode.childNodes[i].attributes.id;
    dvd_list.addItem(dvdID);
  }
}
```

The code starts by removing any existing items from the list. Then it declares a variable that will store the DVD id attribute value. The code loops through the childNodes array using a for loop. You'll notice that the construction is the same as within JavaScript:

```
for (var i:Number=0; i < rootNode.childNodes.length; i++) {
```

As in the previous chapters, the code uses the length property of the childNodes array to determine the end point for the loop.

Within the loop, the code determines the id attribute value using this code:

```
dvdID = rootNode.childNodes[i].attributes.id;
```

This code finds the relevant childNode array element and finds the id property within the attributes collection. Finally, the addItem() method adds the id attribute to the dvd_list List component:

```
dvd_list.addItem(dvdID);
```

The other block of code within the Actions panel responds to the user making a selection from the List component:

```
var dvdListener:Object = new Object();
dvdListener.change = function(evtObj:Object):Void {
  var nodeIndex:Number = evtObj.target.selectedIndex;
  selectedDVDNode = rootNode.childNodes[nodeIndex];
  title_txt.text = selectedDVDNode.childNodes[0].firstChild.nodeValue;
  format_txt.text = selectedDVDNode.childNodes[1].firstChild.nodeValue;
  genre_txt.text = selectedDVDNode.childNodes[2].firstChild.nodeValue;
}
dvd_list.addEventListener("change", dvdListener);
```

The code defines an event listener object called dvdListener and adds it to the dvd_list component, listening for the change event.

When the object detects the event, it determines which item the user selected and stores it within the nodeIndex variable:

```
var nodeIndex:Number = evtObj.target.selectedIndex;
```

It then uses that value to set an XMLNode object to reference the appropriate element in the XML object:

```
selectedDVDNode = rootNode.childNodes[nodeIndex];
```

Finally, the function sets the text property of each TextInput component to the value from the appropriate element in the XML object. For example, the title comes from the first child node (childNodes[0]) of the <dvd> element. You can find the text by using the firstChild property of this element and determining the nodeValue:

```
title_txt.text = selectedDVDNode.childNodes[0].firstChild.nodeValue;
```

Testing the Flash document shows something similar to Figure 10-2. You should be able to select each DVD from the List component and see the title, format, and genre of each.

■ **Tip** If you're not familiar with Flash, you can generate a web page that displays the SWF file by choosing File ➤ Publish. Flash will create the web page in the same folder as the SWF file.

In this example, you saw how to load an XML document into Flash and display it in UI components. You can also use Flash to update content and send it to a server-side file for processing.

Updating XML Content in Flash

As you saw earlier in this chapter, Flash can use methods such as `createNode()`, `appendNode()`, `insertBefore()`, and `cloneNode()` to manipulate an XML tree. The manipulation takes place within Flash, but if you need to update an external data source, you'll have to send the content to a server-side file for processing.

I'll work through an example where I take user input and use it to update the `dvd.xml` document tree within Flash. You can find this example saved in the file `dvd3.fla`. Figure 10-5 shows the interface populated with the `dvd.xml` file.

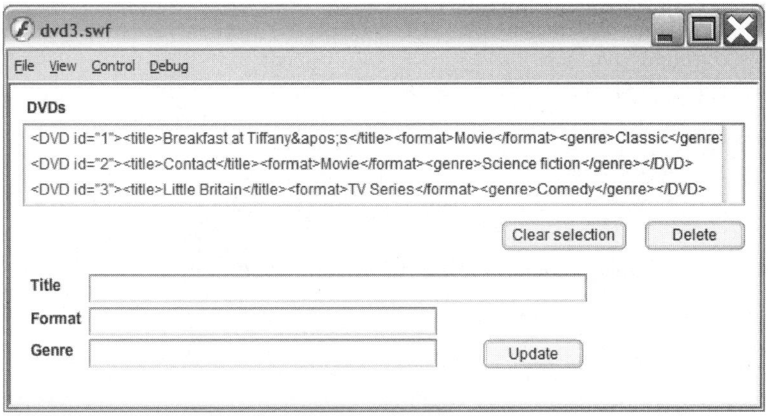

Figure 10-5. *The interface of the dvd3.fla movie*

This interface allows you to view the details of a DVD, add a new DVD to the XML tree, and edit or remove an existing DVD.

If you open Frame 1 of the `actions` layer with the F9 shortcut key, you'll see that it's a little more complicated than the previous example. To start with, there are now three timeline variables:

```
var rootNode:XMLNode;
var selectedDVDNode:XMLNode;
var booNew:Boolean = true;
```

The added third line creates a Boolean variable that determines whether to add a new node or to edit an existing node.

The processXML()function is almost identical to the previous example. When it calls the loadList() function, it passes null, signifying that a DVD has not yet been selected. The loadList() function works a little differently from the previous example. This time it displays a string representation of the complete XMLNode object in the List component. The new and changed lines appear in bold in the following code block:

```
function loadList(theNodeIndex:Number):Void {
  dvd_list.removeAll();
  var dvdNode:XMLNode;
  for (var i:Number=0; i < rootNode.childNodes.length; i++) {
    dvdNode = rootNode.childNodes[i];
    dvd_list.addItem(dvdNode.toString());
  }
  if (theNodeIndex != null) {
    dvd_list.selectedIndex = theNodeIndex;
  }
}
```

The toString() method displays the content of each element within the List component.

The new example includes onRelease handlers for each of the three buttons: Clear, Update, and Delete. The Clear button clears the selection:

```
clear_btn.onRelease = function():Void {
  dvd_list.selectedIndex = undefined;
  selectedDVDNode = null;
  booNew = true;
  clearTextInputs();
}
```

The function starts by removing the selection from the dvd_list component:

```
dvd_list.selectedIndex = undefined;
```

It then clears the selectedDVDNode variable by setting the value to null. The function sets the booNew variable to true and then calls the clearTextInputs() function to remove the text from the interface. The clearTextInputs() function follows:

```
function clearTextInputs():Void {
  title_txt.text = "";
  format_txt.text = "";
  genre_txt.text = "";
}
```

Clicking the Update button calls the doUpdate() function. This function either adds a new record to the XML tree or updates the currently selected element, depending on the value of the booNew variable.

The doUpdate()function follows:

```
function doUpdate():Void {
  if (booNew) {
    if (title_txt.text.length > 0) {
      var newDVD:XMLNode = oXML.createElement("DVD");
      newDVD.attributes.id = rootNode.childNodes.length + 1;
      var newDVDTitle:XMLNode = oXML.createElement("title");
      newDVDTitle.appendChild(oXML.createTextNode(title_txt.text));
      newDVD.appendChild(newDVDTitle);
      if (format_txt.text.length > 0) {
        var newDVDFormat:XMLNode = oXML.createElement("format");
        newDVDFormat.appendChild(oXML.createTextNode(format_txt.text));
        newDVD.appendChild(newDVDFormat);
      }
      if (genre_txt.text.length > 0) {
        var newDVDGenre:XMLNode = oXML.createElement("genre");
        newDVDGenre.appendChild(oXML.createTextNode(genre_txt.text));
        newDVD.appendChild(newDVDGenre);
      }
      rootNode.appendChild(newDVD);
      loadList(null);
      clearTextInputs();
    }
  }
  else {
    var selectedNodeIndex:Number = Number(selectedDVDNode.attributes.id)-1;
    if (title_txt.text.length > 0) {
      selectedDVDNode.childNodes[0].firstChild.nodeValue = title_txt.text;
    }
    if (format_txt.text.length > 0) {
      selectedDVDNode.childNodes[1].firstChild.nodeValue = format_txt.text;
    }
    if (genre_txt.text.length > 0) {
      selectedDVDNode.childNodes[2].firstChild.nodeValue = genre_txt.text;
    }
    loadList(selectedNodeIndex);
  }
}
```

You can divide the function into two areas—the first section adds a new record, and the second edits an existing record. If you're adding a new record (booNew is true), the code tests whether the record has a title. The function won't proceed unless a title exists:

```
if (title_txt.text.length > 0) {
```

If a title exists, the code creates a new <DVD> element and adds an id attribute:

```
var newDVD:XMLNode = oXML.createElement("DVD");
newDVD.attributes.id = rootNode.childNodes.length + 1;
```

It sets the value of the attribute to one more than the number of <DVD> elements in the XML tree.

The next code block creates a new <title> element and uses appendChild() to add the text from the title_txt component:

```
var newDVDTitle:XMLNode = oXML.createElement("title");
newDVDTitle.appendChild(oXML.createTextNode(title_txt.text));
newDVD.appendChild(newDVDTitle);
```

The code repeats this process for the <format> and <genre> nodes:

```
if (format_txt.text.length > 0) {
  var newDVDFormat:XMLNode = oXML.createElement("format");
  newDVDFormat.appendChild(oXML.createTextNode(format_txt.text));
  newDVD.appendChild(newDVDFormat);
}
if (genre_txt.text.length > 0) {
  var newDVDGenre:XMLNode = oXML.createElement("genre");
  newDVDGenre.appendChild(oXML.createTextNode(genre_txt.text));
  newDVD.appendChild(newDVDGenre);
}
```

Finally, the code appends the <DVD> element to the root node, reloads the List component, and clears the values in the text field:

```
rootNode.appendChild(newDVD);
loadList(null);
clearTextInputs();
```

Editing an existing node uses a different block of code that's easier to interpret. First, the code finds the child node index for the selected node so it can select the node again after the update:

```
var selectedNodeIndex:Number = Number(selectedDVDNode.attributes.id)-1;
```

Then it checks whether appropriate text has been entered into the TextField component and changes the nodeValue accordingly:

```
if (title_txt.text.length > 0) {
  selectedDVDNode.childNodes[0].firstChild.nodeValue = title_txt.text;
}
if (format_txt.text.length > 0) {
  selectedDVDNode.childNodes[1].firstChild.nodeValue = format_txt.text;
}
if (genre_txt.text.length > 0) {
  selectedDVDNode.childNodes[2].firstChild.nodeValue = genre_txt.text;
}
```

Finally, the code calls the loadList() function, passing the index of the selected node:

```
loadList(selectedNodeIndex);
```

The remaining button deletes the selected <DVD> element from the List component:

```
delete_btn.onRelease = function():Void {
  selectedDVDNode.removeNode();
  clearTextInputs();
  loadList(null);
}
```

It starts by using the removeNode() method to remove the selected <DVD> element from the XML tree. Then it clears the interface and reloads the list.

As I mentioned earlier, modifying the content within Flash won't change the external data. You can only update the external data by sending the content to a server-side document for processing.

Sending XML Content from Flash

You can use either the send() or sendAndLoad() method to send content from Flash to an external file for processing. The difference between the two is that the latter method receives a response from the external file. This makes it a more robust approach.

Because this method allows you to check that the processing has completed successfully, you can use it to display an appropriate message in the Flash movie. In this section, I'll look at the second of these two methods—sendAndLoad().

The sendAndLoad() method requires two XML objects: one to store the content to send to the server for processing, and one to receive the response after the processing completes. The first XML object calls the sendAndLoad() method, while the second uses an onLoad handler to process the server reply.

The sendAndLoad() method uses POST to send its XML content. It takes two parameters: the path to the processing page and the XML object for the response:

```
oSendXML.sendAndLoad("processingPage.php", oReceiveXML);
```

You need to make sure that you set the content type appropriately using the contentType property:

```
oSendXML.contentType = "text/xml";
```

You can use code similar to the following to update external XML content:

```
var oSendXML:XML = new XML("<DVD>Splash</DVD>");
var oReceiveXML:XML = new XML();
oReceiveXML.onLoad = showResponse;
oSendXML.contentType = "text/xml";
oSendXML.sendAndLoad("http://localhost/apress/updateXML.php", oReceiveXML);
```

You also need to create the showResponse() function.

I won't work through an example because it requires server-side interaction. However, you should note a couple of points:

- You need to use the full server path to the processing page in the first parameter (e.g., `http://localhost/apress/updateXML.php`).
- You must remember to set the content type appropriately for the processing page using the `contentType` property.

In addition to the `XML` class, Flash Professional provides an alternative way to load and display XML content using the `XMLConnector` data component.

Using the XMLConnector Component

If you own Flash Professional and prefer to work visually, you can use the `XMLConnector` data component to load XML content from an external source. The advantage is that you can configure the component using the `Component Inspector` panel. In the previous example, I had to write `for` loops to iterate through the XML document tree. Instead, data components support data binding so that you don't need to write code.

The `XMLConnector` component is one of a family of data components that are available with Flash Professional. The other components allow you to load content from web services or a database, store external content in a `DataSet` component, and track changes so that you can send changed content from Flash. I'll restrict myself to working with the `XMLConnector` component in this section. Figure 10-6 shows how this component works.

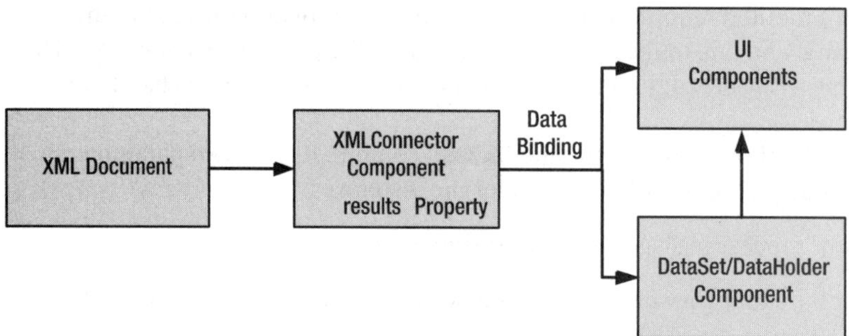

Figure 10-6. *Using the XMLConnector*

The `XMLConnector` component loads the XML document. You can bind the `results` property from the `XMLConnector` component directly to UI components. You can also bind the results to a `DataSet` or `DataHolder` component first. In that case, either the `DataSet` or `DataHolder` component is bound to the UI components. You bind to a `DataSet` if Flash needs to update an external XML document using an `XUpdateResolver` component.

You'll be able to see the process by working through an example. I'll load the `dvd.xml` document into the Flash document `dvd4.fla`. I'll then bind the data directly to several UI components to display the content in Flash. Start by opening the resource file `dvd4.fla`.

Loading an XML Document

You need to add the XMLConnector component to the Flash document. You can find the data components in the Components panel. If you can't see it at the right of the screen, choose Window ➤ Components.

Drag the XMLConnector to the left of the Stage, as shown in Figure 10-7. Data components have no visual appearance, so it doesn't matter where you place them.

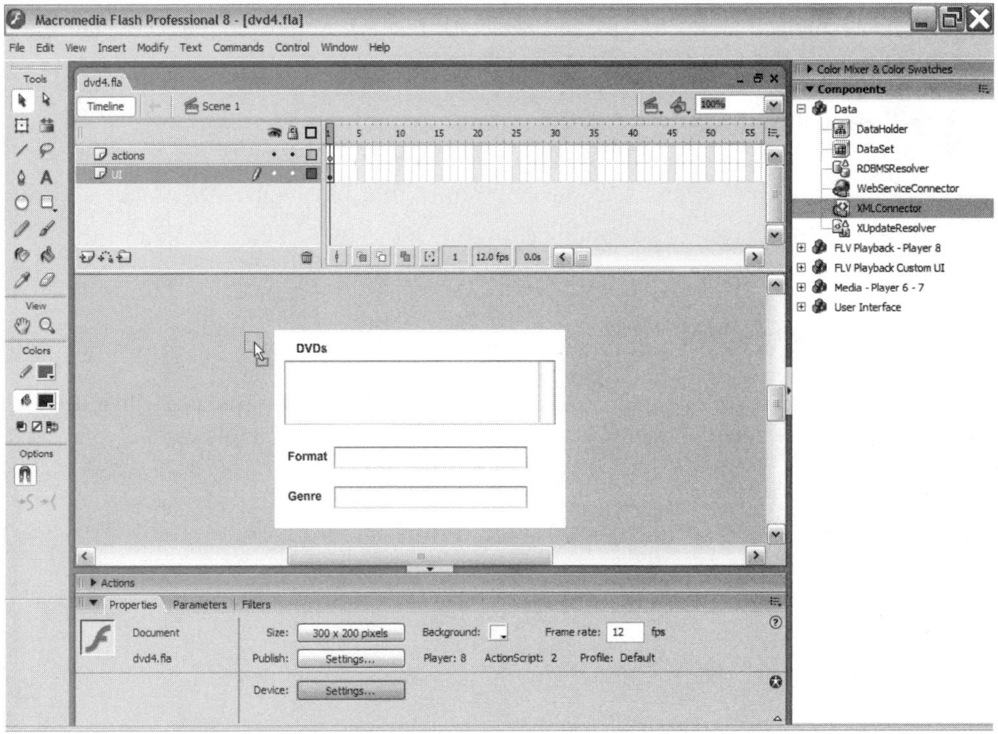

Figure 10-7. *Dragging the XMLConnector component into the Flash movie*

In the Properties panel, give the XMLConnector the name dvd_xc. In the Parameters tab, set the URL to dvd.xml and the direction to receive, as shown in Figure 10-8.

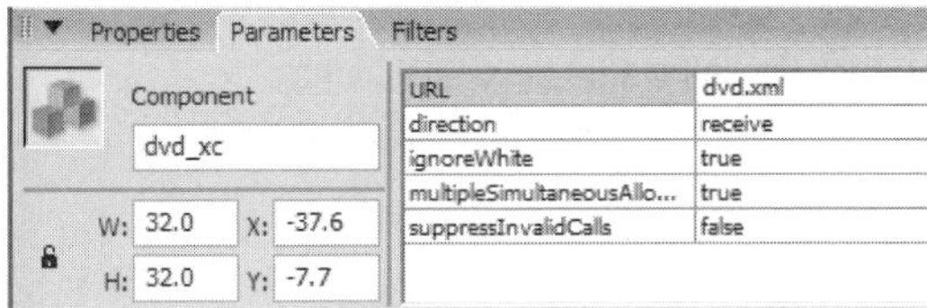

Figure 10-8. *Configuring the component*

The `Component Inspector` panel allows you to work with the `XMLConnector` in more detail. If you can't see the panel on the right, choose Window ➤ Component Inspector. This panel contains three tabs: `Parameters`, `Bindings`, and `Schema`. You've already configured the parameters for the component. Click the `Schema` tab.

The `Schema` tab allows you to build a schema describing the structure of your XML document. You can also infer a schema from an external XML document. You can do this for the `params` property (data sent out of Flash) or for the `results` property (data received from external sources).

I'll infer a schema from the `dvd.xml` file. Select the `results` property in the `Schema` tab and click the `Import a schema` button, as shown in Figure 10-9.

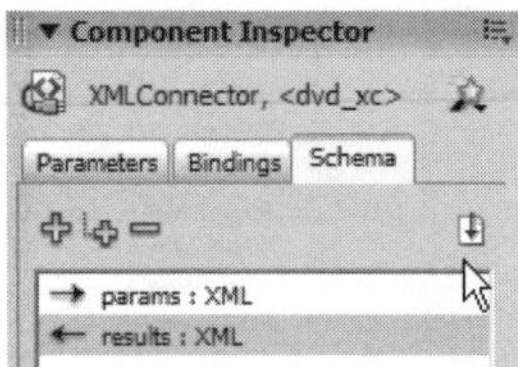

Figure 10-9. *Inferring a schema*

Navigate to the `dvd.xml` document and click `Open`. The `Schema` tab populates with a structure inferred from the document. Figure 10-10 shows the appearance at this point.

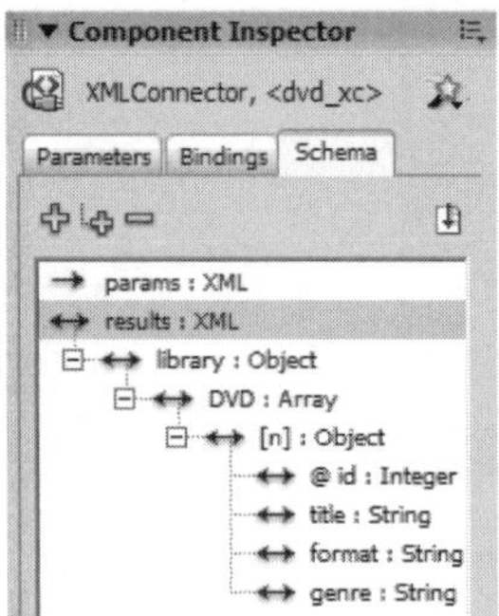

Figure 10-10. *The inferred schema*

■ **Note** Although Flash uses the word *schema*, this process doesn't create an XML schema.

You need to trigger the data component before it loads the XML document. You can do this by adding the following line to Frame 1 of the actions layer:

```
dvd_xc.trigger();
```

If you test the Flash movie at this point, nothing will happen because the data has not yet been bound to the UI components.

Data Binding

You can configure the data bindings for the XMLConnector component within the Bindings tab of the Component Inspector panel. Select the XMLConnector component on the Stage, and click the Bindings tab. It will initially appear empty.

You can add a binding by clicking the Add Binding button. It looks like a blue plus sign. When you click this button, you'll be prompted for the source of the binding. Because I want to display details of each DVD in the list, I need to select the DVD : Array option, as shown in Figure 10-11. When you've done this, click OK.

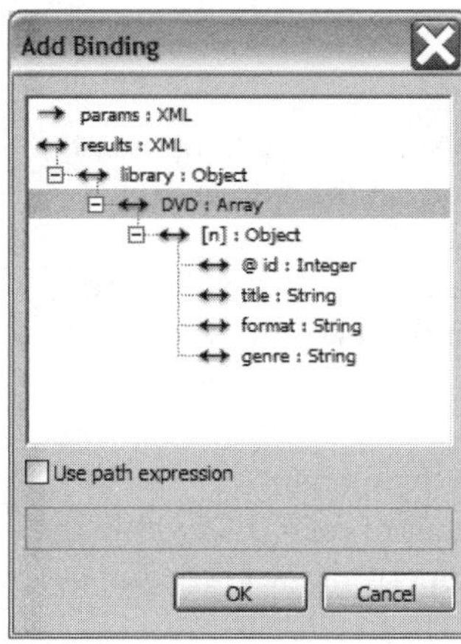

Figure 10-11. *Selecting the source for the binding*

You then need to select a direction and destination for the binding. The binding will operate in one way: out from the XMLConnector and in to the List component. Select out for the direction, and click in the bound to field. This brings up a magnifying glass that you can click to select the List component. You'll bind to the dataProvider property of the List component, as shown in Figure 10-12.

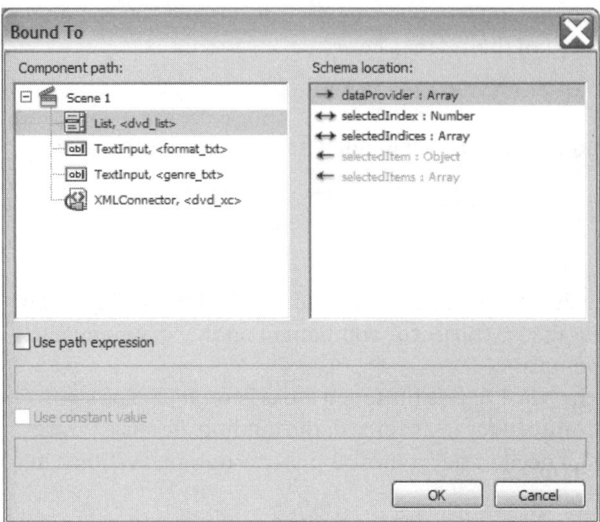

Figure 10-12. *Selecting the destination for the binding*

If you use the Ctrl+Enter shortcut to test the movie now, you'll see the `List` component populates with all content from each `<DVD>` element. You need to format the data to display only the `<title>` element.

Click in the `formatter` field and choose a `Rearrange Fields` formatter. Click within the `formatter options` field and use the magnifying-glass icon to enter the following setting:

```
label=title
```

If you test the movie again, you'll see only the titles in the `List` component.

You can now bind the selected title so that you can see the details of each DVD within the `TextInput` components. You can do this with the `selectedIndex` property of the `List` component. In other words, show the details of whichever item is selected from the list.

Click the `XMLConnector` component and add another binding—this time, from the `format` item in the schema. You'll notice that Flash adds a new field, `Index for 'DVD'`, to the `Bindings` panel. Set the direction of the binding to `out` and bind to the `TextInput` component called `format_txt`.

You can display the correct format by changing the `Index for 'DVD'` field. Click in the field to bring up the `Bound Index` dialog box. Uncheck `Use constant value` and choose the `selectedIndex` property of the `List` component, as shown in Figure 10-13.

If you test the Flash movie now, you'll be able to populate the `format_txt` component by selecting from the list of titles. You'll need to repeat the process for the `genre_txt` component to complete the application. You can find the completed Flash file saved as `dvd4_completed.fla` if you run into any difficulties.

It's worthwhile noting that you can create the `XMLConnector` component and bindings using only ActionScript. I'm not going to cover that in this book.

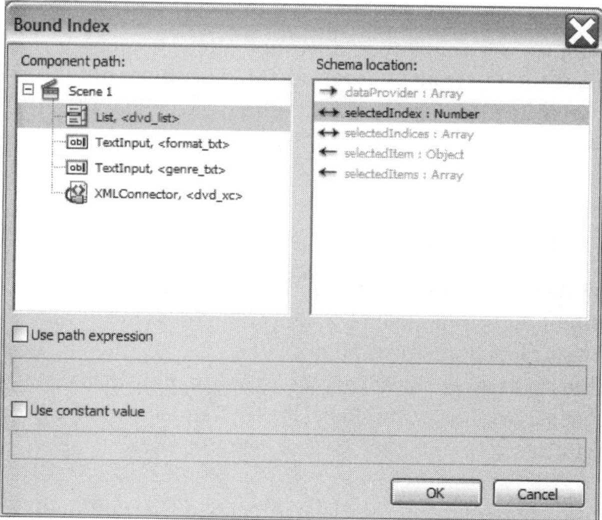

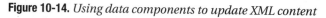

Figure 10-13. *Binding the index to the List component*

Updating XML Content with Data Components

It's beyond the scope of this chapter to show you how to send content from Flash using data components, but you need to know that it's possible. Sending content from Flash requires server-side interaction and is quite a complicated process. Figure 10-14 shows the process for using data components to update external content.

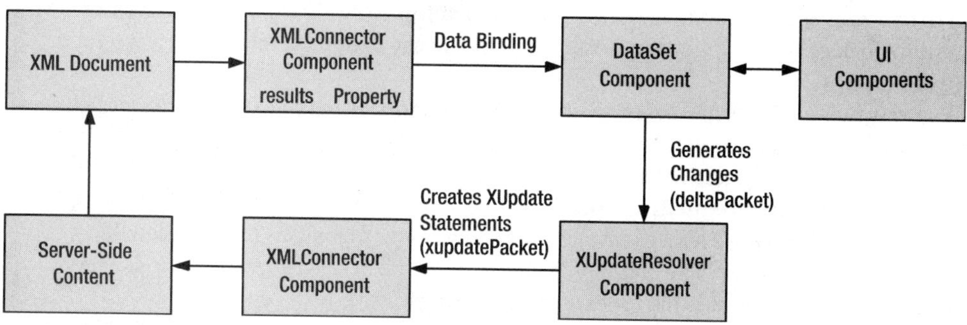

Figure 10-14. *Using data components to update XML content*

The process starts using an `XMLConnector` component to load content from an external source. The component binds the `results` property to a `DataSet` component. The `DataSet` provides content to UI components in a two-way binding. This means that it remains synchronized as UI components update the XML tree.

When requested, the `XMLConnector` generates a `deltaPacket` that contains a list of all changes to the XML tree. It sends the `deltaPacket` to an `XUpdateResolver` component, where the changes are converted into XUpdate statements. The resolver sends these statements to a second XMLConnector, which in turn sends the content externally for server-side processing. As I mentioned earlier, this is a complicated process, so I won't go into more detail here.

In this chapter's examples, I've loaded content from an external XML document into Flash. It's important to understand the security model for working with external data. This model applies to any external data accessed by Flash, including XML.

Understanding Flash Security

From Flash Player 6 and above, restrictions apply to the loading of external data, including XML documents. You can only load content that comes from the same domain as the Flash movie. In Flash Player 7 and above, you can't load data from subdomains.

This means that if the SWF file resides at http://www.apress.com, you can only load content that is also from http://www.apress.com. Users with Flash Player 7 and above won't be able to load data from subdomains such as http://books.apress.com or https://www.apress.com.

The restriction doesn't apply when you're working in the Flash Integrated Development Environment (IDE). However, it comes into effect when the SWF file is located on a web server. You can get around the restriction by including a cross-domain policy file in the root of the web server hosting the data. That topic is a little beyond the scope of this book, but you can find out more in the Flash help files.

Summary

In this chapter, you learned how to use Flash as an alternative mechanism for displaying and manipulating XML content on the client side. One advantage of using Flash is that you don't need to consider cross-browser issues in your application. Flash Lite 2.0 can also display XML content in devices such as phone handsets, making it easy to deploy your application for a range of purposes.

You saw two methods of working with XML documents: using the XML and XMLNode classes, and using the XMLConnector data component. You worked through the properties and methods available through the XML and XMLNode classes. Many of them were similar to the XML DOM methods that you worked with in Chapter 8.

You worked through several examples that allowed you to load and manipulate XML content using a Flash interface. The chapter briefly covered the sendAndLoad() method, which sends content to a server-side file for external updating.

You used the XMLConnector component to work with an XML document visually. You were able to load the document and a schema representation by configuring the Component Inspector panel. You were also able to use data binding to display the content in UI components. I worked through an example that used these concepts, and I only needed to write a single line of ActionScript to include the XML content in a Flash movie. I finished the chapter by looking at the security restrictions that apply to external data.

This chapter concludes the section on working with XML content on the client. In the remaining chapters of this book, I'll look at server-side XML interaction. I'll introduce the concepts in Chapter 11 and compare the .NET 2.0 and PHP 5 code within an application. You'll see two complete server-side case studies: one using .NET 2.0 in Chapter 12, and one using PHP 5 in Chapter 13.

CHAPTER 11

■ ■ ■

Introduction to Server-Side XML

For the remainder of this book, I'll show you how to work with XML on the server. I'll focus on two of the most popular server-side languages—.NET 2.0 and PHP 5.

In this chapter, I'll present the reasons for using server-side XML, and I'll work through some simple server-side code samples. The chapter presents the code samples side-by-side, so you can see how to access XML documents in each language. In the next two chapters, I'll work through two case studies that provide more details about how to use .NET and PHP to build XML applications. Chapter 12 will focus on a .NET 2.0 application, while Chapter 13 will provide a PHP case study.

Server-Side vs. Client-Side XML Processing

So far, you've learned how to work with XML documents using client-side XML processing. The client-side examples showed you how to load XML content and display it within the web browser. You used JavaScript to work with the Document Object Model (DOM), and you transformed XML documents into XHTML using Extensible Stylesheet Language Transformations (XSLT) stylesheets.

In the examples, you may have noticed that I didn't update the XML documents—that's not possible with client-side XML. You also noticed that when you worked with JavaScript, you had to consider the target web browsers and write code appropriate to each. You weren't able to work with client-side XSLT in Opera.

You can overcome some of the limitations of client-side XML by working with XML on the server. Server-side XML processing provides the following advantages:

- *Applications don't need to be concerned with target web browser versions*: Server-side pages deliver XHTML to the client, so you don't need to worry about creating code that works across different browsers. You also don't need to rewrite applications to cope with new browsers or browser versions.
- *Applying transformations server-side can reduce the amount of content downloaded from the server*: Server-side pages only need to provide XHTML to the browser. In the case of XSLT transformations, you don't need to provide both the source XML document and XSLT stylesheet.
- *Server-side processing allows for increased security of data*: Server-side pages can filter potentially sensitive XML data before providing content to a web page.

The downside of server-side processing is an increase in server load. It's possible to overcome this limitation and improve application performance by caching frequently accessed pages.

This chapter contains sample .NET 2.0 and PHP 5 code. I've written the .NET samples in Visual Basic .NET (VB .NET). If you want to work through the code provided in the chapter, make sure you have a web server installed that is capable of running the appropriate language.

For the .NET 2.0 samples, you need to install Internet Information Services (IIS) and the .NET Framework 2.0. You can download the .NET Framework 2.0 from the Microsoft web site; you can search for it at `http://www.microsoft.com/downloads/search.aspx?displaylang=en`—the actual URL is too long to print!

If you're working with PHP 5, you'll need a web server capable of running PHP, such as Apache. You can download PHP from `http://www.php.net/downloads.php`. You can also run PHP through IIS, providing you download the relevant installation files from `http://au3.php.net/install.windows`.

■ **Tip** As an alternative, you can download XAMPP from `http://www.apachefriends.org/en/xampp.html`. This download includes PHP, MySQL, and Perl together in a single, preconfigured file. Simply install the package, and you'll be ready to start working immediately.

Server-Side Languages

Many different server-side languages are capable of working with XML applications. Common languages include VB .NET, Visual C# .NET (C#), PHP, ColdFusion, JavaServer Pages (JSP), and Perl. It can be difficult to choose which language is appropriate for your needs. In this section, I'll cover two of the most popular server-side approaches—the .NET Framework and PHP.

.NET

The .NET Framework is a set of web development technologies from Microsoft. It is the successor to Active Server Pages (ASP) and is part of the .NET platform. It features a common language runtime (CLR) that all Microsoft applications share. This means that developers can write .NET web applications in any language supported by the CLR, including C#, VB .NET, JScript .NET, Perl, and Python. I've written the samples in this chapter in VB .NET.

The .NET Framework offers a managed run-time environment. It includes a range of controls and supports data binding. Tools such as Visual Studio allow developers to work visually.

Microsoft released .NET 2.0 in November 2005. It also released Visual Studio 2005 and SQL Server 2005 at the same time.

Advantages

There are many reasons for working with the .NET Framework, including the following:

- The .NET Framework is free, and you can download it from the Microsoft web site.
- The .NET Framework runs on the Microsoft IIS web server, which is provided with many recent Windows operating systems.
- .NET is documented extensively on the Microsoft Developer Network (MSDN) at `http://msdn.microsoft.com`.
- .NET developers can work in a range of languages.

Drawbacks

Developers working with the .NET Framework need to consider the following:

- .NET requires the Windows operating system and Microsoft IIS web server. It can run on Linux using Mono (`http://www.mono-project.com/`) or DotGNU (`http://www.dotgnu.org/`), but this isn't native.
- .NET 1.0 and 1.1 did not always generate compliant XHTML code. However, .NET 2.0 addresses this problem.

XML Support

The .NET Framework integrates tightly with XML, providing many namespaces, classes, and controls for working with XML. Namespaces in .NET represent a group of related classes. They provide a hierarchical system for organizing code and allow developers to interact with external code libraries. Five namespaces implement the XML core standards. Table 11-1 summarizes these namespaces and their purpose.

Table 11-1. *XML Namespaces in .NET*

Namespace	Purpose
`System.Xml`	Provides the ability to read and write XML content and work with the DOM. Implements DOM Level 1 Core and DOM Level 2 Core.
`System.Xml.Schema`	Applies XML schema constraints. Implements the XML schema 1 (XML Schema Part 1: Structures) recommendation and supports XML schema 2 (XML Schema Part 2: Datatypes) for data types.
`System.Xml.Serialization`	Serializes to plain XML and Simple Object Access Protocol (SOAP).
`System.Xml.XPath`	Allows for navigation of XML documents using XPath. Implements DOM XPath.
`System.Xml.Xsl`	Allows for transformation of XML documents using XSLT stylesheets.

Other namespaces also work with XML, including `System.Web.Services` and `System.Data`.

As you saw in Table 11-1, the .NET Framework supports DOM Level 1 and some of DOM Level 2. The Framework also includes Microsoft additions to the DOM to make working with XML documents easier.

Table 11-2 provides information about some of the most useful classes within the `System.Xml` namespace. You'll notice that some of them are named in a similar way to the DOM interfaces you saw earlier in the book.

Table 11-2. *Useful Classes Within the System.Xml Namespace in .NET*

Class	DOM Interface Equivalent	Purpose
`XmlAttribute`	`Attribute`	Represents an attribute.
`XmlCDataSection`	`CDATASection`	Represents a CDATA section.
`XmlComment`	`Comment`	Represents the contents of an XML comment.
`XmlDataDocument`		Allows structured data to be stored, retrieved, and manipulated through a relational `DataSet`. Appropriate for use with XML database content.
`XmlDocument`	`Document`	Represents an XML document. Appropriate for use with a physical XML document.
`XmlDocumentFragment`	`DocumentFragment`	Represents a lightweight object that is useful for tree insert operations.
`XmlElement`	`Element`	Represents an element.
`XmlEntity`	`Entity`	Represents an entity declaration.
`XmlEntityReference`	`EntityReference`	Represents an entity reference node.
`XmlNamedNodeMap`	`NamedNodeMap`	Represents a collection of nodes that you can access by name or index.
`XmlNodeList`	`NodeList`	Represents an ordered collection of nodes.
`XmlNode`	`Node`	Represents a single node in an XML document.

Class	DOM Interface Equivalent	Purpose
XmlReader		Represents a reader that provides fast, noncached, forward-only access to XML data.
XmlText	Text	Represents the text content of an element or attribute.
XmlTextReader		Represents a reader that provides fast, noncached, forward-only access to streamed XML data.
XmlTextWriter		Represents a writer that provides a fast, noncached, forward-only way to generate XML content.
XmlWriter		Represents a writer that provides a fast, noncached, forward-only way to generate XML content.

Every node type in the .NET DOM inherits from the XmlNode class. This class has a number of member properties and methods that correspond to the DOM scripting methods and properties used client-side. The XmlDocument also includes member properties and methods similar to those in the Document interface within the World Wide Web Consortium (W3C) DOM.

.NET 2.0 simplifies the process of working with read-only XML content, compared with .NET 1.x. Version 2.0 includes the Xml control, which you can use to write out an XML document or the results from an XSLT transformation. You can use the DocumentSource property to specify the XML document, and you can optionally transform the document with a TransformSource. The TransformSource is a valid XSLT stylesheet.

.NET 2.0 also includes the new XMLDataSource control, which allows for declarative data binding to XML files. This control uses a hierarchical data source and binds to hierarchical data-bound controls, such as the TreeView and Menu controls. The XmlDataSource control also allows for binding with list controls, such as GridView, DropDownList, and DataList. You can use XPath expressions to determine the bound data, and it's possible to apply a transformation using a TransformSource with this control. The XMLDataSource control supports very limited updating.

■ **Note** .NET includes a number of server-side controls that provide additional functionality when compared with XHTML controls. These controls generate XHTML and supporting code on the client side, and you can manipulate them programmatically.

PHP

PHP (Hypertext Preprocessor) is an open source server-side scripting language. It was originally designed on Perl scripts in 1995, but has undergone significant changes since that time. PHP 5 was released in July 2004 and provides an object-oriented approach.

Advantages

There are a number of advantages to working with PHP, including the following:

- PHP is open source and is freely available from `http://www.php.net/`.
- PHP is cross-platform.
- PHP includes a large number of free and open source libraries.
- The Linux, Apache, MySQL, PHP (LAMP) architecture is an inexpensive, reliable, and scalable approach to building web applications.

Drawbacks

Developers working with PHP need to consider the following:

- PHP doesn't enforce the declaration of variables, and variables aren't strictly typed.
- PHP 5 is not fully backward compatible with PHP 4.
- The syntax required to connect to different databases is slightly different: .NET abstracts this into the `ADO.NET` layer, while PHP provides the `PEAR` class library for this purpose.

XML Support

PHP 5 provides more XML support than previous versions. The new XML extensions are based on the `libxml2` library from the GNOME project. This library provides for common code shared between all XML extensions. Developers now only need to work with one library for their XML tasks—something not possible in previous versions of PHP. You can find out more about this library at `http://www.xmlsoft.org/`.

PHP 5 has inherited Simple API for XML (SAX) support from PHP 4. The API for this has not changed, so code from PHP 4 should still work under PHP 5. SAX support is now based on the `libxml2` library rather than the `expat` library.

The `domxml` feature from PHP 4 has been completely rewritten. PHP 4 did not follow the standard W3C property and method names. It also had memory leak issues prior to PHP 4.3.

PHP 5 now supports the W3C DOM Level 3 Core standard with the `dom` extension. The new version uses the same method and property names as in the W3C recommendation. You can find out more about these methods and properties in Chapter 8. The rewritten `dom` extension has resolved the memory issues, but it also means that older PHP pages that use `domxml` won't work under PHP 5.

You can load an XML document using a `DomDocument` object:

```
$domDoc = new DomDocument();
$domDoc->load("dvd.xml");
```

You can also use this approach to load an XML stream. You can then manipulate the `DomDocument` using standard W3C DOM methods and properties such as `getElementsByTagName()`, `childNodes`, `firstChild`, `nodeName`, `nodeType`, `createElement()`, `createTextNode()`, and `appendChild()`.

You can traverse the document tree using XPath statements:

```
$xPath = new domxpath($domDoc);
$titles = $xPath->query("/library/DVD/title");
```

PHP 5 supports XSLT using the `libxslt` engine. You can find out more at `http://xmlsoft.org/XSLT/`. PHP 5 no longer supports the Sablotron XSLT processor available to PHP 4. The XSLT API is similar to that used in Mozilla, and you can find code examples in Chapter 8. You can also call PHP functions from within XSLT stylesheets. While doing so may reduce the portability of stylesheets, this approach might be necessary on occasion.

PHP 5 only supports the `libxslt` processor. `libxslt` was chosen because it's also based on `libxml2` and therefore fits with the other XML approaches within PHP 5.

PHP 5 also includes the new `SimpleXML` extension. This extension provides a lightweight approach to working with XML documents by using standard object properties and iterators. The following code shows how to load an XML document into a `SimpleXML` object:

```
$sxe = simplexml_load_file("dvd.xml");
```

`SimpleXML` also includes an `XPath` interface for traversing the XML document tree:

```
$sxe->xpath('/library/DVD/title')
```

`SimpleXML` uses many of the new features available with the Zend Engine 2. Be aware that you may experience bugs with `SimpleXML` because the approach is so new. The code samples provided here don't use this extension.

PHP 5 includes an `xmlreader` extension that processes XML documents as streams, similar to the approach taken in the .NET Framework. It also includes a standards-compliant SOAP extension.

All of the XML extensions are enabled with a standard installation of PHP. You need to configure XSLT and SOAP support within the `php.ini` file before you start using these extensions in your work.

Working Through Simple Examples

You've learned a little about two of the most common server-side languages, so now it's time to move on to an example. I'll work through a simple application that shows the basic XML processing techniques in each language. You'll learn how to read XML content from an external document; transform it with XSLT; and add, edit, and delete content.

For the remainder of the chapter, I'll work on a simple web application that organizes a DVD collection. The application stores the details of your DVD library in the XML document—in fact, the one used throughout the book. It uses server-side XSLT to generate XHTML to display the contents of the library. The application allows you to add a new DVD, edit an existing DVD, and delete a DVD.

Let's get started by looking at the XML document that contains the DVD list.

The XML Document

You've already seen the XML document that contains the DVD list. The following shows the structure of the document with a single DVD:

```
<?xml version="1.0" encoding="UTF-8"?>
<!-- This XML document describes a DVD library -->
<library>
  <DVD id="1">
    <title>Breakfast at Tiffany's</title>
    <format>Movie</format>
    <genre>Classic</genre>
  </DVD>
</library>
```

The document element `<library>` contains a number of `<DVD>` elements. Each `<DVD>` element contains a `<title>`, `<format>`, and `<genre>` element. The `<DVD>` elements are uniquely identified by an `id` attribute. The code uses this attribute to identify each DVD when updating content.

Transforming the XML

The first step is to display the DVD library in a web page. The application does this by transforming the XML content into XHTML using an XSLT stylesheet. It carries out the transformation on the server and displays the DVD list in a table, sorting in order of title. The transformation adds links that allow you to modify or delete an entry.

Figure 11-1 shows the transformed XML document displayed within Internet Explorer (IE).

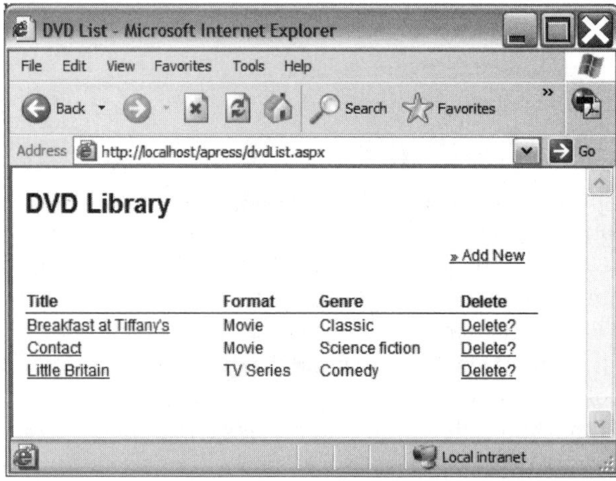

Figure 11-1. *The transformed XML document*

The following XSLT stylesheet, `dvdDetails.xsl`, transforms the content in the .NET application:

```
<?xml version="1.0"?>
<xsl:stylesheet version="1.0" xmlns:xsl="http://www.w3.org/1999/XSL/Transform">
  <xsl:template match="/library">
    <p style="width: 390px; text-align:right;">
    <a href="addDVD.aspx">&#187; Add New</a></p>
    <table cellspacing="0">
      <tr>
        <th>Title</th>
        <th>Format</th>
        <th>Genre</th>
        <th>Delete</th>
      </tr>
      <xsl:apply-templates select="DVD">
        <xsl:sort select="title"/>
      </xsl:apply-templates>
    </table>
  </xsl:template>
  <xsl:template match="DVD">
    <tr>
      <td>
        <a>
          <xsl:attribute name="href">
            editDVD.aspx?id=<xsl:value-of select="@id"/>
          </xsl:attribute>
          <xsl:value-of select="title"/>
        </a>
      </td>
      <td><xsl:value-of select="format"/></td>
      <td><xsl:value-of select="genre"/></td>
      <td>
        <a>
          <xsl:attribute name="href">
            deleteDVD.aspx?id=<xsl:value-of select="@id"/>
          </xsl:attribute>
          Delete?
        </a>
      </td>
    </tr>
  </xsl:template>
</xsl:stylesheet>
```

This simple stylesheet displays the DVD elements in a table. It starts with the XML declaration and <xsl:stylesheet> element:

```
<?xml version="1.0"?>
<xsl:stylesheet version="1.0" xmlns:xsl="http://www.w3.org/1999/XSL/Transform">
```

The stylesheet then matches the <library> document element and writes an Add New link:

```
<xsl:template match="/library">
  <p style="width: 390px; text-align:right;">
  <a href="addDVD.aspx">&#187; Add New</a></p>
```

This link opens the page addDVD.aspx.

The template then goes on to create the table and header elements:

```
<table cellspacing="0">
  <tr>
    <th>Title</th>
    <th>Format</th>
    <th>Genre</th>
    <th>Delete</th>
  </tr>
```

It then applies the template for the <DVD> element and applies a sort order before closing the table:

```
  <xsl:apply-templates select="DVD">
    <xsl:sort select="title"/>
  </xsl:apply-templates>
</table>
```

The <DVD> element template creates a new table row and creates a link around the title element:

```
<xsl:template match="DVD">
  <tr>
    <td>
      <a>
        <xsl:attribute name="href">
          editDVD.aspx?id=<xsl:value-of select="@id"/>
        </xsl:attribute>
        <xsl:value-of select="title"/>
      </a>
    </td>
```

This code creates a link to edit an existing DVD in the page editDVD.aspx. Notice that it passes the id of the <DVD> element to the page.

The code also displays the format and genre of the DVD in the table:

```
<td><xsl:value-of select="format"/></td>
<td><xsl:value-of select="genre"/></td>
```

It finishes by creating a Delete link for each DVD:

```
    <td>
      <a>
        <xsl:attribute name="href">
          deleteDVD.aspx?id=<xsl:value-of select="@id"/>
```

```
          </xsl:attribute>
          Delete?
        </a>
      </td>
    </tr>
  </xsl:template>
</xsl:stylesheet>
```

The link calls the page `deleteDVD.aspx` and passes the `id`.

Note that the links within this stylesheet refer to `.aspx` files. I'll introduce these pages shortly. The file `dvdDetails1.xsl` contains the PHP version of this stylesheet. This stylesheet is slightly different from the .NET version.

The next step in building the application is to create the server-side page that applies this transformation to the XML document.

.NET: Transforming the XML

The `dvdList.aspx` page applies the transformation. This is a simple page written in VB .NET:

```
<%@ Page Language="VB" %>
<%@ Import Namespace="System.Xml" %>
<html>
  <head>
    <title>DVD List</title>
    <link href="styles.css" type="text/css" rel="stylesheet" />
  </head>
  <body>
    <h1>DVD Library</h1>
    <form runat=server>
      <asp:Xml id="dvdXML" DocumentSource="dvd.xml" ➥
      TransformSource="dvdDetails.xsl" runat="server" />
    </form>
  </body>
</html>
```

The code starts by declaring the page language and importing the `System.Xml` namespace:

```
<%@ Page Language="VB" %>
<%@ Import Namespace="System.Xml" %>
```

Then it includes some XHTML tags to create the page and display a header:

```
<html>
  <head>
    <title>DVD List</title>
    <link href="styles.css" type="text/css" rel="stylesheet" />
  </head>
  <body>
    <h1>DVD Library</h1>
```

The page finishes by loading and transforming the XML document using the new .NET 2.0 `Xml` control:

```
    <form runat=server>
      <asp:Xml id="dvdXML" DocumentSource="dvd.xml" ➥
      TransformSource="dvdDetails.xsl" runat="server" />
    </form>
  </body>
</html>
```

Notice that it's possible to specify the `DocumentSource` and `TransformSource` within the control. If you test this document through IIS, you'll see something similar to the screen shot shown in Figure 11-1.

An alternative approach would be to use the `XmlDataSource` control and bind the XML document directly to a web control, such as the `Repeater`. This approach is shown in the page `dvdList1.aspx`. I could apply a transformation during the process, but I've created this page without a transformation so I can show how to use XPath expressions to target parts of the XML document:

```
<%@ Page Language="VB" %>
<%@ Import Namespace="System.Xml" %>
<html>
  <head>
    <title>DVD List</title>
    <link href="styles.css" type="text/css" rel="stylesheet" />
  </head>
  <body>
    <h1>DVD Library</h1>
    <p style="width: 390px; text-align:right;">
    <a href="addDVD.aspx">&#187; Add New</a></p>
    <form runat="server">
      <asp:Repeater ID="Repeater" runat="server" DataSourceID="XmlDataSource1">
        <HeaderTemplate>
        <table cellspacing="0">
          <tr>
            <th>Title</th>
            <th>Format</th>
            <th>Genre</th>
            <th>Delete</th>
          </tr>
        </HeaderTemplate>
        <ItemTemplate>
          <tr>
            <td><a href="editDVD.aspx?id=<%# XPath("@id") %>">
            <%# XPath("title") %></a></td>
            <td><%# XPath("format") %></td>
```

```
          <td><%# XPath("genre") %></td>
          <td><a href="deleteDVD.aspx?id=<%# XPath("@id") %>">Delete?</a>
        </tr>
      </ItemTemplate>
      <FooterTemplate>
        </table>
      </FooterTemplate>
    </asp:Repeater>
    <asp:XmlDataSource ID="XmlDataSource1" runat="server" ➥
    DataFile="dvd.xml" XPath="/library/DVD">
    </asp:XmlDataSource>
  </form>
</body>
</html>
```

This page starts the same way as the previous page. It creates the `Add New` link and specifies the structure for the XML content in a `Repeater` control:

```
<p style="width: 390px; text-align:right;">
<a href="addDVD.aspx">&#187; Add New</a></p>
<form runat="server">
  <asp:Repeater ID="Repeater" runat="server" DataSourceID="XmlDataSource1">
    <HeaderTemplate>
      <table cellspacing="0">
        <tr>
          <th>Title</th>
          <th>Format</th>
          <th>Genre</th>
          <th>Delete</th>
        </tr>
    </HeaderTemplate>
    <ItemTemplate>
      <tr>
        <td><a href="editDVD.aspx?id=<%# XPath("@id") %>">
        <%# XPath("title") %></a></td>
        <td><%# XPath("format") %></td>
        <td><%# XPath("genre") %></td>
        <td><a href="deleteDVD.aspx?id=<%# XPath("@id") %>">Delete?</a>
      </tr>
    </ItemTemplate>
    <FooterTemplate>
      </table>
    </FooterTemplate>
  </asp:Repeater>
```

The Repeater control binds to the data source by specifying the id of the XmlDataSource control (XmlDataSource1). The control uses XPath expressions to target specific portions of the XML document:

```
<%# XPath("@id") %>
<%# XPath("title") %>
<%# XPath("format") %>
<%# XPath("genre") %>
```

The XmlDataSource control loads the file dvd.xml and specifies the context for the XPath expressions using the XPath property:

```
      <asp:XmlDataSource ID="XmlDataSource1" runat="server" ➥
      DataFile="dvd.xml" XPath="/library/DVD">
      </asp:XmlDataSource>
    </form>
  </body>
</html>
```

Figure 11-1 shows how this document should appear when opened in a web browser.

PHP: Transforming the XML

It's relatively easy to load and transform an XML document using PHP 5. This example uses the XSLT stylesheet dvdDetails1.xsl. The stylesheet differs slightly from the .NET version, as it includes the <html>, <head>, and <body> declarations in the first match. This template follows, with the added lines shown in bold:

```
<xsl:template match="/library">
<html>
  <head>
    <title>DVD List</title>
     <link href="styles.css" type="text/css" rel="stylesheet" />
  </head>
  <body>
    <h1>DVD Library</h1>
   <p style="width: 390px; text-align:right;">
    <a href="addDVD.php">&#187; Add New</a></p>
    <table cellspacing="0">
      <tr>
        <th>Title</th>
        <th>Format</th>
        <th>Genre</th>
        <th>Delete</th>
      </tr>
      <xsl:apply-templates select="DVD">
        <xsl:sort select="title"/>
      </xsl:apply-templates>
```

```
    </table>
  </body>
</html>
</xsl:template>
```

The only difference in the remainder of the stylesheet is a reference to `.php` files instead of `.aspx` files.

Applying the transformation is straightforward, providing you've enabled the XSL extension in your `php.ini` file. The file `dvdList.php` shows how:

```
<?php
$xsl = new DomDocument();
$xsl->load("dvdDetails1.xsl");
$inputdom = new DomDocument();
$inputdom->load("dvd.xml");
$proc = new XsltProcessor();
$xsl = $proc->importStylesheet($xsl);
$newdom = $proc->transformToDoc($inputdom);
print $newdom->saveXML();
?>
```

The code starts by loading both the XSLT stylesheet and XML document into `DomDocument` objects:

```
$xsl = new DomDocument();
$xsl->load("dvdDetails1.xsl");
$inputdom = new DomDocument();
$inputdom->load("dvd.xml");
```

It then creates an instance of the XSLT processor and imports the stylesheet:

```
$proc = new XsltProcessor();
$xsl = $proc->importStylesheet($xsl);
```

Notice that this code is similar to the Mozilla client-side transformations used in Chapter 8.

Finally, the code applies the transformation and shows the results in the web page:

```
$newdom = $proc->transformToDoc($inputdom);
print $newdom->saveXML();
```

When you test the page, you should see the same result as shown in Figure 11-1.

Adding a New DVD

The application allows you to add a new DVD to the library. You need to provide information about the title, format, and genre of the DVD and update the external XML document.

When the stylesheet transforms the data, it includes an `Add New` link. Depending on which stylesheet used, the link loads either the page `addDVD.aspx` or `addDVD.php`. Figure 11-2 shows how the `addDVD.aspx` page appears within a web browser.

Figure 11-2. *The addDVD.aspx page*

The page hosts a simple form that includes three text input fields. The code to create this page is a little different in the PHP application compared with the .NET version.

.NET: Adding a New DVD

The `addDVD.aspx` page adds a new DVD and includes processing to update the XML document. The page follows:

```
<%@ Page Language="VB" %>
<%@ import Namespace="System.Xml" %>
<script runat="server">
  Private Sub btnAdd_Click(sender As Object, e As EventArgs)
    Dim myXmlDocument as XmlDocument = new XmlDocument()
    myXmlDocument.Load (server.mappath("dvd.xml"))
    Dim rootNode as XMLElement = myXmlDocument.DocumentElement
    Dim intNewID as Integer = rootNode.childNodes.count + 1
    Dim newDVDElement as XMLElement = myXmlDocument.CreateElement("DVD")
    newDVDElement.SetAttribute("id",intNewID)
    Dim newTitleElement as XMLElement = myXmlDocument.CreateElement("title")
    newTitleElement.appendChild(myXmlDocument.CreateTextNode(txtTitle.text))
    Dim newFormatElement as XMLElement = myXmlDocument.CreateElement("format")
    newFormatElement.appendChild(myXmlDocument.CreateTextNode(txtFormat.text))
    Dim newGenreElement as XMLElement = myXmlDocument.CreateElement("genre")
    newGenreElement.appendChild(myXmlDocument.CreateTextNode(txtGenre.text))
    newDVDElement.appendChild(newTitleElement)
    newDVDElement.appendChild(newFormatElement)
    newDVDElement.appendChild(newGenreElement)
    rootNode.appendChild(newDVDElement)
    myXmlDocument.Save(Server.Mappath("dvd.xml"))
   lblMessage.text = "You have successfully updated the XML document"
```

```
  End Sub
</script>
<html>
  <head>
    <link href="styles.css" type="text/css" rel="stylesheet" />
  </head>
  <body>
    <h1>Add New DVD</h1>
    <form runat="server">
      <asp:Label id="lblMessage" runat="server" forecolor="Blue"></asp:Label>
      <table>
      <tr>
        <td class="emphasis">
          <asp:Label id="lblTitle" runat="server" text="Label">Title:</asp:Label>
        </td>
        <td>
          <asp:TextBox id="txtTitle" runat="server" Width="200px"></asp:TextBox>
            <asp:RequiredFieldValidator id="val1" runat="server"
            ErrorMessage="Please enter a title" Display="Dynamic"
            ControlToValidate="txtTitle"></asp:RequiredFieldValidator>
        </td>
      </tr>
      <tr>
        <td class="emphasis">
          <asp:Label id="lblFormat" runat="server" text="Label">Format:</asp:Label>
        </td>
        <td>
          <asp:TextBox id="txtFormat" runat="server" Width="200px"></asp:TextBox>
          <asp:RequiredFieldValidator id="RequiredFieldValidator2" runat="server"
          ErrorMessage="Please enter a format" Display="Dynamic"
          ControlToValidate="txtFormat"></asp:RequiredFieldValidator>
        </td>
      </tr>
      <tr>
        <td class="emphasis">
          <asp:Label id="lblGenre" runat="server" text="Label">Genre:</asp:Label>
        </td>
        <td>
          <asp:TextBox id="txtGenre" runat="server" Width="200px"></asp:TextBox>
          <asp:RequiredFieldValidator id="RequiredFieldValidator3" runat="server"
          ErrorMessage="Please enter a title" Display="Dynamic"
          ControlToValidate="txtGenre"></asp:RequiredFieldValidator>
        </td>
      </tr>
      <tr>
        <td class="emphasis" colspan="2">
          <asp:Button id="btnAdd" onclick="btnAdd_Click" runat="server"
```

```
          Text="Add New DVD"></asp:Button>
        </td>
      </tr>
      </table>
    </form>
  </body>
</html>
```

I'll work through this code so you can understand what happens. Note that, for simplicity, I've assumed that the new DVD id value is one more than the number of <DVD> elements in the XML document.

The page starts with declarations and a subroutine that responds to the button click. I'll come back to that code block a little later:

```
<%@ Page Language="VB" %>
<%@ import Namespace="System.Xml" %>
```

The page includes the <head> and <body> sections, with a heading and <form> opening tag:

```
<html>
  <head>
    <link href="styles.css" type="text/css" rel="stylesheet" />
  </head>
  <body>
    <h1>Add New DVD</h1>
    <form runat="server">
```

I've included a Label control to display a message to the user after updating:

```
<asp:Label id="lblMessage" runat="server" forecolor="Blue"></asp:Label>
```

I've created each of the input fields with a Label and TextBox control. I'll use the id attribute to identify the controls later in the code. I've also included a RequiredFieldValidator control for each field. The title section of the form follows:

```
<table>
  <tr>
    <td class="emphasis">
      <asp:Label id="lblTitle" runat="server" text="Label">Title:</asp:Label>
    </td>
    <td>
      <asp:TextBox id="txtTitle" runat="server" Width="200px"></asp:TextBox>
      <asp:RequiredFieldValidator id="val1" runat="server"
      ErrorMessage="Please enter a title" Display="Dynamic"
      ControlToValidate="txtTitle"></asp:RequiredFieldValidator>
    </td>
  </tr>
```

The remaining elements use similar code. The block finishes with a Button control and closing tags. When the user clicks the Add New DVD button, it calls the btnAdd_Click subroutine listed at the top of the page:

```
      <tr>
        <td class="emphasis" colspan="2">
          <asp:Button id="btnAdd" onclick="btnAdd_Click" runat="server"
          Text="Add New DVD"></asp:Button>
        </td>
      </tr>
      </table>
    </form>
  </body>
</html>
```

The btnAdd_Click subroutine does all of the processing to add a new DVD. It starts by creating a new XmlDocument object and using it to load the dvd.xml file:

```
Private Sub btnAdd_Click(sender As Object, e As EventArgs)
  Dim myXmlDocument as XmlDocument = new XmlDocument()
  myXmlDocument.Load (server.mappath("dvd.xml"))
```

The code then works with the contents of the file. It sets a variable for the document element and determines the new id by adding one to the total number of DVD elements:

```
Dim rootNode as XMLElement = myXmlDocument.DocumentElement
Dim intNewID as Integer = rootNode.childNodes.count + 1
```

The code then creates a new <DVD> element using the CreateElement method and sets the id attribute:

```
Dim newDVDElement as XMLElement = myXmlDocument.CreateElement("DVD")
newDVDElement.SetAttribute("id",intNewID)
```

Most of the remaining lines create the new elements and text nodes and append them to the appropriate places in the XML document:

```
Dim newTitleElement as XMLElement = myXmlDocument.CreateElement("title")
newTitleElement.appendChild(myXmlDocument.CreateTextNode(txtTitle.text))
Dim newFormatElement as XMLElement = myXmlDocument.CreateElement("format")
newFormatElement.appendChild(myXmlDocument.CreateTextNode(txtFormat.text))
Dim newGenreElement as XMLElement = myXmlDocument.CreateElement("genre")
newGenreElement.appendChild(myXmlDocument.CreateTextNode(txtGenre.text))
newDVDElement.appendChild(newTitleElement)
newDVDElement.appendChild(newFormatElement)
newDVDElement.appendChild(newGenreElement)
rootNode.appendChild(newDVDElement)
```

The code block finishes by saving the XML document and displaying a simple update message in the Label control:

```
  myXmlDocument.Save(Server.Mappath("dvd.xml"))
  lblMessage.text = "You have successfully updated the XML document"
End Sub
```

Note You can only save the XML document if you've set up the appropriate permissions on the folder containing the `dvd.xml` document within IIS.

Figure 11-3 shows how the page appears after adding a new DVD.

Figure 11-3. *Adding a new DVD*

You could probably have used other approaches to add the new DVD, but this represents a simple method of updating the XML document. No doubt, the DOM manipulation methods used here will look similar to you after working through Chapter 8.

PHP: Adding a New DVD

The `addDVDAction.php` page does much the same as the corresponding .NET page. The `addDVD.htm` page contains this form:

```
<html>
  <head>
    <link href="styles.css" type="text/css" rel="stylesheet" />
  </head>
  <body>
    <h1>Add New DVD</h1>
    <form id="frmNewDVD" method="POST" action="addDVDAction.php">
      <table>
        <tr>
          <td class="emphasis">Title:</td>
          <td><input name="txtTitle" type="text" size="30" maxlength="50"/></td>
        </tr>
        <tr>
```

```
        <td class="emphasis">Format:</td>
        <td><input name="txtFormat" type="text" size="30" maxlength="50"/></td>
      </tr>
      <tr>
        <td class="emphasis">Genre:</td>
        <td><input name="txtGenre" type="text" size="30" maxlength="50"/></td>
      </tr>
      <tr>
        <td class="emphasis" colspan="2">
          <input type="submit" id="btnAdd" value="Add DVD"/>
        </td>
      </tr>
    </table>
  </form>
 </body>
</html>
```

For simplicity, I haven't added validation to the form. I'm sure you're familiar with this type of page, so I won't go through an explanation.

The addDVDAction.php page needs to collect the details submitted from the form and use DOM scripting to generate the new <DVD> element. The page also needs to save the updated details to the DVD.xml document. The page follows:

```
<?php
  $title = $_POST['txtTitle'];
  $format = $_POST['txtFormat'];
  $genre = $_POST['txtGenre'];
  $dom = new DomDocument();
  $dom->preserveWhiteSpace = false;
  $dom->formatOutput = true;
  $dom->load("dvd.xml");
  $root = $dom->documentElement;
  $DVDelements = $dom->getElementsByTagName("DVD");
  $newID = $DVDelements->length + 1;
  $newDVDElement = $dom->createElement("DVD");
  $newDVDElement->setAttribute("id",$newID);
  $newTitleElement = $dom->createElement("title");
  $newTitleElement->appendChild($dom->createTextNode($title));
  $newFormatElement = $dom->createElement("format");
  $newFormatElement->appendChild($dom->createTextNode($format));
  $newGenreElement = $dom->createElement("genre");
  $newGenreElement->appendChild($dom->createTextNode($genre));
  $newDVDElement->appendChild($newTitleElement);
  $newDVDElement->appendChild($newFormatElement);
  $newDVDElement->appendChild($newGenreElement);
  $root->appendChild($newDVDElement);
  $dom->save("dvd.xml");
?>
```

```
<html>
  <head>
    <link href="styles.css" type="text/css" rel="stylesheet" />
  </head>
  <body>
    <div id="divMessage">You have successfully updated the XML document</div>
  </body>
</html>
```

You'll notice that the page is functionally similar to the .NET version. It starts by retrieving the values entered in the form controls:

```
<?php
  $title = $_POST['txtTitle'];
  $format = $_POST['txtFormat'];
  $genre = $_POST['txtGenre'];
```

It then creates a new `DomDocument` object and loads the `dvd.xml` document:

```
$dom = new DomDocument();
$dom->preserveWhiteSpace = false;
$dom->formatOutput = true;
$dom->load("dvd.xml");
```

Notice that I've set the `preserveWhiteSpace` property to `false` so that the white space in the XML document is ignored. I've also specified a `true` value for the `formatOutput` property.

The next line sets a variable for the `documentElement` property:

```
$root = $dom->documentElement;
```

The code then retrieves the list of `<DVD>` elements and uses the length to determine the `id` for the new element:

```
$DVDelements = $dom->getElementsByTagName("DVD");
$newID =  $DVDelements->length + 1;
```

Most of the remaining lines create the new elements using DOM scripting. They start by creating the `<DVD>` element and setting the value of the attribute:

```
$newDVDElement = $dom->createElement("DVD");
$newDVDElement->setAttribute("id",$newID);
```

As in Chapter 8, the code uses the `createElement()` and `setAttribute()` methods.

It then creates the `<title>`, `<format>`, and `<genre>` elements and adds the appropriate text:

```
$newTitleElement = $dom->createElement("title");
$newTitleElement->appendChild($dom->createTextNode($title));
$newFormatElement = $dom->createElement("format");
$newFormatElement->appendChild($dom->createTextNode($format));
$newGenreElement = $dom->createElement("genre");
$newGenreElement->appendChild($dom->createTextNode($genre));
```

The next code block appends the child elements to the <DVD> element and then adds the <DVD> element as the last child node of the document element:

```
$newDVDElement->appendChild($newTitleElement);
$newDVDElement->appendChild($newFormatElement);
$newDVDElement->appendChild($newGenreElement);
$root->appendChild($newDVDElement);
```

The final line saves the updated XML document:

```
$dom->save("dvd.xml");
```

The remainder of the file displays a message on the web page. The example should probably include a little more error handling and a return link, but the focus of this sample is on DOM scripting.

Note You need to make sure that the appropriate permissions have been set before you can update the `dvd.xml` file.

Modifying an Existing DVD

The next task for the application is modifying the details of an existing DVD. The application does this with the `editDVD.aspx` and `editDVD.php` files, passing the `id` of the DVD to modify in the `querystring`.

.NET: Modifying DVD Information

The `editDVD.aspx` file works in a similar way to the `addDVD.aspx` file. The main difference is that the page receives the `id` of an existing DVD and displays its details in the form. The body section of this page is almost identical to the `addDVD.aspx` page, so I won't replicate it here. The only difference is in the `id` of the button and its text. When `editDVD.aspx` loads, it needs to display the details of the selected DVD in the form controls. The population is handled in the `Page_Load` subroutine.

The remainder of the page follows:

```
<%@ Page Language="VB" %>
<%@ import Namespace="System.Xml" %>
<script runat="server">
  Dim intDVDID as integer
  Dim myXmlDocument as XmlDocument = new XmlDocument()
  Dim rootNode as XMLElement
  Dim selectedDVD as XMLElement
  Sub Page_Load(Src As Object, E As EventArgs)
    intDVDID = request.querystring("id")
    myXmlDocument.Load (server.mappath("dvd.xml"))
    rootNode = myXmlDocument.DocumentElement
    selectedDVD = rootNode.childNodes(intDVDID-1)
```

```
    if Not Page.IsPostBack then
      txtTitle.text = selectedDVD.childNodes(0).InnerText
      txtFormat.text = selectedDVD.childNodes(1).InnerText
      txtGenre.text = selectedDVD.childNodes(2).InnerText
    end if
  end sub
  Private Sub btnEdit_Click(sender As Object, e As EventArgs)
    selectedDVD.childNodes(0).InnerText = txtTitle.text
    selectedDVD.childNodes(1).InnerText = txtFormat.text
    selectedDVD.childNodes(2).InnerText = txtGenre.text
    myXmlDocument.Save(Server.Mappath("dvd.xml"))
    lblMessage.text = "You have successfully updated the DVD"
  End Sub
</script>
```

This time, the page starts with declarations and creates some variables:

```
<%@ Page Language="VB" %>
<%@ import Namespace="System.Xml" %>
<script runat="server">
  Dim intDVDID as integer
  Dim myXmlDocument as XmlDocument = new XmlDocument()
  Dim rootNode as XMLElement
  Dim selectedDVD as XMLElement
```

It then runs code in response to the page loading. The subroutine retrieves the id from the querystring and loads the dvd.xml document:

```
Sub Page_Load(Src As Object, E As EventArgs)
  intDVDID = request.querystring("id")
  myXmlDocument.Load (server.mappath("dvd.xml"))
```

Next, it sets the rootNode variable and determines which <DVD> element to modify:

```
rootNode = myXmlDocument.DocumentElement
selectedDVD = rootNode.childNodes(intDVDID-1)
```

Notice that the code has to subtract one from the id value because the childNodes list is zero-based.

The subroutine then loads the details of the selected <DVD> element into the interface, using the InnerText property of each child node:

```
  if Not Page.IsPostBack then
    txtTitle.text = selectedDVD.childNodes(0).InnerText
    txtFormat.text = selectedDVD.childNodes(1).InnerText
    txtGenre.text = selectedDVD.childNodes(2).InnerText
  end if
end sub
```

Clicking the `btnEdit` button calls the `btnEdit_Click` sub:

```
Private Sub btnEdit_Click(sender As Object, e As EventArgs)
  selectedDVD.childNodes(0).InnerText = txtTitle.text
  selectedDVD.childNodes(1).InnerText = txtFormat.text
  selectedDVD.childNodes(2).InnerText = txtGenre.text
  myXmlDocument.Save(Server.Mappath("dvd.xml"))
  lblMessage.text = "You have successfully updated the DVD"
End Sub
```

This subroutine sets the `InnerText` value from the values entered into the text fields. It then uses the `Save()` method to update the `dvd.xml` document and displays a message. As before, you need to make sure that you've set the appropriate permissions to allow updating.

PHP: Modifying DVD Information

You can use the form on the page `editDVD.php` to collect the modifications, which will then be processed with the page `editDVDAction.php`. The page `editDVD.php` populates the form with the selected element:

```
<?php
  $id = $_GET['id'];
  $dom = new DomDocument();
  $dom->preserveWhiteSpace = false;
  $dom->formatOutput = true;
  $dom->load("dvd.xml");
  $path = "/library/DVD[@id=" . $id . "]";
  $xPath = new domxpath($dom);
  $selectedNode = $xPath->query($path)->item(0);
  foreach ($selectedNode->childNodes as $child) {
    if ($child->nodeName == "title") {
      $title = $child->textContent;
    }
    elseif ($child->nodeName == "format") {
      $format = $child->textContent;
    }
    elseif ($child->nodeName == "genre") {
      $genre = $child->textContent;
    }
  }
?>
<html>
  <head>
    <link href="styles.css" type="text/css" rel="stylesheet" />
  </head>
  <body>
```

```
    <h1>Edit DVD Details</h1>
    <form id="frmEditDVD" method="POST" action="editDVDAction.php">
      <input type="hidden" name="txtID" value="<?php echo $id; ?>"/>
        <table>
        <tr>
          <td class="emphasis">Title:</td>
          <td><input name="txtTitle" type="text" size="30" maxlength="50"
          value="<?php echo $title; ?>"/></td>
        </tr>
        <tr>
          <td class="emphasis">Format:</td>
          <td><input name="txtFormat" type="text" size="30" maxlength="50"
          value="<?php echo $format; ?>"/></td>
        </tr>
        <tr>
          <td class="emphasis">Genre:</td>
          <td><input name="txtGenre" type="text" size="30" maxlength="50"
          value="<?php echo $genre; ?>"/></td>
        </tr>
        <tr>
          <td class="emphasis" colspan="2">
            <input type="submit" id="btnAdd" value="Update DVD"/>
          </td>
        </tr>
      </table>
    </form>
  </body>
</html>
```

The section within the `<html></html>` tags is similar to the previous PHP example, so I'll focus on the processing code at the top of the page.

The code starts by collecting the `id` from the `querystring`:

```
<?php
$id = $_GET['id'];
```

It creates a new `DomDocument` object, sets the `preserveWhiteSpace` and `formatOutput` properties, and loads the file `dvd.xml`. There is nothing new in this code block:

```
$dom = new DomDocument();
$dom->preserveWhiteSpace = false;
$dom->formatOutput = true;
$dom->load("dvd.xml");
```

The next line creates an XPath expression and stores it in a variable called `$path`:

```
$path = "/library/DVD[@id=" . $id . "]";
```

The expression finds the `<DVD>` element with the matching `id` attribute:

```
/library/DVD[@id=1]
```

The code then creates a new dompath object and uses it to return a NodeList with matching elements. The code selects the first element from the list:

```
$xPath = new domxpath($dom);
$selectedNode = $xPath->query($path)->item(0);
```

The last block is a loop that checks the names of each of the child nodes of the <DVD> element. The code stores each value in a different variable using the PHP shorthand property textContent to access the text inside the element:

```
  foreach ($selectedNode->childNodes as $child) {
    if ($child->nodeName == "title") {
      $title = $child->textContent;
    }
    elseif ($child->nodeName == "format") {
      $format = $child->textContent;
    }
    elseif ($child->nodeName == "genre") {
      $genre = $child->textContent;
    }
  }
?>
```

The page could have located the elements using other coding approaches. Using this approach allows me to show you how to use the domxpath object and different DOM scripting methods and properties.

The page displays the values in the form elements:

```
<form id="frmEditDVD" method="POST" action="editDVDAction.php">
  <input type="hidden" name="txtID" value="<?php echo $id; ?>"/>
  <table>
    <tr>
      <td class="emphasis">Title:</td>
      <td><input name="txtTitle" type="text" size="30" maxlength="50"
      value="<?php echo $title; ?>"/></td>
    </tr>
    <tr>
      <td class="emphasis">Format:</td>
      <td><input name="txtFormat" type="text" size="30" maxlength="50"
      value="<?php echo $format; ?>"/></td>
    </tr>
    <tr>
      <td class="emphasis">Genre:</td>
      <td><input name="txtGenre" type="text" size="30" maxlength="50"
      value="<?php echo $genre; ?>"/></td>
    </tr>
    <tr>
      <td class="emphasis" colspan="2">
        <input type="submit" id="btnAdd" value="Update DVD"/>
```

```
      </td>
    </tr>
  </table>
</form>
```

Notice that I've also passed through the `id` in a hidden form field. Again, I haven't added validation to simplify the code.

Once the user changes the details of a DVD, the form submits to the page `editDVDAction.php`:

```
<?php
  $id = $_POST['txtID'];
  $title = $_POST['txtTitle'];
  $format = $_POST['txtFormat'];
  $genre = $_POST['txtGenre'];
  $dom = new DomDocument();
  $dom->load("dvd.xml");
  $path = "/library/DVD[@id=" . $id . "]";
  $xPath = new domxpath($dom);
  $selectedNode = $xPath->query($path)->item(0);
  foreach ($selectedNode->childNodes as $child) {
    if ($child->nodeName == "title") {
      $child ->firstChild->nodeValue = $title;
    }
    elseif ($child->nodeName == "format") {
      $child->firstChild->nodeValue = $format;
    }
    elseif ($child->nodeName == "genre") {
      $child->firstChild->nodeValue = $genre;
    }
  }
$dom->save("dvd.xml");
?>
<html>
  <head>
    <link href="styles.css" type="text/css" rel="stylesheet" />
  </head>
  <body>
    <div id="divMessage">You have successfully updated the XML document</div>
  </body>
</html>
```

The code starts by collecting the values posted from the form and storing them in variables:

```
<?php
  $id = $_POST['txtID'];
  $title = $_POST['txtTitle'];
  $format = $_POST['txtFormat'];
  $genre = $_POST['txtGenre'];
```

Again, the code creates a new DomDocument and loads the dvd.xml document:

```
$dom = new DomDocument();
$dom->load("dvd.xml");
```

The code uses the same approach as on the previous page, using a domxpath object to find the selected <DVD> element:

```
$path = "/library/DVD[@id=" . $id . "]";
$xPath = new domxpath($dom);
$selectedNode = $xPath->query($path)->item(0);
```

The code loops through the child nodes of the <DVD> element and applies the updates:

```
foreach ($selectedNode->childNodes as $child) {
  if ($child->nodeName == "title") {
    $child ->firstChild->nodeValue = $title;
  }
  elseif ($child->nodeName == "format") {
    $child->firstChild->nodeValue = $format;
  }
  elseif ($child->nodeName == "genre") {
    $child->firstChild->nodeValue = $genre;
  }
}
```

Notice that the code assigns the value to the nodeValue property of the firstChild of the selected element. It's important to do this because the text within an element is the firstChild of that element.

Finally, the code saves the changes:

```
$dom->save("dvd.xml");
?>
```

Deleting a DVD

The last task for the application is removing a DVD from the library. The application passes the id of the element that will be removed to either the deleteDVD.aspx or deleteDVD.php page.

.NET: Deleting a DVD

The deleteDVD.aspx page follows:

```
<%@ Page Language="VB" %>
<%@ import Namespace="System.Xml" %>
<script runat="server">
  Dim intDVDID as integer
  Dim myXmlDocument as XmlDocument = new XmlDocument()
  Dim rootNode as XMLElement
  Dim selectedDVD as XMLElement
  Sub Page_Load(Src As Object, E As EventArgs)
    intDVDID = request.querystring("id")
    myXmlDocument.Load (server.mappath("dvd.xml"))
    rootNode = myXmlDocument.DocumentElement
    selectedDVD = rootNode.childNodes(intDVDID-1)
    if Not Page.IsPostBack then
      rootNode.RemoveChild(selectedDVD)
      myXmlDocument.Save(Server.Mappath("dvd.xml"))
      lblMessage.text = "You have successfully deleted the DVD"
    end if
  end sub
</script>
<html>
  <head>
    <link href="styles.css" type="text/css" rel="stylesheet" />
  </head>
  <body>
    <h1>Delete DVD</h1>
    <form runat="server">
      <asp:Label id="lblMessage" runat="server" forecolor="Blue"></asp:Label>
    </form>
  </body>
</html>
```

This page is very simple. It starts with some declarations and variable definitions:

```
<%@ Page Language="VB" %>
<%@ import Namespace="System.Xml" %>
<script runat="server">
  Dim intDVDID as integer
  Dim myXmlDocument as XmlDocument = new XmlDocument()
  Dim rootNode as XMLElement
  Dim selectedDVD as XMLElement
```

When the page loads, it determines the id of the DVD to delete and loads the XML document:

```
Sub Page_Load(Src As Object, E As EventArgs)
  intDVDID = request.querystring("id")
  myXmlDocument.Load (server.mappath("dvd.xml"))
```

The code sets a variable for the document element and identifies the <DVD> element to delete:

```
rootNode = myXmlDocument.DocumentElement
selectedDVD = rootNode.childNodes(intDVDID-1)
```

It then removes the element, saves the dvd.xml document, and displays a success message:

```
    if Not Page.IsPostBack then
      rootNode.RemoveChild(selectedDVD)
      myXmlDocument.Save(Server.Mappath("dvd.xml"))
      lblMessage.text = "You have successfully deleted the DVD"
    end if
  end sub
</script>
```

PHP: Deleting a DVD from the List

The deleteDVD.php page is also very simple:

```
<?php
  $id = $_REQUEST['id'];
  $dom = new DomDocument();
  $dom->load("dvd.xml");
  $root = $dom->documentElement;
  $path = "/library/DVD[@id=" . $id . "]";
  $xPath = new domxpath($dom);
  $DVDelement = $xPath->query($path)->item(0);
  $root -> removeChild($DVDelement);
  $dom->save("dvd.xml");
  ?>
<html>
  <head>
    <link href="styles.css" type="text/css" rel="stylesheet" />
  </head>
  <body>
    <div id="divMessage">You have successfully updated the XML document</div>
  </body>
</html>
```

The code block starts by determining the id of the <DVD> element to delete and then creates a new DomDocument, loading the dvd.xml document:

```
<?php
$id = $_REQUEST['id'];
$dom = new DomDocument();
$dom->load("dvd.xml");
```

The code then sets a variable, $root, for the document element and creates an XPath expression that targets the appropriate <DVD> element:

```
$root = $dom->documentElement;
$path = "/library/DVD[@id=" . $id . "]";
$xPath = new domxpath($dom);
$DVDelement = $xPath->query($path)->item(0);
```

Finally, the removeChild() method removes the element from the document element variable, and the code updates the XML document:

```
  $root -> removeChild($DVDelement);
  $dom->save("dvd.xml");
?>
```

Summary

In this chapter, I showed you how to use server-side processing to work with XML documents. I examined the advantages of working on the server compared with client-side processing. You saw that you can apply transformations on the server and send only the transformed content to the client. This approach reduces the amount of content sent to the client and avoids the need to code for different browser types and versions.

The chapter gave a brief overview of using .NET 2.0 and PHP 5 to work with XML content. I worked through some simple examples showing how to perform common XML-related tasks. I looked briefly at

- Applying an XSLT transformation to an XML document to create XHTML
- Creating new elements and updating an external XML document
- Modifying existing XML content
- Deleting content from within an XML document

Even though I only covered .NET and PHP, many of the DOM manipulation methods are similar to those used client-side. The techniques demonstrated within this chapter could apply equally to other server-side languages. In the next two chapters, I'll look at each of the two approaches in more detail.

CHAPTER 12

Case Study: Using .NET for an XML Application

In Chapter 11, you learned about many advantages to using XML on the server. You also saw that .NET has good support for XML. In this chapter, I'll work through a .NET case study, so you can see some of the techniques available to you.

In this case study, I'll build a News application to display XML browser news. The application will show XML and web news from a Microsoft Access database, and users will be able to add news items. The site will make the news available as a Really Simple Syndication (RSS) 2.0 feed and will display feeds from other web sites.

This application isn't intended as a secure and robust case study. Rather, it's an example of what you can achieve using .NET and XML on the server. You'll start by learning more about how the application is structured. After that, I'll work through each section of the application in detail.

Understanding the Application

In this case study, I'll work with news items in a database and RSS feeds. If you're not familiar with RSS, it describes news items using an XML vocabulary. Netscape originally developed RSS, and there are actually seven different specifications. In this example, I'll focus on RSS 2.0. You can find out more about the RSS 2.0 specification at `http://blogs.law.harvard.edu/tech/rss`.

The application displays and manages news items stored in an Access database. It generates an RSS 2.0 feed from these news items and uses an XSLT stylesheet to display them on the home page. Users can add, edit, and delete news items. They can also view and consume the RSS feed.

The application allows users to display RSS 2.0 news feeds from other web sites. The same XSLT stylesheet transforms these feeds into XHTML for display on the page.

Figure 12-1 shows the application displaying the current XML browser news from the database. Users see this view when they first enter the site.

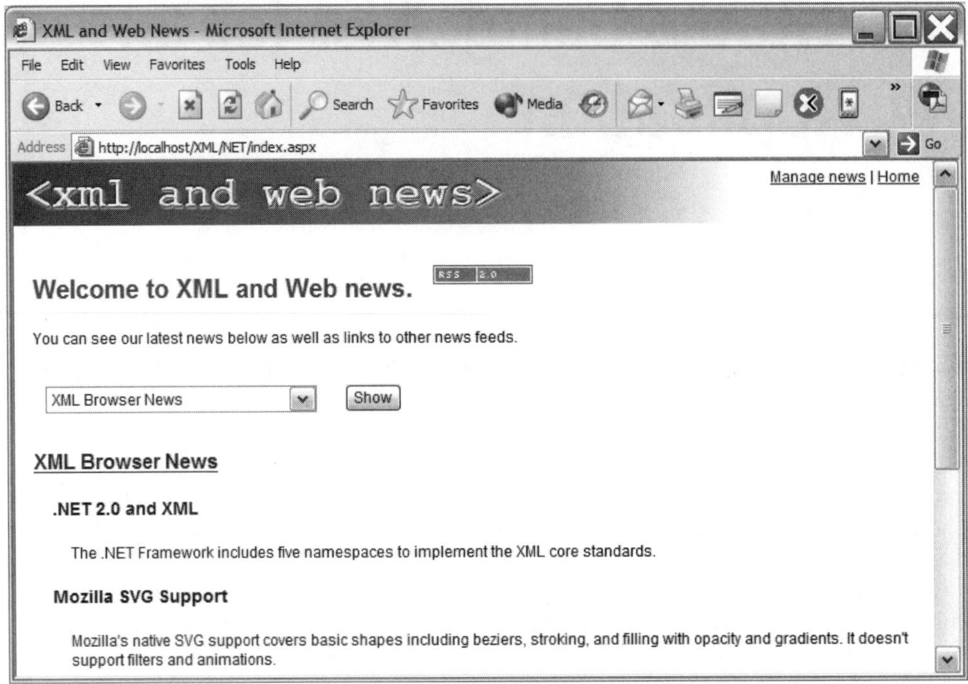

Figure 12-1. *The News application*

You can see that a link at the top right of the page allows users to manage news items. Users can also view the RSS feed by clicking the RSS 2.0 image button. Selecting a different news feed displays the news items on the page.

Setting Up the Environment

The case study uses .NET 2.0, so you need to run the Internet Information Services (IIS) web server on your computer or at your Internet service provider (ISP). You also need to have the .NET Framework 2.0 installed. You can download this at no cost from the Microsoft web site at `http://msdn.microsoft.com/netframework/downloads/updates/default.aspx`. You can't use an earlier version of .NET because the application uses controls that are only available in .NET 2.0. I've written the application using Visual Basic .NET (VB .NET), but you could rewrite it using Visual C# .NET (C#), JavaServer Pages (JSP), or any of the other languages supported by the common language runtime (CLR).

IIS

IIS is Microsoft's web server used to process and display server-side web pages in a web browser. Locally, you can only run IIS under Windows XP Professional or a server operating system such as Windows 2003—it's not available with the home version of Windows XP. In Windows XP Professional, IIS is not installed by default, so you probably have to install it from the CD.

IIS installs a new folder called `InetPub` that contains a `wwwroot` folder. You should create all web sites as folders within the `wwwroot` folder. The `wwwroot` folder is the root directory of the web server, and you can access it in a web browser by loading the URL `http://localhost`. If you create a folder for your web site at `C:\InetPub\wwwroot\Apress`, you can view the site at `http://localhost/Apress`.

The News application uses an Access 2000 database stored in the `App_Data` folder of the application. This folder is specifically designed to store databases and XML documents. It provides extra security for data files, because a web browser can't directly request information from this folder.

The application references the database using the new `AccessDataSource` control. You can use this control to connect to a database and execute SQL statements. The control supports data binding, as you'll see in the application. The new `Xml` control displays the XML content, and the `GridView` control allows for editing of the database content.

The application could use a Microsoft SQL Server 2005 or an Access database to store the news items. SQL Server 2005 provides additional XML support compared with Access, and is obviously better suited to large-scale applications. As the focus here is on scripting XML in .NET, the choice of database isn't important, so I've used Access. If you choose a different database, you'll need to modify the connection strings appropriately.

In this chapter, I haven't described how to use Visual Studio 2005 to set up the application. Rather, I've shown the declarative code that forms the application. You can download the application from the Source Code area of the Apress web site at `http://www.apress.com`. On my computer, I've stored the application in the folder `C:\Inetpub\wwwroot\XML\NET`, so my code references this path. If you set up the application in a different folder, you'll need to remember to change the path. When I'm testing the application, I'll need to use the URL `http://localhost/XML/NET/` to view the pages.

Understanding the Database Structure

This application uses a simplistic database structure with a single table. The database is in Access 2000 format and is called `news.mdb`. Figure 12-2 shows the fields in the `news` table in this database.

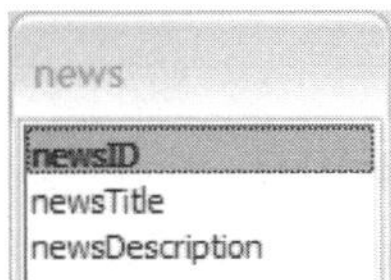

Figure 12-2. *The structure of the news table*

I could have added other fields such as publish and expiration dates, and used them to filter the display. I could also have added links to pages containing more content. However, the aim here is to create a simple application and focus on XML and .NET.

Remember that you need to set appropriate write permissions for the database so that the application can edit and update the news table. In Windows XP, you can do this by turning off Simple File Sharing, right-clicking the App_Data folder, and choosing Properties. Select the Security tab and assign write permission to the appropriate users. Make sure that you give database permissions to the machine account called ASPNET in Windows XP, or the NETWORK SERVICE account in Windows 2003.

Understanding the Structure of RSS 2.0 Documents

The application displays RSS 2.0 feeds from external web sites. It also generates an RSS feed from the database content. Before I get started, it's important to see the structure of an RSS feed:

```
<?xml version="1.0" encoding="UTF-8"?>
<rss version="2.0">
  <channel>
    <title>News feed title</title>
    <link>http://www.newsfeedurl.com</link>
    <description>News feed description</description>
    <item>
      <title>Title of the news item</title>
      <link>Link to the news item</link>
      <description>Description of the news item</description>
    </item>
  </channel>
</rss>
```

I've saved this file as rssStructure.xml with your resources.

As you can see, the news feed is a valid XML document. The news feed exists within a <channel> element. The <channel> element must contain a <title>, <link>, and <description> element as well as <item> elements. The <channel> element can optionally contain elements such as <language>, <copyright>, <pubDate>, and <generator>. See the RSS 2.0 specification at http://blogs.law.harvard.edu/tech/rss for a complete list of optional elements.

Each <item> represents a news item, so you're likely to see more than one of these elements. An <item> element contains one or more child elements. Each child element is optional, but the <item> element must contain either a <title> or <description>. In addition, each <item> can include <link>, <author>, <pubDate>, and <comments> elements. Again, you should check the specification for a complete listing of all optional elements.

Understanding the Components of the News Application

The News application contains many components. The rss.aspx page is at the heart of the application, as it creates an RSS 2.0 news feed from the contents of the news table in the news database. The home page, index.aspx, consumes the rss.aspx news feed when the user first visits the application. The feed is also available to external sites.

The home page includes a list of external RSS news feeds that users can select from a drop-down list. The news items from that feed then display on the home page. The `rss.xsl` stylesheet transforms all news feeds into XHTML for display on the home page.

The `manageNews.aspx` page displays the news items from the database in a `GridView` control and allows users to edit and delete news items. From this page, users can access the `addNews.aspx` page to add a new item.

All `.aspx` pages use the `template.master` page for their structure and global content. Master pages are a new feature in .NET 2.0, and they provide the structure and content for all pages in a site. The `template.master` page links to the stylesheet `styles.css` for formatting and presentation. Figure 12-3 shows how these components interact.

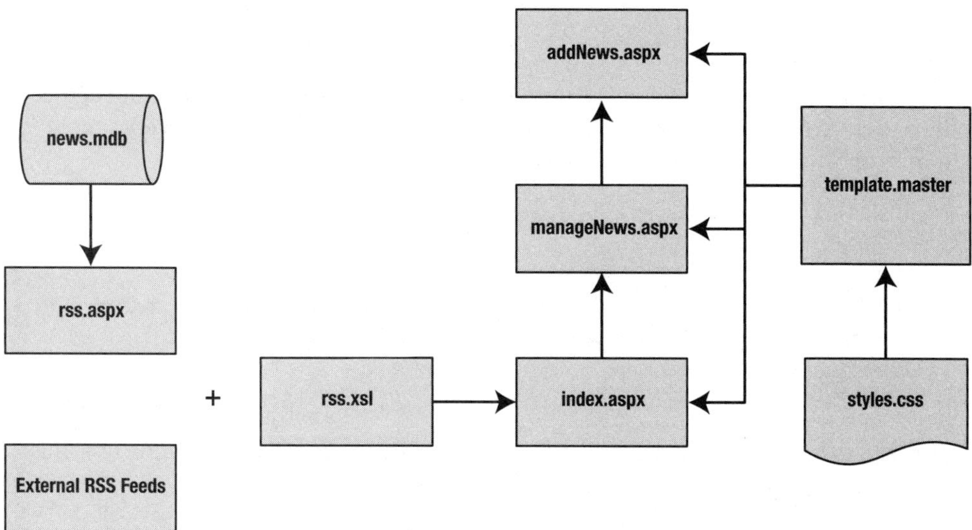

Figure 12-3. *The interaction between the components of the News application*

Table 12-1 lists each of the application components and their purpose.

Table 12-1. *The Purpose of Components in the News Application*

Component	Purpose
`addNews.aspx`	Allows a user to add a news item to the database.
`index.aspx`	The home page of the application.
`manageNews.aspx`	Responsible for displaying, editing, and deleting existing news items.
`rss.aspx`	Generates the RSS 2.0 feed from the news database.
`rss.xsl`	Transforms an RSS 2.0 news feed for display on the `index.aspx` page. Used with `rss.aspx` and external news feeds.
`styles.css`	Provides styling information for the application.
`template.master`	The master page for the application, containing the common elements that appear on each page.

Continued

Table 12-1. *Continued*

Component	Purpose
`web.config`	Contains the global settings for the application.
`App_Data/`	The folder containing the news database.
`news.mdb`	The Access database containing the news items.
`images/`	The folder containing images for the application.

I'll work through the main components of the application so you can understand how they work.

web.config

The `web.config` file stores the custom settings for the application and lives in the root of the application at `C:\Inetpub\wwwroot\XML\NET`. In this application, `web.config` is a very simple file, storing only the connection string for the Access database:

```
<?xml version="1.0" encoding="UTF-8" ?>
<configuration>
    <appSettings>
        <add key="connectionstring" value="Provider=Microsoft.Jet.OLEDB.4.0;➥
          data source=C:\Inetpub\wwwroot\XML\NET\App_Data\news.mdb"/>
    </appSettings>
</configuration>
```

The path to the database is stored in the `connectionstring` key. The application uses this key to connect to the database when adding news items.

In the preceding code, my database is stored in the folder `C:\Inetpub\wwwroot\XML\NET\App_Data\news.mdb`. If you've stored the application in a different location on your web server, you'll need to change the path so that the application works correctly.

template.master

The `template.master` file provides the template for the .aspx pages within the site. As I mentioned, master pages are a great new feature within .NET 2.0 that allow you to maintain a consistent look throughout a site.

The master page follows:

```
<%@ master language="VB" %>
<html xmlns="http://www.w3.org/1999/xhtml">
  <head runat="server">
    <title>XML and Web News</title>
    <link rel="stylesheet" type="text/css" href="styles.css">
  </head>
  <body>
    <div style="float:left;">
      <img src="images/top.jpg" width="600" height="49" alt=""/>
    </div>
```

```
    <div style="float:right; margin: 5px;">
      <a href="manageNews.aspx">Manage news</a> | <a href="index.aspx">Home</a>
    </div>
    <div style="clear: both;"/>
    <form runat="server">
      <asp:ContentPlaceHolder id="PageContent" runat="server"/>
    </form>
  </body>
</html>
```

The page declares the XHTML tags that structure the page, including the linked CSS stylesheet. It sets up the global page elements in a series of <div> tags. The first <div> element contains the image for the top of the page. The second contains the links to manage news items and to return to the home page. I've included a third <div> element to clear the floats from the first two elements.

The master page also includes a <form> element containing the runat="server" attribute. Within the form is the new ContentPlaceHolder control that identifies areas of content that other .aspx pages will supply.

styles.css

The styles.css page contains the presentation styles for the application:

```
body {
  font-family: Arial, Verdana, sans-serif;
  font-size: 12px;
  margin: 0px;
}
td, input, select, textarea {
  font-family: Arial, Verdana, sans-serif;
  font-size: 12px;
  margin: 10px;
}
h1, h2, p {
  margin-left: 15px;
}
h1 {
  font-size: 20px;
  color: #333699;
}
h2 {
  font-size: 16px;
}
h3 {
  font-size: 14px;
  margin-left: 30px;
}
table {
```

```
  margin: 20px;
}
td {
  padding: 5px;
}
.indent {
  margin-left: 45px;
  margin-right: 20px;
}
.emphasis {
  font-weight: bold;
  color: #333699;
}
.error {
  font-weight: bold;
  font-size: 14px;
  color: #FF0000;
}
```

This content is self-explanatory, so I won't go through it in any detail.

index.aspx

The home page for the application initially displays the RSS feed from the news database. It transforms the feed using an XSLT stylesheet to create XHTML content. The page also allows users to select and display other news feeds. The code for the page follows, and I'll walk through it in detail shortly:

```
<%@ Page Language="VB" MasterPageFile="template.master" %>
<%@ import Namespace="System.Xml" %>
<script runat="server">
  Sub Page_Load(Src As Object, E As EventArgs)
    showRSS("http://localhost/XML/NET/rss.aspx")
  End sub
  Sub showRSS(RSSURL as String)
    Dim RSSDoc as XmlDocument = new XmlDocument()
    RSSDoc.PreserveWhitespace = false
    RSSDOC.load(RSSURL)
    displayRSS.Document = RSSDoc
    displayRSS.TransformSource = "rss.xsl"
  End Sub
  Sub chooseRSS(sender As Object, e As System.EventArgs)
    Dim RSSURL as String = RSSList.SelectedItem.Value
    showRSS(RSSURL)
  End sub
```

```
  Sub showRSS2Feed(sender As Object, e As ImageClickEventArgs)
    response.redirect ("rss.aspx")
  End Sub
</script>
<asp:Content id="homeContent" ContentPlaceHolderID="PageContent" runat="server">
  <h1>Welcome to XML and Web news.
  <asp:ImageButton runat="server"
    ImageUrl="images/rss2.gif"
    OnClick="showRSS2Feed"/></h1>
  <p>You can see our latest news below as well as links to other news feeds.</p>
  <p><asp:DropDownList id="RSSList" runat="server">
    <asp:ListItem value="http://alistapart.com/rss.xml">
      A List Apart</asp:ListItem>
    <asp:ListItem value="http://z.about.com/6/g/webdesign/b/rss2.xml">
      About Web Design/HTML articles</asp:ListItem>
    <asp:ListItem value="http://feeds.computerworld.com/Computerworld/XML/News">
      ComputerWorld XML News</asp:ListItem>
    <asp:ListItem value="http://www-128.ibm.com/developerworks/views/xml/rss/➥
      libraryview.jsp">IBM developerWorks XML Feed</asp:ListItem>
    <asp:ListItem value="http://feeds.lockergnome.com/rss/web.xml">
      LockerGnome</asp:ListItem>
    <asp:ListItem value="http://p.moreover.com/page?o=rss002&➥
      c=XML%20and%20metadata%20news">Moreover XML and MetaData News</asp:ListItem>
    <asp:ListItem value="http://localhost/XML/NET/rss.aspx" selected="True">
      XML Browser News</asp:ListItem>
  </asp:DropDownList>
  <asp:Button Text="Show" OnClick=" chooseRSS" Runat="Server"/></p>
  <asp:AccessDataSource id="NewsDS" runat="server"
    DataSourceMode="DataReader"
    DataFile="App_Data/news.mdb"
    SelectCommand="SELECT news.newsTitle, news.newsDescription FROM news ➥
    ORDER BY news.newsTitle"/>
  <asp:Xml id="displayRSS" runat="server"/>
</asp:Content>
```

I'll work through each section of the code so you can understand the page better.

Walking Through index.aspx

The page starts with a language and master file declaration. By specifying a master page, the application needs to include a Content control to specify the variable content for the template. The page also imports the System.Xml namespace:

```
<%@ Page Language="VB" MasterPageFile="template.master" %>
<%@ import Namespace="System.Xml" %>
```

It then includes a Page_Load subroutine:

```
Sub Page_Load(Src As Object, E As EventArgs)
  showRSS("http://localhost/XML/NET/rss.aspx")
End sub
```

This subroutine calls the showRSS sub, passing the URL of the local RSS feed. The showRSS subroutine follows:

```
Sub showRSS(RSSURL as String)
  Dim RSSDoc as XmlDocument = new XmlDocument()
  RSSDoc.PreserveWhitespace = false
  RSSDOC.load(RSSURL)
  displayRSS.Document = RSSDoc
  displayRSS.TransformSource = "rss.xsl"
End Sub
```

The showRSS subroutine starts by creating a new XML document called RSSDoc. It sets the PreserveWhitespace property to false so that extra white space in the RSS feed is ignored. The load method loads the content from the feed specified in the RSSURL variable.

When the user initially loads the page, the path to the feed is http://localhost/XML/NET/rss.aspx. You may need to change the path on your own system if you've set up your application in a different folder on the web server.

The content displays in the displayRSS Xml component. The code assigns the RSSDoc XML document to the Document property of this component. It can apply a transformation by assigning the rss.xsl file to the TransformSource property of the displayRSS component.

The home page allows users to display content from external RSS 2.0 feeds. The page achieves this with the chooseRSS subroutine:

```
Sub chooseRSS(sender As Object, e As System.EventArgs)
  Dim RSSURL as String = RSSList.SelectedItem.Value
  showRSS(RSSURL)
End sub
```

This subroutine starts by finding the value of the selected item from the combo box. The value corresponds to the URL of the RSS feed. The code then calls the showRSS subroutine, passing the URL of the selected RSS feed.

The script block finishes with the following subroutine:

```
  Sub showRSS2Feed(sender As Object, e As ImageClickEventArgs)
    response.redirect ("rss.aspx")
  End Sub
</script>
```

This subroutine responds to the click of the RSS 2.0 image button. When the user clicks the image button, the page redirects to rss.aspx to show the local RSS feed.

The display components on the page are contained within the Content control. Anything placed between the <asp:Content> tags displays within the ContentPlaceHolder control specified in the master page.

The page displays a heading and an image button that links to the local RSS feed on the rss.aspx page:

```
<asp:Content id="homeContent" ContentPlaceHolderID="PageContent" runat="server">
  <h1>Welcome to XML and Web news.
  <asp:ImageButton runat="server"
    ImageUrl="images/rss2.gif"
    OnClick="showRSS2Feed"/></h1>
  <p>You can see our latest news below as well as links to other news feeds.</p>
```

When users click the image button, it calls the showRSS2Feed subroutine that you saw earlier.

The page also hosts a drop-down list containing references to several RSS 2.0 feeds. The users can select an item from the list and click a button to load the selected feed:

```
<p><asp:DropDownList id="RSSList" runat="server">
  <asp:ListItem value="http://alistapart.com/rss.xml">
    A List Apart</asp:ListItem>
  <asp:ListItem value="http://z.about.com/6/g/webdesign/b/rss2.xml">
    About Web Design/HTML articles</asp:ListItem>
  <asp:ListItem value="http://feeds.computerworld.com/Computerworld/XML/News">
    ComputerWorld XML News</asp:ListItem>
  <asp:ListItem value="http://www-128.ibm.com/developerworks/views/xml/rss/➥
    libraryview.jsp">IBM developerWorks XML Feed</asp:ListItem>
  <asp:ListItem value="http://feeds.lockergnome.com/rss/web.xml">
    LockerGnome</asp:ListItem>
  <asp:ListItem value="http://p.moreover.com/page?o=rss002&➥
    c=XML%20and%20metadata%20news">Moreover XML and MetaData News</asp:ListItem>
  <asp:ListItem value="http://localhost/XML/NET/rss.aspx" selected="True">
    XML Browser News</asp:ListItem>
</asp:DropDownList>
<asp:Button Text="Show" OnClick=" chooseRSS" Runat="Server"/></p>
```

The code sets the value property for each list item to the URL for the feed. Clicking the button calls the chooseRSS subroutine that you explored earlier.

The page finishes with an AccessDataSource control that connects to the database and executes a SELECT query:

```
<asp:AccessDataSource id="NewsDS" runat="server"
  DataSourceMode="DataReader"
  DataFile="App_Data/news.mdb"
  SelectCommand="SELECT news.newsTitle, news.newsDescription FROM news ➥
    ORDER BY news.newsTitle"/>
```

This control is new to .NET 2.0 and allows for database connections that don't specify a connection string. To make the connection, the code sets the value of the DataFile property to the relative path to the database—in this case, App_Data/news.mdb. The AccessDataSource control manages the underlying connection to the database.

■**Note** If you secure the Access database with a username and password, you won't be able to use the AccessDataSource control. Instead, you'll need to use the SqlDataSource control, as you are able to specify the complete connection string.

The AccessDataSource control specifies an id (NewsDS), which the code can use as the DataSourceID property for any bound control. The application scripts the binding, so you don't need to set that property here.

The code also specifies that the DataSourceMode is DataReader. A DataReader provides a read-only, forward-only cursor. The code could also specify a DataSet value, which you could use if the bound control needs to support sorting and paging. You'll see an example of this a little later.

Finally, the code specifies a SELECT command that retrieves the records from database. In this case, the statement selects all records from the news table in order of newsTitle.

The page finishes with an Xml control, again new to .NET 2.0. This control displays the transformed XML content from the RSS feed:

```
  <asp:Xml id="displayRSS" runat="server"/ >
</asp:Content>
```

As I mentioned, when the home page first loads, it displays the news feed from the database. The file rss.xsl transforms the feed into XHTML for display.

Using a Proxy Server

If you're using a proxy server, you may need to make a change to the web.config file so that you can access the remote URLs in this example. You can specify a proxy server by rewriting the web.config file as follows; the new lines appear in bold:

```
<?xml version="1.0" encoding="UTF-8" ?>
<configuration>
  <appSettings>
    <add key="connectionstring" value="Provider=Microsoft.Jet.OLEDB.4.0;data
      source=C:\Inetpub\wwwroot\XML\NET\App_Data\news.mdb"/>
    </appSettings>
  <system.net>
    <defaultProxy>
      <proxy usesystemdefault = "false" proxyaddress="http://proxyserver"
        bypassonlocal="true"/>
    </defaultProxy>
  </system.net>
</configuration>
```

Make sure you set the address of the proxy server appropriately. In the preceding code, I've used the address `http://proxyserver`.

rss.xsl

The `rss.xsl` stylesheet transforms any RSS 2.0 feed accessed in the application into XHTML. The code applies the stylesheet to the local RSS feed when the home page first loads, as well as to any other feed selected from the drop-down list. The stylesheet follows:

```
<?xml version="1.0" encoding="UTF-8"?>
<xsl:stylesheet version="1.0" xmlns:xsl="http://www.w3.org/1999/XSL/Transform">
  <xsl:template match="/">
    <xsl:apply-templates select="rss/channel"/>
  </xsl:template>
  <xsl:template match="channel">
    <h2><a href="{link}" target="_blank"><xsl:value-of select="title"/></a></h2>
    <xsl:apply-templates select="item"/>
  </xsl:template>
  <xsl:template match="item">
    <h3>
    <xsl:choose>
        <xsl:when test="string-length(link)>0">
          <a href="{link}" target="_blank"><xsl:value-of select="title"/></a>
        </xsl:when>
        <xsl:otherwise>
            <xsl:value-of select="title"/>
        </xsl:otherwise>
     </xsl:choose>
    </h3>
    <div class="indent">
      <xsl:value-of disable-output-escaping="yes" select="description"/><br/>
      <xsl:choose>
        <xsl:when test="string-length(pubDate)>0">
        <strong>Published: </strong><xsl:value-of select="pubDate"/>
        </xsl:when>
      </xsl:choose>
    </div>
  </xsl:template>
</xsl:stylesheet>
```

This stylesheet is straightforward. It starts with an XML declaration and `<xsl:stylesheet>` element:

```
<?xml version="1.0" encoding="UTF-8"?>
<xsl:stylesheet version="1.0" xmlns:xsl="http://www.w3.org/1999/XSL/Transform">
```

The stylesheet then matches the document element and applies the template for the <channel> element:

```
<xsl:template match="/">
  <xsl:apply-templates select="rss/channel"/>
</xsl:template>
```

The <channel> element template creates the heading information:

```
<xsl:template match="channel">
  <h2><a href="{link}" target="_blank"><xsl:value-of select="title"/></a></h2>
  <xsl:apply-templates select="item"/>
</xsl:template>
```

Here, the stylesheet creates a link around the <title> element so that the user can access it in a new browser window. The stylesheet displays this as a level 2 heading and places the transformation from the <item> elements underneath.

The final template matches each <item> element. It checks to see if the XML document contains a <link> element. If so, the <title> element displays as a hyperlink to the relevant URL; otherwise, it appears as an <h3> element:

```
<xsl:template match="item">
  <h3>
    <xsl:choose>
      <xsl:when test="string-length(link)>0">
        <a href="{link}" target="_blank"><xsl:value-of select="title"/></a>
      </xsl:when>
      <xsl:otherwise>
        <xsl:value-of select="title"/>
      </xsl:otherwise>
    </xsl:choose>
  </h3>
```

Notice that the stylesheet uses <xsl:when> and <xsl:otherwise> to add conditional logic. The built-in XPath function string-length tests the length of the text within the <title> element. If the length is greater than 0, the heading is linked.

Once the stylesheet writes the news item heading, it displays the item content in a <div> element:

```
<div class="indent">
  <xsl:value-of disable-output-escaping="yes" select="description"/><br/>
```

The value of disable-output-escaping is set to yes so that the stylesheet doesn't escape any XHTML tags in the <description> element. As you'll see from some of the news feeds, it's common to add XHTML content in the description.

The stylesheet includes another logical test, this time looking to see if a publish date exists:

```
      <xsl:choose>
        <xsl:when test="string-length(pubDate)>0">
        <strong>Published: </strong><xsl:value-of select="pubDate"/>
        </xsl:when>
      </xsl:choose>
    </div>
  </xsl:template>
</xsl:stylesheet>
```

Again, the test uses the XPath `string-length` function to test the length of the `<pubDate>` element. If the element exists, the publish date is included in the XHTML output. Notice that the stylesheet doesn't contain an `<xsl:otherwise>` element here so that nothing displays if no publish date exists.

The stylesheet is first applied to the `rss.aspx` news feed when the home page initially loads.

rss.aspx

When users view the home page for the first time, it displays the default local RSS feed from the page `rss.aspx`. Users can also view this feed by clicking the RSS 2.0 image button. They can reference the `rss.aspx` page directly to consume the feed.

If you click the RSS 2.0 button, you should see something similar to the image shown in Figure 12-4.

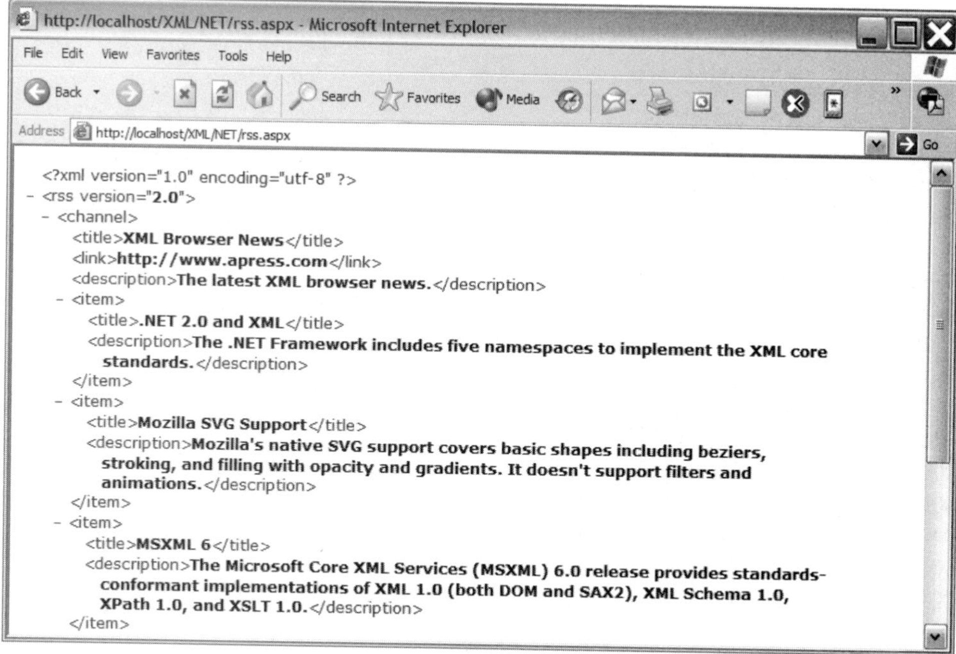

Figure 12-4. *The RSS feed shown in Internet Explorer (IE)*

In this case, the code uses an `XmlTextWriter` object to create the XML stream and generate the content for the news feed. I didn't cover this object in Chapter 11, so Table 12-2 provides a summary of the most important methods.

Table 12-2. *The Most Important Methods of the XmlTextWriter Class*

Method	Explanation
`WriteStartDocument()`	Writes the XML declaration, using version 1.0
`WriteEndDocument()`	Closes open elements or attributes
`WriteComment()`	Writes a comment
`WriteProcessingInstruction()`	Writes a processing instruction
`WriteDocType()`	Writes the DOCTYPE declaration
`WriteStartElement()`	Writes a starting tag
`WriteEndElement()`	Closes the current tag
`WriteElementString()`	Writes an element including text
`WriteStartAttribute()`	Writes the start of an attribute
`WriteEndAttribute()`	Writes the end of an attribute
`WriteAttributes()`	Writes an attribute
`Flush()`	Flushes the buffer to the stream
`Close()`	Closes the XML stream

You'll see many of these methods used in the rss.aspx page, which follows:

```
<%@ Page Language="VB" %>
<%@ import Namespace="System.IO" %>
<%@ import Namespace="System.Data" %>
<%@ import Namespace="System.Xml" %>
<script runat="server">
  Sub Page_Load(Src As Object, E As EventArgs)
    Response.ContentType = "text/xml"
    Dim dv As DataView = CType(NewsDS.Select(DataSourceSelectArguments.Empty), ➥
      DataView)
    Dim XMLFeed as XmlTextWriter = new XmlTextWriter(Response.OutputStream, ➥
      Encoding.UTF8)
    XMLFeed.WriteStartDocument()
    XMLFeed.WriteStartElement("rss")
    XMLFeed.WriteAttributeString("version", "2.0")
    XMLFeed.WriteStartElement("channel")
    XMLFeed.WriteElementString("title", "XML Browser News")
    XMLFeed.WriteElementString("link", "http://www.apress.com")
    XMLFeed.WriteElementString("description", "The latest XML browser news.")
    For Each dr As DataRow In dv.Table.Rows
```

```
      XMLFeed.WriteStartElement("item")
      XMLFeed.WriteElementString("title", dr("newsTitle").ToString())
      XMLFeed.WriteElementString("description", dr("newsDescription").ToString())
      XMLFeed.WriteEndElement()
    Next
    XMLFeed.WriteEndElement()
    XMLFeed.WriteEndElement()
    XMLFeed.WriteEndDocument()
    XMLFeed.Flush()
    XMLFeed.Close()
    Response.End()
  End sub
</script>
<asp:AccessDataSource id="NewsDS" runat="server"
  DataSourceMode="DataSet"
  DataFile="App_Data/news.mdb"
  SelectCommand="SELECT news.newsTitle, news.newsDescription FROM news ➥
    ORDER BY news.newsTitle"/>
```

This page doesn't use the master page, as it contains only XML content. The page starts by declaring the language and importing namespaces:

```
<%@ Page Language="VB" %>
<%@ import Namespace="System.IO" %>
<%@ import Namespace="System.Data" %>
<%@ import Namespace="System.Xml" %>
```

It then runs code in response to the page load event.

The Page_Load subroutine starts by declaring the content type as text/xml:

```
Sub Page_Load(Src As Object, E As EventArgs)
  Response.ContentType = "text/xml"
```

The code then declares a DataView object that takes its content from the NewsDS AccessDataSource control:

```
Dim dv As DataView = CType(NewsDS.Select(DataSourceSelectArguments.Empty), ➥
  DataView)
```

The DataView allows the page to access the contents of the AccessDataSource control programmatically. The code uses the contents to generate the RSS feed.

It starts by creating a new XmlTextWriter object:

```
Dim XMLFeed as XmlTextWriter = new XmlTextWriter(Response.OutputStream, ➥
  Encoding.UTF8)
```

The code sets the stream to Response.OutputStream and the encoding to UTF8. It could also specify a physical file for the XML stream.

The next code section starts writing the XML stream, using the WriteStartDocument() method to generate the XML declaration. The WriteStartElement() method creates the root <rss> element, and sets the version attribute of this element to 2.0:

```
XMLFeed.WriteStartDocument()
XMLFeed.WriteStartElement("rss")
XMLFeed.WriteAttributeString("version", "2.0")
```

Next, the code creates the <channel> element along with the <title>, <link>, and <description> elements:

```
XMLFeed.WriteStartElement("channel")
XMLFeed.WriteElementString("title", "XML Browser News")
XMLFeed.WriteElementString("link", "http://www.apress.com")
XMLFeed.WriteElementString("description", "The latest XML browser news.")
```

The first parameter of the WriteElementString() method specifies the name of the element. The second parameter provides the text content. In this case, the <title>, <link>, and <description> are not taken from the database. The WriteElementString() method generates the closing tag automatically.

At this point, the XML stream contains the following content:

```
<?xml version="1.0" encoding="utf-8" ?>
<rss version="2.0">
  <channel>
    <title>XML Browser News</title>
    <link>http://www.apress.com</link>
    <description>The latest XML browser news.</description>
```

The code generates the remaining <item> elements by looping through the content in the DataView. It accesses each data row in the rows collection. Each time the code finds a news item, it writes a starting <item> element and adds the <title> and <description> elements. The WriteElementString() method creates the opening tag, adds the specified text, and generates the closing tag:

```
For Each dr As DataRow In dv.Table.Rows
  XMLFeed.WriteStartElement("item")
  XMLFeed.WriteElementString("title", dr("newsTitle").ToString())
  XMLFeed.WriteElementString("description", dr("newsDescription").ToString())
  XMLFeed.WriteEndElement()
Next
```

The script block finishes by writing the closing elements for each of the elements created earlier. It also calls the Flush() method to flush whatever is in the buffer to the stream, and it uses the Close() method to close the stream:

```
    XMLFeed.WriteEndElement()
    XMLFeed.WriteEndElement()
    XMLFeed.WriteEndDocument()
    XMLFeed.Flush()
    XMLFeed.Close()
    Response.End()
  End sub
</script>
```

The code creates the following structure:

```
<?xml version="1.0" encoding="utf-8" ?>
<rss version="2.0">
  <channel>
    <title>XML Browser News</title>
    <link>http://www.apress.com</link>
    <description>The latest XML browser news.</description>
    <item>
      <title>.NET 2.0 and XML</title>
     <description>The .NET Framework includes five namespaces to implement
       the XML core standards.</description>
    </item>
  </channel>
</rss>
```

I've only included one `<item>` element in the document for brevity.

The only control on the page is an `AccessDataSource` control:

```
<asp:AccessDataSource id="NewsDS" runat="server"
  DataSourceMode="DataSet"
  DataFile="App_Data/news.mdb"
  SelectCommand="SELECT news.newsTitle, news.newsDescription FROM news ➥
    ORDER BY news.newsTitle"/>
```

The control has the `id` of `NewsDS`, and I refer to this when creating a `DataView` object, as you saw earlier. The code sets the `DataSourceMode` to `DataSet` so the page can access the content programmatically in a `DataView` object. It also specifies the `DataFile` property and `SelectCommand`.

The remainder of the application deals with managing the news content within the database.

manageNews.aspx

The manageNews.aspx page displays the content from the database in a GridView control, as shown in Figure 12-5. Notice that the control renders as a table.

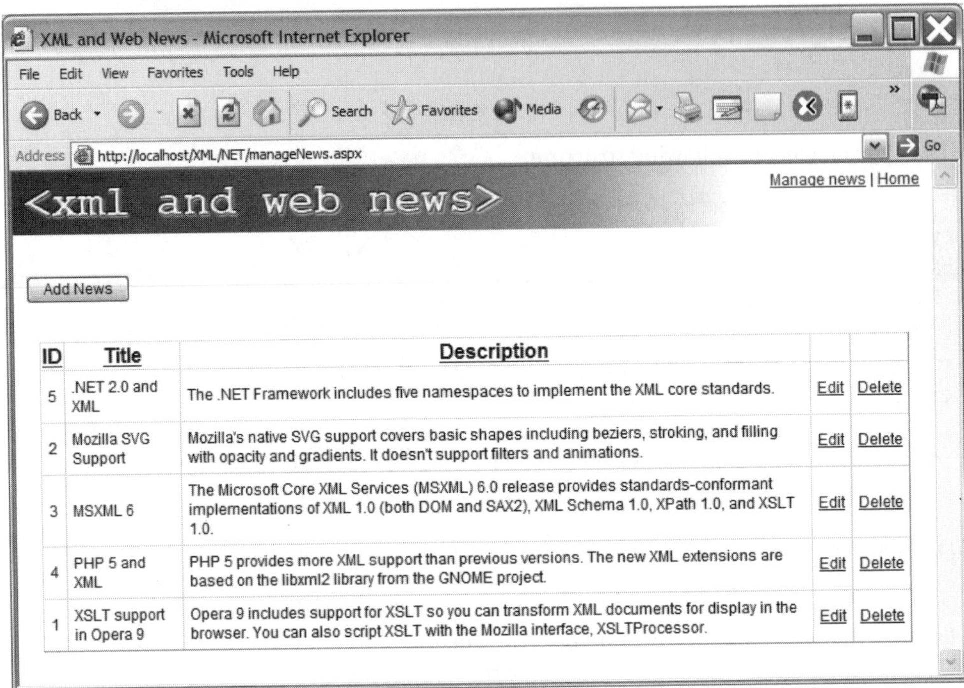

Figure 12-5. *The manageNews.aspx page*

The news items display in a table. Each column represents a field from the news table. The table headings are links that you can click to sort the columns.

This page also includes automatically generated Edit and Delete links. Users need to click the Add News button to add a new item.

The code to create this page follows:

```
<%@ Page Language="VB" masterpagefile="template.master" %>
<script runat="server">
  Sub GridViewUpdated(ByVal s As Object, ByVal e As GridViewUpdatedEventArgs)
    If Not e.Exception Is Nothing Then
      lblError.Text = "<br/>  Error: Could not update row"
      e.ExceptionHandled = True
    End If
  End Sub
  Sub GridViewDeleted(ByVal s As Object, ByVal e As GridViewDeletedEventArgs)
```

```
    If Not e.Exception Is Nothing Then
      lblError.Text = "<br/>  Error: Could not delete row"
      e.ExceptionHandled = True
    End If
  End Sub
  Sub addNews(sender As Object, e As System.EventArgs)
    response.redirect("addNews.aspx")
  end sub
</script>
<asp:Content id="homeContent" ContentPlaceHolderID="PageContent" runat="server">
  <asp:Button runat="server" Text="Add News" OnClick="addNews"/>
  <asp:Label runat="server" id="lblError" cssClass="error"/>
  <asp:AccessDataSource id="NewsDS" runat="server"
    DataSourceMode="DataSet"
    DataFile="App_Data/news.mdb"
    SelectCommand="SELECT * FROM news ORDER BY news.newsTitle"
    UpdateCommand="UPDATE news SET newsTitle=?,newsDescription=? ➥
      WHERE newsID=@newsID"
    DeleteCommand="DELETE FROM news WHERE newsID=@newsID">
    <UpdateParameters>
      <asp:Parameter Type="String" Name="newsTitle"/>
      <asp:Parameter Type="String" Name="newsDescription"/>
    </UpdateParameters>
  </asp:AccessDataSource>
  <asp:GridView ID="NewsGV" runat="server"
    AutoGenerateColumns="False"
    DataKeyNames="newsID"
    DataSourceID="NewsDS"
    AllowSorting="true"
    OnRowUpdated="GridViewUpdated"
    OnRowDeleted="GridViewDeleted">
    <Columns>
      <asp:BoundField HeaderText="ID"
        DataField="newsID"
        SortExpression="newsID"
        ReadOnly="True"/>
      <asp:TemplateField HeaderText="Title" SortExpression="newsTitle">
        <ItemTemplate><%#Eval("newsTitle")%></ItemTemplate>
        <EditItemTemplate>
          <asp:TextBox runat="server" id="txtTitle"
            Text='<%#Bind("newsTitle")%>'
            Width="175px"/><br/>
          <asp:RequiredFieldValidator runat="server" id="TitleRequiredValidator"
            ControlToValidate="txtTitle"
```

```
            Display="Dynamic"
            Text="Please enter a title" />
        </EditItemTemplate>
      </asp:TemplateField>
      <asp:TemplateField HeaderText="Description" SortExpression="newsDescription">
        <ItemTemplate><%#Eval("newsDescription")%></ItemTemplate>
        <EditItemTemplate>
          <asp:TextBox runat="server" id="txtDescription"
            Text='<%#Bind("newsDescription")%>'
            TextMode="MultiLine"
            Columns="100"
            Rows="2"/><br/>
          <asp:RequiredFieldValidator runat="server"
            id="DescriptionRequiredValidator"
            ControlToValidate="txtDescription"
            Display="Dynamic"
            Text="Please enter a description" />
        </EditItemTemplate>
      </asp:TemplateField>
      <asp:CommandField EditText="Edit" ShowEditButton="True"/>
      <asp:CommandField DeleteText="Delete" ShowDeleteButton="True"/>
    </Columns>
  </asp:GridView>
</asp:Content>
```

As you can see, this page contains a lot of code, but it's not complicated. I'll break down each section so you can understand how the page works. The code uses an `AccessDataSource` control to load the content from the database. It binds the data to a `GridView` control and changes the default settings so users can edit or delete each news item.

The code starts with a page declaration and a script block containing a subroutine called `GridViewUpdated`:

```
<%@ Page Language="VB" masterpagefile="template.master" %>
<script runat="server">
  Sub GridViewUpdated(ByVal s As Object, ByVal e As GridViewUpdatedEventArgs)
    If Not e.Exception Is Nothing Then
      lblError.Text = "<br/>  Error: Could not update row"
      e.ExceptionHandled = True
    End If
  End Sub
```

This subroutine handles the `OnRowUpdated` event, which is broadcast when users update a row. The code displays an error message in a `Label` control called `lblError` if the update was not successful. Figure 12-6 shows how the error message appears.

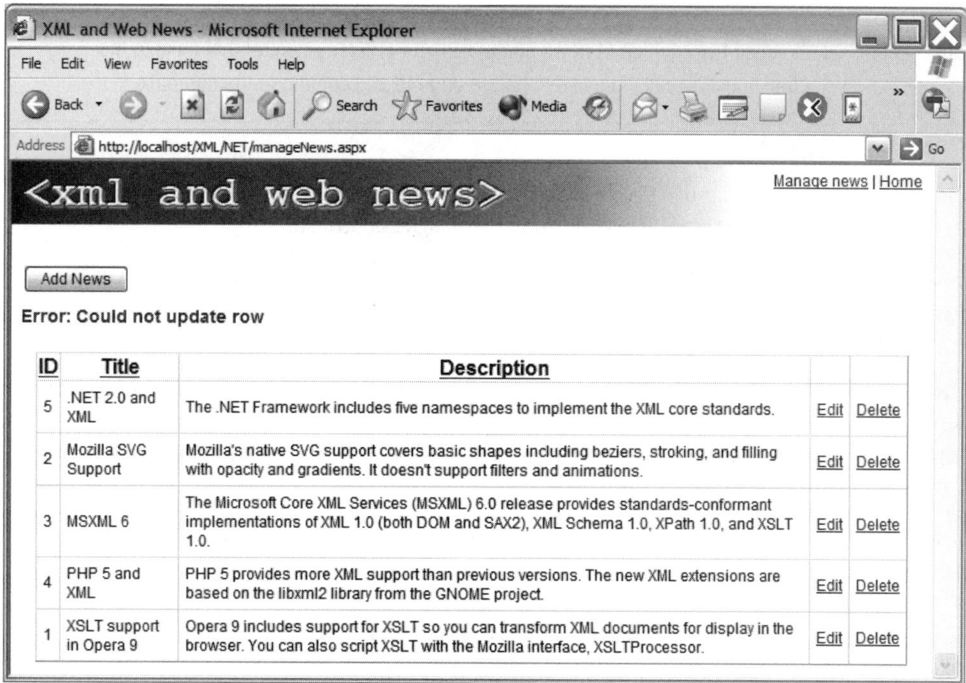

Figure 12-6. *Handling updating errors*

The next subroutine, GridViewDeleted, is similar:

```
Sub GridViewDeleted(ByVal s As Object, ByVal e As GridViewDeletedEventArgs)
  If Not e.Exception Is Nothing Then
    lblError.Text = "<br/>  Error: Could not delete row"
    e.ExceptionHandled = True
  End If
End Sub
```

Again, the page displays an error if it can't delete a row.

The code block also contains a subroutine called addNews. This subroutine handles the Add News button click event:

```
  Sub addNews(sender As Object, e As System.EventArgs)
    response.redirect("addNews.aspx")
  end sub
</script>
```

When users click the Add News button, the browser redirects to the addNews.aspx page. The page adds new content to the database.

Note I could have handled the addition of news items using a `FormView` control that links to the `GridView`. However, I find it just as easy to use a separate page to add content to the database.

As with other pages that use the `template.master` master page, all content for the page exists within the `Content` control. This contains the `Add News` button:

```
<asp:Content id="homeContent" ContentPlaceHolderID="PageContent" runat="server">
  <asp:Button runat="server" Text="Add News" OnClick="addNews"/>
  <asp:Label runat="server" id="lblError" cssClass="error"/>
```

You saw the click handler `addNews` earlier. The page also includes a `Label` control for displaying error messages arising from updates.

It then includes an `AccessDataSource` control called `NewsDS`. The opening tag of this control follows:

```
<asp:AccessDataSource id="NewsDS" runat="server"
  DataSourceMode="DataSet"
  DataFile="App_Data/news.mdb"
  SelectCommand="SELECT * FROM news ORDER BY news.newsTitle"
  UpdateCommand="UPDATE news SET newsTitle=?,newsDescription=? ➥
    WHERE newsID=@newsID"
  DeleteCommand="DELETE FROM news WHERE newsID=@newsID">
```

The code sets the `DataSourceMode` property to `DataSet` so that users can sort the `GridView`. The `AccessDataSource` control draws content from the `news.mdb` database using the SQL statement contained within the `SelectCommand` property.

The code also specifies two additional SQL commands: `UpdateCommand` and `DeleteCommand`. These commands specify which SQL statement to run when users click the `Update` or `Delete` links.

The `UpdateCommand` attribute refers to an `UPDATE` statement. Notice that the code uses the wildcard character ? to specify that it will receive update parameters. The `@newsID` placeholder specifies the `newsID` from the current row. The `DeleteCommand` refers to a `DELETE` query that also uses `@newsID`.

Because the `UPDATE` SQL command contains parameters, the page must include an `<UpdateParameters>` section within the control:

```
  <UpdateParameters>
    <asp:Parameter Type="String" Name="newsTitle"></asp:Parameter>
    <asp:Parameter Type="String" Name="newsDescription"></asp:Parameter>
  </UpdateParameters>
</asp:AccessDataSource>
```

Each parameter contains a `Name` property. The page uses this property when binding a `GridView` to the `AccessDataSource` component. The `UpdateParameters` values are bound to the columns with the same name as those specified in the `Name` property. The parameters also specify a `Type` that specifies the data type of each parameter.

The next control in the code is the `GridView`. This control is bound to the `AccessDataSource` to display the news items in a table structure. I'll start by looking at the opening tag of the `GridView` control:

```
<asp:GridView ID="NewsGV" runat="server"
  AutoGenerateColumns="False"
  DataKeyNames="newsID"
  DataSourceID="NewsDS"
  AllowSorting="true"
  OnRowUpdated="GridViewUpdated"
  OnRowDeleted="GridViewDeleted">
```

In this tag, the code indicates that the columns won't be generated automatically with the attribute `AutoGenerateColumns="False"`. It also specifies the `newsID` as the data key for the edit and delete queries. The code binds this control to the `id` of the `AccessDataSource` component `newsDS` through the `DataSourceID` property.

Because the `AccessDataSource` component is in `DataSet` mode, it allows for sorting of the records by setting the `AllowSorting` property to `true`. The code can also assign event handlers—`GridViewUpdated` and `GridViewDeleted`—to respond when you update or delete a row. If either process throws an error, it displays an error message in a `Label` control, as you saw in Figure 12-6.

The next step is to specify the columns for the `GridView`. You can use any of the column field types shown in Table 12-3.

Table 12-3. *Column Field Types for Use Within a GridView*

Column Field Type	Explanation
`BoundField`	The default column type; displays the field value from the data source
`ButtonField`	Displays a button for each item
`CheckBoxField`	Displays a checkbox for each item
`CommandField`	Displays predefined options to select, edit, or delete rows
`HyperLinkField`	Displays a hyperlink for the field value
`ImageField`	Displays an image for each item
`TemplateField`	Uses a template to display user-defined content for each item

In this application, I'll use the `BoundField`, `TemplateField`, and `CommandField` types:

```
<Columns>
  <asp:BoundField HeaderText="ID"
    DataField="newsID"
    SortExpression="newsID"
    ReadOnly="True"/>
  <asp:TemplateField HeaderText="Title" SortExpression="newsTitle">
    <ItemTemplate><%#Eval("newsTitle")%></ItemTemplate>
    <EditItemTemplate>
      <asp:TextBox runat="server" id="txtTitle"
        Text='<%#Bind("newsTitle")%>'
```

```
          Width="175px"/><br/>
        <asp:RequiredFieldValidator runat="server" id="TitleRequiredValidator"
          ControlToCalidate="txtTitle"
          Display="Dynamic"
          Text="Please enter a title" />
      </EditItemTemplate>
    </asp:TemplateField>
    <asp:TemplateField HeaderText="Description" SortExpression="newsDescription">
      <ItemTemplate><%#Eval("newsDescription")%></ItemTemplate>
      <EditItemTemplate>
        <asp:TextBox runat="server" id="txtDescription"
          Text='<%#Bind("newsDescription")%>'
          TextMode="MultiLine"
          Columns="100"
          Rows="2"/><br/>
        <asp:RequiredFieldValidator runat="server"
          id="DescriptionRequiredValidator"
          ControlToValidate="txtDescription"
          Display="Dynamic"
          Text="Please enter a description" />
      </EditItemTemplate>
    </asp:TemplateField>
    <asp:CommandField EditText="Edit" ShowEditButton="True"/>
    <asp:CommandField DeleteText="Delete" ShowDeleteButton="True"/>
  </Columns>
</asp:GridView>
```

The application uses a `BoundField` type for the `ID` column, as it's bound directly to a field in the database and users won't need to edit this value:

```
<asp:BoundField HeaderText="ID"
  DataField="newsID"
  SortExpression="newsID"
  ReadOnly="True"/>
```

The label for the column is set using the `HeaderText` property. The bound field is specified with the `DataField` property. The code also specifies a sort expression that will apply if users click the header. The column is set to read-only because you won't be updating the autonumber primary key in the database.

The next column refers to the title of the news item. Because the page displays custom editing controls, this column is a `TemplateField`. This allows the code to specify different templates for the display and editing of the data:

```
<asp:TemplateField HeaderText="Title" SortExpression="newsTitle">
  <ItemTemplate><%#Eval("newsTitle")%></ItemTemplate>
  <EditItemTemplate>
    <asp:TextBox runat="server" id="txtTitle"
      Text='<%#Bind("newsTitle")%>'
      Width="175px"/><br/>
    <asp:RequiredFieldValidator runat="server" id="TitleRequiredValidator"
      ControlToValidate="txtTitle"
      Display="Dynamic"
      Text="Please enter a title" />
  </EditItemTemplate>
</asp:TemplateField>
```

When users aren't in editing mode, the title displays normally, using the `<ItemTemplate>` element. When users edit the title, the `<EditItemTemplate>` element specifies the display. This template uses a `TextBox` control with a `RequiredFieldValidator` control, which prevents users from adding blank entries. Notice that the code uses `Bind` to display the contents in edit mode.

The third column displays in much the same way:

```
<asp:TemplateField HeaderText="Description" SortExpression="newsDescription">
  <ItemTemplate><%#Eval("newsDescription")%></ItemTemplate>
  <EditItemTemplate>
    <asp:TextBox runat="server" id="txtDescription"
      Text='<%#Bind("newsDescription")%>'
      TextMode="MultiLine"
      Columns="100"
      Rows="2"/><br/>
    <asp:RequiredFieldValidator runat="server" id="DescriptionRequiredValidator"
      Controltovalidate="txtDescription"
      Display="Dynamic"
      Text="Please enter a description" />
  </EditItemTemplate>
</asp:TemplateField>
```

This time, the contents appear in a multiline `TextBox`, specifying the `Columns` and `Rows` properties. Again, a `RequiredFieldValidator` ensures that users don't leave the content blank.

The code generates the last two columns as command fields:

```
      <asp:CommandField EditText="Edit" ShowEditButton="True"/>
      <asp:CommandField DeleteText="Delete" ShowDeleteButton="True"/>
    </Columns>
  </asp:GridView>
</asp:Content>
```

These columns display `Edit` and `Delete` links automatically because the `ShowEditButton` and `ShowDeleteButton` properties are set to `true`. The `EditText` and `DeleteText` properties set the text for these links. Figure 12-7 shows what happens when users click the `Edit` link.

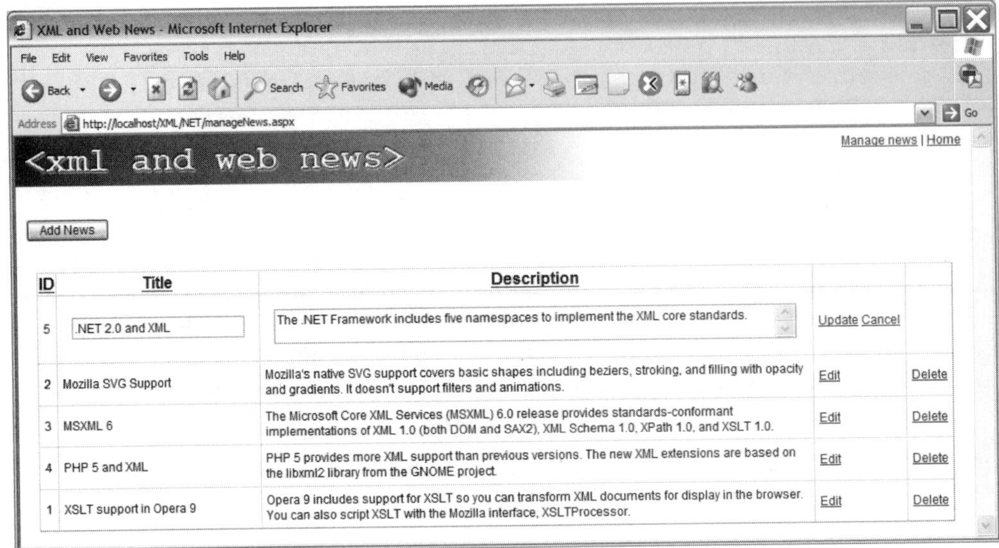

Figure 12-7. *Clicking the Edit link within the GridView control*

The `GridView` shows the editable content in the controls specified in the template. It also changes the `Edit` link to `Update` and `Cancel`, and it removes the `Delete` link for the selected row. Users can click the `Delete` link to remove an item from the `GridView` and the database.

When users click the `Add News` button, the `addNews.aspx` page loads.

addNews.aspx

The `addNews.aspx` page displays an update form and handles the database updating:

```
<%@ Page Language="VB" masterpagefile="template.master" %>
<%@ import Namespace="System.Data" %>
<%@ import Namespace="System.Data.Oledb" %>
<script runat="server">
  Sub Page_Load(Src As Object, E As EventArgs)
    if page.isPostBack then
      Dim strTitle as String = txtTitle.text
      Dim strDescription as String = txtDescription.text
      Dim dbConn as OleDbConnection
      dbConn=New OleDbConnection(ConfigurationSettings.➥
        AppSettings("connectionstring"))
      dbConn.Open()
      Dim sql As String = "INSERT INTO News (newsTitle, newsDescription) ➥
        Values ('" & strTitle & "', '" & strDescription & "')"
```

```
      Dim objCmd As New OleDbCommand(sql, dbConn)
      objCmd.ExecuteNonQuery()
      dbConn.Close()
      response.redirect("manageNews.aspx")
    end if
  End sub
</script>
<asp:Content id="homeContent" ContentPlaceHolderID="PageContent" runat="server">
  <h1>Add news item</h1>
  <table><tr>
    <td><asp:Label runat="server" id="lblTitle" cssClass="emphasis">Title
    </asp:Label></td>
    <td><asp:TextBox runat="server" id="txtTitle" width="400px"></asp:TextBox>
      <br/>
      <asp:RequiredFieldValidator runat="server"
        ControlToValidate="txtTitle"
        ErrorMessage="Enter a title"
        Display="Dynamic"/>
    </td>
  </tr>
  <tr>
    <td><asp:Label runat="server" id="lblDescription" cssClass="emphasis">➥
    Description
    </asp:Label></td>
    <td><asp:TextBox runat="server" id="txtDescription"
      TextMode="MultiLine"
      Columns="75"
      Rows="2"/>
      <asp:Button runat="server" Text="Save"></asp:Button><br/>
      <asp:RequiredFieldValidator runat="server"
        ControlToValidate="txtDescription"
        ErrorMessage="Enter a Description"
        Display="Dynamic"/>
    </td>
  </tr></table>
</asp:Content>
```

Again, this page looks complicated but is relatively simple.

The page starts with declarations and namespaces:

```
<%@ Page Language="VB" masterpagefile="template.master" %>
<%@ import Namespace="System.Data" %>
<%@ import Namespace="System.Data.Oledb" %>
```

It continues with a `Page_Load` subroutine that responds only when the page posts back to the form. I'll come back to that subroutine a little later.

The content of the page includes a heading and a table. It displays a `Label` and `TextBox` for the title and description, along with a `Save` button, as shown in Figure 12-8.

Figure 12-8. *The addNews.aspx page*

Each of the controls has a `RequiredFieldValidator` to make sure that users don't insert blank entries into the database.

When users click the `Save` button, the page calls the code within the `Page_Load` subroutine:

```
<script runat="server">
  Sub Page_Load(Src As Object, E As EventArgs)
    if page.isPostBack then
      Dim strTitle as String = txtTitle.text
      Dim strDescription as String = txtDescription.text
      Dim dbConn as OleDbConnection
      dbConn=New OleDbConnection(ConfigurationSettings.➥
        AppSettings("connectionstring"))
      dbConn.Open()
      Dim sql As String = "INSERT INTO News (newsTitle, newsDescription) ➥
        Values ('" & strTitle & "', '" & strDescription & "')"
      Dim objCmd As New OleDbCommand(sql, dbConn)
      objCmd.ExecuteNonQuery()
      dbConn.Close()
      response.redirect("manageNews.aspx")
    end if
  End sub
</script>
```

The code responds when the page has been posted back:

```
<script runat="server">
  Sub Page_Load(Src As Object, E As EventArgs)
    if page.isPostBack then
```

It collects the values from the form and stores them in the variables `strTitle` and `strDescription`:

```
Dim strTitle as String = txtTitle.text
Dim strDescription as String = txtDescription.text
```

The subroutine then declares and opens a database connection using the `connectionstring` key in the `web.config` file:

```
Dim dbConn as OleDbConnection
dbConn=New OleDbConnection(ConfigurationSettings.➥
AppSettings("connectionstring"))
dbConn.Open()
```

It creates a SQL `INSERT` statement, which executes, closing down the database connection:

```
Dim sql As String = "INSERT INTO News (newsTitle, newsDescription) ➥
  Values ('" & strTitle & "', '" & strDescription & "')"
Dim objCmd As New OleDbCommand(sql, dbConn)
objCmd.ExecuteNonQuery()
dbConn.Close()
```

Finally, the code redirects back to the `manageNews.aspx` page:

```
      response.redirect("manageNews.aspx")
    end if
  End sub
</script>
```

■ **Note** In a real-world application, I'd probably be a little more stringent in testing for apostrophes and other reserved SQL characters. I'd also want to protect my application against SQL injection attacks where users can modify the database maliciously by passing SQL statements through the `querystring`. However, for simplicity, I haven't addressed those issues here.

If users execute the code, they'd see the new item within the GridView control. Figure 12-9 shows adding the news item and the updated grid.

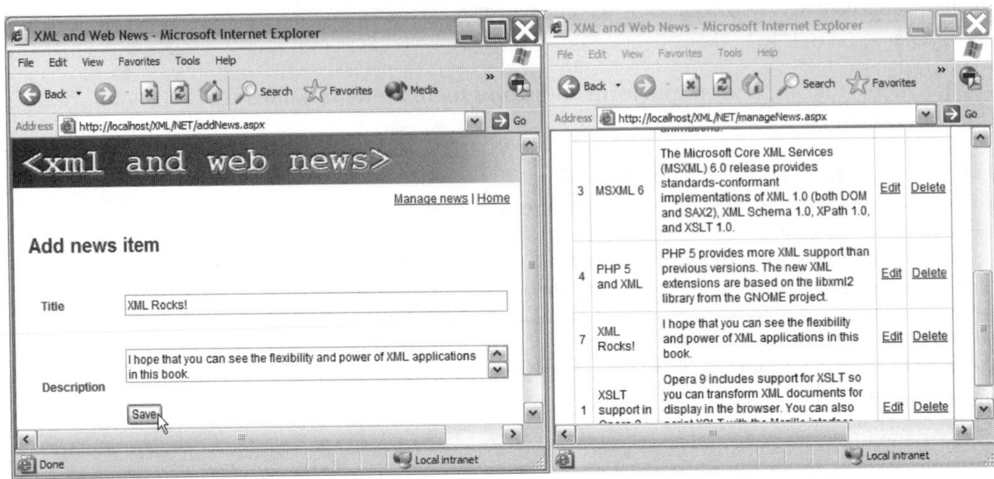

Figure 12-9. *Adding a news item*

Summary

In this chapter, I walked through a .NET 2.0 XML application. The application created and displayed a news feed from an Access database. It also included methods for editing, deleting, and adding news items.

The application generated an RSS 2.0 feed using an XmlTextWriter. It made this feed available to external sources by providing a link to an .aspx page. The application also generated XHTML from the RSS feed using an XSLT stylesheet. The stylesheet included conditional logic to determine which elements to display.

Users can consume external RSS 2.0 feeds within the application. Because the application generates a valid RSS 2.0 feed, it can use the same XSLT stylesheet to display the external news items.

In the next chapter, I'll look at a PHP case study. Rather than replicate this example, you'll see a community weather portal application that uses a MySQL database, DomDocument objects, and XSLT stylesheet transformations.

CHAPTER 13

■ ■ ■

Case Study: Using PHP for an XML Application

In the last chapter of this book, I'll work through a real-world application that uses XML with PHP. Chapter 11 introduced you to using PHP 5 with XML and XSLT stylesheets. This case study will extend your knowledge further. I'll use PHP to take content from a database, convert the results into an XML document, and generate XHTML content for a web browser.

I'll start by exploring the sample application, and then I'll break down the code and work through each section. You can download the resource files from the Source Code area of the Apress web site (`http://www.apress.com`).

Understanding the Application

This case study focuses on a sample web application, the Community Weather Portal. The application maintains a database of weather conditions collected from community users. Users can navigate to their city and display the current weather conditions from entries that other users have added. Users can add cities that aren't in the database. They can also add the current weather conditions for any city.

The application uses a breadcrumb navigation system to allow users to select their location. They start by choosing a continent, then a country, and then an area before selecting the city. Once they reach the city level, they see the current weather conditions. At any time, a complete navigation path leads back to the area, country, or continent.

Setting Up the Environment

This application uses PHP 5 and MySQL, and I tested it on a clean installation of both. The application uses the `libxslt` extension, and I haven't enabled any other related extensions. As I mentioned in Chapter 11, the `libxslt` extension is installed by default with PHP 5, but you need to enable it within the `php.ini` file. Make sure that you uncomment the following line in the file:

```
extension=php_xsl.dll
```

PHP.INI SETTINGS

If you're using PHP to output files with an XML header, and you have the `short_open_tag` directive turned on in your `php.ini` file, you're likely to run into problems. This directive allows you to use `<?` as the opening tag for a PHP code block. These are the same two characters that you'll find at the beginning of the XML declaration:

```
<?xml version="1.0" encoding="iso-8859-1"?>
```

Therefore, the XML directive will be interpreted as PHP code and will generate an error.

The application uses a MySQL database to store the weather information, so you need to run some SQL scripts to create the tables and enter content. I've assumed that you have the MySQL database installed and that you're using phpMyAdmin to administer the database. You can download phpMyAdmin from `http://www.phpmyadmin.net/home_page/index.php`. If you prefer, you can use an alternative database, but the remainder of the chapter covers the use of MySQL.

Before I get started, it's important to understand the structure of the database that stores the weather data.

Understanding the Database Structure

Because the application is likely to store large volumes of data, it's more appropriate to store the application information within a database rather than relying on XML documents. As XML documents increase in size, they become harder to work with and take longer to load. The application can streamline this process by accessing the database and generating the relevant XML content as required.

The database uses a relational structure to describe the relationships between data. The continents sit at the top data level. Within each continent, there are many countries, and within each country, there are many areas. Areas are divided into cities, and each city can have multiple weather items. Weather items include a weather type, and this data is held in a separate table. Figure 13-1 shows an entity-relationship diagram (ERD) describing these relationships.

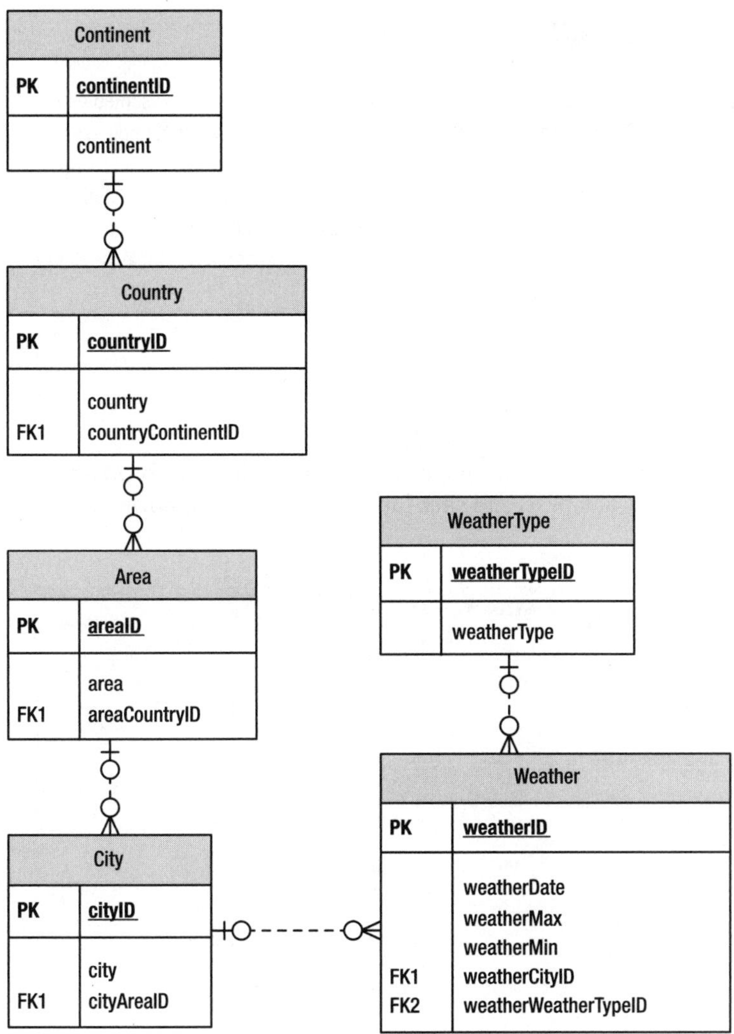

Figure 13-1. *An ERD for the Community Weather Portal*

UNDERSTANDING THE ERD

If you're not familiar with ERDs, you might find the diagram a little confusing. Each table is represented as a square box containing a list of all fields. Primary keys are represented with the letters PK, and foreign keys are represented with the letters FK. The lines describe the relationships between the tables.

The symbols at the end of each line have specific meanings to describe the different types of relationships. In Figure 13-1, the lines are all the same, so all tables have the same type of relationships. One end of the line contains a vertical line and circle symbol. This symbol indicates that one record in this table is related to zero or more records in the table on the other end of the line.

MySQL

You need to start by creating the weather database. Open phpMyAdmin in a web browser. Enter `weather` as a name for the new database, and click the `Create` button, as shown in Figure 13-2.

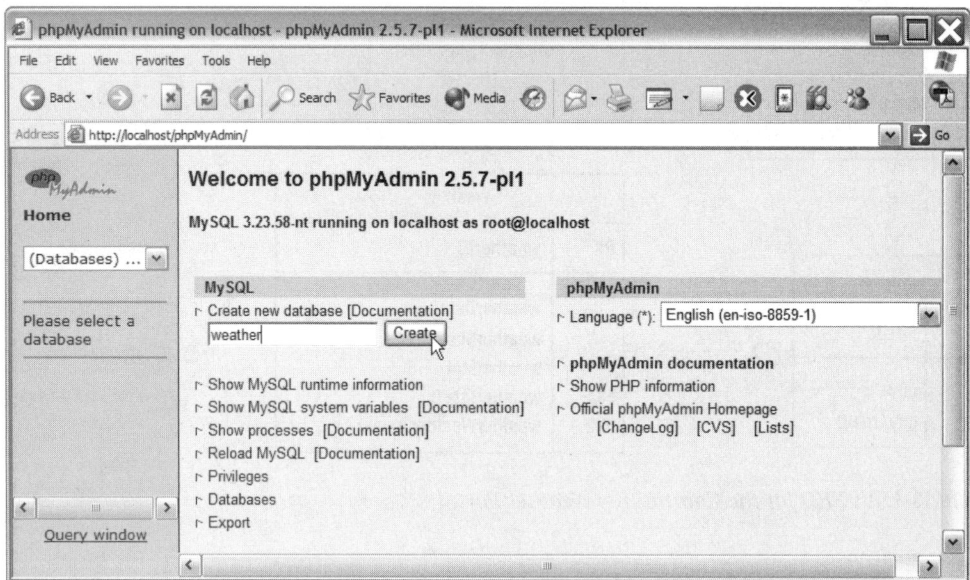

Figure 13-2. *Creating the weather database using phpMyAdmin*

You create the database tables using a SQL script. The script creates the relevant tables and inserts some sample content. You can find the complete script saved as `weather.sql` with your resources. Before you run the script, I'll work through each section so you can understand what's happening.

To start with, the script creates the continent, country, area, and city tables:

```
CREATE TABLE continent (
  continentID int(11) NOT NULL auto_increment,
  continent varchar(20) default NULL,
  PRIMARY KEY (continentID)
) TYPE=MyISAM;

CREATE TABLE country (
  countryID int(11) NOT NULL auto_increment,
  country varchar(100) default NULL,
  countryContinentID int(11) default NULL,
  PRIMARY KEY (countryID),
  FOREIGN KEY (countryContinentID) REFERENCES continent (continentID)
) TYPE=MyISAM;

CREATE TABLE area (
  areaID int(11) NOT NULL auto_increment,
  area varchar(100) default NULL,
  areaCountryID int(11) default NULL,
  PRIMARY KEY (areaID),
  FOREIGN KEY (areaCountryID) REFERENCES country (countryID)
) TYPE=MyISAM;

CREATE TABLE city (
  cityID int(11) NOT NULL auto_increment,
  city varchar(100) default NULL,
  cityAreaID int(11) default NULL,
  PRIMARY KEY (cityID),
  FOREIGN KEY (cityAreaID) REFERENCES area (areaID)
) TYPE=MyISAM;
```

Each table has a primary key ending with the letters ID. The script also defines foreign keys that specify the relationships between each table.

The individual city forecasts appear within the weather table:

```
CREATE TABLE weather (
  weatherID int(11) NOT NULL auto_increment,
  weatherDate int(11) default NULL,
  weatherMax int(4) default NULL,
  weatherMin int(4) default NULL,
  weatherCityID int(11) default NULL,
  weatherWeatherTypeID int(11) default NULL,
  PRIMARY KEY (weatherID),
  FOREIGN KEY (weatherCityID) REFERENCES city (cityID),
  FOREIGN KEY (weatherWeatherTypeID) REFERENCES weatherType (weatherTypeID)
) TYPE=MyISAM;
```

This table stores the date of the forecast, the maximum and minimum temperatures, and the current weather conditions.

The current conditions come from values in the `weatherWeatherTypeID` field. This foreign key is associated with the `weatherType` table:

```
CREATE TABLE weatherType (
  weatherTypeID int(11) NOT NULL auto_increment,
  weatherType varchar(40) default NULL,
  PRIMARY KEY (weatherTypeID)
) TYPE=MyISAM;
```

The last section of the SQL script inserts the default weather conditions into the `weatherType` table:

```
INSERT INTO weatherType VALUES (1,'hot');
INSERT INTO weatherType VALUES (2,'sunny');
INSERT INTO weatherType VALUES (3,'windy');
INSERT INTO weatherType VALUES (4,'cloudy');
INSERT INTO weatherType VALUES (5,'rain');
INSERT INTO weatherType VALUES (6,'rainstorms');
INSERT INTO weatherType VALUES (7,'snow');
INSERT INTO weatherType VALUES (8,'snowstorms');
```

Each of these weather types has an associated image in the `images` folder.

In phpMyAdmin, switch to the SQL section and copy and paste the contents of the `weather.sql` file into the `Run SQL queries` section of the page, as shown in Figure 13-3.

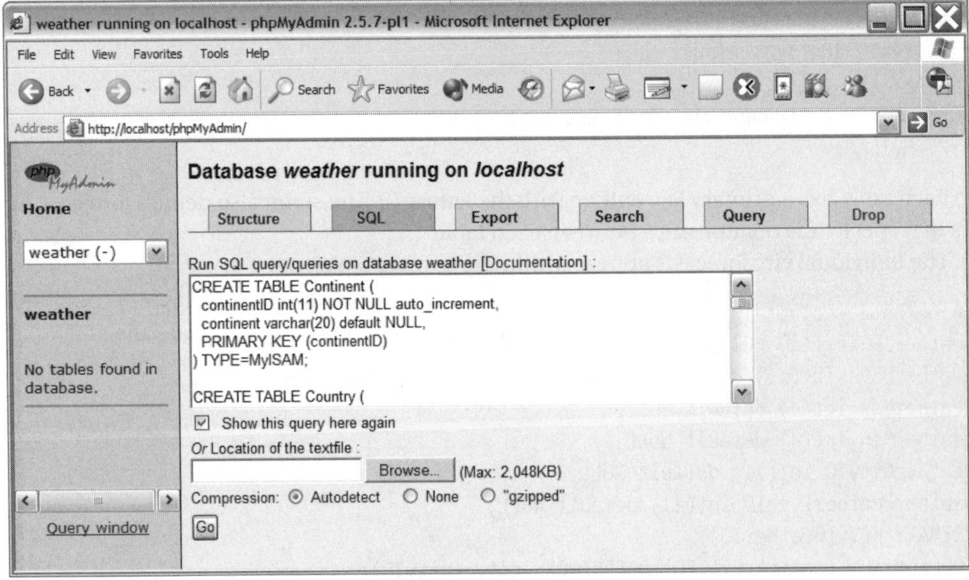

Figure 13-3. *Running the SQL script in phpMyAdmin*

Click the Go button to run the script. You should see a message stating that the SQL query has been executed successfully. The left-hand side of the page should show the names of six tables, as in Figure 13-4.

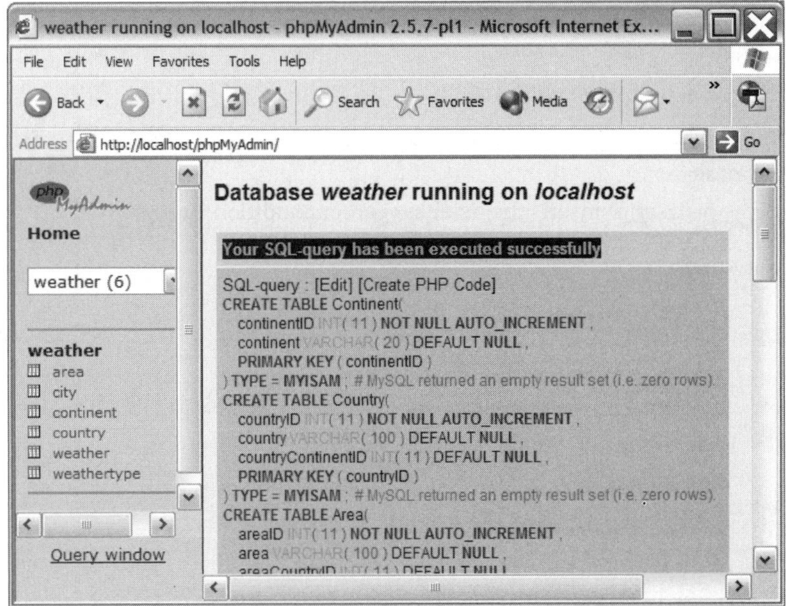

Figure 13-4. *The completed database*

You also need to set the permissions and user details for the database. The connection details are stored within the file weather.php:

```
$wdb_host = 'localhost';
$wdb_user = 'user_weather';
$wdb_pass = 'weatherpassword';
$wdb_name = 'weather';
```

You may need to alter the host setting for your own system.

In phpMyAdmin, switch back to the databases section by choosing (Databases) from the drop-down list on the left of the screen. Click the Privileges link in the central pane and choose Add a new User.

Enter the details from `weather.php`. The default username is `user_weather`, and the default password is `weatherpassword`. Enter the host details and assign the privileges, as shown in Figure 13-5.

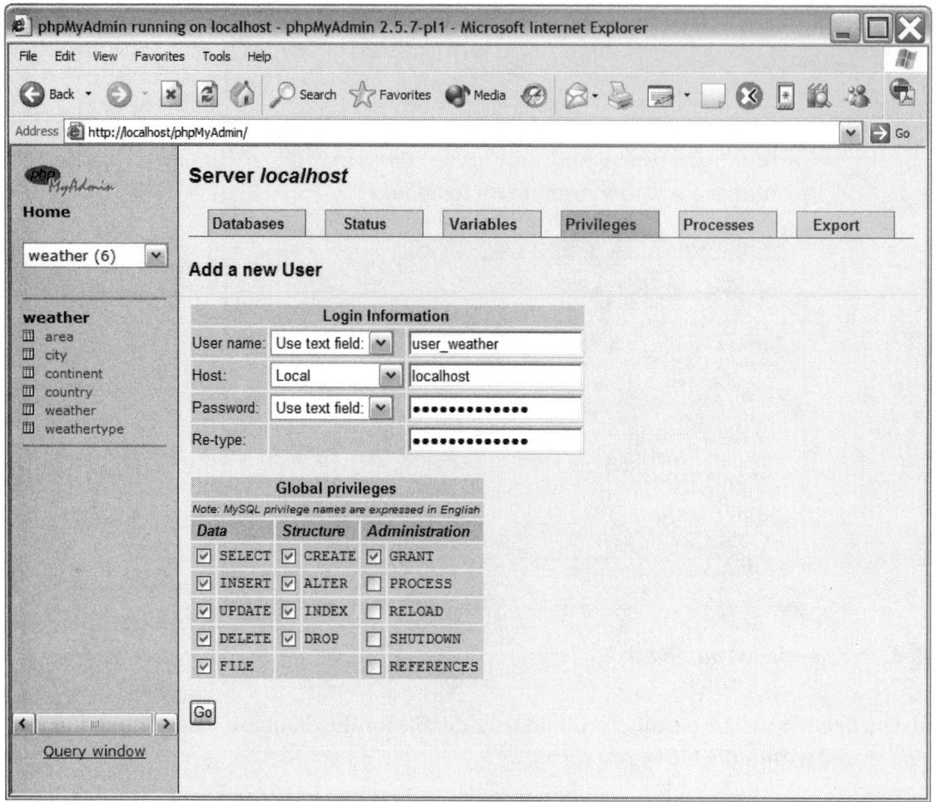

Figure 13-5. *The privileges for the user_weather user*

Click `Go`, then set the same database-specific privileges on the weather database. You may also need to restart MySQL to apply the permissions.

Understanding Components of the Weather Portal Application

Before I work through the application, let's look at its component parts. The home page, `index.php`, is made up of `sidebar.php` and `standard.php`. The file `standard.php` is constructed from `mk_navxml.php` and `mk_weather.php`. These pages interact with the XSLT stylesheets `nav.xsl` and `weather.xsl`, and the pages `addnew.php` and `addweather.php`. Figure 13-6 shows the interaction between these pages.

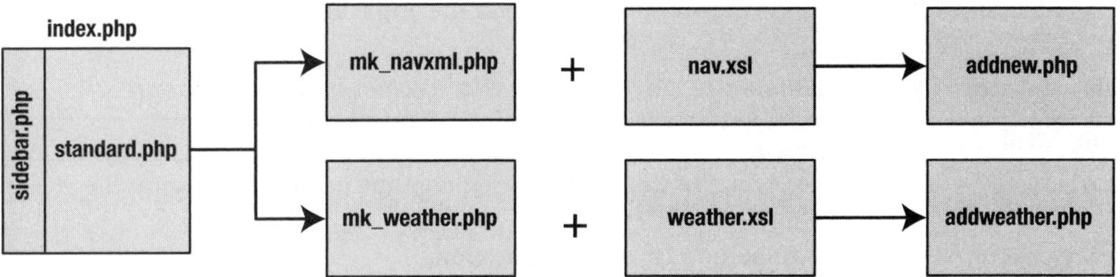

Figure 13-6. *The interaction between the components of the Community Weather Portal application*

Figure 13-7 shows the finished application displaying the temperature for a city.

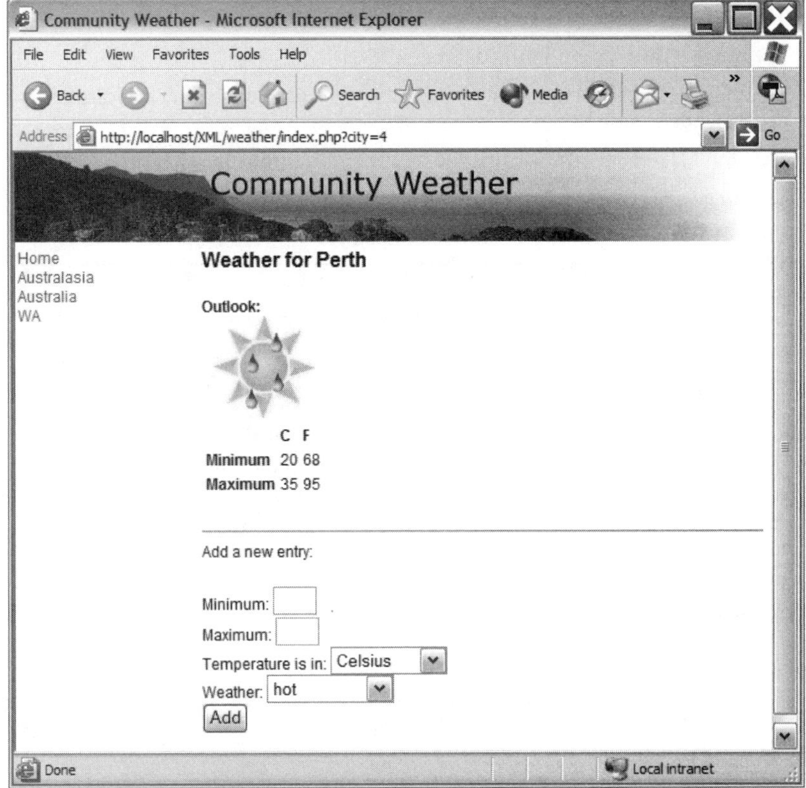

Figure 13-7. *The Community Weather Portal*

Table 13-1 summarizes the purpose of each part of the application.

Table 13-1. *The Purpose of Components in the Community Weather Portal Application*

Component	Purpose
`weather.php`	This page contains the database username and password, as well as the database connection code.
`index.php`	This is the home page of the application.
`standard.css`	This CSS stylesheet adds styling to XHTML elements.
`sidebar.php`	This page contains the sidebar for the application, which provides a breadcrumb style of navigation through the locations to the home page.
`standard.php`	This page determines the content to display.
`mk_navxml.php`	This page queries the database and returns an XML document determining the next level of navigation.
`nav.xsl`	This XSLT stylesheet transforms the navigation XML into XHTML.
`addnew.php`	This page adds content to the database.
`mk_weather.php`	This page queries the database and returns the current weather conditions as an XML document.
`weather.xsl`	This XSLT stylesheet transforms the weather conditions into XHTML.
`addweather.php`	This page adds a new weather record to the database.
`/images/`	This folder contains images for the application.

I'll examine these components in more detail in the next section.

weather.php

As I mentioned previously, the `weather.php` script contains settings for the application. It contains details for connecting to the database along with the code to make the connection:

```
<?php
$wdb_host = 'localhost';
$wdb_user = 'user_weather';
$wdb_pass = 'weatherpassword';
$wdb_name = 'weather';
mysql_connect($wdb_host, $wdb_user, $wdb_pass);
mysql_select_db($wdb_name);
?>
```

Storing the details in a single place means that you can update the settings more easily. The settings shown here relate to my own environment. If you changed the password or have a different host, your settings may be a little different.

index.php

The `index.php` page shows all of the content for the application. The content depends on the arguments passed to the script through the querystring in the address bar.

The application identifies four navigation areas: continent, country, area, and city. By passing these arguments to the script, the application can filter the content displayed on the `index.php` page. It determines which value(s) are passed and then extracts the filter from the `$_GET` array.

If you test the page before populating the database content, you'll see something similar to the image shown in Figure 13-8.

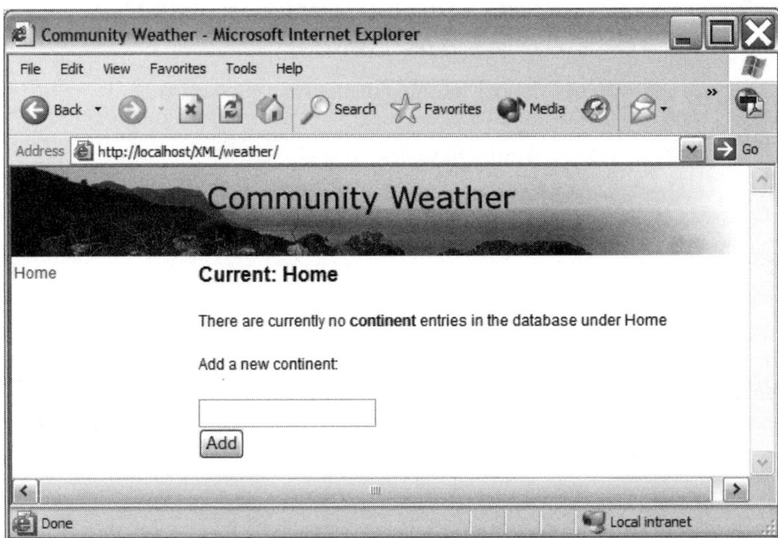

Figure 13-8. *The Community Weather Portal without database content*

The `addnew.php` script allows users to enter content for the portal. I'll work through that page shortly. The code within the `index.php` page follows:

```
<?php
if (isset($_GET['continent'])) {
    $continent = intval($_GET['continent']);
}
if (isset($_GET['country'])) {
    $country = intval($_GET['country']);
}
if (isset($_GET['area'])) {
    $area = intval($_GET['area']);
}
if (isset($_GET['city'])) {
    $city = intval($_GET['city']);
}
?>
```

The content displayed on the page is determined by your position in the navigation system. Therefore, the application needs to figure out which values have been passed into the page through the querystring. It uses these variables to determine what data to extract and display from the database.

The remainder of the page follows:

```
<!DOCTYPE html PUBLIC "-//W3C//DTD XHTML 1.0 Strict//EN"
    "http://www.w3.org/TR/xhtml1/DTD/xhtml1-strict.dtd">
<html xmlns="http://www.w3.org/1999/xhtml">
  <head>
    <title>Community Weather</title>
    <meta http-equiv="Content-Type" content="text/html; charset=iso-8859-1" />
    <link href="standard.css" rel="stylesheet" type="text/css" />
    <style>
      #layHeading {
        position:absolute;
        left:0px;
        top:0px;
        width:600px;
        height:70px;
        z-index:1;
      }
      #layNavigation {
        position:absolute;
        left:2px;
        top:75px;
        width:140px;
        z-index:2;
      }
      #layContent {
        position:absolute;
        left:150px;
        top:75px;
        width:450px;
        z-index:3;
      }
    </style>
  </head>
  <body>
    <div id="layHeading">
      <img src="images/header.jpg" width="600" height="70" alt="Page Heading"/>
    </div>
    <div id="layNavigation">
      <?php include 'sidebar.php'; ?>
    </div>
    <div id="layContent">
      <?php include_once 'standard.php'; ?>
    </div>
  </body>
</html>
```

This code sets up the page, links to an external stylesheet, and embeds some stylesheet declarations associated with the ids of <div> elements.

The <body> section of the page contains a series of <div> elements. The first, layHeading, contains the heading image:

```
<div id="layHeading">
  <img src="images/header.jpg" width="600" height="70" alt="Page Heading"/>
</div>
```

The second, layNavigation, contains the navigation on the left side of the screen. The navigation comes from the page sidebar.php, which I'll look at shortly:

```
<div id="layNavigation">
  <?php include 'sidebar.php'; ?>
</div>
```

The final <div> element encloses the content from the page, which comes from standard.php:

```
<div id="layContent">
  <?php include_once 'standard.php'; ?>
</div>
```

The standard.php page determines whether to display additional levels of navigation—either countries, areas, or cities. If users select a city, this page displays the weather conditions. I'll work through the page shortly.

standard.css

The CSS stylesheet standard.css provides formatting for index.php. It contains a set of standard declarations for elements on the page:

```
body {
  font-family: Arial, Helvetica, sans-serif;
  font-size: 12px;
  font-weight: normal;
  color: #000000;
}
strong {
  font-size: 12px;
  font-weight: bold;
}
a {
  color : #0066FF;
  text-decoration : none;
}
a:hover, a:active {
  text-decoration : underline;
}
```

sidebar.php

The sidebar.php script builds the breadcrumb navigation for the left of the index.php page. Figure 13-9 shows the navigation system. Notice that I've used Australasia in the example, which isn't, strictly speaking, a continent.

Figure 13-9. *The index.php page showing the breadcrumb navigation*

The sidebar.php page starts with a link to the home page:

```
<a href="index.php">Home</a><br />
```

The page needs to connect to the database, so it must include the weather.php file:

```
<?php
include_once 'weather.php';
```

The next block of code determines which of the three navigation variables have been set: $country, $area, or $city. The page doesn't need to test for the $continent variable, as the home page is above continent level, and that page has a fixed link.

If users are at country level, the page will need to provide a link to the continent containing that country:

```
if (isset($country)) {
  $sql = 'SELECT country.countryContinentID, continent.* ➥
    FROM country, continent WHERE countryContinentID=continentID ➥
    AND countryID=' . $country;
  $cRes = mysql_query($sql) or die(mysql_error());
  if (mysql_num_rows($cRes) == 1) {
    $cRow = mysql_fetch_array($cRes);
    echo '<a href="index.php?continent=' . $cRow['continentID'] . '">' . ➥
      $cRow['continent'] . '</a><br />';
  }
}
```

The SELECT statement determines the country. If the database contains a valid country, the page provides a link.

The application uses the same approach for the area level, where it provides links back to the area's country and continent:

```
if (isset($area)) {
  $sql = 'SELECT area.areaCountryID, country.*, continent.* ➥
    FROM area, country, continent WHERE areaCountryID=countryID ➥
    AND countryContinentID=continentID AND areaID=' . $area;
  $cRes = mysql_query($sql) or die(mysql_error());
  if (mysql_num_rows($cRes) == 1) {
    $cRow = mysql_fetch_array($cRes);
    echo '<a href="index.php?continent=' . $cRow['continentID'] . '">' . ➥
      $cRow['continent'] . '</a><br />';
    echo '<a href="index.php?country=' . $cRow['countryID'] . '">' . ➥
      $cRow['country'] . '</a><br />';
  }
}
```

Finally, when users are at a city level, they need to be able to link back to the area, country, and continent:

```
  if (isset($city)) {
    $sql = 'SELECT city.cityAreaID, area.*, country.*, continent.* ➥
      FROM city, area, country, continent WHERE cityAreaID=areaID ➥
      AND areaCountryID=countryID AND countryContinentID=continentID ➥
      AND cityID=' . $city;
    $cRes = mysql_query($sql) or die(mysql_error());
    if (mysql_num_rows($cRes) == 1) {
      $cRow = mysql_fetch_array($cRes);
      echo '<a href="index.php?continent=' . $cRow['continentID'] . '">' . ➥
        $cRow['continent'] . '</a><br />';
      echo '<a href="index.php?country=' . $cRow['countryID'] . '">' . ➥
        $cRow['country'] . '</a><br />';
      echo '<a href="index.php?area=' . $cRow['areaID'] . '">' . ➥
        $cRow['area'] . '</a><br />';
    }
  }
?>
```

You'll notice that the SQL statements become more complicated as the page determines more levels in the navigation hierarchy.

standard.php

The standard.php page determines what content to display on the page. If the page has set the $city variable, the users have chosen a city and wish to see the weather. Figure 13-10 shows the content that displays when the $city variable is set but when there are no weather entries.

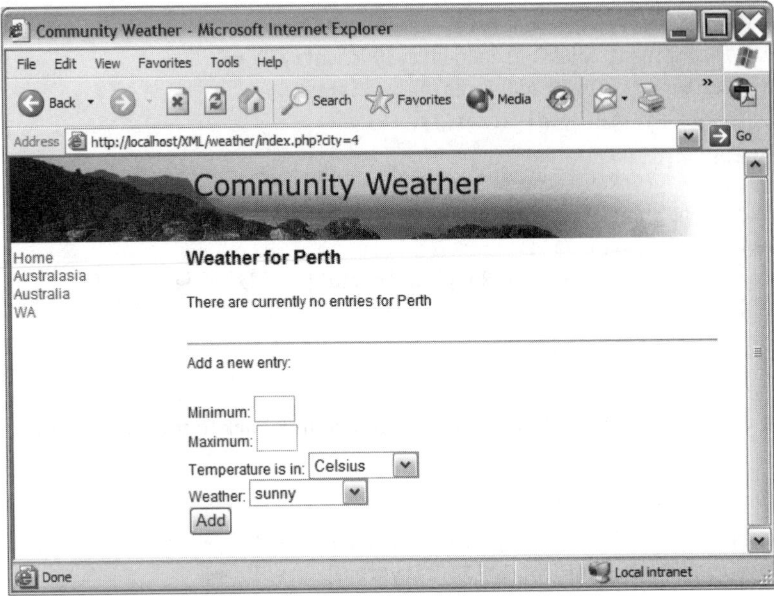

Figure 13-10. *Displaying city details where no weather is entered*

If the $city variable hasn't been set, the page needs to display further navigation so users can navigate to the city level.

The standard.php page follows:

```
<?php
  $xml = new DomDocument();
  $xsl = new DomDocument();
  if (isset($city)) {
    include 'mk_weather.php';
    $xsl->load('weather.xsl');
}
  else {
    include 'mk_navxml.php';
    $xsl->load('nav.xsl');
}
$xml->loadXML($xml->saveXML());
$proc = new XsltProcessor();
$xsl = $proc->importStylesheet($xsl);
$xml = $proc->transformToDoc($xml);
echo $newdom->saveXML();
?>
```

Let's work through the code in a little more detail. First, the page creates two DomDocument objects for the XML and XSL documents:

```
$xsl = new DomDocument();
$inputdom = new DomDocument();
```

Then it tests to see if the $city variable is set and includes the appropriate document. The code also loads the related XSLT stylesheet:

```
if (isset($city)) {
  include 'mk_weather.php';
  $xsl->load('weather.xsl');
}
else {
  include 'mk_navxml.php';
  $xsl->load('nav.xsl');
}
```

The next code block loads the XML content and creates a new XsltProcessor:

```
$xml->loadXML($xml->saveXML());
$proc = new XsltProcessor();
```

The code then imports the stylesheet and applies the transformation, displaying the output in the page:

```
$xsl = $proc->importStylesheet($xsl);
$newdom = $proc->transformToDoc($xml);
echo $newdom->saveXML();
```

mk_navxml.php

The mk_navxml.php script is a complicated page responsible for much of the work in the application. This page creates the XML document that the application uses for the navigation in the site.

The variables passed to the page determine the navigation system. There are four types of navigation to display:

1. The $area variable is set, so the navigation should display the cities.
2. The $country variable is set, so the navigation should display the areas.
3. The $continent variable is set, so the navigation should display the countries.
4. No variables are set, so the navigation should display a list of continents.

The application uses the following template for the XML document built from the database content:

```
<?xml version="1.0" encoding="UTF-8"?>
<entries>
  <current type=""></current>
  <items>
    <linksto> </linksto>
    <entry id=""> </entry>
  </items>
</entries>
```

The document element is `<entries>`. The `<current>` element specifies the user's current position in the navigation system. The `<items>` element contains a `<linksto>` element. This element specifies the links from this level. The `<items>` element also contains a list of `<entry>` elements, one for each navigation item at this level. An XSLT stylesheet uses the values in the `<entry>` elements to create the links to the subsequent levels of navigation.

The structure of the XML document built by the application needs to take into account the following scenarios:

1. There are no subnavigation items to display.
2. The values in the querystring change and cause an error.
3. There are subnavigation items to display.

The last scenario is the most likely, but I'll look at the XML structure that the application needs to produce for each option.

Scenario 1: No Subnavigation Items

The first situation I'll look at is where the users have reached a point in the navigation where there are no subnavigation items. A sample XML file structure for this scenario follows:

```
<?xml version="1.0" encoding="UTF-8"?>
<entries>
  <current type="area" id="8">WA</current>
  <items>
    <linksto>city</linksto>
  </items>
</entries>
```

In this structure, I've navigated to Western Australia (WA), a state in Australia. The `<current>` element shows that I'm in an area called `WA`. However, the `<items>` element doesn't contain `<entry>` tags, as no cities are specified within the area.

Scenario 2: Changing Querystring Variables

Users might change the values in the querystring, perhaps changing one of the variables to see what happens. Let's assume that the URL to generate the XML document in scenario 1 was `http://localhost/weather/index.php?continent=1`.

If users change the URL to http://localhost/weather/index.php?continent=7643, one of two things can happen. Either the value 7643 refers to a continent in the database, or the id is invalid. In the first case, the application can display the subnavigation for that continent, but in the second case, it needs to display an error message.

The application uses the following XML document structure for this scenario:

```
<?xml version="1.0" encoding="UTF-8"?>
<entries>
  <current>Error</current>
  <error>You appear to have selected an invalid continent</error>
</entries>
```

Instead of an <items> element, the document includes Error as the value of the <current> element. It also includes an <error> element with an error message that displays to the user.

Scenario 3: Dealing with Subnavigation Items

The most likely scenario is that the application displays subnavigation items. The structure of this type of XML document is similar to that shown in scenario 1. The difference is that the <items> element contains multiple <entry> elements:

```
<?xml version="1.0" encoding="UTF-8"?>
<entries>
  <current type="area" id="8">WA</current>
  <items>
    <linksto>city</linksto>
    <entry id="1">Albany</entry>
    <entry id="2">Bunbury</entry>
    <entry id="3">Geraldton</entry>
    <entry id="4">Perth</entry>
  </items>
</entries>
```

Each <entry> element has an id that corresponds to the id field in the database. It also contains the name of the navigation item—in this case, the name of the city.

Now let's see how to build the XML document to cope with these different scenarios.

Building the XML Document

The mk_navxml.php document starts by including weather.php:

```
<?php
  include_once('weather.php');
```

The page uses a variable called $xml to build the XML document. It starts by creating a new DomDocument:

```
$xml = new DomDocument('1.0', 'UTF-8');
$xml->xmlStandalone = false;
```

The code then sets the document element using the createElement() and appendChild() methods:

```
$root = $xml->createElement('entries');
$root = $xml->appendChild($root);
```

The next code block tests which variable has been set: $area, $country, or $continent. It does this in an if/else statement that starts with the lowest navigation level, area:

```
if (isset($area)) {
```

If the $city variable is set, the code in standard.php will branch to include the mk_weather.php script instead.

The code starts by retrieving the current area information from the database:

```
$sql = 'SELECT * from area WHERE areaID=' . $area;
$tres = mysql_query($sql) or die(mysql_error());
```

It also tests that the area id is valid:

```
if (mysql_num_rows($tres) == 0) {
  $current = $xml->createElement('current', 'Error');
  $current = $root->appendChild($current);
  $error = $xml->createElement('error', 'You appear to have selected ➥
    an invalid area');
   $error = $root->appendChild($error);
}
```

If the query returns no rows, the application knows that the area id is invalid and the page can generate an <error> element.

If the query returns rows, the area name is stored in a variable for later use:

```
else {
  $row = mysql_fetch_array($tres);
  $area_name = $row['area'];
```

Once the page determines the area, it then needs to select the subnavigation city items:

```
$sql = 'SELECT * FROM city WHERE cityAreaID =' . $area . ' ORDER BY city';
$cres = mysql_query($sql) or die(mysql_error());
```

The code can then use DOM methods to create the <current> element and set the attributes:

```
$current = $xml->createElement('current', $area_name);
$current->setAttribute('type', 'area');
$current->setAttribute('id', $area);
$root->appendChild($current);
```

It also creates the <items> and <linksto> elements:

```
$items = $xml->createElement('items');
$root->appendChild($items);
$linksto = $xml->createElement('linksto', 'city');
$items->appendChild($linksto);
```

Finally, it loops through the results and creates a set of <entry> elements. Obviously, if there are no cities, it doesn't create any elements:

```
while ($crow = mysql_fetch_array($cres)) {
  $entry = $xml->createElement('entry', $crow['city']);
  $entry->setAttribute('id', $crow['cityID']);
  $items->appendChild($entry);
}
```

Note that I've left out the closing brackets to simplify the code.

The code repeats this process for the country. This time, it returns the areas with the country as <entry> elements instead of the cities:

```
else if (isset($country)) {
  $sql = 'SELECT * from country WHERE countryID =' . $country;
  $tres = mysql_query($sql) or die(mysql_error());
  if (mysql_num_rows($tres) == 0) {
    $current = $xml->createElement('current', 'Error');
    $current = $root->appendChild($current);
    $error = $xml->createElement('error', 'You appear to have selected ➥
      an invalid country');
    $error = $root->appendChild($error);
  }
  else {
    $trow = mysql_fetch_array($tres);
    $country_name = $trow['country'];
    $sql = 'SELECT * FROM area WHERE areaCountryID =' . $country . ' ➥
      ORDER BY area';
    $cres = mysql_query($sql) or die(mysql_error());
    $current = $xml->createElement('current', $country_name);
    $current->setAttribute('type', 'country');
    $current->setAttribute('id', $country);
    $root->appendChild($current);
    $items = $xml->createElement('items');
    $root->appendChild($items);
    $linksto = $xml->createElement('linksto', 'area');
    $items->appendChild($linksto);
    while ($crow = mysql_fetch_array($cres)) {
      $entry = $xml->createElement('entry', $crow['area']);
      $entry->setAttribute('id', $crow['areaID']);
      $items->appendChild($entry);
    }
  }
}
```

The page then repeats the process for continents:

```
else if (isset($continent)) {
  $sql = 'SELECT * from continent WHERE continentID =' . $continent;
  $tres = mysql_query($sql) or die(mysql_error());
  if (mysql_num_rows($tres) == 0) {
    $current = $xml->createElement('current', 'Error');
    $current = $root->appendChild($current);
    $error = $xml->createElement('error', 'You appear to have selected ➥
      an invalid continent');
    $error = $root->appendChild($error);
  }
  else {
    $trow = mysql_fetch_array($tres);
    $continent_name = $trow['continent'];
    $sql = 'SELECT * FROM country WHERE countryContinentID =' . $continent . ➥
      ' ORDER BY country';
    $cres = mysql_query($sql) or die(mysql_error());
    $current = $xml->createElement('current', $continent_name);
    $current->setAttribute('type', 'continent');
    $current->setAttribute('id', $continent);
    $root->appendChild($current);
    $items = $xml->createElement('items');
    $root->appendChild($items);
    $linksto = $xml->createElement('linksto', 'country');
    $items->appendChild($linksto);
    while ($crow = mysql_fetch_array($cres)) {
      $entry = $xml->createElement('entry', $crow['country']);
      $entry->setAttribute('id', $crow['countryID']);
      $items->appendChild($entry);
    }
  }
}
```

If none of the variables has been set, users are at the top level of navigation, and the application must display a list of continents from the database:

```
else {
  $sql = 'SELECT * FROM continent ORDER BY continent';
  $cres = mysql_query($sql) or die(mysql_error());
  $current = $xml->createElement('current', 'Home');
  $current->setAttribute('type', 'home');
  $root->appendChild($current);
  $items = $xml->createElement('items');
  $root->appendChild($items);
  $linksto = $xml->createElement('linksto', 'continent');
  $items->appendChild($linksto);
  while ($crow = mysql_fetch_array($cres)) {
```

```
      $entry = $xml->createElement('entry', $crow['continent']);
      $entry->setAttribute('id', $crow['continentID']);
      $items->appendChild($entry);
    }
  }
```

By the time the script finishes running, it has built an XML document that is transformed in the `standard.php` script, as you saw earlier.

nav.xsl

Let's look at the XSLT stylesheet, `nav.xsl` in more detail. This stylesheet transforms the XML document from the `mk_navxml.php` page.

The stylesheet starts with an XML declaration and the opening `<xsl:stylesheet>` element:

```
<?xml version="1.0"?>
<xsl:stylesheet version="1.0" xmlns:xsl="http://www.w3.org/1999/XSL/Transform">
```

The code creates some XSLT variables to store values that the stylesheet will use:

```
<xsl:variable name="linksto">
  <xsl:value-of select="entries/items/linksto"/>
</xsl:variable>
<xsl:variable name="numLinks">
  <xsl:value-of select="count(entries/items/entry)" />
</xsl:variable>
```

It uses the `linksto` variable to determine the link type, and the `numLinks` variable to determine whether any links exist.

The page uses the `<xsl:choose>` element to provide some conditional logic. To start with, it identifies errors:

```
<xsl:template match="/">
  <xsl:choose>
    <xsl:when test="//entries/current='Error'">
      <h4>Error</h4>
      <xsl:value-of select="entries/error" />
    </xsl:when>
```

When the application has an error, the stylesheet displays it in a level 4 heading.

If there is no error, it displays the requested details:

```
<xsl:otherwise>
  <h4>Current: <xsl:value-of select="entries/current" /></h4>
```

The stylesheet uses another `<xsl:choose>` element to see if there are any subnavigation links:

```
<xsl:choose>
  <xsl:when test="$numLinks=0">
```

If there are no links, it displays a message to that effect:

```
    There are currently no <strong><xsl:value-of select="$linksto" />
    </strong> entries in the database under
    <xsl:value-of select="entries/current" />
  </xsl:when>
```

Otherwise, it displays the links, using the value of the `$linksto` variable to create the URL:

```
  <xsl:otherwise>
    <p>Please select a <xsl:value-of select="$linksto" />:</p>
    <xsl:for-each select="entries/items/entry">
      <a><xsl:attribute name="href">index.php?<xsl:value-of select="$linksto" />➥
        =<xsl:value-of select="@id" /></xsl:attribute><xsl:value-of select="." />
      </a><br />
    </xsl:for-each>
  </xsl:otherwise>
</xsl:choose>
```

This portion of the template generates XHTML similar to the following:

```
<p>Please select a country:</p>
<a href="index.php?country=1">Australia</a><br/>
<a href="index.php?country=2">New Zealand</a><br/>
```

After the stylesheet displays the subnavigation links, it displays a form that allows users to add a new entry at the current level:

```
<p>Add a new <xsl:value-of select="$linksto" />:<br />
  <form action="addnew.php" method="POST">
```

The code needs to pass the level at which you're adding this entry, the `id` of the parent record, and the current navigation level. It does this using hidden form fields:

```
        <xsl:text disable-output-escaping="yes">
          &lt;input type="hidden" name="current" value="</xsl:text>
        <xsl:value-of select="entries/current/@type" />
        <xsl:text disable-output-escaping="yes">" /&gt;</xsl:text>
        <xsl:text disable-output-escaping="yes">
          &lt;input type="hidden" name="parent" value="</xsl:text>
        <xsl:value-of select="entries/current/@id" />
        <xsl:text disable-output-escaping="yes">" /&gt; </xsl:text>
        <xsl:text disable-output-escaping="yes">
          &lt;input type="hidden" name="into" value="</xsl:text>
        <xsl:value-of select="$linksto" />
        <xsl:text disable-output-escaping="yes">" /&gt; </xsl:text>
```

The current level determines which table receives the new record. The code then inserts the parent `id` value into the record. The current navigation level redirects users to the current page after inserting the record.

The remainder of the block creates the visible text field and Add button:

```
      <input type="text" name="entry" /> <br />
      <input type="submit" value="Add" />
    </form>
  </p>
 </xsl:otherwise>
</xsl:choose>
```

The form appears within the <xsl:choose> element, so it only displays if a valid record exists. Figure 13-11 shows the form as it appears when working at the city level.

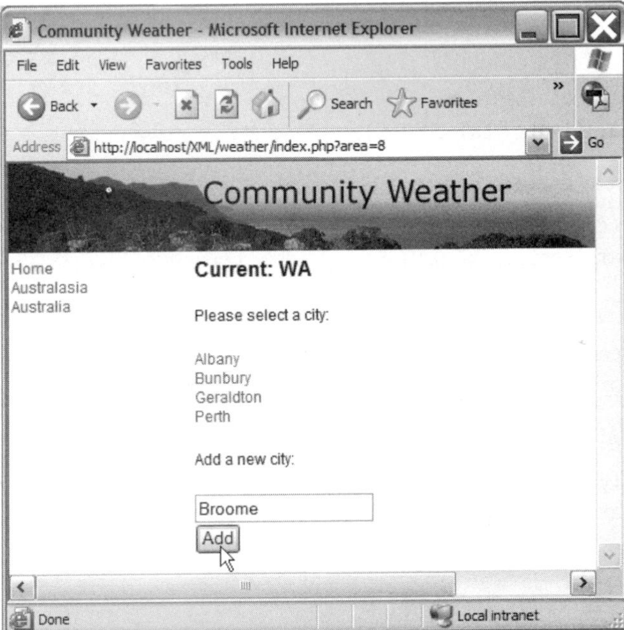

Figure 13-11. *Adding a new city*

addnew.php

If you add new details, the form action calls the addnew.php script. This script inserts the new record into the appropriate table in the database. I'll break down the page and discuss each section.

To start with, the page includes weather.php to access the database:

```
<?php
include_once 'weather.php';
```

It then retrieves the details from the form, including the values in the hidden fields:

```
$into = $_POST['into'];
$current = $_POST['current'];
$parent = $_POST['parent'];
$entry = $_POST['entry'];
```

The page tests to see that users have entered details into the form:

```
if (strlen(trim($entry)) > 0) {
```

If so, it uses the `$into` variable to determine the appropriate `INSERT` statement and stores it in the variable `$sql`:

```
switch ($into) {
  case 'continent':
    $sql = 'INSERT into continent (continent) ➥
      VALUES ("' . htmlspecialchars($entry,ENT_QUOTES) . '")';
    break;
  case 'country':
    $sql = 'INSERT into country (country, countryContinentID) ➥
      VALUES ("' . htmlspecialchars($entry,ENT_QUOTES) . '",' . $parent . ')';
    break;
  case 'area':
    $sql = 'INSERT into area (area, areaCountryID) ➥
      VALUES ("' . htmlspecialchars($entry,ENT_QUOTES) . '",' . $parent . ')';
    break;
  case 'city':
    $sql = 'INSERT into city (city, cityAreaID) ➥
      VALUES ("' . htmlspecialchars($entry,ENT_QUOTES) . '",' . $parent . ')';
    break;
  default:
    $sql = '';
    break;
  }
}
else {
  $sql ='';
}
```

Finally, the code checks for a SQL statement, in which case the length of the `$sql` variable must be greater than `0`. It then inserts the new record and redirects to the previous navigation position:

```
  if (strlen($sql) > 0) {
    mysql_query($sql) or die(mysql_error());
  }
  header('Location: index.php?' . $current . '=' . $parent);

?>
```

The `$current` variable contains the previous navigation level, while `$parent` contains the `id` of that entry. I've now worked through the code that builds the site navigation.

The remainder of the application handles the weather details. The `mk_weather.php`, `weather.xsl`, and `addweather.php` scripts deal with the weather details. The application uses the same approach as it did with the navigation. The `mk_weather.php` script generates the weather XML, which `weather.xsl` transforms into XHTML. The `addweather.php` page allows users to add new weather details.

mk_weather.php

The `mk_weather.php` page generates the XML document containing current weather details. It uses the following template:

```
<?xml version="1.0" encoding="UTF-8"?>
<weather>
  <city id=""> </city>
  <temperature>
    <minimum></minimum>
    <maximum></maximum>
  </temperature>
  <outlook>hot</outlook>
  <weathertypes>
    <type id=""> </type>
  </weathertypes>
</weather>
```

There are three possibilities for the structure of the XML document that the application generates:

1. There is no current weather report.
2. The values in the querystring change and cause an error.
3. There is a current weather report.

I'll work through each scenario.

Scenario 1: No Current Weather Reports

In the first scenario, the selected city has no current weather reports. Figure 13-12 shows how this appears to users.

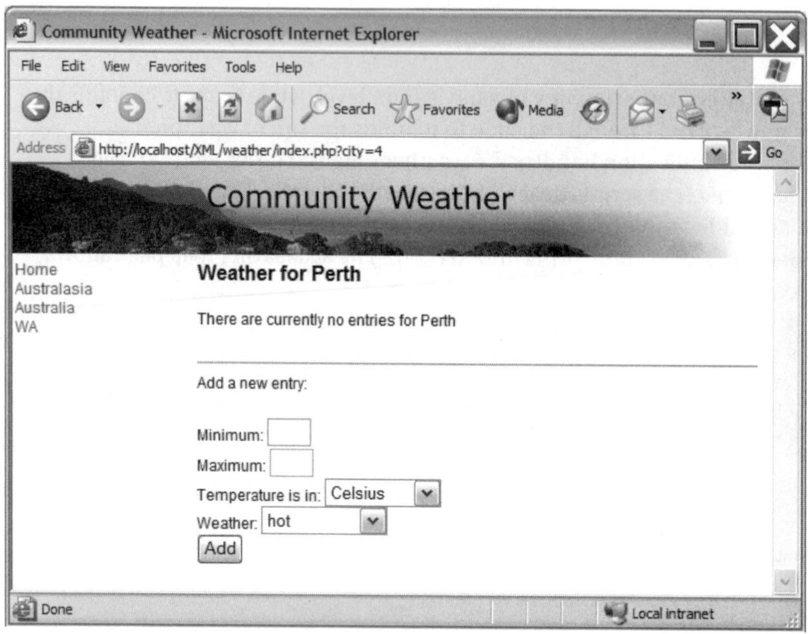

Figure 13-12. *There is no current weather report to display.*

The XML document describing the weather in this scenario would appear as follows:

```
<?xml version="1.0" encoding="UTF-8"?>
<weather>
  <city id="4">Perth</city>
  <weathertypes>
    <type id="1">hot</type>
    <type id="2">sunny</type>
    <type id="3">windy</type>
    <type id="4">cloudy</type>
    <type id="5">rain</type>
    <type id="6">rainstorms</type>
    <type id="7">snow</type>
    <type id="8">snowstorms</type>
  </weathertypes>
</weather>
```

The `<weather>` element is the document element. This element includes the `<city>` element, which contains the city name as text and an attribute with the `id` from the database.

The page also contains a form that allows users to add a new weather report. To make life easier, the application provides a list of weather types in a drop-down list. This information comes from the <weathertypes> element.

Scenario 2: Changing Querystring Variables

The second possibility occurs when users edit the querystring to add an invalid city code. This would produce the following XML document:

```
<?xml version="1.0" encoding="UTF-8"?>
<weather>
  <city>Error</city>
  <error>You appear to have selected an invalid city</error>
</weather>
```

This document provides users with an error message.

Scenario 3: Current Weather Reports Available

The final scenario shows a current weather report for the selected city. The XML document needs to include the current weather conditions with the possible weather types:

```
<?xml version="1.0" encoding="UTF-8"?>
<weather>
  <city id="4">Perth</city>
  <temperature>
    <minimum>20</minimum>
    <maximum>35</maximum>
  </temperature>
  <outlook>hot</outlook>
  <weathertypes>
    <type id="1">hot</type>
    <type id="2">sunny</type>
    <type id="3">windy</type>
    <type id="4">cloudy</type>
    <type id="5">rain</type>
    <type id="6">rainstorms</type>
    <type id="7">snow</type>
    <type id="8">snowstorms</type>
  </weathertypes>
</weather>
```

The <temperature> element provides the minimum and maximum temperatures. The <outlook> element is the current outlook for the city. It contains one of the predefined weather types.

Now that you've seen the XML document structures, I'll look at the code that builds these structures from the database.

Building the XML Document

The mk_weather.php script starts by including the weather.php page and creating a new DomDocument:

```
<?php
include_once 'weather.php';
$xml = new DomDocument('1.0', 'UTF-8');
```

It then adds the XML declaration and the <weather> element:

```
$xml->xmlStandalone = false;
$root = $xml->createElement('weather');
$root = $xml->appendChild($root);
```

The page needs to query the database to find out the city name. This code also tests whether users have passed in a valid id for the city:

```
$sql = 'SELECT * FROM city WHERE cityID =' . $city;
$cres = mysql_query($sql) or die(mysql_error() . "\n<br />" . $sql);
```

If the id is not valid, the code generates an error:

```
if (mysql_num_rows($cres) == 0) {
  $cityElement = $xml->createElement('city', 'Error');
  $root->appendChild($cityElement);
  $error = $xml->createElement('error', 'You appear to have selected ➥
    an invalid city');
  $root->appendChild($error);
}
```

If the application has a valid city id, it retrieves the name of the city and adds it to the XML document:

```
else {
  $crow = mysql_fetch_array($cres);
  $city_name = $crow['city'];
  $cityElement = $xml->createElement('city', $city_name);
  $cityElement->setAttribute('id', $city);
  $cityElement = $root->appendChild($cityElement);
```

The code uses the createElement(), setAttribute(), and appendChild() methods to add the content.

Because the application should only show the current weather reports, you can filter the details to show only current entries. In this application, entries added in the last eight hours are current. The variable $weatherWindow has a value of the current time minus eight hours, or 28800 seconds:

```
$weatherWindow = time() - 28800;
```

As the application shouldn't store the outdated weather entries in the database, the code uses the `$weatherWindow` variable to delete the old records. That way, the code can just select the remaining records:

```
$sql = 'DELETE FROM weather WHERE weatherCityID=' . $city . ' ➥
AND weatherDate < ' . $weatherWindow;
mysql_query($sql) or die(mysql_error() . "\n<br />" . $sql);
```

The application also determines the forecast, based on how many people select each weather type. If 10 people indicate that the weather is sunny, and one person adds that it's raining, the application can probably assume that the weather is sunny. It could extend the logic and analyze weather changes over time, but that's beyond the scope of this application. The application determines weather type by counting the number of each type of entry:

```
$sql = 'SELECT count(weather.weatherWeatherTypeID) AS tOrder, ➥
  weathertype.weatherType FROM weather, weathertype ➥
  WHERE weatherWeatherTypeID=weatherTypeID and weatherCityID =' . $city . ' ➥
  GROUP BY weatherWeatherTypeID ORDER BY tOrder DESC';
$wres = mysql_query($sql) or die(mysql_error() . "\n<br />" . $sql);
```

If the query returns no records, there are no current weather reports. It doesn't need to add any weather data to the XML document. It will only proceed if there are more than zero rows of data:

```
if (mysql_num_rows($wres) > 0) {
  $wrow = mysql_fetch_array($wres);
```

The code retrieves the minimum and maximum values by averaging the temperatures. It rounds the averaged value to display a whole number:

```
$sql = 'SELECT ROUND(AVG(weatherMax)) AS maxavg FROM weather ➥
  WHERE weatherCityID =' . $city;
$wMaxRes = mysql_query($sql) or die(mysql_error() . "\n<br />" . $sql);
$wMaxRow = mysql_fetch_array($wMaxRes);
$sql = 'SELECT ROUND(AVG(weatherMin)) AS minavg FROM weather ➥
  WHERE weatherCityID =' . $city;
$wMinRes = mysql_query($sql) or die(mysql_error() . "\n<br />" . $sql);
$wMinRow = mysql_fetch_array($wMinRes);
```

The page needs to add these elements to the XML document:

```
$temp = $xml->createElement('temperature');
$temp = $root->appendChild($temp);
$min = $xml->createElement('minimum', $wMinRow['minavg']);
$min = $temp->appendChild($min);
$max = $xml->createElement('maximum', $wMaxRow['maxavg']);
$max = $temp->appendChild($max);
```

The application also adds the outlook to the document. Because the code sorts the query in reverse count order, it displays the first record, which contains the highest number of responses:

```
$outlook = $xml->createElement('outlook', $wrow['weatherType']);
$outlook = $root->appendChild($outlook);
```

As the page finishes with the weather report, it can output the available weather types. You've seen this code before:

```
  $types = $xml->createElement('weathertypes');
  $types = $root->appendChild($types);
  $sql = 'SELECT weatherTypeID, weatherType FROM weatherType';
  $tRes = mysql_query($sql) or die(mysql_error() . "\n<br />" . $sql);
  while ($tRow = mysql_fetch_array($tRes)) {
    $type = $xml->createElement('type', $tRow['weatherType']);
    $type->setAttribute('id', $tRow['weatherTypeID']);
    $type = $types->appendChild($type);
  }
}
```

weather.xsl

The application needs to transform the XML content using the XSLT stylesheet `weather.xsl`. The stylesheet starts in the following way:

```
<?xml version="1.0"?>
<xsl:stylesheet version="1.0" xmlns:xsl="http://www.w3.org/1999/XSL/Transform">
```

It then checks that there are weather results by counting the number of temperature elements and storing the value in a variable:

```
<xsl:variable name="numTemp">
  <xsl:value-of select="count(weather/temperature)"/>
</xsl:variable>
```

The value is `1` if users have entered a forecast, and `0` if there are no database results.

The stylesheet can then test to see if an error occurred:

```
<xsl:template match="/">
  <xsl:choose>
    <xsl:when test="//weather/city='Error'">
      <h4>Error</h4>
      <xsl:value-of select="weather/error"/>
    </xsl:when>
```

If there is an error, the stylesheet displays the details; otherwise, it displays the weather title:

```
<xsl:otherwise>
  <h4>Weather for <xsl:value-of select="weather/city"/></h4>
```

The stylesheet needs to check the value of the $numTemp variable. If the value is 0, there are no weather records, and it will display an appropriate message:

```
<xsl:choose>
  <xsl:when test="$numTemp=0">
    There are currently no entries for
    <xsl:value-of select="weather/city"/>
  </xsl:when>
```

If the value isn't 0, there are weather details that the stylesheet can display. As I'm writing this from Australia, I use the Celsius temperature scale. The database stores the temperatures in Celsius, but the application needs to display both Celsius and Fahrenheit values. The stylesheet converts the existing Celsius temperatures to Fahrenheit values and stores them in variables:

```
<xsl:otherwise>
  <xsl:variable name="MinF">
    <xsl:value-of select="round(((weather/temperature/minimum * 9) div 5)+ 32)"/>
  </xsl:variable>
  <xsl:variable name="MaxF">
    <xsl:value-of select="round(((weather/temperature/maximum * 9) div 5)+ 32)"/>
  </xsl:variable>
```

The stylesheet displays the weather outlook using images designed by Gavin Cromhout. You can find them in the images folder. It chooses the images in the following way:

```
<strong>Outlook:</strong><br/>
<xsl:text disable-output-escaping="yes">&lt;img src="images/</xsl:text>
<xsl:value-of select="weather/outlook"/>
<xsl:text disable-output-escaping="yes">.jpg" width="100" height="80" ➥
alt="</xsl:text>
<xsl:value-of select="weather/outlook"/>
<xsl:text disable-output-escaping="yes">" /&gt;</xsl:text><br/>
```

It then displays the minimum and maximum temperatures in a table:

```
<table border="0">
  <tr>
    <td/>
    <td><strong>C</strong></td>
    <td><strong>F</strong></td>
   </tr>
   <tr>
     <td><strong>Minimum</strong></td>
     <td><xsl:value-of select="weather/temperature/minimum"/></td>
     <td><xsl:value-of select="$MinF"/></td>
   </tr>
  <tr>
    <td><strong>Maximum</strong></td>
    <td><xsl:value-of select="weather/temperature/maximum"/></td>
```

```
        <td><xsl:value-of select="$MaxF"/></td>
      </tr>
    </table>
  </xsl:otherwise>
</xsl:choose>
```

The stylesheet also includes a form so users can add a new weather report:

```
<p>
  <hr/>Add a new entry:<br/>
  <form action="addweather.php" method="POST">
```

The form needs to pass the current city id, so the application can store the value in the database:

```
<xsl:text disable-output-escaping="yes">
  &lt;input type="hidden" name="city" value="</xsl:text>
<xsl:value-of select="weather/city/@id"/>
<xsl:text disable-output-escaping="yes">" /&gt; </xsl:text>
```

The rest of the form provides appropriate inputs as well as a drop-down list showing the different weather types:

```
            Temperature is in:
            <select name="temptype">
              <option value="C">Celsius</option>
              <option value="F">Fahrenheit</option>
            </select><br/>
            Weather:
            <select name="weather">
              <xsl:for-each select="weather/weathertypes/type">
                <xsl:text disable-output-escaping="yes">
                  &lt;option value="</xsl:text>
                <xsl:value-of select="@id"/>
                <xsl:text disable-output-escaping="yes">"&gt;</xsl:text>
                <xsl:value-of select="."/>
                <xsl:text disable-output-escaping="yes">&lt;/option&gt;</xsl:text>
              </xsl:for-each>
            </select><br/>
            <input type="submit" value="Add"/>
          </form>
        </p>
      </xsl:otherwise>
    </xsl:choose>
  </xsl:template>
</xsl:stylesheet>
```

addweather.php

The final part of the application processes the weather details entered by users and adds the content to the database. As I mentioned earlier, the database stores all values in Celsius degrees. The page addweather.php starts with a conversion function that converts Fahrenheit temperatures to Celsius:

```
<?php
  function alterTemp($temperature, $current) {
    if ($current=='C') {
        $newtemp = $temperature;
    } else {
      $newtemp = ((($temperature -32) * 5) / 9);
    }
    return $newtemp;
  }
```

It then includes the weather.php file and collects the values from the weather details form:

```
include_once 'weather.php';
$city = $_POST['city'];
$min = $_POST['min'];
$max = $_POST['max'];
$weather = $_POST['weather'];
$temptype = $_POST['temptype'];
```

The page needs to make sure that there are valid minimum and maximum temperatures before entering the information into the database:

```
if (is_numeric($min) && is_numeric($max)) {
  $sql = 'INSERT INTO weather (weatherCityID, weatherDate, weatherMin, ➥
    weatherMax, weatherWeatherTypeID) VALUES (' . $city . ',' . time() . ',' . ➥
    alterTemp($min, $temptype) . ', ' . alterTemp($max, $temptype) . ','➥
    . $weather . ')';
}
else {
  $sql = 'SELECT (1+1)';
}
mysql_query($sql) or die(mysql_error() . $sql);
```

Finally, it needs to redirect back to the weather page for the current city:

```
  header('Location: index.php?city=' . $city);
?>
```

Figure 13-7 earlier in the book shows how the completed application appears when viewing the weather for a city.

Summary

In this chapter, I worked through an application that uses PHP, MySQL, XML, and XSLT to display and manage weather content. The application stores all of the data within a MySQL database. The application retrieves the relevant database records with PHP 5. It uses the new PHP 5 `DomDocument` object to generate the XML document. The structure of the generated XML documents is flexible enough to cope with several different scenarios.

In order to display the XML content within the application, I used XSLT stylesheet transformations to generate XHTML. You saw how to use XSLT variables and include conditional logic in the stylesheets.

This chapter wraps up the book. I hope you've enjoyed reading about XML and that you've expanded your knowledge. XML is a flexible approach to building both client- and server-side web applications, and I hope the contents of this book will make you as enthusiastic about XML as I am!

Index

Symbols

A

D

G

H

I

J

L

M

N

O

P

Q

R

S

T

U

V

W

X

Z

eBookshop

ASP Today

Apress®
THE EXPERT'S VOICE™